S E R G E I   P R O K O F I E V

A Soviet Tragedy

Prokofiev's last portrait, Fall 1952

Sergei Prokofiev

A SOVIET TRAGEDY

The case of Sergei Prokofiev, his life & work,

his critics, and his executioners

by Victor Seroff

A Crescendo Book

TAPLINGER PUBLISHING COMPANY

New York

A Crescendo Book, published in 1979 by
TAPLINGER PUBLISHING CO., INC.
New York, New York

Library of Congress Catalog Number: 78-73657
ISBN 0-8008-7067-0 (cloth)
ISBN 0-8008-7068-9 (pbk)

Printed in the United States of America

9 8 7 6 5 4 3 2 1

To Joan Kennedy

"Tu montrera ma tête au peuple; elle en vaut bien la peine."

—Danton to his executioner

FOREWORD

This is not just another biography of a musician: it is a case history of what can and did happen even to a world-famous creative artist in Soviet Russia—a country that prides itself on treating talented men as a privileged class of society. (Stalin referred to these creative artists as "the engineers of the human soul.") Therefore, I feel compelled to bring to the reader's attention the importance of every contributing detail in Prokofiev's personal and professional life. For what may seem to us unexceptionable can be of grave importance in the eyes of the Communist authorities in Russia.

Under the Soviet system the people, along with all other forms and products of national wealth, are the property of the state. No Soviet citizen, no matter how humble or imposing his achievements, can enjoy freedom as we know it in the free world. He is given ample opportunities for his work so long as it serves the interest of the state. But he is denied free access to information, since he has *no* access to anything unauthorized by the government. Not even his personal matters can safely be regarded as private—his home may be searched, his correspondence censored. Indeed, his choices of work and marriage must be approved by the government.

My treatment of the subject of this book is based not only on materials published outside of Russia but on Sergei Prokofiev's own autobiography, and on documents, letters, and memoirs published within Soviet Russia. It is also based on unique and revealing documents in my possession.

A list of the abovementioned works and sources is given in the Bibliography, and photostats of the documents appear in the Appendix.

V. S.

PART ONE

1891-1917

1

"The devil only knows what this is, but it is not music!" This was one of the comments on his work that pursued Sergei Prokofiev through most of his life. Sometimes it was voiced by the music critics, but more often by indignant members of audiences, by men who stalked out of concert halls or even engaged in fistfights with those who dared approve of Prokofiev's compositions.

In 1932, during his concert tour in the United States, Prokofiev attended a concert in New York in which Bruno Walter conducted Portraits, a suite from Prokofiev's opera *The Gambler*. During the intermission the composer stepped out of his box into the corridor and saw a man who, leaving the adjoining box, was shaking his fist and shouting angrily, "I would like to meet that guy! I would tell him a thing or two about his compositions!" "He was an excellent specimen of the American physique," Prokofiev related later, "and I thought it wise to disappear in a hurry."

It would be useless, however, to seek in Prokofiev's background plausible reasons for his becoming such an *enfant terrible* of twentieth-century music. He was not like Andersen's Ugly Duckling: "It had no feathers, and its legs were long and gawky. 'What if it's a turkey!' exclaimed the mother duck in terror."

On the contrary, he was a perfectly normal, healthy boy who had a happy childhood and adolescence. Psychiatrists would look in vain to these two periods of his life for an explanation of what some critics called his "mischievous, prankish musical nature."

He was born at five o'clock in the afternoon on Wednesday, April

3

23, 1891, in Sontsovka* in the Ekaterinoslav district of the Ukraine. Sontsovka was an estate of about eighteen thousand acres that belonged to Dmitri Sontsov. Sontsov and Sergei's father had been friends since their student days at the Agricultural Academy in Moscow, and as Sontsov preferred to live on his much smaller estate near the town of Kursk, he had asked Sergei's father to take charge of administering Sontsovka, and do with it whatever he wished. While the salary he offered was very small, Sontsov agreed to pay Sergei's father 20 per cent of the income derived from the estate.

It was an attractive challenge to the young agriculturist, who was anxious to try out in practice the theoretical knowledge he had acquired at the Agricultural Academy. Thus it happened that the Prokofievs made their home in a little village some thirteen miles from the nearest railroad station, ten miles from the nearest hospital, and five miles from the post office, which functioned only twice a week.

Had Sergei Prokofiev's life been spent outside Russia and had he not returned at the age of forty-five to Soviet Russia, where he was to remain until his death, the backgrounds of his parents and grandparents would have been relatively unimportant. In Czarist Russia, for example, it was no one's concern that Anton Chekhov's grandfather was a serf and that the author "took years to squeeze from his veins the last drop of serfdom," as he said about himself. That was merely his personal attitude. But after the Revolution, when the Soviet government assumed complete responsibility for the citizens' social status, the question of social origin became important. It affected in no small measure the composer's personal life and, consequently, his work.

Sergei Prokofiev had very scant knowledge of his paternal grandparents, for they were seldom mentioned in his family. He knew that they were. fairly well-to-do—they owned a small factory—but not particularly well educated, and that his father, who was born in Moscow on July 20, 1846, was fourteen years old when both his parents died in the cholera epidemic then raging in Moscow. The boy and his brother Peter, three years younger, were taken by their elder sister Nadezhda, already married to Michael Smirnoff, to live with them and their four daughters.

The two boys were educated in a commercial school, which offered a less general and classical education than the gymnasium. Peter showed little interest in his studies and was merely anxious to complete the courses at the school so that he could start his own business, for which he had many plans. But he failed in his enterprises and re-

* Now Krasnoe Selo.

mained for the rest of his life the general business manager for his four nieces, Nadezhda's daughters. "He was not of a particularly refined character, but rather amiable," the composer remarked. "He was my godfather, and for my birthdays and name days always presented me with gold coins."

The composer's father, whose name was also Sergei, took his studies very seriously. Not satisfied with the limited curriculum offered at the commercial school, he later entered the university. But when the time came for him to choose a profession, he could not decide whether to become a doctor of medicine or to study chemistry. Finally, because of its well-equipped Department of Chemistry, he became a student at the Petrovsko-Razumovskoe Agricultural Academy near Moscow.

Although he did not take part in the students' revolutionary activities in the early 1870's, Sergei Prokofiev was punished by the government authorities for refusing to name the accused students. He was either arrested—the composer was not certain about this—or was denied some privileges to which he would have been entitled upon his graduation from the Academy. That left a definite scar, and for the rest of his life he tried to avoid any entanglements with government authorities.

Thus ends the composer's record of his father's background. Nevertheless, the fact that his father had been "persecuted" by the Czarist government placed him, in the eyes of the Soviet authorities, among those who had "suffered" under the old regime; his family was therefore entitled to special consideration.

The composer's mother, Maria, came from peasant stock. That is, according to the Soviet classification of social origin, she had a proletarian background—something that confers great privileges in Soviet society. Originally, Maria's ancestors were peasants in Serebryaniye Prudy, a village near Yasnaya Polyana, Leo Tolstoy's estate.

At that time peasants "belonged" to a landlord, and since they had no civil rights, they were virtually slaves whom he had the right to dispose of as he pleased. Because of his stubborn and rebellious character, Maria's grandfather, Nikita, was sent to the Saratov district, where he became a serf of Count Sheremetyev. But his son Gregori, Maria's father, was brought to St. Petersburg, where at first he worked in Sheremetyev's home; after 1861, when the peasants were granted "freedom," he was given the last name of Zhitkov (most probably derived from the word zhito, meaning rye) and became a solicitor in legal cases, although he had no law degree.

In his business, however, Gregori was so unsuccessful that one of his five daughters, while still a youngster, committed suicide. "Not because of an unhappy love affair," the composer explained, "but because of the burden of their poverty." But despite their destitute situation, the other girls strove for a better life. Maria and her sister Ekaterina entered a gymnasium, while Varvara and Tatyana, the two younger sisters, studied as best they could at home.

The Zhitkovs lived either in St. Petersburg or Moscow, depending on Gregori's business, and it was in a Moscow gymnasium that Maria and her sister became close friends of Nadezhda Smirnoff's daughters. The Smirnoffs, who were well-to-do, looked down on the poor Zhitkov sisters, although the latter were far better educated. "Or perhaps," the composer commented, "this fact unconsciously attracted the Smirnoff young ladies to the Zhitkovs. Maria was gay and witty, Ekaterina was good-looking and had an angelic disposition, while the Smirnoffs apparently were not particularly brilliant in any way."

Actually, Maria's good nature and vivacity were her chief characteristics at the age of fifteen, for she was not exceptionally handsome: she had a slightly turned-up little nose, lips that were much too full, a protruding jaw, and straight, short hair. She gained in looks after her marriage, but she always had a good figure and a small foot that she liked to show off. She danced well and was usually surrounded by a group of her classmates. She was the leader in all their amusements, and they readily submitted to her dominating nature.

These young people brought unusual noise and commotion into the Smirnoffs' home and disturbed the studies of the composer's father, then a serious student, who, lifting his head from his books, glanced disapprovingly at the girls. And the girls were afraid of his severe appearance, his beard, and his gold-rimmed spectacles.

But several years went by, and when Maria graduated from the gymnasium with a gold medal, she came up to the young student, who had also just completed his studies at the Academy, and putting her arms behind her back, announced to him, "I am no longer afraid of you!"

With this remark their romance began. But its further development met with obstacles. First of all, after his graduation Sergei's father bought a small estate—Nikolaevka—in the Smolensk district (he had inherited approximately fifteen thousand gold rubles from his parents), where he had moved in order to manage it, while the Zhitkovs once again returned to St. Petersburg. Their meetings grew rare.

But what was far more serious, the Smirnoffs, who had enjoyed the company of the vivacious Zhitkov sisters as long as they were their daughters' schoolmates, looked disdainfully on the idea of the young Prokofiev marrying a penniless girl. They would have preferred one who brought a substantial dowry.

That not unusual reasoning had particular point in this case: in order to bring sufficient income, the newly acquired estate, Nikolaevka, needed investment in additional work buildings and agricultural implements, and Sergei's father was hesitant to involve himself in marriage and the rearing of a family.

The composer kept his mother's letter written to his father at the time of their engagement on November 10, 1876. "To my deep sorrow I can offer you only myself, and I expect only the same in return from you," Maria had written. "As before, so now, I repeat: I am not attracted by your future wealth. In fact, it is repugnant to me, because it has separated us."

"Yes, there were obstacles indeed," commented the composer, "but love triumphed. And several months later, on May 7, 1877, they were married. But without secret pride I would like to add that in her family my mother was the intellectual, and so was my father in his."

This last remark, which the composer made in summarizing their background and which he included in his autobiography written after he returned to Soviet Russia, was no doubt to stress to the authorities the important fact that his parents were not merely bourgeois, but belonged to the intelligentsia, the intellectual class of society.

The composer's father was thirty-one years old when he married, but for some unaccountable reason Maria, in her later years, kept her age so secret that at her death her passport claimed her to be fifteen years younger than she actually was. Only through some discreet inquiries and calculations did her son succeed in establishing approximately the date of her birth: December 25, 1855. Thus she was twenty-three when, after spending a year at Nikolaevka, she and her husband drove in a four-horse carriage to Sontsovka, along narrow roads lined with poplars, willows, and cherry trees, and on to a manor house on the hill.

It was a white one-story building with a green roof. On one side of it stood a large chestnut tree under which, as a child, the future composer found refuge from the summer heat, and on the other side a long row of acacias. There were nine rooms (not counting storerooms and an office), with low ceilings, yellow floors, and white walls. All the furniture was slip-covered because the upholstery was old and worn, and in every corner there were ficus, philodendra, and small palm trees in large tubs. The kitchen and the servants' quarters were in an adjoining small building, beyond which were three stables (Dmitri Sontsov bred horses), four granaries, a smithy, and a pigsty.

Sontsovka was inhabited by about a thousand peasants and workmen who lived in small thatched clay huts on the five streets that spread like a spider web from the center of the village. Some of these streets were a mile long and led to the forest, which was rapidly being thinned under the axes of the impoverished woodsmen; and that was all there was to Sontsovka—the rest was steppe and uncultivated fields.

Sergei's father knew that the estate was in the black-soil district and that the extremely fertile land would yield, if properly managed, a handsome income for its owner. And, indeed, he succeeded in his project so well that before he died at the age of sixty-four, the net profit rose to some sixty thousand rubles a year, which, with the share agreed upon by Sontsov, made him quite well off.

But the beginning was very hard. He had to start from scratch to divide the property into sections (and not merely on paper), stipulating which were to be used for sowing grain and which for grazing sheep, goats, cows, and pigs; to build roads and paths; and to select and engage a staff of workers capable of handling the modern equipment that he was to import.

Fortunately, Maria was helpful in this pioneering work in which both of them had great faith. She also organized a school for the peasants' children in which she taught; and with her own and her husband's little knowledge of medicine, they were able to take care of the sick—of course, only with primitive drugs like quinine, castor oil, iodine, and bromides, the latter administered for their calming effects both to those who were unhappy in love and to those who were on the verge of insanity. And Maria never failed to mention that in her *Apteka* (pharmacy) she also had some medicine containing a real poison, entrusted to her by a visiting doctor. "The poison in Mama's *Apteka* always made a big impression," remarked the composer.

Perhaps the location of Sontsovka was an important factor in Sergei's father's great success. Sontsovka was pleasant only during the late spring and summer months. The rest of the time it was covered with snow or had its roads made impassable by the early spring thaw and autumn rains.

The black-soil zone has always been the envy of farmers, but they must pay a price for this fertile land. No one who has not seen it can imagine what mire the earth turns into after it has been soaked by spring or autumn rains. It was not unusual for the peasants to lose cattle and horses that were mired too deeply to be saved. During World War II the German motorized units and their army supply lines were bogged down on their march through southern Russia because of these muddy roads.

The Prokofievs' few neighbors were wealthy landowners who lived some twenty miles away. Because of this isolation the young Prokofievs were seldom interrupted in their work by idle visitors. Actually, Sergei's father never sought a close relationship with his neighbors. Not very sociable, he shied away from being treated with familiarity, so that after living at Sontsovka for some thirty-three years he could count only two friends: a doctor and a veterinarian.

If this isolation from the more civilized parts of the country was beneficial for the work the young couple was doing at Sontsovka, it also may have been partly responsible for the two events that marred their happiness. During the thirteen years before Sergei was born, his parents lost two daughters; the death of both girls was caused by teething. Maria, the elder child, died at the age of two, while her sister, Lubov, lived only nine months. It is understandable that when Sergei was born he became the object of his parents' particular care, for he too inherited his mother's formation of mouth and teeth.

Fearing that something might happen to him, they decided to keep him at home as long as possible and to teach him themselves the subjects he would have learned in the first grades of a public school. They found no difficulty in working with him, for he was an obedient and reasonable child, and he accepted the discipline and systematic division of his time for study and relaxation as easily as he did the wholesome but not elaborate menu in their home. He was not a capricious or mischievous boy, although like everybody else he had his likes and dislikes.

His sensitive ears were irritated by anyone shuffling his heels as he walked, and particularly by noisy drinking and champing at the table—*khlupanie* and *chavkanie*, the Russians call it. The Russians' extraordinary capacity for consuming large quantities of food during long hours at the table and the gusto with which they drink countless glasses of tea might well unnerve someone less sensitive than Sergei was. On such occasions, to keep him from making faces at the unfortunate guest at the table, Maria had to whisper a promise of some chocolate later if he behaved himself.

Sergei's father did not believe in punishment, and on the few occasions when Maria felt she simply had to "lecture" the boy, his father preferred to go his study rather than witness the "execution," as Sergei called it. On the whole, his parents succeeded in winning their son's confidence, for he never had to lie or conceal things from them.

"They were torturing me for six hours a day," the composer remarked later, but "torturing" referred only to his general education. "My mother loved music, my father respected it," he said. "Most probably, he too loved music, but in a philosophical way, as a manifestation of culture, a lofty expression of the human spirit. Once, when I was still a little boy, my father heard me play the piano; he listened for a while, and then said, 'These are noble sounds.' I have always felt that *there* was the key to his attitude toward music."

Sergei's mother, on the other hand, not only loved to listen to music but devoted hours to playing the piano. Although she was handicapped by lack of technique, she had other advantages—sincere enjoyment, persistence in her work, and good taste. She was afraid of playing before strangers, and yet she practiced as diligently, trying to perfect her repertory, as if she were preparing for a performance.

Every year Maria went to St. Petersburg to visit her relatives—sometimes for as long as two or three months in the winter—and while she was there, she took piano lessons from her old teacher. After she had played the pieces she had been working on, they would go through a whole list of new compositions, so that Maria would return home with another program for the following year. She was interested exclusively in serious music, and this had a definite influence on her growing son. By the age of twelve he "sincerely despised so-called popular music."

"While my mother was awaiting my birth, she played the piano for as long as six hours a day," Sergei Prokofiev said. "Thus, the future little human being was formed to the accompaniment of music." And his earliest memories connected with music took him back to the times when, as a child, he would be put to bed early and would listen to the sounds of the piano four rooms away instead of going to sleep.

Maria liked to play Beethoven sonatas, Chopin preludes, mazurkas, and waltzes, some pieces by Liszt that were not too difficult technically, and among the Russian composers she preferred Tchaikovsky and Anton Rubinstein. Rubinstein was then at the peak of his fame, "and mother was convinced," Prokofiev remarked sarcastically, "that he was far greater than Tchaikovsky." A large portrait of Rubinstein hung over the upright piano in their sitting room.

As a rule, Maria began her daily practicing with Hanon exercises and Czerny études, and it was then that the four-year-old Sergei would timidly nestle near the keyboard and try to strike the keys. Sometimes, while playing in the middle register, Maria would leave the two octaves in the treble free for Sergei's pianistic experiments, and this "barbarous ensemble," as the composer later called it, eventually stimulated the boy to play on his own.

What did he try to play? Although he loved to listen to his mother at the piano, his attitude was rather critical. Not all her "little songs," as he referred to the compositions she played, pleased him. But the melodies he liked he retained in his memory and later tried to pick out on the piano by ear. This eventually led to his "improvising"—trying to play a "little song" of his own. But here his creative ability met with a new obstacle: he wanted to write down what he managed to play on the piano, but he did not know how.

Sitting at a desk, he used to cover pages of paper with the musical signs he had seen; he drew notes and clefs as other children drew cats, ducks, or trains. Unfortunately, the collection of musical signs that he scrawled did not have any meaning. Once, according to Maria, when she had finished practicing, he brought her a whole page covered with these "music notes," and said, "Here, I have composed Liszt's rhapsody. Play it for me." (It has never been firmly established whether the piece was "Liszt's rhapsody" or "Chopin's mazurka," because of the discrepancy between the composer's and his mother's version of the story.)

Placing the page on the music rack before her, Maria began to play one of Liszt's rhapsodies. "No, no," Sergei interrupted her. "That's not it." Maria started on another, and then still another, but each time Sergei stopped her, saying it was not the one, until finally he said, "Play the one I composed." Embarrassed, Maria began to explain that she could not play what he had written because one did not write music that way, but seeing that he was about to burst into tears, she changed the subject and told him that a rhapsody is a piece of music, and that Liszt was the man who composed Liszt's rhapsodies. Sergei must have gone to bed more bewildered than ever.

Still, when he was only five years old, he composed a melody of his own, eight bars long, which he called an "Indian Gallop." "One could not think up a more absurd title," the composer remarked when he spoke later of his first composition, but apparently it was inspired by his parents' discussions of the famine that was raging at the time in India. Maria wrote down the melody while Sergei watched and tried to learn the process. This attempt was followed by the compositions Waltz, March, and Rondo, all in about the same vein as the Indian Gallop.

A year and a half later Sergei had an opportunity to hear even more music. The Prokofievs were visited by a young woman who played the piano better than Maria did. She gave Maria a few lessons, and the two often played duets. This four-hand playing intrigued Sergei, and he told his mother that he was going to write a march for four hands. "But that is going to be very difficult," Maria tried to dissuade him. "You will have to have separate music for each person." It was a problem indeed.

Nevertheless, Sergei used a great deal of paper and a few days later brought her a march for four hands in C major with a glissando over two octaves at the end, thus closing the composition with "chic" and overcoming all obstacles.

When he heard as a whole what he had picked out for each part separately, Sergei was enchanted. He made a rather mature observation: "Each of them plays a different thing at the same time, and yet together it does not sound badly at all." This, after all, was his first *partitura*—an orchestral score—although at that age he did not yet know the meaning of the word.

All these compositions were later taken to St. Petersburg by Sergei's Aunt Tanya, Maria's younger sister, who had an experienced musician copy them. They were bound into an album, with *Seregenki Prokofieva Composizii* printed in gold letters on the cover.

"This album," the composer said later, "contained three stages in the development of my creative activities: music written down by a third person, music written down by the composer, and music for four hands, which could not have been picked out at the piano but had to be composed in his mind."

The album survives to this day. The originals were thrown away by the copyist, for, as he sagely remarked, "they were of no use to anybody."

2

But music was not yet all-absorbing. Sergei's parents felt that he should receive as good a general education as they could give him; they stressed particularly a knowledge of foreign languages. Therefore, while Maria was on one of her regular winter visits to St. Petersburg, she looked for a governess to teach him French. She grew very discouraged, because those she interviewed were either "positively repulsive," as she said, or had poor pronunciation, until she learned that there was an employment office in Warsaw directly connected with Paris.

Not in the least disturbed by the extra thousand kilometers she had to travel out of her way, she went to Warsaw, where, indeed, she found a young French girl who had just arrived from Paris. Louise Roblin's father was a veteran of the Franco-Prussian War, and when the family's means began to dwindle, Louise was forced to seek her fortune in the "country of white bears," where the knowledge of little besides the French language was worth more than in France.

Actually, Maria was not looking for a governess in the strict sense of the word—someone to take charge of her son's upbringing—for this role she reserved exclusively for herself. She merely wanted to find a young girl who, while spending much time with Sergei, could teach him French. The slender, petite Louise was sixteen, good-natured, and impressed Maria as being rather naïve. At first, however, Louise would not even listen to Maria's proposition. Hoping to find a position in St. Petersburg or in Moscow, she could not see herself buried in a wilderness like Sontsovka. But when Maria promised to teach her to play the piano and told her that in the summer she could gallop on thoroughbreds over the steppe, Louise agreed to come. "Most probably," said the composer later, "it was my mother's personality that made the proper impression. She was an intelligent woman who could charm when she wished." Thus, after having tasted the Russian way of traveling—they journeyed for three days and nights, changing trains six times, and riding two hours in a sleigh through a snowstorm on the last stretch of their route—frozen and exhausted, Louise was revived with several cups of hot tea in the Prokofievs' dining room on the evening of January 21, 1899.

She was placed next to her future pupil. Sergei, surprised to find himself with anyone who did not know a single word of Russian, immediately began to teach her the Russian for the few words he already knew in French: "*Éléphant—slon; lion—lev.*" And Louise, overwhelmed by the unusual journey and the new surroundings, blinked and repeated, "*Slone—lef.*"

Maria spoke French fairly well, and Sergei's father claimed to know the language "theoretically"—that is, he could read and understand the few French books on agriculture he had in his library, but his pronunciation, according to his son, was atrocious.

Louise acclimatized herself very soon. In fact, she became so enthusiastic about playing with Sergei's toys that often their games ended in quarrels and tears. To avoid these scenes, Maria and her husband had to buy as many playthings for Mademoiselle as they did for their son.

Sergei was forbidden to teach Louise Russian, and instead was told to read aloud *Les Malheurs de Sophie*, a story by Mme. de Ségur, which he did with difficulty, not quite knowing whether it was meant as a lesson or a pleasure. But it was not long before Sergei, taking *Les Malheurs de Sophie* as an example, began to write his own *Mademoiselle's Adventures*, in which he described Louise mistaking the caviar for jam or losing herself hopelessly in Sontsovka's muddy roads.

Maria taught Louise the piano for an hour every day without any thought that Mademoiselle's acquired knowledge of music would be useful to Sergei. (Louise turned out to be a wonderful copyist for his manuscripts.) No one knows anything about the second promise Maria made when she hired Louise—galloping over the steppe—nor has it been mentioned anywhere whether Sergei rode horseback. But it may be taken for granted that any boy who was brought up on an estate where there were stables rode, although Maria was overanxious about the safety of her son's hands and for this reason even worried about his walking on stilts, one of his favorite games.

Louise was not Sergei's only playmate: the housekeeper's children, three boys and a girl, were his other companions. The girl was six months younger than he, and one of the boys a year and a half younger. "The other two boys were small fry and did not count," although they followed them everywhere.

And there was Marfusha, whom Sergei credited with more intellect than the others. Before coming to the Prokofievs, she had worked as a servant for one of the neighboring landowners. Sergei was fascinated by Marfusha's stories about her master, who apparently spent the evening hours playing the piano. "Then," Marfusha said, "he would go to the cupboard and fetch a large box of chocolates and eat one after the other without a stop." "And then?" Sergei would interrupt, his mouth watering at the thought of so much chocolate. "And then," Marfusha continued, "he would go back to the piano and this went on until the early morning hours."

It was Marfusha with whom Sergei shared his musical impressions of pieces he heard his mother play. Later, he played for Marfusha The Evening Star from *Tannhäuser*, trying to impress her with the beauty of the composition. But although he played it for her over and over again, Marfusha remained deaf to Wagner's composition. Sergei was very unhappy that he had failed to prove that "good music is good."

Their favorite entertainment was to play "theatre," to stage plays. Sergei, who produced the plays, did not lack imagination in concocting plots that he would then explain to his friends. Once they understood the main theme of a drama, each one would act his own part, inventing his own dialogue. These *commedie dell'arte* were produced simply, and the performances were amazingly natural and vivid.

Each Sunday a new play was given. In the morning, large posters were hung, announcing the title of the play, the characters, and the names of the actors—everything painted in bright colors. One could not miss it, as one could not miss the art director's (Sergei's) devotion to his job. For the whole week the young servants and the children were engaged in preparations for the forthcoming event.

Maria had given them permission to make use of anything that was necessary, and the doors of storerooms stood ajar while the children carried out old hats, coats, dresses, and lampshades that in an emergency could serve as hats. Even the summer heat did not stop them from pulling fur coats out of the trunks to be used by an actor who was to represent a bear attacking a hunter. The wearing of a mask, of which there was ample variety, would complete the illusion of a vicious beast. Tubs with oleanders and ficus were brought "on stage"—these were the forest—and to create the effect of a waterfall, water was poured from one set of buckets into another. Naturally, the water often missed its aim and the floors were inundated, but to mop

up the floors afterward was no great chore for the enthusiastic servants. A whole arsenal of arms was on display: old rifles, guns, and
pistols that could be fired with blanks, and daggers and weird rusty
knives. For facial make-up, the actors used burnt cork for beards,
mustaches, and eyebrows.

And what was most important, they had an appreciative audience:
all who worked on the estate, with their wives and children, never
missed a performance, never missed a cue to applaud and cheer the
young artists. But no one was more enthusiastic than Sergei and his
little troupe of actors. Already at this early age Sergei showed with
what passion he would work at something that aroused his interest. He
was actor, producer, and of course, author of the plays.

A drama that includes a duel was the traditional subject. Children's
stories about magicians, monsters, and other fairy-tale characters were
not even considered. Here is a description of one of the scenes as recounted in the composer's autobiography.

As the curtain rises (the doors opened into the adjoining room, which
was the stage), one hears a terrific noise, cries and voices backstage,
where presumably a train is being wrecked. Wheels, large pieces of
iron and wood, and wounded and dead passengers fall on the stage.
("Vasya, you must fall on the stage as if you were thrown by the
shock out of the window of one of the carriages," was the stage direction Sergei had given one of his friends.) Then the survivors enter,
the wounded leaning on each other for support. Suddenly a bear runs
across the stage. One of the passengers bemoans a dead friend, while
another discovers that his wallet has been stolen. Although it is obvious who has committed the crime, it is impossible to prove the male-
factor's guilt. A noisy quarrel. A duel. The guilty one kills the innocent
victim, but as he rejoices in his triumph, the bear jumps on the stage
and devours him. Thus, virtue is upheld.

Sometimes, however, the plays ran into difficulties with Sergei's father, usually for reasons of safety. The play called *The Fire* could not
pass his censorship no matter how much Sergei argued that there was
no danger in performing it. He had to go back to his friends and,
sulking, tell them of the "mean decision." The already painted posters
had to carry an announcement—"Due to unexpected circumstances
the performance has been canceled"—and the children had to resort to
a less hazardous occupation, playing chess.

For some time Sergei had been intrigued by a box containing a
Chinese chess set that his father liked to show to his friends. They
were beautifully chiseled ebony pieces, and each time they were

brought out Sergei asked, "How does one play with them?" But, carefully rewrapping them in cotton, his father always explained that chess was a difficult game, not for Sergei, and that the pieces were not to be used anyway, that they were much too delicate. Then Sergei's cousin, a student at Moscow University, arrived in Sontsovka to spend the summer, and Sergei at once asked him whether he knew how to play chess. He not only knew the game but was willing to teach Sergei, who was already on his way to get the pieces. Reluctantly, his father gave him another set of chessmen, repeating, "This business is not for your brain." "But *he*," Sergei said, referring to his cousin, "says it is."

In this way, Sergei was introduced to a game that absorbed him all his life to such a degree that he often said that had he not become a musician, he would most probably have become a professional chess player.

Either because Sergei knew that when his cousin departed he would be left without a partner or because always being beaten is never much fun for anybody, he taught all his little friends to play, including Louise and Marfusha. Maria provided them with several sets of chessmen, and the house became a sort of chess club. They all played badly, sometimes even continuing the game after one of the players was already checkmated, but they played.

Sergei's game, however, gained an extra professional air because he had learned from his cousin how to write down the moves during the game. And, they organized chess matches, in which he already showed one of his main characteristics: an unusual interest in competitions and sports. Later, as a grown man, he was not content to play bridge for the fun of it, but insisted on organizing bridge matches with his partners; when he lived in the country much later, shortly before his death, whenever he fed the chickens, he would have them race for their feed.

Since Marfusha was his only serious chess opponent, Sergei challenged her to a match of twenty games. The match lasted for months, every game duly recorded in a large accounting copybook that Sergei acquired from his father's office.

The score was in Sergei's favor: he had won twelve games, Marfusha six, and two were draws. In one of the later games Sergei was left with a rook, a knight, and a bishop, while Marfusha had only one knight. There were no pawns left on the board, yet after half an hour of laborious maneuvering, Sergei agreed to a draw. Under an extremely long list of moves he wrote: "It is very difficult and most probably impossible to win." Many years later, the composer re-marked that this ending of the game indicated the level of his knowl-edge of chess at the time.

Sergei was also fascinated by the encyclopedia he discovered in his father's library. He could read it for hours, and when he saw the flags of various nations all done in colors, he kept nagging his mother to make him a few: Russian, Italian, and French. "But of course," he said, "the most interesting of all is the one of the United States, with all those stars, but . . . I suppose, very difficult to make."

A few days later he walked into the sitting room and found his mother and his aunt there sewing, but before he could see what they were working on, Maria told him to leave the room. "Why?" he asked. "Because the window is open, it is too cold." While saying this, Maria actually opened the window, and Sergei pondered the discrepancy be-tween her words and action as Maria gently turned him around and led him into the adjoining room.

On the following morning, for his birthday, he was presented with the American flag, which he and his playmates with great ceremony placed on the top of the garden fence. To his sorrow, the flag was sto-len during the night by the boys from the village, who must have found it as attractive as he did.

3

Maria took Sergei's musical education seriously and was cautious about his piano lessons. Her main aim was to develop in the boy a true love for music and not destroy his early enthusiasm by the constant practicing of exercises. In working with him, she devoted most of the time to introducing him to the musical literature. At the age of seven, Sergei's daily lessons never lasted more than twenty minutes, but as he grew older, the lessons became longer, until at the age of nine they were one hour long.

From a volume of collected short compositions, she selected those that were most beautiful and interesting, and once Sergei was acquainted with the original version of the composition, he had to transpose it into two or three different keys—a process that was supplemented by their discussions of which of the keys was the most suitable for the composition and why. Then the piece was laid aside, and Sergei proceeded to the next one.

Although Sergei Prokofiev later thought that "too-anxious mothers of future musicians" should refrain from forcing their children to practice the same pieces over and over again, he had to admit that while his mother's method both introduced him to an exceptionally large and varied number of compositions and taught him to read music at sight with extreme ease, his technical skill at the keyboard lagged behind. Her method developed a certain carelessness in his playing. As he said, "The thoughts were ahead of the fingers, which followed any old way." And later on, when he decided to become a pianist, he had to pay dearly for this unfortunately acquired habit.

Nevertheless, he was grateful to his mother's method, for his early knowledge of a vast number of compositions led to his musical maturity: at the age of ten he already had his own "point of view" toward each work that, as he said, he could defend.

The "method," of course, was applied only during his lessons, leaving him free to play whenever and as often as he liked, particularly after the Prokofievs bought a beautiful new grand piano. "The Prokofievs must have lost their minds. Why do they need a second piano?" said the villagers, as at first they watched the careful, almost ceremonial transportation of the instrument over the bumpy roads, and as they later learned of the arrival of a piano tuner—piano tuning was an unheard-of profession in Sontsovka.

The new piano had a much richer, fuller tone than the old one. Sergei loved playing it. He loved the sound of it; it made him not merely pick out the melodies he heard, but improvise, transforming the visions of his fantasy into sounds. Often, after playing for their guests the pieces he had recently learned, he would improvise, sometimes carried away so completely that either his father or mother would have to come up to him and whisper something into his ear to make him finish the endless piece quickly.

At about this time, when he was nine years old, his parents took him along on a visit to Moscow. There he was given a great treat: he was taken to the opera to see Gounod's *Faust*. Before the performance Maria tried to explain the plot of the opera in a few sentences. "You see, there was a man named Faust; he was a scientist. He was already an old man and spent his time reading books. And then the devil came to see him and said, 'Sell me your soul and I will make you young again.' Well, Faust sold him his soul, and the devil made him young, and they began to have a good time. . . ."

Although Sergei was at first very intrigued, he grew bored because they arrived at the opera house long before the start of the performance, and he became rather skeptical about the whole thing.

"At last they played the overture and the curtain rose," the composer later described his first impressions. "Indeed, there were books everywhere and Faust with a long beard read something in a fat volume, then he sang something, and then read again. But where was the devil? How slow everything was! Well, at last—the devil. But why was he in a red costume and with a saber, and so elegant? For some reason I expected him to be black, half-naked, and with hooves and a tail. Later, when they began to 'have a good time,' I recognized the waltz and the march I had heard mother play at home, but could not understand what 'the fun' was all about." Also, Sergei could not understand why sometimes a white spotlight was directed at Marguerite and a deep-red light at the devil, particularly when he sang for a long time.

But on the whole the spectacle made a greater impression on him than Borodin's *Prince Igor* or Tchaikovsky's ballet *The Sleeping Beauty*, which he saw before they returned to Sontsovka. Neither the music nor the production of these was to be blamed, for this time Sergei sat in a box with his cousins where the fresh fruit, chocolates, and sweetcakes brought by their parents drew his attention from what was taking place on stage.

"Mama, I want to write my own opera," Sergei said shortly after their arrival home.

"How would you write an opera?" Maria asked, with what Sergei thought was a rather disrespectful attitude and lack of faith in him. "Why talk about something you couldn't possibly do?"

"Oh, well, you'll see."

They talked about it for a while, and Maria thought that was the end of the project, but Sergei would not give up the idea so easily. For days everything else—his regular lessons and his piano playing—became of secondary importance in his mind, until one day he called in his playmates. He had the title, *The Giant*, and the plot was contrived in the same way as for their plays—that is, he and his friends developed the action and dialogue as they progressed from one scene to the next.

"Stenya," Sergei said to the girl who was to play the leading role in the opera, "you sit there as though you were reading a book. Suddenly the giant goes by. Frightened, you ask 'Who is there?' He says, 'This is I, this is I,' and then he wants to catch you. Just then Vasya and I walk in and we hear you scream. Vasya says, 'Well, then, shall I shoot him?' 'No, not yet.' "

Vasya broke into Sergei's improvisation, "The giant sees me and quickly retreats."

"And I faint," concluded Stenya.

In the same manner, the following scenes involved a king who sent an army against the giant, but failing to subdue him, committed suicide, while the heroes of the play celebrated the giant's victory.

Actually, Sergei had his first "political" problem on his hands. The dénouement of his opera met with his father's objections: there was no sense in a nine-year-old boy behaving unconsciously as a revolutionary. Apparently, his father still remembered the unpleasant consequences of his student days, and he very delicately and diplomatically asked Sergei whether there could not be another ending to the opera: for instance, could the king make peace with the giant?

But such a variant would not fit into Sergei's plot. It seemed to him rather dull, and besides, he would not know what to do about the king's pathetic recitative. In short, his father's puzzling intrusion upset him so that the text of the dénouement never was written into the third act.

Thus, completely ignorant of such things as kings and their privileged position in society and of revolutionaries—obviously a disturbing element that on no account should be allowed to triumph—Sergei at this early age for the first time experienced the cruel hand of the censor.

Neither the story nor Sergei's music was very successful. Having seen *Faust*, he thought that an opera must have a waltz and a march, and every character at least one short aria and one long one. Since Sergei did not know yet how to write vocal parts, the text was written above the treble-clef part. Also, though overtures are usually written after an opera score is completed and are based on the most characteristic themes of the whole composition, Sergei began by writing the overture—first things first.

Nevertheless, the opera pleased Sergei's audience. His admiring aunt took the "manuscript" to be copied and bound in St. Petersburg, and when, during the following summer, Maria and Sergei were visiting their relatives, it was performed at his uncle's home.

Directing his cousins through the first act, Sergei became so transported that Maria thought it better to end the spectacle with the close of the first act, "or Sergei is going to be sick," she said. But his uncle was enchanted by the performance and congratulating the young composer, said, "Well, Seryozha, when they present your works at the Imperial theatres, don't forget that your debut was at my home."

"Speaking this way, my uncle hardly thought he was predicting my future," the composer once told me. "But I remembered his words when some twenty years later (my uncle was no longer alive, and there were no more Imperial theatres in Russia), my opera, not this one but another one, was given its first performance in Chicago." (Prokofiev meant his opera *The Love for Three Oranges*, which had its world premiere in Chicago in 1921.)

Encouraged by his success, Sergei immediately started on his second opera, *On Deserted Islands*. The subject, the composer said later, was even more childish than *The Giant*, something about an expedition and a ship wrecked by storms. But by the time he had his heroes on a "deserted island," he did not know what to do with them and how to end the thrilling adventure. He worked on it for more than a year, so that the score reached large dimensions—all the short piano pieces he composed "on the side" were incorporated into the opera.

Meanwhile, Sergei continued his lessons with his parents, who divided between them history, geography, and arithmetic. After two years in Sontsovka, Louise returned to Paris for a visit, but the German governess who took her place was not as successful with Sergei as Mademoiselle, so that his early knowledge of the German was not as good as his command of French.

After the usual short winter visit in St. Petersburg, Maria and her son arrived in Moscow in January, 1902, and it was then that Sergei came into his first contact with professional musicians. At the home of the Pomerantsevs, old friends of Sergei's parents, the twenty-year-old Yury Pomerantsev, student at the Moscow Conservatory, put Sergei through all kinds of tests of his ability to play the piano, read music at sight, play a short composition on the piano after looking over the piece away from the instrument, write down what he heard played, call out the chords or single notes that Pomerantsev struck on the piano.

Although Sergei did not pass all the tests, Pomerantsev promised to speak about him to his teacher, Sergei Taneyev. And he kept his word, to the great suprise of the aspiring ten-year-old composer.

Sergei Taneyev, whose compositions and theoretical treatises are known to comparatively few outside of Russia, was a significant figure in the history of Russian music. He was a pupil of Tchaikovsky, but so far surpassed him in his theoretical knowledge that it was Tchaikovsky who sought his advice and criticism rather than vice-versa. Taneyev was considered such an extraordinary man (which indeed he was—a scientist, a mathematician) that rumors circulated about his incredible knowledge of the mysterious, of the mathematical calculations with which he was to conquer the theory of sound; and this reputation in turn created an almost superstitious fear of him, as though he were a medieval alchemist or a sage. Because he did not drink, he was regarded as an ascetic who sacrificed every pleasure in life for the sake of music. He never married but led an isolated life, at first in a little house on Sivsev Vrashka, and later, on the Mertvy Perulok, the "Blind Alley of the Dead," an address that seemed to add a peculiar ghostly accent to his personality.

His little house there, like all those in which he liked to live, had neither electricity nor running water; it was a house with a sign permanently attached to its front door, "Sergei Taneyev is not at home," regardless of whether he was in or out.

Among the few privileged visitors was Leo Tolstoy. Tolstoy's wife was an ardent music lover; who devoted several hours a day to practicing the piano and often organized informal musicals at their home. A number of world-famous musicians performed at the Tolstoys', and it was even insinuated that Tolstoy's novel *The Kreutzer Sonata* was a product of Tolstoy's jealousy of Taneyev.

Had Maria known even a little of all this, she would have been even more nervous than she was on the late afternoon at the end of January when she and Sergei, carrying in his briefcase everything he had ever composed, walked up to the porch of Taneyev's house.

Taneyev's nurse, who took care of him all his life, opened the door. Of large proportions, she walked as a rowboat rides the waves, Sergei thought as she showed them into her master's study. The many books, the quiet atmosphere of the room, as if it were completely isolated from the rest of the world, and the benevolent voice of the tall, heavy-set Taneyev made the visitors feel as if they had entered a temple. But when Taneyev offered Sergei some chocolate, Sergei no longer found him as terrifying as he expected a celebrity to be.

Sergei played the overture to *On Deserted Islands*, "a friable piece" that he would not have chosen had he known that this was all he was going to be asked to play. Taneyev glanced through *The Giant* and then told Maria that although the boy was only ten, they should not waste any more time but that he should start immediately to learn harmony and counterpoint, or he would acquire bad habits that would be difficult for him to correct later. He suggested they take advantage of their visit to Moscow by having Sergei study with Yury Pomerantsev. Thus Sergei's musical education began in earnest. And he did not like it at all.

Just as Sergei Rachmaninoff, also Taneyev's pupil, at the age of sixteen balked at the strict rules because, as he had told me, "I could not take the faintest interest in counterpoint in the strict style, in all these imitations and inversions," so did the ten-year-old Sergei Prokofiev, who was anxious to compose operas with marches, sea storms, duels, and blood-curdling scenes. "Instead," Sergei grumbled, "they are binding me hand and foot with 'this is not allowed,' and 'this is unnecessary,' forcing me to write twaddle that is useless to anyone." Just as Rachmaninoff shirked his assignments, so did Prokofiev, who, upon his return to the hotel where he lived with his mother, would rather spend hours sitting by the window and writing down the numbers of trolley cars passing by.

But before they went back to Sontsovka, Maria called on Taneyev again. He told her that these lessons with Pomerantsev were the merest beginning, that to learn the art of composition Sergei should work with a composer whom they should invite to Sontsovka for three summer months. He suggested Reinhold Glière.

4

Of Belgian origin, born in 1874 in Kiev, where his father manufactured wind instruments, Reinhold Glière, who is best known for his ballet *The Red Poppy* and his Third Symphony, *Ilya Murometz,* was then twenty-eight. He had been graduated from the Moscow Conservatory with the gold medal and had had several compositions published, some of which had won him prizes.

Even as a student he had begun to give private lessons in harmony, often tutoring those who lagged behind in their studies at the Conservatory. With this pedagogical experience and a suitcase containing a modest variety of personal effects and a large amount of music paper, Glière arrived at Sontsovka at the beginning of the summer of 1902.

Sergei had overheard his parents talking about the forthcoming visitor, but paid little attention. "He'll surely turn out to be just another Pomerantsev with all those dull and useless exercises," Sergei pouted. And only when he saw his mother and Marfusha preparing a room for his teacher with unusual care was he, too, caught up in the general excitement.

Not because of any lack of respect for Glière, but because of a certain decorum they felt they should preserve, Sergei's parents did not believe they should all "pour out" to welcome their guest. Instead, they told Sergei to meet him and take him to his room. It was an unusual procedure, Sergei thought, and he reluctantly went to the porch, where, while waiting for the return of the carriage that had been sent to fetch Glière from the station, he busied himself by cutting off thorns from three large thistle stalks he brought from the garden.

"He'll see me cutting off the thorns," Sergei shrugged. "So what? Let him see it—there is nothing wrong with it. Or is there?"

When Glière stepped down from the carriage and greeted him, at the same time inquiring, "Seryozha?" Sergei noticed that the slender young man with the broad face, dark mustache, and heavy eyebrows carried a violin case in his hand. If he is going to teach me composition and to play the piano, why then the violin? Sergei wondered after he had left Glière in his room and returned to his parents for further instructions.

"Let him rest for a while from his long journey," Maria said, "and then go and invite him to join us for lunch on the terrace in the garden. And meanwhile go and clean up the mess you made on the porch."

All this unaccustomed formality disconcerted Sergei, and he was ready to take a definite dislike to the strange intruder into his pleasant life. But he turned out to be a nice fellow, Sergei decided later.

Although Glière's room was small, everything was neatly arranged for his comfort and his work; the windows opened onto the garden, a large lilac bush was in full bloom in front of one of them, and farther on he could see flower beds, fruit trees, and beautifully kept little paths. From his first days in Sontsovka, Glière felt as if he were one of the Prokofiev family.

In Maria, whom he met for the first time, he found an intelligent and interesting companion who knew how to create a simple and pleasant atmosphere. He observed her extraordinary love for her son, but also realized that her pride in his talent was not merely a blind adoration. She was aware of her responsibility for his education and was both stern and demanding with him. At the end of each day, during their supper, she would ask him how he had passed the day, what he had accomplished, and whether he was satisfied with it.

Glière saw less of Sergei's father, who was extremely busy either in his study or in the fields, or was away on short trips to various towns in connection with the sale of the products of the estate. But he, too, was very serious about Sergei's education.

And even when he did see him, Glière never succeeded in establishing a close relationship with Sergei's father, for as Maria remarked on several occasions, her husband was one of those men who are very shy and who, although capable of deep feeling, seldom reveal their thoughts.

Glière thought the strict program of the family's daily life unusual but wise. They rose early and before breakfast went swimming in the river, which was within walking distance of the house. From ten to eleven Glière worked with Sergei. Then Sergei had his lessons with his father in Russian and arithmetic, followed by the lessons in French or German with his mother. Dinner was at three in the afternoon, and the time after that was reserved for relaxation—long walks in the fields or games of croquet. (Russian croquet differs from that which is played elsewhere because it is played on a field as smooth as a tennis court, with wickets firmly cemented into the ground; both the mallets and the balls are larger, requiring more strength from the players.)

Like Louise before him, Glière easily fell in with the general way of living at Sontsovka, so that he, too, after having finished his own work—he was writing a string quartet—was ready to play a game of chess or accept Sergei's challenge to a duel, thus winning the boy's heart once and for all.

Later in the afternoon Sergei had one more hour of music with Glière, a piano lesson. Maria always sat in at those sessions, so that, as she said, she could continue teaching Sergei according to Glière's methods after Glière's departure at the end of the summer. At that time Sergei particularly liked the two last movements of Beethoven's First and "Moonlight" Sonatas, because of their "stormy character."

Sometimes after supper, during the long quiet summer evenings, Glière would bring out his violin and play Mozart and Haydn sonatas with Sergei. At the first strains of the music Sergei's father would emerge from his study and tiptoe to a far corner of the room, where in an easy chair he would remain listening until the concert ended. Maria would call Marfusha to look after a domestic chore (such as making cherry jam to be sent to her sisters in St. Petersburg) so that she could sit by the open window of the drawing room, where the servants would join her in listening to the music.

During Glière's two summers at Sontsovka, combining the teaching of harmony with free composition, he also explained to Sergei the rudiments of orchestration. All this Glière successfully accomplished during the long sessions at the piano when they played four-hand arrangements of the compositions of Haydn, Mozart, Beethoven, and Tchaikovsky. By this time Sergei not only did not object to working on theoretical exercises, but with the enthusiasm of a true creator, was absorbed in solving the problems of harmony.

By the end of Glière's first summer at Sontsovka and despite his arguments against it, Sergei composed a symphony in G major in four movements. It was orchestrated with Glière's help, and when later in the year Sergei went again with his mother to Moscow, he showed it to Taneyev.

Taneyev was amused and remarked that it was harmonically "a bit commonplace." "This remark touched me to the quick," Sergei Prokofiev said later, while reminiscing about this initial turn in his development as a composer. "Although I was on the verge of tears I didn't cry, did not spend a sleepless night, but somehow I could not get rid of the idea: the harmonic treatment was much too simple, 'commonplace.' The microbe had penetrated into the organism but it had to have a long incubation period."

Four years later Sergei's experiments in harmony provoked interest among his friends, but when eight years later he played his Études (Op. 2) for Taneyev, the old master, obviously displeased, said, "Far too many false notes. . . ." Sergei reminded him of his remark about the first symphony, and Taneyev laughed: "So it was I who pushed you onto this slippery road!"

Far from abandoning the "slippery road," Sergei made it more and more his own, and this despite the fact that later on, after hearing some of his compositions, his own mother argued with him until they finished by not speaking to each other for days. Still later, Nikolai Medtner, Prokofiev's contemporary composer, was to declare publicly, "If this is music, I am not a musician."

But Glière was not in the least at fault, for he instructed Sergei in the theoretical subjects just as they were taught at the Moscow Conservatory or at any other. It was Sergei's own language that he had created and that he preferred for the expression of his musical ideas. Nor could Glière be held responsible for Sergei's poor piano technique. While working with him, Glière realized that although Sergei played with a great deal of freedom and assurance, the lack of good schooling caused a large number of missed notes and an uneven and sloppy execution. Actually, Glière was surprised that with his long fingers and clumsy way of using his hands Sergei managed to play some of the more complicated passages while at the same time he could barely master accurately a simple run of a few notes.

Glière, however, could not help him much with practical advice, for he himself was a violinist and not an accomplished pianist.

Besides, although Sergei was an obedient student of theoretical subjects, he was very argumentative and stubborn whenever Glière offered him some advice about his playing. Occasionally, to win the argument, Sergei would point to the difficult passage in question and maliciously say, "Let's see you do it," which, of course, only embarrassed Glière.

"Sergei was fortunate," Glière related later, "that eventually, at the Conservatory, he was admitted into Anna Essipova's class. It is well known that it took her a long time to teach him to use his hands correctly, but during the first years of her work with him it often came to sharp conflicts between the famous pedagogue and the young student, until one day, losing her temper, Essipova shouted, "Either you are going to hold your hands at the piano as you should, or leave my class!"

Such was later to be Sergei's beginning both as a composer and a pianist. If his relationship with eminent teachers occasionally suffered from discord, his preparatory work with Glière at Sontsovka was most harmonious.

5

The eleven-year-old Sergei found a sympathetic friend in Glière, who knew how to guide him through the problems of composition and who even succeeded in making the "dull and useless" exercises in harmony and counterpoint interesting and challenging to Sergei's imagination.

Using the analogy of "subjects and predicates," Glière explained the structure of the three-part song and those "songs without words," short piano pieces Sergei called "Ditties" for lack of any better name. He seemed to enjoy composing them and, in fact, continued writing them during the following six years in such quantity—close to seventy —that he later grouped them into a series.

Glière also taught him orchestration, although living in Sontsovka, Sergei had no opportunity to hear a symphony orchestra and therefore had only a vague idea of the sound of the various instruments. Before leaving Sontsovka, Glière marked in Anton Arensky's book on harmony a number of exercises for Sergei to work on during the winter, and which he was to send to Glière for correction.

This work by correspondence, however, did not prove successful. Once no longer under Glière's watchful eye, Sergei grew less diligent.

"Did you look through the corrections and try to understand your mistakes?" Maria would ask him. The boy would reluctantly play what Glière had sent him. But later on Maria discovered several envelopes that had not even been opened.

It is possible that Sergei's loss of enthusiasm in his homework was caused by the length of time (between ten days and two weeks) that would lapse before Glière's reply could reach him. Meanwhile, Sergei would either forget the exercises, or "they were pushed aside" by the one he was currently working on. Maria understood this and refrained from scolding or forcing him.

During the winter she took Sergei along on her annual visit to Moscow, and there Sergei resumed his daily lessons with Glière. But Sergei enjoyed even more going with his teacher and friend to concerts and operas. It was then that he heard a symphony orchestra for the first time, and he was fortunate to hear it conducted by such eminent conductors as Arthur Nikish and Vasily Safonoff. Sergei sat as if bewitched by the sound of the orchestra, the conductor's gestures, and the festive atmosphere of the concert hall. Sergei wrote to his father:

It is one o'clock in the morning—we have just come home from a concert. Nikish is a famous and elegant conductor who has been driving the audiences in Moscow and St. Petersburg mad. The concert was magnificent. Nikish was presented with two wreaths and three or four baskets of flowers. I thought that Nikish conducted the overture to Glinka's *Russlan and Ludmilla* much better than Safonoff, whom I heard two days ago. We liked Grieg's Suite, and apparently everybody else did too, because they made him repeat the second and fourth parts.

Glière played the viola in the orchestra—he wanted so much to play under Nikish's direction, but there was no vacancy among the violins and therefore he had to play viola. After the concert, Nikish was called back at least eight or ten times and they applauded so much that he bowed in every possible manner and even threw kisses at them besides, they were waving handkerchiefs, hats, and programs at him, offered him flowers and shouted *bravo* terribly!!! Even Mama did too, and my hands are sore from clapping.

Three days later he was taken to the Bolshoi Theatre to hear Wagner's *The Valkyrie*. This time he was less enthusiastic. "It is a terribly boring opera," he reported again to his father, "without any melodies, or dramatic action, but with a great deal of noise."

Later, commenting on this early critical reaction, Prokofiev said that while he could easily understand that the absence of scenic action would bore an eleven-year-old boy, the remark about "great deal of noise" must have been picked up from those who took him to the opera, for the loud orchestration would have intrigued rather than frightened him.

Now that Sergei was growing older, the Prokofievs were faced with a new problem: for his general education he had to enter a gymnasium. But the question was, where? The provincial schools were notoriously poor—the best among them were at Ekaterinoslav, some eight hours from Sontsovka.

Maria, who had observed so much interest in Sergei by musicians in Moscow, tried upon their return home to persuade her husband to send Sergei to a school there. The boy, she argued, could be living with their relatives, and Maria could come for short visits, or she could stay with him during the school year and her husband could visit them. Christmas and Easter vacations they could spend together in Sontsovka.

Whatever the final decision, it meant breaking up the happy quiet life of the family in their little village. Their debates over the problem were so lively that Sergei remembered being awakened one morning by a "stormy discussion" in his parents' bedroom. Through the open door he heard his father saying, "In this case there is nothing else left for me to do but to shoot myself."

Sergei took his father's threat literally and burst into loud sobs. The embarrassed parents tried to calm him, and for a while the final decision was put off. But not so far as Sergei's daily schedule of lessons was concerned. Sergei was not yet well prepared enough to pass the required examinations, and he had to undergo a far more intensified program of studies.

To make things even more unnerving, Sergei overheard stories of teachers who would conceive a prejudice against the applicant for no reason at all, of perfectly sadistic men who took delight in seeing young boys fail in their examinations. Actually, there was another reason for the extreme difficulty in entering the schools. At that time in Russia there were not enough schools to accommodate all the applicants; the maximum number of pupils in each class was already established. (There was great competition among, for instance, twenty-five applicants for the third grade—Sergei's level—and perhaps only five vacancies.) Facing such a dismal prospect, Sergei's parents worked with him for five to six hours a day. And Sergei still hated it.

Thus it was a relief, when in June, Glière arrived for his second summer in Sontsovka, and Sergei was allowed to spend more time on music. Glière made several corrections in the violin sonata Sergei had written during the winter, but found nothing wrong with the latest collections of Ditties. For Sergei's major summer work he suggested a string quartet or sextet, but Sergei's heart was set on writing another opera. Glière argued against it, said it was much too complicated, but finally gave in. After two days of leafing through several volumes of Pushkin, he chose *Feast During the Plague* for Sergei's opera.

This choice of subject was not particularly wise, because the action in the play could not stir the young boy's imagination, but there were some aspects in its favor. First of all, since it was a play, there was no need to write a libretto, but simply to make cuts in the dialogue; there was no love intrigue to be handled by a twelve-year-old boy; and finally, it was in one act and could be written during the three summer months.

"And you will use the best themes of the opera in the overture," Glière said as he handed the book to Sergei, who looked as if he were already composing the overture in his mind. "We'll do the overture as it should be—in sonata form, not just any old way."

Guided by Glière through every detail of the opera, Sergei worked on it all summer long. This time the opera, written with an orchestral score and vocal parts, had a professional look. The overture, on which Sergei worked by himself after Glière's departure, turned out to be much too long. Following Glière's advice to use the best themes, Sergei incorporated into the overture practically half of the opera. This gave his new opus the aspect of a large head on a small body. Nevertheless, it showed a definite step forward in comparison with his first symphony. (Prokofiev's lifelong habit of never discarding any music he had written must already have been established, for six years later, when graduating from the composition course at the Conservatory, he completely rewrote this opera score.)

By coincidence, at about this time Cesar Cui, already a well-known composer, one of the Mighty Five (Balakirev, Borodin, Cui, Moussorgsky, and Rimsky-Korsakov) had also composed an opera on the same subject. When Glière returned to Moscow, he sent Cui's published score to Sergei. "I examined the score with obvious jealousy, but very critically," Prokofiev said later. Having discovered that one of the arias in Cui's score closely resembled his own setting of the same passage, he played both versions to his mother.

"Don't you like mine better?" he asked.

"Yes, of course," Maria said sympathetically, "only you would do better not to try to play Cui's opera so badly."

"That Cui's was a master's work, I did not understand at the time," Prokofiev admitted later, when speaking of the "professional jealousy" that was already then characteristic of his nature. It often led to embarrassing situations when, for example, after having criticized someone's playing of a certain composition, Sergei would venture to show how superior was his own interpretation, and only fail miserably because of his lack of the necessary pianistic technique. But these occasional "setbacks" did not discourage him—professional jealousy was a part of his passionate young nature—but they could not have failed eventually to develop in him a sense of self-criticism, for he was an intelligent and proud boy.

From habit picked up as a youngster, his music manuscripts were not only sloppy, but dirty. He was careless because he could depend on Louise, who had learned to make a beautiful, clean copy. Often he would draw in the margins little figures of devils, monkeys, or men waving their hands—these were to indicate the corrections, to serve as signals for Louise to consult him first where this or that correction belonged.

But Louise was going to leave the Prokofievs in order to teach at a school in St. Petersburg, and Maria told Sergei he had better learn to write his music properly so that he would not be ashamed of showing it to men like Taneyev. This remark was sufficient to prompt Sergei to develop such a beautiful handwriting that when later on he would be asked to show his rough draft, he could nonchalantly say, "This is it."

He also began to be more orderly about his clothes, and being an observant child, he formed definite ideas about "proper appearance."

During the winter of 1904 Maria again took him along to St. Petersburg. Soon after their arrival, Maria managed to have an interview for them with Alexander Glazunov, who, then thirty-nine, had been conducting classes in orchestration and score reading at the Conservatory for the past five years. Maria knew even less about Glazunov than about Taneyev, although Glazunov's reputation had been established since he had composed his first symphony at the age of sixteen.

Glazunov had originally been Rimsky-Korsakov's pupil and at one time had joined Mili Balakirev's group of disciples, which Balakirev had acquired in the last period of his life when he was no longer associated with the Mighty Five, whose leading force and mentor he had been from 1859 to 1870. Not particularly influenced by the Russian national school of thought, Glazunov's music showed traces of Brahms, and was accepted, although without any spectacular enthusiasm, by the two opposing musical circles in Moscow and St. Petersburg.

He was no innovator, nor was he interested in any new, progressive ideas in music; and his uneventful career as a composer suited perfectly his uneventful life—the comfortable and responsible position of a professor. Even his general appearance and behavior conformed to this prototype. He was of large build and early inclined to stoutness due, according to some, to his weakness for alcohol.

Sergei played the overture to *Feast During the Plague* and Glazunov, who listened as if he were half-asleep, mumbled something about his impression. "He is not at all like dear Taneyev," Maria said to Sergei after they left Glazunov's home.

Sergei, too, was less moved by his first meeting with the composer than he was embarrassed a few days later when Glazunov called on them unannounced while Maria was not at home. "I was annoyed," Prokofiev said later, "because of the disorder in the room: on the table was the remains of my plate of *kasha*, next to it a textbook and a copybook in which I was working on an arithmetic problem, and a rubber pistol. Our rented upright piano was covered with music. My sailor shirt needed a button sewed on, and my hair was all mussed up because I had been taking a nap on the couch."

Glazunov took no notice of the disorder. "Tell your Mama that I am sorry not to have seen her, but that I'll come the day after tomorrow at the same time. Now, don't forget to tell her." And Glazunov was about to leave when he saw a score of Beethoven's symphonies arranged for four hands on the music rack.

"Who plays these?" he asked in his gruff voice.

"I play them with Mama."

"Which other symphonies have you played?"

"Haydn's."

"Have you played Schumann's?"

"No."

"Then buy Schumann's," Glazunov ordered, and walked out.

When Sergei told her about it, Maria became very excited that so eminent a personage as Glazunov had come to see her and that he was coming again. It was decided to serve him tea with "delicious cakes and expensive fruit," as Sergei observed his mother running back and forth to her relatives to borrow nice cups and saucers for the occasion and a vase for flowers from their landlady.

Neither Maria nor Sergei could have had any idea that Glazunov's visit was to have a decisive influence on Sergei's future.

Glazunov arrived punctually, declined to take tea because of lack of time, and asked Maria to listen attentively to what he had to say. "I came to try to persuade you to send your son to the Conservatory."

Maria argued against it. It would be all very well, she said, if Sergei were endowed with such talent that he would become a great artist. But if not, what then? What would be his prospects? To remain for the rest of his life a secondary teacher of music? This is why she and her husband would prefer that Sergei become a civil engineer or an architect—professions that would necessitate his living in a large city where he would have an opportunity to continue his interest in music, to attend concerts, and to keep up his contacts with musicians.

Glazunov was not moved by these arguments. On the contrary, he told Maria, in the end Sergei would be neither a good architect nor musician, and he said that she would never forgive herself for letting Sergei remain merely an amateur.

"Your son will be admitted into the composition class," Glazunov continued, "and at the same time he could attend the classes in general education at the Conservatory. They are not as comprehensive as those of the gymnasium, but you could have extra tutoring at home." And this final argument succeeded in persuading Maria. There would be no more nightmarish worries over Sergei's passing the examinations or not being accepted at the gymnasium. Glazunov suggested that Maria consult her husband and left.

A lively correspondence between Maria and her husband followed the long discussions Maria had with her relatives and friends and with Glière, who came from Moscow to attend a performance of his works in St. Petersburg. Glière spoke about Sergei to Rimsky-Korsakov, who was the leading professor in the composition class at the Conservatory in St. Petersburg, told him about their summer work, Sergei's libretto in verse for *The Giant*, about the theatrical performances with his little friends in the country, and even about Sergei's passion for chess.

" 'Sergei must go to a Conservatory,' drones everyone," Maria wrote to Sontsovka. But Sergei's father preferred the Moscow Conservatory because his relatives lived in the city and could be both of assistance and company to his wife and son, while Maria insisted on St. Petersburg just because of this. She had never gotten over her in-laws' snobbish attitude before her marriage and her own superior feeling, developed since, toward their purely bourgeois existence and lack of intellectual interests.

Eventually she persuaded her husband at least to give it a try. She would move with Sergei to St. Petersburg and rent a small apartment, and he could visit them whenever he managed to get away from his work.

It looked like the final decision to Sergei when he saw his mother buying furniture at an auction and acquiring from the landlady the vase she had borrowed for Glazunov's visit. A rather cumbersome article, it somehow reminded Sergei and Maria so much of the large dimensions of Glazunov's figure that it remained in the Prokofiev family with the nickname "Glazunov's vase."

Sergei showed very little interest in what should have been an exciting prospect—entering the St. Petersburg Conservatory. He had no idea of what a conservatory was like. One good thing about it, he thought, was that at least that dreadful question of exams and entering a gymnasium was finally solved. He never had cherished the idea of going to a gymnasium because there, he had heard, the boys liked fist-fights and poking fun at and taunting the newcomers, and Sergei was not strong and did not know how to fight. At home his friends were given strict orders never to fight with him, and they treated him with "due respect." "You are a sweet butterball," Maria used to say as she caressed his pale cheeks.

And so, it was decided that in the autumn of 1904, at the age of thirteen, Sergei should go to the Conservatory in St. Petersburg for his examinations.

6

At home again, Maria plunged into the busiest summer she had ever had. Since she would be leaving Sontsovka for the whole winter, she had to see to it that her household would continue to function as usual and that her husband's daily schedule would not be interrupted, lest it add extra pain to the breaking up of their family life.

Glière did not come to Sontsovka, and what free time Sergei had was spent in composing *Undine*, an opera that had been suggested to him by Maria Kilshtet, a friend of his relatives in St. Petersburg. About fifty years old, Madame Kilshtet was a poet whose poems were published in the newspapers. She had offered to write a libretto in verse based on the original by Friedrich de la Motte-Fouqué, and soon after returning home, Sergei received the first act. This time, according to Sergei's plans, the opera was to be in five acts and six scenes.

But by the end of August, Sergei was caught up in the general excitement over the final preparations for their departure. Every other time, sitting next to his mother in the carriage that was taking them to the nearest station on their way to Moscow or St. Petersburg, Sergei had swallowed his tears, and, trying to alleviate the pain of parting with everything dear to him at Sontsovka, he had concentrated on a promised "real engine" or some other new toy. Now, entering his adolescence, he was in an exhilarated mood, savoring in advance everything new and interesting awaiting him in the capital. He was not afraid of the exams, he kept saying to himself, and his father had promised to visit them within a month.

But his heart did not beat quite so calmly when his mother took him to the Conservatory for the examinations in composition and theoretical subjects. And the longer he had to wait before being called into the director's office in which the examinations were being held, the more nervous he became. There were altogether about twenty young applicants, all much older than Sergei. One of them, a man in his thirties with a great beard, who had brought with him only one song without any accompaniment, was examined just before Sergei. Then Sergei walked into the director's office carrying two bulging briefcases, one under each arm, holding manuscripts of four operas, two sonatas, a symphony, and a large number of piano pieces. (Perhaps this contrast with the single work offered by the preceding applicant made the members of the jury take immediate notice.)

Rimsky-Korsakov, assisted by Glazunov and Anatol Lyadov, conducted the examinations while ten other professors of the Conservatory sat at a table on the other side of the room drinking tea and eating buttered buns and jam.

"Are all these your own compositions?" Rimsky-Korsakov asked, as he opened one of the briefcases Sergei laid on the desk before him.

"Yes," Sergei answered in a quavering voice.

"Do you play the piano?"

"I do."

Rimsky-Korsakov, after glancing through one of the compositions, said, "I like this one. Come along," and he led Sergei to the piano.

Pointing to a Mozart sonata on the music rack, he said, "Play this for me."

It was a sonata Sergei had played through some years before. As he began, Rimsky-Korsakov interrupted him: "Very well . . . how about this one?" and he turned several pages to another sonata that Sergei had never seen before.

"He is Glière's pupil," Glazunov told Rimsky-Korsakov who knew this already. "Oh . . . and what did you do with him?" Rimsky-Korsakov asked Sergei.

"He was staying with us two summers, and . . ."

"What did you do in theoretical subjects, I mean," Rimsky-Korsakov interrupted again.

"We worked on harmony, using Arensky's textbook," Sergei began, and hesitatingly added, "but because I was going to study harmony at the Conservatory, last summer I didn't work on harmony any more . . . not at all."

"We should test his ear for music," suggested one of the professors who was chewing a bun.

"Do you have perfect pitch?" Rimsky-Korsakov asked.

"I think so," Sergei answered with a little more assurance.

At random, Rimsky-Korsakov struck first several keys and then a few chords on the piano. Sergei named them all accurately.

"How about his *solfeggio?*" asked the professor, who had finished eating buns and now, leaning across the table, looked sternly at Sergei.

Sergei's heart sank. "I . . . I . . . never sang," he blushed.

"Never mind," Rimsky-Korsakov said. "Here, sing to me this bass part."

It was too low for Sergei's childlike voice, and he tried to sing it an octave higher, but fumbled.

"Obviously he cannot sing. . . . He should have been taught. . . ." Sergei overheard the professors whispering at the tea table, and suddenly all the stories he had heard about the examiners who failed the applicants to the gymnasia flashed through his mind. Was this the ignominious end? What would Mama and Papa say? What would the boys in Sontsovka say?

A few horrifying minutes passed before Alexander Bernhard, the director, who until then had merely watched the proceedings, suggested, "Ask him to sing something from the keys of different instruments, transposing into the right key."

"Do you know the keys?" Rimsky-Korsakov asked.

"Of course he knows," answered Glazunov, who obviously was going to "pull Sergei through" the tests. "He has written orchestral scores."

"Orchestral scores?" the professors at the tea table asked doubtfully.

"And operas." Glazunov added.

"And operas?" Sergei heard as if he were in a daze. He did not notice the professors leave their table and go to the piano where, taking one of the orchestral scores, they were searching for something suitable for Sergei's high voice. Finally, putting the volume on the music rack, they pointed to a passage in a symphony score.

"Oh, no . . . this is much too virtuoso," Glazunov protested.

"It doesn't matter," Rimsky-Korsakov said, and Sergei began to sing: "O-o-o." "No, no," Rimsky-Korsakov stopped him. "Don't sing 'Do-do-do . . .' when it is not *do* at all. Just sing without naming the notes."

By this time Sergei was on the verge of tears. He wanted, but did not dare, to say that he was not singing *do* even if it sounded as if he were.

"Now, let's see your compositions." Rimsky-Korsakov returned to the director's table. With a shaking hand, Sergei opened one of the briefcases.

On the top of his manuscripts Rimsky-Korsakov noticed a piece of paper. "What is this?" he asked.

"It's the list . . . the list of my compositions." Sergei's voice was barely audible.

"A list of your compositions?" Rimsky-Korsakov laughed. And picking the score of *Undine* from the pile of music before him, he told Sergei to play it.

"And tell him to sing the vocal parts," insisted one of the professors.

"Now, how can he?" Rimsky-Korsakov asked.

"Oh . . . he can, he can," Glazunov interrupted. "He sings his own music very well—I have heard him." Sergei did not look at Glazunov —he had never sung anything for him.

After Sergei played the three pages of the score, Rimsky-Korsakov stopped him. "That will do," he said. "How much of the opera have you completed?"

"One act."

"Why only one?"

"Because I have not yet received the libretto of the second act."

"And who is writing your libretto?"

"She is a poet."

"Let him play one of his own compositions," one of the professors suggested.

Sergei played a short piece, "Vivo," which he believed was one of his best. That ended his examination.

The professors moved back to their tea table and began to discuss how best Sergei could combine his musical studies with his general education. Somehow they could not agree until Rimsky-Korsakov, who was a free-thinker and who considered the "everlasting" studies of religious subjects a waste of time, finally interrupted them. "Perhaps he can do without religious instruction. Is he Greek Orthodox?"

"Yes, he is," Glazunov replied.

"Does he know foreign languages?" Rimsky-Korsakov changed the subject.

"Do you know French?" Glazunov asked Sergei.

"I do."

"Do you speak it?"

"I can."

"And what about German?"

"Also."

Glazunov turned to Rimsky-Korsakov. "You see, he knows them both."

When finally Sergei was told that he might leave the room, he found his mother in a corridor talking to Rimsky-Korsakov and Gla-zunov. As they all said good-by, Glazunov, shaking hands with Sergei, added, "Come tomorrow morning at ten for your harmony lesson."

Many years later, when Sergei Prokofiev was reminiscing about the ten years he had spent at the St. Petersburg Conservatory, he said, "With that long exam my short-lived honeymoon with that music school ended," for his troubles began almost in the first week of his studies there.

7

As Glazunov had told Maria, the demands in general education at the Conservatory were less rigorous than at the gymnasium. Sergei easily passed the tests, and he looked back with regret at all the hours he had spent "cramming" during the past summer months at Sontsovka. He could have devoted this utterly wasted time, he thought, to something far more interesting, his music, or even playing with his friends. But Maria did not see it that way. Far from agreeing with him, she considered his general education very important, and realizing how elementary was the instruction the Conservatory provided, she had immediately engaged a private tutor. She reasoned that in addition to gaining a superior education he would do well on the simple examinations required at the end of each year at the Conservatory.

On Glazunov's suggestion Sergei was to take the harmony courses from the beginning under Anatol Lyadov.

In Lyadov's class, there were five other students, all of them older than Sergei. The eldest among them was a heavy-set man with a mop of luxurious blond hair parted in the middle. According to the current vogue, he wore a slightly varicolored velvet waistcoat, had a rather frivolous attitude toward his work, and looked down on Sergei: "I've started on my fourth decade, I have two children, and there, if you please, is *Prokosha*, who is only thirteen." The others barely noticed Sergei, but he felt that they resented a thirteen-year-old boy's being admitted into such a "serious" class. Only the nineteen-year-old Alexander Kankarovich, who played the violin, composed very little (mostly short pieces), and studied theoretical subjects in the hope of eventually becoming a conductor, treated Sergei in a comradely way.

Anatol Lyadov, a talented composer, always gave the impression of being bored. This may have been his attitude toward teaching at the Conservatory, his "serfdom," as he called it, which kept him away from his favorite occupation—composing; it was hard to tell. With a sort of lazy elegance and a condescending air, barely enunciating the words, he would write a theoretical problem on the blackboard, or with an expression of suffering play his pupils' works on the piano, sarcastically exaggerating each mistake.

He was not at all interested in developing individuality in his students and scorned every manifestation of originality. An excellent theoretician of the Rimsky-Korsakov school, he believed that each young composer should profit first of all by the experience of the classics, and only then try to invent something new. "You there," he would address a student with utter disdain, "you may despise all these rules of harmony and counterpoint, but you must understand that music is based on these laws. You cannot disregard them before creating new laws."

Lyadov recognized Sergei's unusual talent, but he treated his work as he did that of the rest of his class—that is, according to the prescribed program of the Conservatory; he inevitably awakened in Sergei his old distaste for harmony exercises. Later on, when Lyadov allowed his pupils to compose short pieces, he became annoyed with anyone who "dared" to disobey the rules he taught. Putting his hands in his pockets, he would sway back and forth on his smooth, heelless woolen shoes and say, "Perhaps you should be teaching *me*, and not I you." Raising his voice, he would add, "I don't understand why you come to me. Go to Richard Strauss or Debussy!" This he would say as if he were saying, "Go to the devil!" And speaking of Sergei to others, he invariably would wave his hand hopelessly and say, "He'll write himself out of his nonsense."

Sergei's studies under Rimsky-Korsakov were not much happier. Teaching counterpoint along with orchestration, Rimsky-Korsakov combined two of his two-hour classes into one four hours long. He no doubt thought that his pupils would profit especially from his corrections of the work of others as well as their own. But unfortunately the class was crowded; the students surrounded him at the piano so closely that it was difficult to see or hear his remarks if you stood in the back. Besides, the four-hour lesson was very tiring.

Unlike Lyadov, Rimsky-Korsakov enjoyed his work: with minute attention, he examined his students' problems, giving to each the necessary time and sharing his knowledge and experience generously. Those who realized the value in such association with a great composer profited by these lessons. They were a kind of laboratory of art, but Sergei was much too young to appreciate them.

He found uninteresting the four-hand Marches by Schubert that Rimsky-Korsakov asked his students to orchestrate, and he was careless in his work.

"Instead of giving serious thought to it, you simply guess—'should it be a clarinet or an oboe?'" Rimsky-Korsakov would tell him as he looked at his manuscript. "And why is this melody played by only one cello?"

"Because I don't like it when it is played by the orchestra," Sergei replied.

"*You don't like it!* Have you ever heard it?"

"Yes, I heard it last night in Sibelius' symphony."

"Heavens above! Why do you listen to Sibelius? What about Glinka? Have you heard *Russlan and Ludmilla?*"

"I must admit," Prokofiev confessed later, "that during those two years I learned nothing from Rimsky-Korsakov, and barely passed the exam in orchestration."

"Talented, but completely immature," Rimsky-Korsakov wrote on Sergei's examination papers.

Sergei's disrespect for Rimsky-Korsakov the teacher however, was in strange contrast with his admiration for Rimsky-Korsakov the composer. He applauded the performances of his compositions until his hands ached and never missed a production or rehearsal of one of his operas.

Sergei had been but a few months at the Conservatory when his studies were interrupted by the first Russian Revolution, which broke out in January, 1905.* The Russo-Japanese War, which was less than a year old, was bringing crushing and humiliating defeats to the Russians. In the autumn of 1904 the Russian Army lost a battle at Liaoyang and several months later was defeated again at Mukden, while the fleet sent from the Baltic Sea all the way to the Far East around Africa was annihilated at Tsushima. The cruel mismanagement and irresponsibility in conducting the military campaign, leading to senseless losses in men at the front and catastrophic economic conditions in the land, roused resentment against the government throughout Russia.

The war had caused prices to rise, for the basic necessities of food and clothing were lacking, and the state of the workers, whose nominal wages had fallen, grew steadily worse. Exhausted by labor, riddled with alcohol, disease, and hunger, living in filth and misery, with no

* The following sketch of political conditions in Russia follows substantially the account given in my *Rachmaninoff* (New York: Simon & Schuster, 1950).

civil rights whatsoever and no assurance of steady work—since corruption and bribery ruled the choice of employed—they were fertile soil for any scheme that might better their lot.

While the war with Japan was the outward cause of the first Revolution, the internal motives for the widespread dissatisfaction among the diverse groups of the population lay deep in social conditions. "Bloody Sunday," as the tragic event was called, became the decisive turning point in the history of the working classes.

The sporadic strikes throughout the country gained momentum under the leadership of the revolutionaries, culminating in the autumn of 1905 in a general strike that left the cities without communications, food, and medical supplies, as well as without electricity and water; with the exception of the line between St. Petersburg and Moscow, all railroads came to a standstill.

It is self-evident that these events affected directly the peaceful life at the Conservatory, where Sergei was a student. Because its "revolutionary spirit" was akin to that of the University, which in the eyes of the government authorities was a breeding ground of revolutionary activities, the Conservatory was temporarily closed. The government reprisals were brutal and senseless; students had been traditionally branded as a dangerous element. The illiterate Russian soldier was taught to answer the question, Who were the enemies of his Czar and fatherland? with, "External—Germans and Turks; and Internal—Poles, Jews, and students."

Thousands of students all over Russia were expelled and hundreds were arrested, regardless of their guilt or connection with events. Throughout the history of Czarist Russia many, if not most, of the outstanding men who dared to criticize the Czarist regime and the ruling society were marked as "revolutionaries and security risks" by the authorities. Lermontov and Pushkin were censored, Dostoyevsky was exiled, Tolstoy was excommunicated by the Church, and many others went into voluntary exile abroad, deciding that it was too difficult to live under existing conditions in which their main energies had to be expended not on the work itself, but on the struggle for the right to work. All of them were in the way. None of them was wanted.

In Moscow the government authorities, fearing public demonstration, did not dare to permit the performance of Glinka's *A Life for the Czar* without a strong guard of soldiers, and in St. Petersburg the insurrection scene in Rimsky-Korsakov's version of Moussorgsky's *Boris Godunov* was deleted. Rimsky-Korsakov himself was eventually dismissed from his post as a leading professor at the Conservatory because he was accused of siding with the students, the revolutionary

element. In protest, Lyadov and Glazunov resigned, while Anna Essipova, the eminent professor in the piano class, went abroad.

Sergei Taneyev left the Conservatory in Moscow because of the director Vasily Safonoff's repressive attitude toward the students, and
Sergei Rachmaninoff resigned his post as a conductor at the Bolshoi
Theatre and also went abroad. Life within the walls of the Bolshoi in
Moscow and the Maryinsky Theatre in St. Petersburg, as well as in
the opera houses and theatres in Russia was only an echo of what was
taking place in the cities.

In view of this situation, which was simply a reflection of what was
happening in Russia as a whole, can one accept the statements made
repeatedly by the Soviet music critics and musicologists eager to find
any alibi for Sergei Prokofiev's apparent lack of interest in the Revo-
lutions—of both 1905 and 1917—by saying, "He was much too young
to comprehend the meaning of these events"? What, then, did he
think of the sudden arrival of a detachment of soldiers at the Conservatory, where he went for his lessons whenever it was reopened, or of a
sudden absence of his professors? It is most unlikely that an intelligent
boy at the age of fourteen was so "deaf and blind."

Besides, Sergei was living with his mother, and the Soviet music
critics and musicologists would certainly not go so far as to suggest
that Maria was also ignorant of the "meaning of these events," that she
would conceal from her son that there was "something rotten in the
State of Denmark." Or would they?

On the contrary, Sergei joined his classmates in signing a protest
against the reprisals taken by the government. That his father was
very much disturbed when he heard about this is another story. Having never forgotten the price he himself had had to pay for his sense
of solidarity with fellow students in his own student days, and knowing only too well that "being too young, etc.," would hardly be
accepted as a valid excuse by the authorities, he wrote Sergei a long letter, advising him to stay away from any entanglements with the revolutionary activities at the Conservatory. While Sergei followed his
advice, the seeds of his eventual and permanent rebellion against accepted "traditional principles" in any form were well sown.

In order not to lose time, Sergei continued his theoretical studies
privately with Lyadov, so that when the 1905 Revolution had been
crushed, and the Conservatory reopened and the professors returned
to their posts, he was admitted into the next grade without examination.

It was then, during the autumn of 1905, that Sergei met the composer Nikolai Miaskovsky, who had entered Lyadov's and Rimsky-Korsakov's classes. The son of a Russian Army general, Miaskovsky at first had followed in his father's footsteps as an officer in the engineering corps, but at the age of twenty-three, like Moussorgsky and Rimsky-Korsakov, had forsaken his military career to become a musician.

Miaskovsky, who is chiefly remembered for the unusually large number of his symphonies, twenty-seven, was at that time twenty-five and still wearing the uniform of an officer in a sapper regiment. He was of small stature, shy, and soft-spoken. His dark beard made him look older, and the large bulging briefcase, with which he never seemed to part, gave him an air of importance, somehow justified by his extraordinary erudition on artistic subjects.

At first, Miaskovsky paid no attention to Sergei, whose latest idea of keeping score of the marks received by his classmates only further alienated them. But when, at a concert of Max Reger's compositions, he discovered that the mischievous boy was sincerely interested in contemporary music, he came to Sergei to play four-hands with him from the orchestral score of Reger's Serenade in G major. Impressed by Sergei's ability to sight-read, he soon returned to play Beethoven's Ninth Symphony. According to Miaskovsky, he had not till then found anyone capable of playing it with him to the end.

"I was very proud that such a man, an officer, should take the trouble to come to me," Sergei said, and he timidly showed Miaskovsky his latest collections of Ditties, which he had now rechristened "Puppies" because one of his friends had said that they were "apt to bite." A few days later, referring to these pieces, Miaskovsky remarked, "I didn't realize what a little viper we were warming in our bosoms," but noticing the smile under his mustache, Sergei believed that Miaskovsky approved of his "darings."

Thus began a friendship that lasted some forty years, until Miaskovsky's death in 1952.

Miaskovsky not merely approved but actually encouraged Sergei's "darings," which simply amounted to his desire to compose in his own way. The cultivated young officer did not cry "anathema" when Sergei confessed that he did not like Mozart because of his "oversimple harmonization" or Chopin because he was "much too sweet."

There was nothing particularly revolutionary in Sergei's musical thinking. In fact, he was far from following the "modernists," and in 1906—that is, after Debussy's *Pélléas et Mélisande*, and after the Arnold Schoenberg of the Gurre-Lieder had composed *Pierrot Lun-*

aire—Sergei told Lyadov that his favorite composers were Tchaikovsky, Wagner, and Grieg.

"I spoke of Tchaikovsky," Prokofiev explained later, "although I didn't know many of his compositions. I knew his Second Symphony, one or two of his operas, and some piano compositions, but was completely ignorant of his chamber works. I mentioned Wagner from pure snobbism—I had heard that his works were interesting and much discussed in musical circles, but I myself had heard neither his *Ring* nor *Tristan*, and I knew very little of the *Meistersinger*. But I was well acquainted with Grieg's piano works."

After Miaskovsky and he had played together many classical scores and some works of Tchaikovsky, Rimsky-Korsakov, and Glazunov, often arguing bitterly as they analyzed them, Miaskovsky introduced Sergei to the music of the contemporary foreigners. Sergei's early enthusiasm for Grieg, Rimsky-Korsakov, and Borodin now was succeeded by an even more pronounced admiration for Debussy, Richard Strauss, and Max Reger.

Their mutual understanding and respect led the two friends to establish a sort of tradition of consulting each other about their own works, a tradition that lasted all their lives. This procedure was not even interrupted by Sergei's vacations at Sontsovka, for they continued their consultations about the form, harmonization, and orchestration of their compositions by mail.

At that time they were both writing two kinds of compositions: for Lyadov, written to satisfy the requirements of his course, and others for themselves, free from any restrictions.

8

It would be a mistake to think that Sergei was so absorbed in his work that he missed all the fun a young man his age can have in extra-curricular activities. Russian gymnasia have separate schools for boys and girls, but in the coeducational conservatories the boys have far more opportunities to make friends with girls their own age. While there were mostly young men in Rimsky-Korsakov's and Lyadov's classes, in the general education classes there were almost as many girls as boys, and Sergei soon made friends with several of them.

Tall and slender, dressed in a well-kept uniform, with his blond hair carefully combed, he carried himself with distinction. In his gray astrakhan cap and long uniform-overcoat with its black astrakhan collar he walked through the Conservatory's corridors as if he expected everyone to give him the right-of-way, which caused more resentment than respect among the students. Tutored at home, he showed a superior knowledge in all subjects, but his straightforward and often condescending manner in answering the teachers' questions annoyed his classmates, and they thought him haughty and arrogant. That Glazunov spoke of him as a talented young composer, thus showing him special consideration, only added fuel to their animosity. Somehow, the boys near his own age did not like him, but the girls did, and Sergei, who sensed this, was naturally drawn closer to them. One of them certainly gained his preference.

Vera Alpers, who eventually became a pianist and a professor at the St. Petersburg Conservatory, was his classmate, and despite those years that Prokofiev spent outside of Russia, remained his close friend to the last days of his life. Vera was a year younger than Sergei and the youngest among the girls in their class. At fifteen she was still a little girl, full of mischief, who liked to play ball and go dancing.

But because of her family background she was also very musical. Her father, Vladimir, was a composer, pianist, and a music critic on the newspaper *Slovo*, her mother, Ludmilla, was a singer, and her three brothers sang, played the piano, and improvised, so that their home seldom knew silence. Their father spent his evenings with his friends, playing four-hand arrangements from a large repertory of orchestral works, and the children at an early age acquired an unusual knowledge of musical literature.

It was a congenial atmosphere for Sergei, but his friendship with Vera developed slowly. Vera was afraid of him: she was overwhelmed by his exuberance, by his desire to miss nothing in life, as he told her—which actually did not amount to anything more at that time than his playing chess with anyone he could find for a partner; his carrying on an extensive number of games by correspondence with opponents whom he could not reach across the table; his persistent study of languages, often working on the conjugation of Italian verbs on streetcars on his way to the Conservatory; and finally, his claim of a friendship with several girls at the same time.

When Vera became a little older, she saw in all this a great deal of boyishness, immaturity, and braggadocio: "See, this is the kind of a fellow I am!" But when Sergei had first joined the last grade of the school, Vera still felt uneasy in his presence.

It was the pleasure they both derived from ballroom dancing that brought Sergei and Vera together. "Sergei loved to dance at every opportunity, at the Conservatory balls and students' parties, but he was not a good dancer," Vera observed. "His movements were flabby, and so was his rhythm. He seemed to lack the necessary capacity of submitting his body to the rhythm of the dance. He gave his partner full freedom, and was very attentive during the dance, but . . . he did not know how to lead."

They spent the traditional New Year's ball at the Conservatory dancing together or sitting and conversing on a couch in a cozy corner of one of the halls. But Vera, unlike Maria, who had said to Sergei's father, "I am no longer afraid of you," and thus started their romance, apparently said nothing so challenging to Sergei and kept her awakening feelings to herself. If they flirted, it was in subdued tones and with delicate insinuations.

After Sergei had left for his vacation in Sontsovka, Vera sent him a postcard on which she wrote a few bars of the music to which they had danced. She neither added a word to it nor signed it. Sergei did not acknowledge the message, but when he returned to school and she asked him about it, he raised his head and sternly remarked, "Why do you ask, since it was meant to be anonymous?"

They were still children, but Vera noted in her diary the year of 1908 as the beginning of their close friendship, and Sergei kept the postcard in an album that he showed her much later, when they both were nearing their sixties.

Now they met daily at the Conservatory, lunched together in the students' dining room, and then walked home. Or, if Sergei happened to be detained, he would catch up with her by taking a streetcar. They agreed to meet before Vera's harmony lesson so that Sergei could correct her homework. At Sergei's suggestion they joined Professor Sakketti's class in esthetics, and they sat at the same desk. But they were not attentive to his lectures, played ticktacktoe or worked on problems of modulations, wrote each other little notes, or just simply talked. They carried this so far that on one occasion Vera noticed a sudden silence in the classroom. She lifted her head and saw Sakketti's sarcastic smile. "My dear young lady," he said, "I am merely waiting for you to finish your discussion."

Vera was no longer too shy to play the piano four-hands with Sergei, and they spent hours, either at her home or in one of the rooms at the Conservatory, going through the orchestral literature: Glazunov's symphonies, Rimsky-Korsakov's "Antar," they even tried Scriabin's "Divine Poem."

Beside their lessons at the Conservatory they went together to the students' parties, concerts, and rehearsals, and shared and discussed their impressions. "It became customary for us to tell each other in detail everything we had done in the short span of time when we could not see each other." Vera recalled later, since for a while Sergei was too preoccupied elsewhere to be with Vera; at about that time Miaskovsky and he were introduced into a musical circle called the "Evenings of Contemporary Music," which gave an additional impetus to Sergei's interest in "new" music.

This was a group of musicians and music lovers headed by Alfred Nurok, an admiralty official and art critic, and Walter Nuvel, an independently wealthy lover of the arts, both close friends and collaborators of Sergei Diaghilev, the famous leader of the Ballet Russe.

They were enthusiastic followers of Diaghilev's theory of "pure art for art's sake," free from the shackles of the notion that art should serve society. They were prejudiced against Tchaikovsky's and Rachmaninoff's "naked emotionalism" as easily accessible to the general public, and even in Moussorgsky's compositions they recognized only the novelty of their form, denying that they had any social significance. They considered devotion to a specifically national character in the arts old-fashioned, and just as the painters worshiped the Impressionists and contemporary French art, so the organizers of the "Evenings of Contemporary Music" admired the works of Reger, Richard Strauss, Schoenberg, and the "modern" French composers. According to Diaghilev's precept, "to follow the contemporary Western culture was the only course toward progress and rebuff to old routine."

The group gave seven or eight concerts monthly between October and April in various concert halls in St. Petersburg. Since the organization received a large number of compositions, some published and many still in manuscript, a most meticulous examination of every score preceded its acceptance for a public performance. And as the organization barely maintained itself on its modest membership and entrance fees, it had to forego orchestral works and could present only chamber and instrumental music.

Along with works of the French composers (Debussy, Paul Dukas, Gabriel Fauré, Ernest Chausson, Vincent d'Indy, and Henri Roussel) and the German (Arnold Schoenberg, Max Reger, Hugo Wolf, and Richard Strauss), some Russian works by Scriabin, Stravinsky, and Tcherepnin were also occasionally performed. The most prominent vocalists and instrumentalists offered their services free of charge, and their names attracted a large segment of the St. Petersburg audience as well as the critics, whose "pro" and "con" reviews made these performances popular and important.

Although Vera saw Sergei less frequently now, she never missed any of Sergei's appearances at the students' concerts. She remembered particularly well one of them in December of 1908 when Sergei played two Études in C major—one by Anton Rubinstein, the other by Chopin—and Schumann's Toccata. "He played brilliantly," Vera recalled, "but he was terribly nervous. I was afraid he was going to faint or have a nervous breakdown. I saw him rush off the stage, and then sit on the stairs leading into the green room, trying to catch his breath. Then, as if he had lost his mind, he jumped up, almost knocking down Anna Essipova, who happened to be passing by, slammed the door, and was gone. During the intermission he returned and when he saw me smiled and looked as happy as if he had not seen me for weeks."

Later that evening, as they walked home together, Vera expected Sergei to tell her what had gone wrong—had they not agreed to tell each other "everything"? Sergei said nothing and Vera did not ask, but watched him anxiously, her heart skipping a few beats with compassion.

Vera was also in the audience at one of the "Evenings of Contemporary Music" concerts on December 31, 1908, when Miaskovsky made his debut with Six Songs, and Sergei played, for the first time in public, seven of his own piano compositions still in manuscript: Fairy Tale, Snowflakes, Reminiscence, Élan, Prayer, Despair, and Diabolic Suggestions. The first six compositions showed the young composer's ability in various moods, but the last in the group brought the audience to its feet. Since then it has become a favorite virtuoso showpiece of many leading concert pianists, but to appreciate fully the tremendous effect this piece produced on the audience, one must remember that when Sergei played it at his debut in 1908, the public was not yet used to such piano compositions.

"It seemed as if the hall was ablaze and we were ready to perish alive in the fire of the music," the poet Vladimir Mayakovsky said of the event. "The young master burned ferociously at the grand piano with whose keys he tussled. He was playing with a captivating elemental ascent at full tilt. Something like this can be witnessed only once in a lifetime, when one sees and feels that the master has gone insane in a super-ecstasy, as if he were going into mortal combat and as if this attack can never again be repeated."

Sitting not far away from Maria, who was also in the audience, Vera was as nervous as Sergei, for this was his first public appearance outside the students' concerts at the Conservatory, and it was an important event. Vera was very proud of him. "And how young he looked," she recalled later. "A mere boy dressed in his school uniform with a silver buckle on his wide black leather belt with the initial SPK [St. Petersburg Conservatory], and especially when, after he had finished playing, he joined his mother in the audience and sat next to her with his head resting on her shoulder."

Thus began Sergei's public career, and Maria, obviously more excited than her son, anxiously looked for reviews, which she then carefully pasted in a special album:

Sergei Prokofiev's short piano pieces, performed by the author himself, are extremely original. Though he has not yet completed his musical education, he belongs to the group of extreme modernists and in his "daring" and "eccentricity" surpasses the contemporary French composers'. An indisputable talent is evident in all the oddity of his rich creative fantasy. It is a talent which still lacks equilibrium, a talent which is easily given to every élan.

Sergei was not particularly impressed by these lines, for he knew that they were written by one of the members of their circle who therefore had to praise his own "merchandise." The only other reference, in the *Petersburg Listok*, was more moderate in its appreciation: "If one regards all these generally somewhat muddled compositions as first attempts, one may, perhaps, discover some signs of a certain talent."

Two months later, on February 23, 1909, Sergei heard for the first time an orchestral performance of his work, his E-minor symphony (the Second Symphony in three movements). During the previous summer, while at Sontsovka, he had written this work in close consultation by mail with Miaskovsky. Upon his return to the Conservatory, he had shown the score to Glazunov, who since the 1905 Revolution had become the director.

"Glazunov must have heard from Lyadov about my extracurricular musical activities," Sergei said, "and must have thought that he had indeed 'warmed a little viper in his bosom.' " The director, who had been so active in getting Sergei into the Conservatory, now showed very little interest in the manuscript, and consented to examine it only after repeated requests. Having made several unimportant changes in the score, he said to Maria, "It is written with enthusiasm and fire. So what?" Obviously, the music was alien to him. Still, he agreed to have the symphony played through at a private rehearsal—no one except close friends and the members of the Conservatory's staff were allowed to attend.

"It is hard to say," Sergei said later, "whether or not such a performance was useful, for one could not tell why the work sounded so bad: was it because it was badly orchestrated or because the orchestra was reading the music for the first time? But it did sound bad and it left a nebulous impression."

Miaskovsky, on the other hand, thought it was a charming piece that deserved success on the concert stage, but agreed that the orchestration should be revised. "The trouble is," he told Sergei, "you should not be entrusted with the reorchestration; you'd ruin it with your tricks."

Clearly, Sergei needed a more intimate knowledge of the instruments, which he was to acquire later by joining Nikolai Tcherepnin's conducting class.

But before this happened, in May, 1909, despite his grades, which were far from brilliant, Sergei was graduated from the composition class. At the examinations he offered one of his early sonatas (which has since been lost) and a recently written new scene for the *Feast During the Plague*, the opera on which he had been working with

Glière. In it he tried to portray a priest condemning and damning a "Godless Feast." Both works provoked his examiners' wrath: "They all want to become Scriabins!" Lyadov exclaimed, and his colleagues at the examiners' table nodded in agreement.

The Conservatory professors were evidently only too glad to be rid of such a restless and troublesome student. But they did not succeed entirely, for Sergei was to remain for several years at the Conservatory before final graduation from the piano and conducting classes. His barely satisfactory marks in composition left him indifferent, for by now he was consumed by an ambition to win the Anton Rubinstein Prize. This prize, awarded to the best graduating piano student, in addition to the honor, presented the winner with a grand piano; but it was the sportive, feverish atmosphere created by the competition that attracted Sergei.

He had to nurse this ambition in secret, however, for the mere mention of it would have made his professors laugh. But he knew that if there was anyone at the Conservatory who could help him improve his playing and prepare him for his task, it was Anna Essipova.

As a professor at the piano class Anna Essipova, of the famous Theodore Leschetizky school, was held in an esteem similar to that accorded Rimsky-Korsakov and his class in composition. What Sergei did not know was that after hearing his performance at the students' concert in December, 1908, Madame Essipova was so impressed by his playing that she had gone backstage to tell him that she would accept him in her class. But he had behaved so erratically, almost knocking her off her feet as he rushed from the green room slamming the door, that Essipova did not have a chance to speak to him. When he heard later of Essipova's interest in him, he felt that he had already won half his forthcoming battle for the prize.

In a happy frame of mind and full of plans for his piano work Sergei, shortly before he left for Sontsovka, attended with Vera a performance of Rimsky-Korsakov's *May Night* which was given by the opera class at the Conservatory. "That evening has remained in my memory," Vera said later, "as the most happy page in our friendship." She said nothing more about that evening, but the few lines she wrote in her diary after Sergei went to Sontsovka explain clearly how she had begun to feel about him:

Oh, what a night! Seryozha already has gone to the station, and in less than half an hour will be speeding to his village, with the scent of the spring, to the singing of nightingales. . . . He is lucky! . . . The train is thundering away, through an open window the wind is blowing the fresh evening air into his face, and he . . . perhaps he remembers the faraway Conservatory, or . . . what is more likely, he is playing chess with someone on the train. . . .

Sergei kept Vera waiting for a letter for ten whole days:

I have been here a week, and I am ready to leave my bear's den. I'll go for a few days to visit an old friend, a musician and a chessplayer. Sontsovka is a frightful wilderness. Up to this day I have not seen a soul—actually there isn't anybody to see. I haven't even seen the village priest. I spend all my time at the piano or at chess.

Essipova would hardly approve of my piano work, but it doesn't really matter, it is only because I have just begun. Actually, I play a great deal, but it makes very little sense. I practice exercises for half an hour and then play all kinds of music beginning with Le Coq d'Or and ending with Scriabin, Glazunov, Balakirev's Islamey, and the Divine Poem, which I play *solo* from the four-hand arrangement.

Vera must have skimmed quickly through this matter-of-fact-report, hoping for something more personal. She got the first inkling of it in the underlined word *solo* in the last sentence. They had played the Divine Poem together, and now he was playing it alone. It was not like him to say anything more, or would he? She went on reading the rest of the letter.

As for what concerns chess, during this week I have mailed seventeen chess letters, and received twelve—so that in our usually quiet post office now reigns a great excitement.

This was still unimportant to Vera, but starting with the next sentence, she read what she wanted so much to hear.

But when in the evening my head aches from chess, and my fingers from playing Scriabin, then I enjoy our May nights, which are truly bewitching: the bright moonlight, the shadowy garden. There is only one annoyance—the fact that the nightingales are joined by a whole chorus of frogs, in a nearby pond. And then I remember another May Night, the Grand Conservatory Hall, and you there. . . . Where are you? In Pavlovsk, Saratov, Pskov, or perhaps again somewhere in Yaroslavl? Do you still have to rest for two hours every day? And do they have to serve you two soft-boiled eggs every morning when you wake up feeling nervous? Please write to me and don't be angry with me because I haven't written you sooner. You have an extremely kind heart and therefore you should not be angry.

Vera was not angry. She had been anxious, but now she forgot about it, and all that summer they kept up a lively correspondence. Two weeks later Sergei started a letter by telling her that he had spent two whole days reading Dostoyevsky's The Possessed, which he apparently did not like, and then went on to say, "I feel sorry for your tender white little fingers which have become so wooden for playing the piano. When will come the day when you can again start practicing the piano? Write me more—you should be able to with your inborn discipline, and don't ever doubt for a minute that I think of my 'sweet friend.' " And a few days later he wrote Vera a short note: "I begin to miss you. Please send me your photograph. I want so much to see you!" But when Sergei received the coveted photograph, he thought it did not do Vera justice and tore it up.

And at the end of July it was Sergei's turn to complain:

You have not written me for so long, my dear Verochka, that I am beside myself with grief. Recently civilization has penetrated our wilderness. One of the peasants has bought himself a gramophone. And now every evening this invention of the devil is placed outside his hut, and begins to gurgle its horrible songs. A crowd of spectators roars with delight and joins in with their own false rendition of the songs, dogs bark and wail, the cows returning from the fields moo and run in all directions, and someone in a neighboring hut accompanies in a wrong key on his accordion. At first I closed my windows and tried to play the piano, but it was of no use. I had to run away on a bicycle from this company. Verochka, please write me—addiò. All yours, Sergei Prokofiev.

But when Sergei returned to St. Petersburg, Vera discovered that he had made several new friends among the girls. This, however, did not disturb her much, for he faithfully reported to her how he had spent his time with them, and Vera and Sergei had fun in discussing them. Vera would voice her critical opinion of each girl, which Sergei would repeat to them just to taunt them. "He liked to tease, vex, cause jealousy, and even annoyance," Vera said. "Sometimes he carried on this game openly in front of everybody. Just before our winter vacation I decided to do the same thing to him, and at the yearly ball at the Conservatory I danced most of the time with my old friends. Sergei was puzzled by this sudden change, but our 'quarrel' was not serious."

On the contrary, from then on he began to come more often to Vera's home, no longer looking for some excuse for his visits; he would drop in after a concert or at any time during the day, sit himself at the tea table, and serve tea from the samovar as if he were in his own house. Or he would go to the piano and play his own compositions, or with Vera's father play a four-hand arrangement of Ravel's Ma mère l'oye, which he liked very much. He liked particularly the part in which the frog is transformed into a prince—good triumphing over evil.

The Alperses enjoyed Sergei's informal behavior and his unannounced visits, but Vera was often upset by so many contradictory aspects of his high-strung character: he could be timid, silent, given to daydreaming, but more often he was excited, curt and "biting," and yet sometimes he was as affected as a capricious girl. Often after the most intimate conversation with Vera or after a sweet little note he had written her, he would on the following day act indifferent, look serious and proud, and greet her ceremoniously from afar.

There was enough for Vera to think about. Fortunately, her misgivings were dispelled when her friends told her that after an evening at their home they saw him turning somersaults, throwing off his galoshes, rolling in the snow, and behaving like a mischievous boy— not like the "serious professor" they had liked to call him.

Although not an expert skater—Maria used to say that on skates he resembled a spider—Sergei suggested to Vera that they go skating together. "Our friendship was growing," Vera observed. Every morning, regardless of the freezing weather, sometimes at −20° C. they met at the skating rink, then later went down to the rehearsals of Siloti's or Nikish's concerts; afterward, swinging their skates in the air, they walked all the way to the Conservatory, thus spending almost entire days together.

Sergei's new friends however, began to disturb the harmony of their relationship, Vera noticed. Besides, a grave misfortune fell upon the Prokofiev family that prevented Sergei from having fun and spending much time with Vera.

Sergei's father had become seriously ill and was brought to St. Petersburg for treatments. For three months Maria and Sergei lived in constant despair, with only slight hope for the sick man's recovery. After the end of the school year the Prokofievs did not go to Sontsovka, but remained in the city, while the Alperses went for the summer to Pavlovsk, a suburb of St. Petersburg. Sergei visited them several times, and Vera took him on long sightseeing tours to the beautiful park with its carefully kept green lawns framed by well-chosen trees. They looked into many pavilions and admired the old monuments and statues; they remained almost in awe before the Temple of Friendship, as if it had a special meaning to them, and then walked in silence over the bridge across the river Slavyanka and up the staircase with the statues of lions; in the evenings they listened to the military band in a park. Everything connected with Pavlovsk enchanted Sergei. Little did he know that in a few years the very name of Pavlovsk would evoke the bitterest memories of his artistic career.

After two operations Sergei's father died on July 23, 1910. He had been suffering from cancer of the liver. A week later Vera received a few lines from Sergei:

My dear Verochka, I am sending you my last greetings from St. Petersburg. Because of my father's death, we are going to Sontsovka tomorrow. Please write me much and often. I will be very grateful to you. My best regards to all of you.

"Thus our youth had come to an end," Vera noted in her diary.

9

Sergei loved his parents, and the loss of his father and his mother's grief weighed heavily upon him. The happy days at Sontsovka had come to an end with his father's death. Ever since his childhood, Sontsovka had been to Sergei his and his parents' own estate. Now, besides being deprived of his father's large income, Maria and Sergei had to leave their home with all its sentimental associations.

Dmitri Sontsov sent a man to try either to sell the property or to find another manager for the estate, and Maria was busy packing their belongings to be sent to St. Petersburg. Meanwhile, Sergei practiced the piano that last summer at Sontsovka more than ever before.

When Sergei returned to the Conservatory in the fall, Madame Essipova, recognizing his talent, was primarily concerned with correcting the bad habits of careless playing that he had acquired in his childhood, since Maria was not competent enough to give him a proper foundation for piano technique.

For a while Madame Essipova overlooked Sergei's disrespectful attitude toward certain composers: "They say one cannot give a piano recital without playing Chopin, and I am going to prove that one can." He treated Mozart with even more disdain: "What primitive, monotonous harmony."

Unwilling to dispense with his own sweeping and bold but far from accurate style of playing, he also often disregarded the composer's text in pieces he was studying, omitting what he considered "superfluous," or writing into the score accents, *accelerandos*, and *staccatos*, as well as introducing extra notes into the chords, thus altering them harmonically.

At first Sergei paid little attention to Essipova's gentle criticism. "She tries to part everybody's hair in the same way, using the same comb," he said. But he so stretched her patience that she became firm in her warning that she would expel him from her class unless he followed her instructions. From then on, Sergei behaved.

While in her class, Sergei learned a number of major piano works, among them Liszt's Sonata and Schumann's F-sharp-minor Sonata, as well as Medtner's Fairy Tales and some Rachmaninoff and Tchaikovsky piano compositions. Essipova forced him to play Mozart, Schubert, and Chopin, insisting on finely polished execution of every piece.

The years of Essipova's disciplined and meticulous work with Sergei were not in vain. To his own steel-like touch and extremely individual way of playing she added clarity to his finger technique, a singing tone, and an unusual elasticity of his wrist. These were characteristics of Essipova's school. And if eventually Sergei developed into a brilliant virtuoso, it was mainly due to the wisdom and patience with which Essipova treated her often argumentative student.

Sergei was less argumentative and much happier in Tcherepnin's conducting class, which he had joined at the same time as he had Essipova's class. At one time a pupil of Rimsky-Korsakov, Nikolai Tcherepnin was a composer, conductor, and teacher whose taste in music was influenced by his wide education and liberal attitude toward everything new in the arts, including Impressionism. It mattered little that he composed more eclectically than he spoke about music both old and new, that he conducted less convincingly than he taught the art of conducting; the association with him was most beneficial to his students. His pupils used to say that working with him was extremely instructive and fascinating, for with him "one could breathe freely."

Sergei was still too young, still too lacking in the necessary authority to lead an orchestra, and Tcherepnin took his time before permitting Sergei to take his place at the conductor's desk. When finally Sergei did face an orchestra and timidly waved his baton, it seemed to him that the members of the orchestra were far away and that his signals never reached them.

Observing him, Tcherepnin quickly appraised his limited ability and pronounced his verdict: "You have no talent for conducting. But because I have faith in you as a composer and know that sometimes you will have to conduct your own works, I am going to teach you."

"Thus I fell into the category of students devoid of talent," Sergei said later. "And although during my Conservatory days I managed to conduct the school orchestra in public performances of Schubert's

Unfinished Symphony, Beethoven's Seventh Symphony, and even Mozart's *The Marriage of Figaro*, I didn't feel 'at home' at the conductor's desk." Only much later, after his graduation from the Conservatory, did Sergei acquire sufficient experience in leading an orchestra. But what was more important, through his work in the conducting class under Tcherepnin, he mastered the art of orchestration.

"Tcherepnin's role in my general education was of paramount value to me: he spoke of innovations in compositions in such a way that I felt like a backward musician; his analytical remarks on opera became very useful in my writing of operas. With a score in his hands, sitting next to me at innumerable rehearsals of the school orchestra, he would point out: 'Listen to how beautiful the bassoon sounds here' or, 'Did you notice the English horn?' I began to acquire a taste for the scores of Haydn and Mozart, hence later on came my Classical Symphony."

Thus the art of orchestration, which he had failed to learn in Rimsky-Korsakov's class, he now acquired in his work under Tcherepnin in direct association with the school orchestra. To this early period belong the five-part Sinfonietta in A major (1909), two symphonic poems, Dreams and Autumnal (1910), and two pieces for female chorus and orchestra, The Swan and The Wave (1911).

In the Sinfonietta he tried to write a "transparent" piece for small orchestra, but this experiment failed, as he himself said later, because he still lacked the necessary mastery for "transparent" writing, and only after he had revised it twice, in 1914 and in 1929, did the piece acquire a satisfactory form. (It was published as Op. 48, in 1931.)

Dreams, written for large orchestra, was more flabby than sensitive. It was first performed under Sergei's direction at a students' recital on November 22, 1910, and the composer never forgot the barbed comment of the critic of *Theatre and Sports*: "Such unsuccessful works should be created . . . only in one's dreams."

Autumnal was also pensive in character and even more gloomy, obviously influenced by Rachmaninoff's The Island of Death and his Second Symphony. This composition he also revised twice, in 1915 and finally, in 1934. "The critics," Sergei told Miaskovsky, "wrote about the drizzle, falling leaves, and quoted poetry, but not one of them understood that it was an inner world and that the autumn feeling can happen in the spring and summer as well."

But at this initial period in his career Sergei could not easily dismiss the critical reaction toward his compositions. Until his father's death he knew nothing about financial problems, but because of his mother's limited means, Sergei had to find some way for his chosen profession to support him. It was difficult to have his works performed and even

harder to have them published. His manuscripts were invariably returned by conductors and publishers who were swamped with manuscripts and had no time to examine works of new composers. No one
wished to be bothered with an "unknown" Conservatory student.

This situation led Sergei to the idea of writing a piano piece that he
would endeavor to perform himself; thus he would double his chances
of attracting attention as composer and pianist. It was to be a short
concertino in one movement for piano and orchestra.

Just as the "Evenings of Contemporary Music" in St. Petersburg
had been an organization affiliated with the magazine *The World of
Arts,* so a group of music lovers in Moscow interested in modern
music was closely associated with the magazine *Music,* published by
Vladimir Derzhanovsky, which adhered to the same principles as those
of their colleagues in St. Petersburg. The magazine's editors declared
proudly that it was the only bulwark of "modern" tendencies, and
they sought to popularize the works of Schoenberg, Stravinsky, and
the later Scriabin. Derzhanovsky's circle had its own forum, the off-
season summer symphonic concerts conducted by Konstantin
Saradzhev in Sakolniki Park. There for the first time in Russia were
heard the works of Debussy, Ravel, and Dukas, as well as those of
many Russian composers; and performers heretofore unknown to the
public at large were presented.

It was to this organization that Miaskovsky, the ardent promotor of
Sergei's music, had appealed to Derzhanovsky in his letter of September 25, 1911. "Prokofiev has been working on a charming, sprightly
concertino of unusually fascinating quality. But the orchestration of
the work had developed it into a regular concerto with a virtuoso
piano part. It would be wonderful if you could include its performance in Saradzhev's program for the next summer's concerts. It will
be a sensation, although I cannot predict what kind—there is so much
of the fantastic in it."

Sergei dedicated the concertino to Tcherepnin, under whose supervision he orchestrated the work and put it in final form for the performance, which took place under Saradzhev's baton in Sakolniki on
July 25, 1912. This was Sergei's first public appearance with an orchestra, and though he acquitted himself brilliantly from a purely
pianistic point of view, the performance divided both the public and
critics into two camps: ardent admirers and their enraged opponents.

Leonid Sabaneyev, the well-known critic, wrote in *Golos Moskvy*

The energetic, rhythmic, harsh, coarse, primitive cacophony hardly deserves
to be called music. In his desperate search for novelty utterly alien to his

nature, the composer has definitely overreached himself. Such things do not happen with real talent.

A week later, Sergei repeated the performance at Pavlovsk, where two years before he had visited with Vera. The work was directed by A. P. Aslanov and caused a reaction similar to that in Sakolniki. Bernstein wrote in the *Peterburgskie Vedomosti* (August 5, 1912):

His professor, Tcherepnin, has been quoted as saying that Prokofiev's concerto is incredibly talented. So far, the incredible dominates the talent of the composer who has written a score full of "musical dirt."

Other reporters noted that on the same program Cesar Cui's two symphonic scherzos were played, and that the works of this representative of the Mighty Five sounded like childish babbling in comparison with Prokofiev's concerto. And as if in duet with Bernstein, the critic of the *Petersburg Gazette* declared that what young Prokofiev needed was a strait jacket.

Sergei was not in the least disturbed by what he read in the newspapers; in fact, he had by now began to collect the reviews that abounded in particularly nasty remarks, while he cheerfully continued his studies in the Essipova and Tcherepnin classes.

Inspired by Schumann's Toccata he had been working on with Essipova, he composed one of his own: a bombshell that has become one of the favorite pieces among the concertizing piano virtuosi, along with Diabolical Suggestion. At the end of the year he was in the throes of his Second Piano Concerto, a composition in four movements, almost twice as long as the First Piano Concerto, and very different in character. Having heard enough criticism, which even went so far as to compare his compositions, to "machines" and "soccer," he tried for more inner content. He paid little attention to those who protested that his compositions were devoid of themes and melodies—"they don't know how to listen," he said; he was far more concerned with the form of his concertos.

"It seems to me," Prokofiev commented later, "that in general piano concertos (excluding the most perfect and the utterly unsuccessful) are of two kinds: in the first, the composer succeeds in writing an ensemble for the solo instrument with the orchestra, but the solo part is not particularly interesting (as in Rimsky-Korsakov's); in the second, the solo is excellent, while the orchestral part serves merely as an adjunct to the whole (as in Chopin's). My first concerto is closer to the first kind, my second—to the second." Sergei Prokofiev considered these concertos his first mature works.

The performance of the Second Piano Concerto stupefied the audience as much as the First had challenged it. "A youngster who could have been from a fashionable high school appears on the stage," the *Petersburg Gazette* reported. "This is Sergei Prokofiev." This critic evidently felt that a description of the composer's physical appearance was necessary, in fact, this was the first one to appear in print. The critic went on:

He takes his place at the piano and seems to be either dusting the keys or striking high or low notes at random. He has a sharp, dry touch. The public is bewildered. Some indignant murmurs are audible. One couple gets up and stalks toward the exit: "This music is enough to drive you mad!" The hall empties. The young artist concludes his concerto with a relent-lessly discordant combination of brasses. The audience is scandalized. The majority hiss. With a mocking bow, Prokofiev resumes his seat and plays an encore. The audience flees to the exits, exclaiming: "To hell with all this futuristic music! We came here for enjoyment. The cats on our roof make better music than this!" while the enchanted progressivists try to drown them with: "This is the work of a genius!"—"How fresh, how new!"— "What temperament! What originality!"

Out of twelve reviews eight were, to put it mildly, "negative." The concerto was branded as a deliberate slap in the face to the public and an impudent anarchistic attack. Although obviously a groundless criticism, the event was associated with the scandals caused by literary performances by modern poets in many cities in Russia and the ultra-leftist tendencies in literature and painting.

Needless to say, these initial performances, instead of launching Prokofiev's career as composer and pianist, actually closed doors to him that would have led to the halls in which the regular Winter season concerts were given. No one was interested in engaging Sergei Prokofiev, nor was anyone willing to perform his compositions. Repeatedly, he sent his manuscripts to conductors of the leading orchestras in St. Petersburg and Moscow, and to Alexander Siloti and Sergei Koussevitzky; they all rejected them. The letters of recommendation by Miaskovsky, Taneyev, Glière, and Tcherepnin carried little weight against the scorching reviews in the press.

But three articles by Vyacheslav Karatygin, the eminent Petersburg critic, that appeared almost simultaneously in *Rech, Theatre and Art,* and *Apollon* (September 25, 1913), not merely disagreed with the other critics but predicted for the young composer a brilliant career:

The audience booed. This means nothing. Some ten years hence the same audience will pay for this booing with unanimous applause for the then famous composer who will be recognized in all of Europe.

But it was too early for Sergei to think about the conquest of European audiences. He still had before him the final graduation examinations and the competition for the coveted Anton Rubinstein Prize.

Unfortunately, Madame Essipova died in 1913, a year before Sergei's graduation. Seriously ill during Sergei's last school year, she could not assist him in his final preparations for the examinations, and although Sergei was chagrined by the death of such a remarkable musician, he was rather content to be "left on his own." "It may have been a catastrophe for her other pupils," Prokofiev said later, "but I could prepare myself without unnecessary conflicts and even carry through some of my own plans. Instead of the customary fugue from Bach's "Well-Tempered Clavichord," I chose one of the lesser-known fugues from his "Art of the Fugue." Also, instead of a classical concerto, I decided to play my own—the First. I felt that with a classical concerto I perhaps would have little chance to surpass the other competitors, while my own concerto would startle the jury by the novelty of the technique; perhaps they would not even understand how I managed to play it. On the other hand, should I fail, it would not be clear why: whether it was the fault of the concerto or of my poor playing."

With this shrewd scheme in mind, Sergei went to Boris Jurgenson, who had until then published only four of Sergei's opuses, paying him, as Prokofiev much later said to Jurgenson, ten kopeks per pood* of music. He persuaded Jurgenson to bring out his concerto in time for the competition. Then he bought twenty copies of the score and distributed them among the jury.

"When I mounted the platform, the first thing I saw was my concerto spread out on twenty pairs of knees. What an unforgettable sight for a composer who had just succeeded in getting some of his works published!" Sergei recalled later.

Reminiscing about his colleagues who took part in the competition —there were seven—Prokofiev said that Nadezhda Golubovskaya, Sergei Lyapunov's pupil, about as old as Prokofiev, was his most serious rival, a very intelligent and unusually sensitive pianist. "We all behaved toward each other with the greatest chivalry. On the eve of the competition we inquired about each other's health, hands, and fingers, and during the long exhausting hours while the jury was in session we played chess."

After long controversial debates the jury split into two camps: Essipova's group and a number of progressive young professors were in

* Approximately forty pounds.

Sergei's favor; the powerful academic group led by Glazunov was against him. Finally, the jury awarded the prize to Sergei. Glazunov, beside himself, refused to announce the results of the contest—it would be tantamount, he raved, to his approving the "harmful tendencies" reflected in Sergei's work. With difficulty he was persuaded to read the announcement, but he read it in a sluggish, barely audible voice.

On May 11, 1914, at the graduation exercises, Sergei played his concerto, with Tcherepnin conducting the orchestra. It had great success. The entire St. Petersburg press reported the event, and even his severest critics were compelled to recognize that the twenty-three-year-old Sergei Prokofiev was an outstanding musician. He had been booed and applauded, his music was published, and he had even been paid for it.

10

It is not surprising that Prokofiev's debut as a composer caused such consternation in Moscow and St. Petersburg musical circles. He struck a dissonant chord, which could not have been welcome in an atmosphere pervaded by Chopin, Tchaikovsky, and Rachmaninoff emotionalism on one side, and the soul-searching and confused mysticism of Scriabin on the other. Prokofiev's hearty laugh, his dry humor, his vigor and exuberance did not fit into a decaying salon romanticism. It was a challenge to every form of convention; it threatened to destroy tradition.

It was at about this time that Scriabin's music was brought to the attention of audiences at large, thanks to Sergei Koussevitzky. Originally a double-bass virtuoso, Koussevitzky had become an orchestra conductor through his second marriage to the daughter of the millionaire Konstantin Ushkov, owner and chairman of the largest tea firm in Russia. After a short period of study under Arthur Nikish in Berlin, Koussevitzky had returned to Moscow to conduct his own orchestra.

He was ambitious and rich, thus independent in his choice— qualities not particularly conducive to winning the sympathy of his former orchestra colleagues at the Bolshoi Theatre. That he had already founded a publishing firm in Berlin and was planning to buy up Russian music-publishing firms were added to the rumors that he was going to build his own concert hall. It furthered a suspicion that he intended to monopolize Russian music and, in fact, Russian musical life in all its forms. This idea was not welcome by the Moscovites, and his first appearances with his orchestra were sparsely attended. But Koussevitzky knew how to attract an audience. He presented *his* discovery, Alexander Scriabin, which he knew would cause controversy, if not a sensation, and thus place him in the foreground of musical life in Russia.

In 1908, Koussevitzky paid Scriabin, who was living in Lausanne, a visit, to find out about his current work as well as his plans for the future. Scriabin spoke to him (as he did to everyone else) about his writing a Mystery (a Passion Play), that he said, would end the world "as we know it."* Not in the least frightened, Koussevitzky patiently listened to Scriabin's disclosure (not quite clear to himself) of the Last Festival, at which Scriabin planned to lead mankind to a specially erected temple on a lake somewhere in India. Intoxicated by the grandeur of his own vision, Scriabin spoke in a language justified by his dream, a language cluttered with quotations from Nietzsche and the Hindu prophets, mixed with his own belief in the divinity of man and himself.

Not only music, Scriabin tried to impress on Koussevitzky, but all the arts were to be part of his Mystery, in which the material and spiritual polarities would eventually meet in an act of love from which would come a return to the primordial state of chaos, followed by a "new breath of Brahma."

At times half-closing his eyes as though he were looking into the distance, Scriabin spoke gently, almost in a languishing voice. But he was in dead earnest about what he was saying, while a happy smile lit up his face, with its childish, excited eyes: ". . . One has only to start. . . . For I will have there seven days. But they are not going to be just ordinary days. . . . Just as during the creation of the world the seven days meant the passing of whole eras, whole lives of races, so then will. . . ." Scriabin paused for a second to look at Koussevitzky's puzzled expression, and then went right on: "But they will also be at the same time just like our days. . . . Time itself will be accelerated and in these days we will live through millions of years. It will be like a curve." Scriabin illustrated with his hand. "Time will gradually quicken the tempo, because it has been slowed up by the process of materialism. But then the dematerialization will set in."

Having recently gained power in the materialistic world, Koussevitzky was the last person to appreciate Scriabin's prophecy, but Scriabin changed the subject before his guest could say a word.

"What strikes me as significant," Scriabin continued in a confidential tone, "is that in observing nature, I see that the vegetation, the trees and flowers, are silent and immovable. And all around them lives the

* This account of Scriabin's Mystery is taken from my *Rachmaninoff, op. cit.*

world of animals, that world which is in constant movement from the slowest motion to the most rapid, from a straight line to a curve. It is a dance of movement against a background of the motionless vegetation. . . . Did this ever occur to you?"

Koussevitzky did not understand a word he said, but nodded in agreement, and Scriabin continued: "In nature the animals correspond to the activity of the masculine and the vegetation to the feminine—will-less, passive." And raising his forefinger and with a sly expression he whispered: "These are polarities, and there might be some kind of love act between the two—some kind of polar act." After a few minutes of silence Scriabin began to explain: "All the animals and vegetation are nothing but the creation of our psyche. They are merely symbols. . . . Don't you feel . . . don't you think that the animals correspond to the caresses of men and women during their act of love and that every caress has its corresponding animal—the birds correspond to the light caresses that have wings . . . and then there are the torturing kind of caresses—these are the wild beasts. How mistaken are those who believe that the wild beasts are merely wild beasts!" Scriabin added with a superior air.

"The caresses of mice are very bad," Scriabin changed the tone of his voice; he was mortally afraid of mice, and his imagination was affected by the common Russian superstition. "The mice correspond to disaster and something terribly unpleasant. They have probably another existence and another significance. . . ." Obviously affected by what he was saying, Scriabin took a deep breath and remained motionless for a long time before he breathed out the air he had just inhaled. "This is the purifying breath," he explained. "In science everything is divided, analyzed. There is no synthesis . . ." Scriabin was leading up to the crux of his argument. "But how else can it be, how else can I invite this world to my Mystery? Because the animals, birds, and insects *must* be there. How wonderful it would be to torture the world with millions of eagles and tigers, to peck at it with caresses and to burn it with the caresses of the wings of tiny, tiny moths and the bites of the snake! . . . As in my *Extase*, on this last day of my Mystery, at this last dance, I will fragment myself into millions of tiny, tiny moths—not only I, but all of us. . . . Perhaps, by the end of the Mystery, we will cease to be human but will become caresses, beasts, birds, moths . . . snakes. . . ."

Scriabin argued his thesis as the natural, inevitable, and logical sequence to the "principles of the whole." He also added that he would need at least five years to complete his *magnum opus*. Apparently he was convinced that by the end of this time, his diabolical scheme to destroy a society based on bourgeois principles would be ready, and he would then square his accounts with this harsh and miserable world.

Koussevitzky listened to him solemnly and was puzzled by his fantastic project for whatever one might have said about Koussevitzky, he could never have been accused of being a mystic. He probably thought that Scriabin was speaking of some kind of large composition he had in mind that he, Koussevitzky, would publish with his new firm, conduct at one of his concerts, and then forget entirely. Two years later Koussevitzky said to Sabaneyev, "It was only Scriabin who expected that after the performance of *Extase* [the composition Scriabin mentioned in his long exposé] everyone right then and there would be suffocated with ecstasy. Actually, we all, including Scriabin, went to a restaurant where we had an excellent dinner and enjoyed ourselves. The same would have happened with his Mystery. We would have played it and then gone to dinner."

But Scriabin was just the kind of trump card that Koussevitzky needed at the beginning of his game against his opponents in Russian musical circles, and proclaiming Scriabin the genius of Russia, Koussevitzky split the concertgoers and musicians into two camps. They fought as bitterly for their cause as the Mighty Five, the founders of Russian National Music, had fought their adversaries in the latter part of the last century. On one side, led by Taneyev, was a party of "conservatives," which had just begun to recognize Brahms and Wagner and was still against the St. Petersburg group and the Mighty Five. And on the other, much smaller in number, were the so-called modernists, and later the Scriabinists. For many among the musicians and music lovers were so impressed with Scriabin's ideas that they were ready to see in him a prophet, if not an outright Messiah. Needless to say, Sergei Prokofiev did not share their admiration. To him all such things as the esoteric, esthetic dreams of Scriabin were sheer nonsense, and he evaluated Scriabin's works purely from a musician's point of view.

Besides Rachmaninoff, Glazunov, Lyadov, and Arensky, Nikolai Medtner was also drawn into the group of "conservatives." The Russian critics, as well as those abroad, maintained that Medtner could be considered a Russian composer only through a misunderstanding. It is almost impossible to name another composer who in his creative ability remained so wholly outside the "influence of the environment" in which he was born and brought up. His compositions show his national origins, German, but the Moscovites accepted Medtner as one of their own, perhaps because, in addition to the German classical tinge, they found in his music something that might have come from the Taneyev school.

Medtner himself neither knew nor understood, nor was even interested in modern music. He did not like the French composers, and he refused to accept anything written after Brahms and Wagner. He was indifferent to Scriabin's later work, and Scriabin seldom looked through Medtner's compositions, for their classicism merely depressed him. Scriabin believed that there should be no music *per se*, but that music had only one *raison d'être*—a sort of nucleus, a part of a whole of the *Weltanschauung*, as he liked to say. He found that Medtner's music was crowded with notes for no particular purpose. "I do not understand how one can in our time write 'mere music'—this is not in itself interesting," he said.

The Russian composers were far from what might be called a happy family. If they did not criticize each other's compositions, they criticized each other as pianists—all of them were first-rate pianists, and most of their music was written for that instrument.

It was only natural that the persistently growing rumble of a new musical volcano, Sergei Prokofiev, challenged both conservatives and Scriabinists to fight a new and perhaps more formidable foe, one even Scriabin could not add to the list of the pianists he hated because, he said, they played as though they were washing laundry or smelling the instrument.

11

At this point, when Sergei had "arrived," when his talent was at last being recognized, it is appropriate to ask how he felt about the crushing criticism that his works received, what he himself thought of his compositions and the "slippery road" that he had chosen to follow determinedly.

His childhood and adolescence were not the kind that produce a rebel. On the contrary, he knew no privations, was brought up in luxury, relatively speaking, on a private estate, like a prince in his own kingdom, and was attended by governesses and a staff of servants.

His example serves as another argument against the naïve assumption that only the "have not" circumstances condition the rebellious spirit. Late-nineteenth-century Russia had produced a long list of intellectuals and authors, wealthy noblemen like Prince Kropotkin, Count Leo Tolstoy, Alexander Herzen, to name only a few, who devoted their lives to working against the accepted concepts of morality and traditions. Perhaps Prokofiev's name would have joined their ranks had he not been a born musician dedicated to his work.

"I have always felt compelled to follow my own way of thinking," Sergei said, "and never to do anything merely because of the accepted rules." This was already evident in his attitude toward his early studies under Glière and later at the Conservatory, where his endeavors to find his "own way," were considered the mischievous pranks of a spoiled boy. Was he? His early musical maturity led to his own judgments of right and wrong in his other activities as well, and since his adoring parents were apt to "understand and forgive" his often unusual behavior, he grew up a spoiled mama's boy indeed.

Traits of character that were overlooked in the exceptionally gifted youngster were to be ascribed as he grew older to arrogance and rudeness. Actually, they were aspects of his self-assurance, his only shield against the many who criticized him, and it must be admitted that for a gentle, sweet mama's boy who was terrified of childish fights with his playmates, Sergei showed remarkable stamina. Small wonder that while tolerating the unceremonious abuse from his critics, he retaliated in the same uncontrolled manner when given an opportunity. Once, rather good-humoredly, he remarked, "I suppose that I, too, might have become a critic and surely would have been as nasty."

Unlike Moussorgsky, who was guided in his compositions solely by his intuition, Prokofiev recognized that his own musical language could neither have validity nor be convincing unless he mastered its delivery. "After I had been graduated from the class of composition at the Conservatory," Sergei said, "I had far too many plans for my work, but not enough technical skill and experience. Therefore, every year I kept composing at least one large orchestral work until, after five or six years of tenacious struggle, I felt that I had gained the necessary freedom in composition. Without being presumptuous, I may say that I never follow anyone else's ideas. In everything I write, I follow two major principles: clarity and brevity, avoiding everything superfluous in the expression of my ideas."

According to Prokofiev's analysis, there were four major characteristics of his works that were either completely overlooked or misunderstood by his critics. "The first," he said, "was the classical, born in my childhood when I heard my mother play Beethoven sonatas. It took a neoclassical turn in my gavottes and sonatas.

"The second—innovation, which started after Taneyev's mocking remark about my 'much too simple' harmony. At first it led to a search for harmonies to suit my own language, and later to a search for a language to express strong emotions, as in The Ghost, Desperation, Diabolical Suggestion. Although this search was mainly concerned with harmonization, it was also influential in the intonation of melodies.

"The third—toccatalike character, or if you prefer to call it so, machine, or motorlike. This had its roots in Schumann's Toccata, which made a great impression on me at the time and is expressed in my Études (Op. 2), Toccata (Op. 11), Scherzo (Op. 12), and in the Scherzo in the Second Piano Concerto. This characteristic is of less importance.

"The fourth—a lyrical principle, at first expressed as a feeling not bound to the melodies in my Fairy Tale (Op. 3), Dreams, Autumnal, and Legend (Op. 12). This characteristic was never noticed, or not until much later. For a long time, my critics denied me any lyricism, and without any encouragement it developed very slowly. But later I paid more attention to it.

"I would like to limit the characteristics in the development of my creative ability to these four," Prokofiev continued, "and to consider the fifth, the so-called 'grotesque,' as a sideline of the four. In fact, I am very much against this term 'grotesque,' which in Russian is a mistranslation of the original French word. In referring to my work I would prefer to use 'scherzando,' meaning simply an effort to express a joke, laughter, or mockery."

These characteristics in his compositions were not overlooked or misunderstood by all critics. Prokofiev had gained a number of admirers who already watched his development with keen interest. Boris Asafiev, a former classmate under Lyadov and Rimsky-Korsakov who had become a music critic (he wrote under the pen name of Igor Glebov), was among the early enthusiasts of Sergei's career as a composer. Already at that date comparison of Prokofiev's and Stravinsky's works led to the appraisal of their significance from the point of view of changing trends in contemporary music.

Stravinsky is the last representative of the most refined and at the same time outdated satiating culture [Asafiev wrote in *Musica*, (1914, No. 203)].

The beauty of the sound of his compositions has its integral beauty, but it almost lacks a "look into the future."

In Stravinsky's works there are no advanced ideas, but rather a refined synthesis of past accomplishments. Stravinsky is all in the past. Despite all his fanciful harmonies, one feels that his strength is in his weakness—with his intuitive insight he captures the spirit and the meaning of the past epoch and stylizes it with astute contemporary means. But everywhere he remains sincere, because in all varied cultures he is at home—all of them have left definite traces on his mind. When one listens to Stravinsky's music it appears that his word is the last, that everything has been achieved and that nothing remains to be accomplished, it would be senseless. And indeed it would be senseless if one would follow his route, the route of refined synthesis and poisonous, but seductive "modern" ideas.

And now the works of Prokofiev are making their appearance. They are fresh and invigorating and speak in a language of a self-confident man conscious of his powers. One feels an enormous creative will, an irresistible creative élan. The composer's fantasy is limitless, his effortless writing is astounding; you hear nothing that was achieved by a struggle, nothing immaterial; on the contrary, one sees in it the author amusing himself with the tone-images in his mind, and one can neither see the end nor predict the character of his future inventions.

Prokofiev's creative ability cannot be forced into any already existing frame, nor can it be measured by the accepted standards—it must be judged by his own rules. There is no doubt that his compositions are imbued with a true beauty, perhaps austere and tart for our sensitive taste. Nevertheless, it is no less acceptable than the refined charm of Stravinsky's music. It seems to me that Prokofiev has the right not only "not to love" but actually to hate the old culture and the old music. He has to believe only in himself, even if it limits him, for in this limitation is his force. What if he appears to be a wild and terrifying creature to those who fear that a new conception of beauty may kill the old, to which they cling so fast, as if beauty, old or new, can ever be limited by its varied manifestations?

With a clear vision of his future work, Sergei Prokofiev began a new phase of his life, that of an independent artist, by going abroad in July, 1914, a present that Maria gave him for having successfully graduated. Since the death of his father, Sergei had not returned to Sontsovka, and except for a short trip to the Caucasus, he and Maria had spent most of their summers in St. Petersburg, only occasionally visiting their friends and relatives in the country nearby, and once taking a brief trip abroad.

"Do you remember," Glière would ask him, "how nice it was in Sontsovka?" Sergei missed the carefree life, the early-morning swims in the river, the fishing, and the picnicking. Life was so natural and easy in the country and so complicated, almost prohibitive, in a large city like St. Petersburg.

The only compensation for the loss of such pleasures was chess, for there had been a dearth of interesting partners at Sontsovka; but in St. Petersburg he had unlimited opportunities. He had been studying chess and had improved so much that when José Capablanca announced an exhibition of simultaneous games at the National Chess Club, Sergei joined the list of his opponents.

The twenty-six-year-old Capablanca—a member of the Cuban diplomatic mission in Russia who several years later (in 1921) became a world champion—was then a rising new chess star, and to play against him, no matter what the result, was a great distinction. Sergei came to this session accompanied by five friends from the Conservatory who were excited and much concerned about the outcome of Sergei's game, for he was entrusted with the honor of defending the "chess prestige" of their school.

"I lost the game," Sergei duly recorded in his notebook. "Capablanca moved his knight, threatening the inevitable loss of my rook."

But his excited friends did not watch the game for nothing as they stood around Sergei's chair. Apparently imbued with the Sontsovka kind of chess sportsmanship, they advised Sergei to save his rook by making a substitute move as Capablanca walked away toward his next opponent, hoping that the chess master would not notice. When Capablanca returned and looked at Sergei's board, he smiled and said nothing; shortly afterward he won the game despite the new *variante*.

After this first encounter Sergei became a close friend of Capablanca, whom he later met on his travels in Europe as well as in the United States. And whenever Capablanca returned to Russia, Sergei attended the chess tournaments.

Chess was Sergei Prokofiev's most passionate hobby. "Chess for me," Prokofiev once said, "is a special world, a world of struggle, plans, and passion. I don't merely follow the games played at tournaments, but I'm also intensely interested in the lives of the masters."

After he played against Capablanca Prokofiev was invited to a banquet in honor of another chess master, Eduard Lasker. This was not his first meeting with the man who held the title of the world champion for twenty-six years. At the age of eighteen Sergei was one of the amateurs who had taken part in an exhibition of simultaneous games given by Lasker on March 2, 1909, in St. Petersburg. "Yesterday," Sergei hastened to inform his friends with well-deserved pride, "I have played against His Majesty King Eduard, and after five hours of struggle we called it a draw—this is certified by newspaper reports, and Lasker's inscription to me on his photograph."

During the evening at this banquet Prokofiev was repeatedly congratulated. "What are they congratulating you for?" Lasker asked him. "Yesterday," Prokofiev replied, "you received the first prize at the chess tournament, and I the first prize at the Conservatory."

"I don't know how well you play the piano," Lasker said, "but I am delighted that the Rubinstein Prize was awarded to a chess player."

A week later Sergei went abroad. This was his second trip outside Russia. During the previous summer he had accompanied his mother on a short journey to France. Like most Russians, he was enchanted by the vigor and tempo of Parisian life and the high standard of culture of the French people. But because of his own forthcoming public appearance in Pavlovsk and his preparation for the final examinations at the Conservatory, his mind had not been free to absorb all the new impressions the strange city offered, including several Diaghilev productions.

At the *pension* in which they had stayed Sergei met the Andreyevs: Anna Zherebzova-Andreyeva, a singer and professor at the St. Petersburg Conservatory, and her husband, Nikolai Andreyev, a singer at the

Maryinsky Theatre who had been engaged by Diaghilev for several guest performances in London. Only after it was agreed that he could use a studio at Otto Klinge's music shop in London so that he would not lose a single day's piano practice, did Sergei accept the Andreyevs' invitation to accompany them to London. Unfortunately, the four days he spent there left but a fleeting impression. In the mornings he worked at the piano diligently, and in the evenings he was taken to concerts and Diaghilev productions. He even attended a boxing match, the brutality of which startled him—"many teeth were knocked out, some boxers lay unconscious, and the public howled with delight," he reported to his mother.

Now it was all to be different, for when Maria offered him the trip, he chose London, where Diaghilev was having one of his brilliant concert and ballet seasons.

Sergei Diaghilev, who probably did more than anyone else to popularize Russian art abroad, did everything on a grand scale. He had started in 1907 by impressing Parisian audiences with such artists as Rimsky-Korsakov, Scriabin, Chaliapin, Rachmaninoff, and Nikish; he also presented a production of Moussorgsky's *Boris Godunov*, the equal of which has never, reputedly, been seen since. In the same season he unveiled the dazzling artistry of Nijinsky, Karsavina, and Pavlova in the Ballet Russe.

"If the theatre were to burn down tonight, the best artistic brains and talents, and the most elegant women of Europe would perish in the audience," he remarked before each triumphal night.

During the following years Diaghilev, no longer insisting on having exclusively Russian artists, produced the works of many outstanding European composers, including Maurice Ravel and Claude Debussy. Although not a painter, dancer, or an accomplished musician, he had left an imprint on the painting, dance, and music of his time. To be associated with Diaghilev was a distinction; to have one's work performed by this glamorous group of elite artists was a unique opportunity and honor. For Diaghilev, with his constant "new discoveries" and the almost legendary presentations of their work, for more than twenty years wielded the most powerful influence on the trend of artistic activities in the Western world.

But Diaghilev's was a complex personality. His irresistible charm and skill at organization won him countless admirers and many devoted friends, while his autocratic manner, often bordering on foolhardiness, estranged an equal number of men of value. He could have remained a dilettante with excellent taste, given that none of his many talents was developed to a professional degree. But his tremendous energy and his genius for choosing the right men to collaborate with him changed him from a *bon vivant* to a patron of art par excellence and a super-Barnum rolled into one.

"His 'season' in London was most interesting indeed," Prokofiev reported. "Chaliapin sang, Richard Strauss conducted, and there were many new productions. Diaghilev himself was a magnificent sight in his superbly cut frock coat, top hat, white gloves, and a monocle, which he constantly adjusted in his eye with the air of a blasé aristocrat."

Walter Nouvell, who accompanied Prokofiev on this trip to London, took him to meet Diaghilev. Prokofiev played his Second Piano Concerto while Diaghilev examined him as though he were a new horse brought to his stables to be groomed for a forthcoming race. He listened benevolently to Prokofiev's composition, but was interrupted by José Sert, the painter, who happened to be present: "But this is some kind of wild beast!" (Sert quickly apologized when he learned that Prokofiev understood French.)

Instead of discouraging him, Sert's remark stirred Diaghilev's imagination: Why not "produce" the concerto with Prokofiev at the piano while a ballet was being performed on stage? He even thought of a fairy-tale hero, "somebody like Lel in Rimsky-Korsakov's *Snow Maiden*," who would be created to the accompaniment of a part of the finale in the concerto. But after further discussions with Prokofiev, he agreed that the subject "somehow does not fit the score" and abandoned the project. Prokofiev took this opportunity to tell him of his desire to write an opera on Dostoyevsky's novel *The Gambler*.

At that time in Russia several plays adapted from Dostoyevsky novels—for example, *The Brothers Karamazov*, *The Possessed*, and *The Idiot*—had been presented at the Moscow Art Theatre, a practice severely criticized by Maxim Gorky, who maintained that these subjects were bound only to upset further the nerves of a society that was already uneasy about the general political situation in Russia. Nevertheless, influenced by these theatrical experiments, Miaskovsky was planning to use *The Idiot* for an opera, while Prokofiev had chosen the dramatic plot of the novel *The Gambler*.

But Diaghilev would not even hear of it. "Opera is passé," he said. "Contemporary taste demands ballet and pantomime." And whether he spoke convincingly on his favorite subject, or more probably because he was willing right then and there to commission Prokofiev to write a ballet on a "Russian fairy tale or a prehistoric subject," Prokofiev agreed.

Patting Prokofiev on the shoulder, Diaghilev closed the interview by telling Nouvell to put the young man in touch with a poet in St. Petersburg, Sergei Gorodetsky, immediately. He spoke with an air of great urgency, as if he expected Prokofiev to return to Russia at once. But Sergei did not have the vaguest idea of what sort of music was expected of him, and he assiduously attended all Diaghilev productions, hoping to find a key to his problem. Over and over again he saw Stravinsky's *Petroushka* and *The Firebird*, and Ravel's *Daphnis and Chloé*.

This was not Sergei's first introduction to Stravinsky's works. Two years before, at one of the contemporary music performances in Moscow, Sergei heard the composer play his *Firebird* in a piano arrangement. Afterward he told Stravinsky that he did not like the music: "There is no music in the introduction, and if there is any, what little there is, is from Rimsky-Korsakov's *Sadko*." Sergei admitted later that this and similar blunt expressions of his opinion did not endear him to Stravinsky, who, like many others, could not consider Prokofiev's lack of respect and impudent behavior a charming trait.

In Paris with his mother, he had seen Diaghilev productions of both ballets, *Petroushka* and *The Firebird*, and his initial impressions were not much changed when he saw them again in London. He found *Petroushka* amusing, vivid, gay, witty, and interesting. "The music," he said, "illustrates very well every detail of action on stage, just as the action conforms with the minute details of each orchestral phrase. The orchestration is excellent and, when necessary, most amusing."

"But now," Sergei continued as he tried to answer the vital question he must ask of himself, "Is there any music in this ballet, or not? Yes and no. Doubtless there is some music in more than one place, but the large part of the score is mere *remplissage*. Actually, when is such filling-in permissible? It seems to me only in the most boring places of an unsuccessful scenario. But Stravinsky, in the most interesting moments, in the most vivid scenes, does not write music, but something that illustrates this or that action exceptionally well. That is nothing but *remplissage*. And if he cannot write music for the most important parts of the scenario but fills them in with any old stuff, then this indeed shows his musical limitations. Thus, if we still insist that Stravinsky has cut a new door into the music of the future, then we must also admit that he has done this with a small knife and not with an ax, which would rightly have bestowed on him the title of *Titan*."

After seeing *The Firebird* several times more in London, Sergei modified his first opinion, but only slightly. "What vivid, almost blinding colors in the score, what inventiveness in all these grimaces, and how sincere is the creation!" he said. "But I could not for a moment be captivated by the music. Where is the music? Nothing but deadwood."

And Sergei was even more critical of Ravel's *Daphnis and Chloé*, which he said was "incredibly boring, thin and watery, soporific when it touches on poetry, and laughable when it concerns drama or scenic action. Its success is due entirely to the enchanting choreography."

During his stay in London, Prokofiev was so engrossed in Diaghilev's productions ("they are so interesting," he said, "that I shall go again and again")—that he almost missed the beginning of World War I and returned home only a few days before Russia entered.

Miaskovsky, as an officer in a sapper regiment, was sent to the front, but Sergei—as the only son of a widow—was not called up. He did not give up the idea of writing an opera on the subject of *The Gambler*, but he put it aside while he was working with Gorodetsky on Diaghilev's projected ballet.

12

Neither Prokofiev nor Gorodetsky knew much about ballet dramaturgy, and they found it very difficult to invent a plot and a suitable scenario. Diaghilev's desire to have the ballet based on a "prehistoric" Russian subject pointed, or so they thought, to a trend very much in vogue at the time: the literati and artists, tired of languishing bedroom themes and everlasting aesthetic self-adoration, were turning to the primitive man and his era. In their works they claimed to oppose the recherché of the Symbolists. Their idealization of the savagery of the prehistoric man, with his superstitions and fear of natural forces, found their expression in Nicholas Roerich's paintings and eventually in Stravinsky's *Le Sacre du Printemps*.

"I understood nothing of it at all," Sergei said after he heard the composition for the first time in concert form performed by Sergei Koussevitzky and his orchestra. Was this the style Diaghilev wanted for his ballet? *Sacre* was no help to him and to Gorodetsky. Prokofiev did not share Stravinsky's lofty idea that his *Sacre* was in the nature of an ideological statement of principles, a glorification of the elemental forces of nature, a revival of savage, pagan instincts, an antidote against the morbid, sensual atmosphere created by the Symbolists. All this was alien to Sergei.

In the Western world, in which no one concerned himself too deeply with Stravinsky's soul-searching, *Sacre* caused a sensation just because it was accepted as another manifestation of Russian exoticism. Prokofiev's plans for his own ballet were comparatively simple: to use this opportunity to express his own ideas in his own idiom.

Some critics later claimed, however, that they found definite traces of *Sacre* in Sergei's composition.

After Gorodetsky had spent long hours reading source books on Russian mythology and in repeated, lengthy discussion, the two collaborators finally concocted a plot: "The Scythians are worshiping the Sun God, Veles, and Ala, a wooden idol, when one night a cunning stranger, Chuzhbog, aided by the dark forces of evil, tries to abduct Ala. Chuzhbog's spell, however, works only in the darkness; under the pale light of the moon he is powerless. Lolli, the warrior, comes to Ala's rescue. Chuzhbog is about to slay him, but timely intervention saves him when the Sun God smites Chuzhbog with his blinding rays."

That there was an echo from Sergei's own childish plot of *The Giant* is of little importance. More noteworthy are the echoes of Rimsky-Korsakov's *Snow Maiden*.

During the months when Gorodetsky was writing the scenario, Sergei occupied himself with other work: a vocal piece called *The Ugly Duckling* after Hans Christian Andersen's fairy tale. He treated the fairy tale allegorically, as the story of a man facing the ugly world of narrow-minded Philistinism. And Sergei found relaxation from the violent sound effects of the ballet in the sketches he composed for *The Ugly Duckling* whenever Gorodetsky supplied him with some fragments of the scenario.

"I have written an 'enormous' *Romance*,* some fifteen pages long," Prokofiev told his friends. He had adapted Andersen's narrative, but had shortened the text to be recited † by a singer, while the piano would accompany the text descriptively. Thus the text presents both the words spoken by the characters of the fairy tale and the emotional attitude of the narrator who describes the misfortunes of *The Ugly Duckling*.

In the piano part Prokofiev succeeded in depicting the atmosphere of a peaceful day, an amusing procession of newborn ducklings (reminiscent of Moussorgsky's ballet of chicks in his *Pictures at an Exhibition*), a wild dog chase after *The Ugly Duckling*, and finally, a cold winter's day. The main theme of the composition is the leitmotiv expressing *The Ugly Duckling's* own sad realization of the source of all his misfortunes: "It is because I am so ugly."

This Op. 18 was performed for the first time at the "Evenings of Contemporary Music" in Petrograd on January 17, 1915, by Anna Zherebzova-Andreyeva, the singer with whom Sergei had gone to

---

* *Romance* is the Russian equivalent of the German *Lieder*.
† The Russians refer to such recitatives as "melodeclaimed."

London in the summer of 1913. Some in the audience found the Romance merely another of Prokofiev's grotesque compositions, but Asafiev praised it, calling it a pearl in contrast to the soporific works
offered by the contemporary Impressionists.

Other critics said that Prokofiev's *Duckling* was not at all *"Ugly,"*
that it showed the composer's fantasy and talent for invention, and
that the usual Prokofiev sharpness was well disguised. Vyacheslav
Karatygin, the eminent critic, remarked that the final episode in
which the text tells of the duckling's turning into a swan was lacking
in more poetic and romantic music. But Asafiev, commenting on
Karatygin's criticism, said, "If Prokofiev has not entirely succeeded in
the final scene, perhaps it happened because he himself has not yet
turned into a swan."

"Why, he has written that composition about himself," Maxim
Gorky said when he heard the piece performed, so human was *The
Ugly Duckling*.

But in the ballet Prokofiev was striving for sharp "barbarous" images that would overwhelm the audience. "You have made everything
much too nice, much too beautiful," he reproached Gorodetsky. Sergei, inspired by the vision of a wild bacchanal of evil forces, imagined
all kinds of chimerical monsters and unheard-of reptiles, influenced no
doubt by Moussorgsky's "Night on Bold Mountain." Gorodetsky, the
poet, daydreamed of songful, plastic music in Rimsky-Korsakov's and
Tchaikovsky's style, but Sergei overwhelmed him with shocking,
loud, discordant, and stormy impressions.

The constant arguments between the two collaborators slowed the
progress of the ballet; it occupied Sergei all through the winter of
1914–15. To friends in Moscow who regretted the time wasted on the
Diaghilev project, Sergei wrote: "I have not given up the idea of
The Gambler; in fact, I think of it more than ever but first I must
complete the ballet. If you really believe a ballet is a second-rate composition, then may God forgive you your utter ignorance."

Finally, Sergei played the score for Alfred Nurok and Walter Nouvell, Diaghilev's close friends, who later reported to Diaghilev: "Prokofiev is writing muddled music on a muddled subject." Nevertheless,
promising to arrange a concert for him in Italy and to pay for his trip,
Diaghilev asked Sergei to come to Rome, where because of the war
he had set up his headquarters.

Traveling through Rumania, Bulgaria, and Greece—countries that
had not yet entered the war—Prokofiev arrived in Rome in February,
1915. Diaghilev listened to the still-unfinished score and did not approve of either the music or the subject "on stilts." "You must write

another ballet," he told Sergei—but he kept his word and arranged a concert for him in Rome.

On March 7, 1915, Sergei played for the first time outside Russia. His performance of the Second Piano Concerto, under the direction of Bernardino Molinari, had a mixed reception but caused no demonstration such as the one he had witnessed when he presented the work for the first time in St. Petersburg.

Despite the war Diaghilev was preparing his next "season." He discussed some new projects with the Italian Futurists, and invited Stravinsky, who was then in Switzerland, to join him. Considering Sergei's first meeting with the composer, both Diaghilev and Sergei were a little apprehensive about Stravinsky's attitude. But Stravinsky was "well-disposed," praised Sergei's concerto, and the two composers played a four-hand arrangement of *Petroushka* for the Futurists.

Filippo Tomaso Marinetti, the founder of the European Futurist movement, advocated the destruction of classical culture and a deliberate perversion of the literary language. "He spoke French incredibly fast, quoting long passages both in verse and prose, so that it was difficult to follow his ideas," Sergei said. "It was new and unusual for me, and I even felt a sense of pride in being in close contact with such a 'terribly advanced' personage, but his theories were over my head."

Since the present "avant-garde" movements are still closely related to the ideas of their early leaders, it is interesting to learn Sergei Prokofiev's views on this subject. "One of the main factors in the Futurists' beliefs is their worship of current technical progress. Idolizing speed, the Futurists admire machines," Sergei noted. "This leads to their poetic claim concerning the beauty to be found in noise—the noise of trains, of propellers, and so on. Searching for these 'beautiful noises,' they invent new 'musical instruments.' Having heard about this, I expected to find a variety of percussion instruments, but I was mistaken, because their newly invented instruments have rather long-drawn sounds from the very lowest to the highest registers."

Sergei then described some of these instruments, which were still in as primitive a stage of development as were the motorcars at that time. Speaking objectively of the whole Futurist idea, he said that the new instruments were capable of producing the sounds of sirens, bowling balls, or rain falling on a windowpane, that the sounds were wild and lacked clear intonation. The Futurists believed that they could form orchestras using these instruments, but in Prokofiev's opinion, they were much too limited in their possibilities for that, not even to mention their technical immaturity.

After Stravinsky's departure Diaghilev and Sergei sat down to ex-

plore a collection of Russian fairy tales by the nineteenth-century eth-
nographer Alexander Afanasiev that Stravinsky had left with them.
They chose two stories from a series about a buffoon, and easily concocted a scenario for a ballet in six scenes. It was to depict a young
village boy, a practical joker who sells to seven other practical jokers
of the village a magic whip that has supernatural powers to revive the
dead. To prove this, he first stages the killing of his wife and then
brings her back to life. After killing their wives the seven men try the
magic whip, but in vain. Their wives are dead. The story had striking
characterizations of the village priest, his wife, and a rich merchant,
but Diaghilev, who was not interested in any anticlerical satire, deleted
the priest and his wife from the scenario.

This time Diaghilev signed a regular contract for three thousand rubles: "Only please write me Russian music," he asked Sergei, "because
in your rotten Petrograd you have completely forgotten how to write
Russian music!"

Now that Sergei was better acquainted with Diaghilev, he was even
more impressed than before by the man's knowledge of the arts. His
opinions, whether on musical compositions or painting, sculpture or
choreography, were sharply defined. In exchange, Diaghilev scoffed at
Sergei's many-sided love of music. "In art you must learn to hate, or
your own art, music, will lose its character," he told Sergei.

"But this inevitably will lead to limitations," Sergei protested.

"A gun fires far because its aim is narrow," Diaghilev replied.

Upon his return to Petrograd, Prokofiev began to work on the thematic material for *The Buffoon*, trying to give it a true Russian character. During his childhood in Sontsovka he had often heard the
peasant girls singing in the village on Saturdays and Sundays, but
whether because the Sontsovka region was poor in original songs, or
whether Sergei was irritated by the vocal technique of the local divas,
who showed no mercy for their voices, he did not remember any of
these songs. "And yet," he said, "I must admit that those melodies must
have penetrated my subconscious," for he had no difficulty in adjust-
ing his style to the national character.

That summer he completed the six scenes. He had agreed to return
to Italy to work with the choreographer, but because of the war the
route through the Balkan countries now was closed to him, and because of the mines he hesitated to travel through the Mediterranean.
Besides, the musical life of Petrograd attracted him far more than the
radiant prospects abroad of which Diaghilev wrote. Accordingly, he
remained in Petrograd, but he sent the manuscript with a choreographer who was on his way to see Diaghilev.

While he was working on *The Buffoon*, Prokofiev once more reviewed the score of *Ala and Lolli*, which Diaghilev had so scornfully rejected. Omitting some less interesting sections, he carved out of the score an orchestral suite, the Scythian Suite, in four parts. After completing the orchestration, he showed it to Siloti. And Siloti, who only a year before had refused to conduct Prokofiev's music—saying that "Debussy's music has a divine aroma, while Prokofiev's stinks"—now invited him to conduct the Scythian Suite at one of his concerts during the following season.

The general tone of the press after Sergei's successful graduation from the Conservatory, and Diaghilev's interest in him, had favorably influenced the attitude of several musicians in Petrograd. Siloti introduced Prokofiev to Albert Coates, the Russian-born English musician who had taken over the post of opera conductor at the Maryinsky Theatre. Coates was not afraid of "novelties" and told Prokofiev, "You write your *Gambler* and we'll produce it."

Nevertheless, some composers among Sergei's contemporaries were less ready to accept him. Sergei Rachmaninoff, condescendingly extending his "large, soft paw," chatted graciously enough when they first met. Later, Prokofiev attended the concert that Rachmaninoff gave as a memorial to Scriabin, who had died during the summer of 1915. Among other Scriabin compositions he played the Fifth Sonata.

"When Scriabin played this sonata," Prokofiev remembered later, "everything flew up and up, somehow, while in Rachmaninoff's delivery every note sat firmly on the ground." Although Scriabin ranked Rachmaninoff very highly, as a pianist he reproached him for the quality of his tone. Prokofiev recalled Scriabin's having said that, "Everything he plays has that same quality as his own music. In his 'sound' there is so much materialism, so much meat . . . almost some kind of boiled ham."

Scriabin's admirers were so disturbed by this performance that they had to hold one of them, Ivan Alchevsky, the famous dramatic tenor at the Maryinsky Theatre, by his coattails while he kept shouting, "Just wait, let me have a word with him." Sergei tried to calm him, tried to reason with him and the excited group of Scriabin devotees by saying that although they all, including Prokofiev himself, were accustomed to Scriabin's own interpretation, there can always be different ways of understanding the same work.

After the concert Prokofiev went to see Rachmaninoff in the green room. "Well," Sergei said, "despite everything, you've played very well."

Rachmaninoff smiled at him in utter disdain: "And you there, perhaps, expected me to play badly?" Then, turning his back on Sergei, he spoke to someone else in the room.

"With this brief exchange," Prokofiev said later, "our initial good relationship ended. This no doubt was affected by his disapproval of my music, which was a source of irritation to him."

Shortly afterward, Sergei unintentionally hurt Nikolai Medtner's feelings. At Medtner's piano recital of his own compositions, Prokofiev had hoped to hear his A-minor sonata, which interested him particularly. But Medtner played one of his less complicated works that Sergei thought could easily be read at home without Medtner's assistance. After the concert Sergei told Medtner that he regretted his choice of sonata. "And what about the one I played?" Medtner asked. "Oh, that one," Sergei replied, "that one is more for home consumption."

Later on, according to Medtner, Rachmaninoff used to say that Prokofiev divided sonatas into two groups: regular sonatas and those for "home consumption."

Nor did Sergei fare any better with Glazunov, whom he had called on especially to invite him to hear the Scythian Suite, which he was going to conduct at one of Siloti's concerts on January 29, 1916. The suite was greeted with an uproar similar to that created by the memorable first performances of his concertos. Glazunov's enthusiasm for Prokofiev's talent had been responsible for getting him into the St. Petersburg Conservatory. Later, he was so disappointed in his protégé that as a member of the Rubinstein Prize jury he had voted against Sergei, and had been so beside himself that he was unwilling to announce the prizewinner. Now once more he was so "beside himself" that he left the hall before Prokofiev had reached the end of the Scythian Suite.

Nor were the members of the orchestra especially happy about playing Sergei's composition. The tympanist, following Prokofiev's relentless demands, broke through the head of the kettledrum, and Siloti promised to send the torn bits of leather to Sergei as a souvenir. "Only because I have a sick wife and three children to support was I willing to submit to this hell," said one of the cellists, whose ears were battered by the deafening sounds coming from the trombones behind him.

In high good humor Siloti walked up and down the hall after the concert exclaiming, "What a slap in their faces! What a slap in their faces!" meaning that his concert organization and Prokofiev were insulting their critics. "A real scandal in a noble family," the critics reported with glee.

Meanwhile, Prokofiev continued to work on *The Gambler*. Encouraged by the controversy evoked by the Scythian Suite, Sergei kept searching for an even more advanced language for his opera. "Have you any idea what in God's name you are hammering out on your piano?" Maria asked her son when she could no longer tolerate the crashing sounds that filled their apartment.

"We quarreled, and didn't speak to each other for two days," Prokofiev remembered later.

He completed the score in five and a half months, in time to show it to Vladimir Telyakovsky, director of the Imperial Theatres. Knowing, however, that the committee that chose the repertory for the following season included such conservatives as Cesar Cui and Alexander Glazunov, Coates had never mentioned *The Gambler* until these men had left the city for their vacations. Then an extraordinary session was called at Telyakovsky's home, with several young conductors of the opera present, including Siloti and Nikolai Malko besides Coates. Telyakovsky was bewildered by the composition, but persuaded by the others to take a "great risk," he signed a contract, and sent Prokofiev flying home to prepare the work for production.

Sergei spent most of the summer orchestrating the score. "How much do you orchestrate per day?" Maria asked Tcherepnin. "Sometimes one single chord," Tcherepnin replied (obviously "showing off," Prokofiev remarked later, "with what thoroughness he worked."). "Why, my son tosses off as many as eighteen pages!" Maria proudly informed him.

Despite the continual criticism of Prokofiev's works, Koussevitzky had scheduled a performance of the Scythian Suite for December 25, 1916. The score called for a large orchestra, and because many men were called into the army shortly before the concert, Koussevitzky had to postpone its performance until the following season, substituting for it the work of another composer.

Nevertheless, on the day after this concert a Moscow newspaper published a review of the Scythian Suite written by Leonid Sabaneyev under the title "The Novelties of the Season."

Sergei was Sabaneyev's *bête noire*, relentlessly pursued in his reviews ever since he had first heard Prokofiev's compositions, saying among other things that Sergei, like Petroushka, had nothing but wood shavings inside him instead of a soul. In reviewing the Scythian Suite, he tore it to shreds, often using words like "barbarous" to describe it. He closed his lengthy analyses by saying, "The composer himself conducted the work with barbarous enthusiasm."

Obviously Sabaneyev had written the review without attending the concert and was unaware of the change in program. Acknowledging Sabaneyev's right to his own opinion, Sergei remarked that although Sabaneyev had never seen the score, he seemed to be so well informed about it that had Koussevitzky actually played it and had Sabaneyev heard it, he would not have changed a single word in his review.

Sabaneyev's review was an unforgivable faux pas for a responsible critic, and Prokofiev did not miss the opportunity to publish a letter in the newspapers stating what had happened.

In disgrace Sabaneyev had to resign his post, and for a while the incident served as a weapon against the malicious outbursts of Prokofiev's adversaries, certainly rendering utterly worthless any further comments Sabaneyev might make about his music.

Many years later, in the mid-1920s, Sergei met Sabaneyev in Paris. "I have no feeling of hatred for him for what happened in the past," Sergei wrote Miaskovsky, "but I am conscious of the fact that he is a man who was passionately mistaken all his life and who changed his opinions every other year. I had such vague recollection as to what he looked like that when we finally met, I didn't recognize him. His appearance is pitiful, sweaty, decayed. He mumbled something about the change in his views, trying no doubt to please me. He wanted us to be friends, but evoked only a sense of distaste. I hope fate preserves me from further meetings with him."

At that time Sabaneyev had written a book on Russian contemporary composers.* Although it is informative, as often happened, Sabaneyev overwrote, overworking the point he was trying to emphasize, and thus at the end of his essays he sometimes contradicted what he had said at the beginning. In his essay on Prokofiev, while admitting Prokofiev's talent and the merits of his compositions, he somehow left the impression that he had never forgotten the unfortunate incident in Moscow. Even as late as 1948, when I visited him in Nice, his attitude toward Prokofiev was still influenced by that episode.

The "Evenings of Contemporary Music," in which Sergei had made his debut and had found so much encouragement, no longer existed, and the activities of this progressive organization were taken over by a magazine, *Contemporary Music*, which also organized public performances. At one of these, in Moscow, on February 18, 1917, the program of chamber music was devoted entirely to Prokofiev's works. Among the invited guests were Medtner and Rachmaninoff. Medtner was boiling with indignation, while Rachmaninoff sat through the concert like a statue, so that the Moscow public, which as a rule received

* *Modern Russian Composers* (New York: International Publishers, 1927).

Prokofiev well, was rather subdued this time, watching their idol's attitude.

A week later Prokofiev's works were again presented, but this time to the Petrograd public. In a gallery in which many contemporary painters exhibited, "musical-literary" evenings were often organized in which many well-known authors and musicians participated. On February 12, 1917, in the first part of the program, Maxim Gorky read from his *Childhood* and Jascha Heifetz played Chopin's Nocturne in B-major and Paganini's Auer Étude No. 24.

The second part of the program was given over to Prokofiev's works: the Scherzo for four bassoons, *The Ugly Duckling*, and the four Études Op. 2, and *Sarcasms*, which Sergei played.

One of the newspaper reports, upbraiding Prokofiev for his mischievous habit of "sticking out his tongue" at the audience, said, ". . . And meanwhile his talent keeps fermenting like new beer in a barrel. When it is poured into a glass it foams higher and higher . . . so high, in fact, that after taking a sip, one discovers that there is very little beer indeed, or perhaps none at all . . . alas, man loses the vices of his youth every minute but never recovers its virtues."

Still a controversial musician, Sergei Prokofiev encountered the Russian Revolution on the streets of Petrograd, a revolution welcomed by those circles in which Sergei moved. No. 19 in his *Fleeting Thoughts*, composed at about this time, expressed his first impressions: the hopeful excitement of the crowds, rather than the meaning of the upheaval itself.

13

During the early months of the Revolution, Prokofiev shared the lot of everyone in Petrograd. It was not unusual for salvos of bullets to crisscross the city streets, sometimes to "discipline" the population, but more often to fire on human targets in deadly earnest. On such occasions Sergei too had either to hide behind a tree or run for cover to the nearest doorway. Aside from such incidents his personal life was not directly affected, except for a call into the army. (The old regulations exempting the only sons in a family from military service were no longer valid.)

Sergei's friends did whatever they could to prevent his conscription, and when their influential connections failed, he was advised to enroll once more in the Conservatory, where as a student he could hope for temporary deferment. Since he had completed the full course at the Conservatory, there was only one class for which he was eligible—that in organ. But Maxim Gorky, the most popular writer during that early period of the Revolution, wrote to the War Ministry on Prokofiev's behalf: "We are not so rich that we can afford to sole soldiers' boots with nails of gold."

Sergei was excused from the service.

Maria went for a cure to Kislovodsk, a health resort in the northern Caucasus, while Sergei spent the summer in a small village near Petrograd. He lived by himself, continuing his reading of philosophical works which he had become interested in through the literary evenings in which he occasionally participated as a musician. This new interest, however, did not lead to systematic studies of Kant and Schopenhauer. "In the latter's works I was more interested in the principles of practical action," Sergei admitted, "than in the analogy of pessimism and the failure of the will." His major preoccupation was always his music.

The performance of *The Gambler* was postponed indefinitely because Siloti could not succeed in interesting either the members of the orchestra or the singer in the work. Therefore Prokofiev went to the country, this time intentionally without a piano; he wanted to try to compose without one. Until then he had principally composed at the piano, but he noticed that whenever his thematic material was written away from the instrument, it gained in quality. For some time he had been considering the idea of writing a whole symphonic work without using the piano, believing that he would thus obtain greater clarity in the orchestral coloring.

"This is how the project of writing a symphony in the style of Haydn was born," Prokofiev said. "Haydn's technique had become especially clear to me after my work with Tcherepnin, and in that familiar channel it was, I felt, much easier to venture into dangerous waters without the piano. It seems to me that had Haydn continued to live into our time he would have retained his own way of writing and at the same time added something 'new.'"

In the modest structure of his Haydnesque symphony Prokofiev wanted to combine the transparent orchestration with "attacks of new harmonies." Several of his short piano pieces—Rigodon, Capriccio, and Gavotte (Op. 12)—already reflected this idea. Now, he said, "I wanted to compose a symphony in a classical style, and as soon as I began to progress in my work, I rechristened it the Classical Symphony, first, because it sounded much more simple, and second—out of pure mischief—'to tease the geese,' and in secret hope that eventually the symphony will become a classic."

During the previous year (1916), Prokofiev had composed the Gavotte in D-major, which now became the third movement of the symphony, and he had already made several sketches for the first and second movements. For the finale he did not use the material he had sketched the year before, but completely rewrote the whole movement, trying to avoid chords in minor tonality.

In this symphony he wished to resurrect the good old times of tradition, farthingales, and powdered wigs, as he said. But thanks to his own characteristic sense of humor and irony, as expressed in piquant harmonies, he avoided the mere "museum restoration" of the picture he was trying to evoke. And the Classical Symphony was the first work to gain universal recognition.

That summer he was also working on the Violin Concerto (Op.

19), the first theme of which he had already written in 1915; he often regretted that the preoccupation with other works had hindered his return to "the poetic, daydreaming beginning of the Violin Concerto." While writing the Classical Symphony, he had had another idea: to compose a miniature Russian Symphony in a similar vein and to dedicate it to Diaghilev because of his concern for Sergei's true Russian style. But this idea was superseded by still another: to compose something monumental, music that would reflect the events stirring all of Russia.

"I wanted to, but didn't know how, and my efforts took a rather strange turn—a turn toward ancient subjects. The old themes that have survived through the centuries stirred my imagination," Prokofiev said.

He chose some verses from Konstantin Balmont's (1867–1943) poem "Chaldean Invocation," based on an engraved inscription in cuneiform on the walls of an ancient Accadian temple which had been deciphered by the German archeologist Hugo Winkler (1863–1913). Sergei planned to compose "Seven, They Are Seven," a contata in one movement for dramatic tenor solo, a mixed chorus, and a full orchestra with an enlarged percussion section.

He became so engrossed in this work that during the first week of September of 1917 he completed the skeleton of the whole composition—that is, he selected the text, marked the parts of the poem he intended to use, sketched the melodies and accompaniments, and planned the characteristics of the orchestration. At times he was so enthusiastic about this work, visualizing so clearly certain parts of the composition, that he would as he said, "become breathless" and had to take long walks in the forest to calm down.

And Prokofiev had indeed written a hair-raising score. A few lines from the text will give a general idea of the composition:

> Charity they know not,
> Shame they have none,
> Prayers they heed not, to entreaties they are deaf.
> Earth and heaven shrink before them,
> They clamp down whole countries as behind prison gates,
> They grind nations, as nations grind grain.
> They are seven! Seven! Seven! *

From the very start of the cantata the listener is assailed by a hurricane of deafening sounds portraying cosmic catastrophe. With scream-

* Quoted in Israel V. Nestyev: *Sergei Prokofiev, His Musical Life,* Rose Prokofieva, trans. (New York: Alfred A. Knopf, 1946). The translator is not related to the composer.

ing trills in the brass, terrifying roars in the basses, glissandos in the harps, and tremolos in the strings, the score builds to a climax that Prokofiev marked *feroce*—the rhythm quickens, the orchestra and the chorus reaching a state of frenzy. Then, amid sudden silence, the tenor pronounces his invocation. Only at the very end of the cantata do the screaming outbursts of the chorus and the thundrous orchestra give way to an almost devout, psalmlike melody sung by the tenor against barely audible strains from the orchestra.

It need scarcely be said that such an interpretation of the current "revolutionary upheaval" could not have been greeted favorably by the Russian critics.

What had the composer to oppose to this colossal force that held the world in thrall? Naught but savage, heathen invocations, the witch doctor's mumblings, the mystic malediction: "Tetal, tetal, curse, curse, curse!" The cantata ends on this despairing note to the furious glissando shriekings of the horns and trombones, the thunder of kettledrums and tomtoms. Such music would only leave the annihilating and morbid impression of some incredible nightmare.*

This was written by Israel V. Nestyev in his book on Sergei Prokofiev published in Moscow in the early 1940s, when Sergei after some fifteen years outside Russia had returned and been admitted into the family of the Soviet composers. The author bends over backward to present Prokofiev as a bona-fide Soviet composer as he chronicles Sergei's life abroad. In analyzing Prokofiev's works, Nestyev prefers to consider this composition an example of "the composer's failure to grasp the true significance of events." Well aware of the government's watchful eye, Nestyev was obliged to criticize the composition adversely, and he limited himself to a gentle reprimand, blaming "foreign, bourgeois influence." "Thus," concludes Nestyev, "while striving intuitively to give musical expression to his presentiment of the titanic social upheavals that were about to shake the world, the composer became entangled in the ugly web of symbolic mysticism."

The cantata, which Sergei later rechristened "The Chaldean Invocation," was given its first performance by Koussevitzky in Paris on May 29, 1924, and although the original score was published in Soviet Russia in 1922, and a revised version in 1933, to the best of my knowledge it has never been performed in Russia.

The collapse of the Russian front against the Germans temporarily interrupted Prokofiev's work on the cantata. There were rumors of

* *Ibid.*

the threatening occupation of Petrograd by the German Army. Maria, who was in Kislovodsk, decided to remain there for the autumn; Sergei joined her.

At Essentuki, another health resort near Kislovodsk, he completed the orchestration of the Classical Symphony, but in Kislovodsk he resumed work on the cantata. He found the second stage—the writing of music to an already fixed skeleton—very difficult, and sometimes was so discouraged that he felt he had accomplished nothing beyond the initial idea of the composition.

The October Revolution started the civil war, dividing the country into several fronts on which the Reds fought the Whites. Kislovodsk was in the hands of the Whites, and what little information about conditions in Petrograd and Moscow reached the little spa was so nebulous that Sergei decided to go back to Petrograd to attend the first performance of his Violin Concerto previously scheduled by Siloti, and to give his own already planned piano recitals.

"You are utterly mad to think of going to these cities," he was told repeatedly by the refugees who arrived in trains scarred by bullets and with windows broken. "There is shooting in the streets of Petrograd and Moscow. You'll never reach either of them."

It was clear to Sergei that under such circumstances, there would be hardly any interest in concerts, so he stayed on in Kislovodsk struggling further with the score of his cantata. And it was then that for the first time he thought of going to the United States. "Obviously Russia will not be much concerned with music," Sergei decided, "while there is a lot to see, a lot to learn, and perhaps a chance to present my own compositions in the United States."

Sergei remembered that during the past summer in Petrograd he had met Cyrus McCormick—one of the members of a delegation headed by Senator Reid that had gone to Russia "to congratulate us on becoming a republic"—the wealthy manufacturer of agricultural implements whose name Sergei had seen ever since his childhood on the reapers his father had imported to Sontsovka. Cyrus McCormick was seriously interested in music, and he had asked Prokofiev to prepare for him a list of worthwhile new compositions. He had also requested that Prokofiev make him a copy of the Scythian Suite, for which he would pay. When he said good-by to Prokofiev, McCormick had added, "If you should ever decide to come to the United States, cable me. I have connections in the musical world there."

When by the end of March the Reds had occupied Kislovodsk, Sergei saw no reason to remain there any longer. Armed with a sort of *laissez-passer* from the newly organized Soviet of Worker's Deputies, he started on his way to Petrograd. It took the train eight days instead of four to reach Moscow. "Here and there they were still shooting," Sergei said, "but on the whole the journey was not marred by any incidents."

In Petrograd, Prokofiev gave two piano recitals, on April 15 and 17; and on April 21, 1918, he conducted the first performance of his Classical Symphony. Among others in the audience was Anatol Lunacharsky, the Soviet government's first Minister of Education and Arts. At that time his office was in the Winter Palace, and Maxim Gorky, who often visited him, took Sergei along to introduce him to Lunacharsky.

"I have been working very hard and would now like to breathe a little fresh air," Prokofiev said to Lunacharsky.

"Don't you find we have enough fresh air here?" Lunacharsky asked.

"Yes, indeed I do, but I would like some ocean air."

Lunacharsky had little difficulty in reading Prokofiev's intentions. "You are a revolutionary in music, and we—we are revolutionary in life. We should be working together. But if you want to go to the United States, I wouldn't stand in your way."

It was a bold move on Prokofiev's part, for the money Koussevitzky had advanced him was barely enough for his journey. What was he to do, then? Could he risk being alone in a strange country? But Prokofiev was young and extremely sure of himself. He received a passport and a supplementary document stating that he was going abroad on business and for his health. No length of journey was stated in the document.

"You are running away from events," he was told, though he never gave the source of this comment, "and these events will never forgive you when you return; you will not be understood."

"I didn't listen to these words," Sergei Prokofiev said. "I took with me the scores of the Scythian Suite, the Classical Symphony, the First Piano Concerto, and some piano compositions; and on May 7, 1918, I started my journey, which was to take me abroad for only a few months . . . or so I thought."

PART TWO
1918-1936

14

Since World War I was still going on in Europe, Sergei Prokofiev had to travel via Japan. Only much later did he realize how hazardous the trip across Siberia had been. The country was in the throes of a civil war, each fighting army trying to keep or get possession of the Trans-Siberian railroad on which Prokofiev's train moved slowly toward Vladivostok. Instead of the usual eight to ten days, it took him eighteen to reach his destination; the postcards he kept mailing to his mother and his friends arrived a year later.

Because of the difference in seasons, Prokofiev had been planning to go first to South America, where he would arrive in time for the winter concert season, and on his journey he diligently studied Spanish. But when he arrived in Tokyo on June 1, the ship for Rio de Janeiro had already left, and the next one was not due for some six or seven weeks. It was much too early for the winter concert season in the United States, and because his American visa took two months to reach him, Prokofiev stayed on in Tokyo.

But he was lucky, for he had arrived in Tokyo shortly after publication of Otaguro's book on modern European music in which one chapter was devoted to Sergei Prokofiev. Trusting that the Japanese would be very much interested in hearing the young Russian musician in person, an enterprising concert manager arranged two piano recitals, one in Tokyo, the other in Yokohama.

Along with his own compositions Prokofiev played Chopin's Ballade in A-flat major, and a selection of his Mazurkas and Études, in addition to Schumann's short piano pieces. In Tokyo his audience was mostly Japanese; in Yokohama it was European.

"Both understood little of music," Prokofiev said later, "but I preferred to play for the Japanese—they listened attentively, sat remarkably quiet . . . and applauded the bravura technique." His audiences
were small and he earned just as small an amount of yen.

From Yokohama via "the most enchanting stay at Honolulu," as he
repeatedly said later, Prokofiev went to San Francisco. During the
long journey across the Pacific he kept himself busy planning an
opera, *The Love for Three Oranges*.

As early as 1914 Carlo Gozzi's witty comedy had aroused unusual
interest among the Russian dramatists, who were attracted not so
much by the improvisation of the *commedia dell' arte* as by its grotesque parody in Gozzi's play. *The Love for Three Oranges* (or *Fiabe
dell' amore delle tre melarance*, as the comedy was originally called)
was written as a satire in which Gozzi, one of the wittiest drama critics of his time, dealt a final blow to Carlo Goldoni, his contemporary
playwright and the founder of the new Italian comedy.

Gozzi belonged to the Granelleschi Society, a group that aimed to
preserve the pure Italian (Tuscan) language from any foreign influence in both literature and drama. He favored the *commedia dell' arte*,
while Goldoni and Pietro Chiari used dialect and followed in their
plays the example of the new French school, that of Molière, bringing
innovations to the theatre.

It has been reported that Goldoni and Gozzi once met at a bookstore in Venice, and that Goldoni remarked to his adversary that it
was much easier to criticize a play than to write a good one. Thus
challenged, Gozzi promised to satisfy the Venetian public with a
purely childlike fantasy. Shortly after this encounter, Gozzi's favored
traveling company, Antonio Sacchi's Commedia Dell' Arte, presented
on January 25, 1761, the *Fiabe dell' amore delle tre melarance*.

This comedy is based on an old Italian fairy tale, but Gozzi managed to weave into its fantasy a satire of Goldoni's and Chiari's dramatic ideas, as well as to hold up to ridicule the personalities of both
writers. Although Goldoni's friends caused a disturbance in the theatre with their protests, the Venetian audience lost its heart to Gozzi's
humor.

The Russians found in Gozzi's comedy an excellent vehicle to mock
the triteness of the contemporary classical theatre. In fact, in their admiration of Gozzi a group of modern dramatists headed by Vsevolod
Meyerhold had brought out in 1914 a magazine called *The Love for
Three Oranges: Doctor Dapertutto's Journal*, in the first issue of
which a scenario of Gozzi's play was published.

Shortly before Prokofiev's departure from Russia Meyerhold had suggested that he write an opera on the subject of Gozzi's play and had given him a copy of the magazine in its motley cover. Prokofiev did not quite grasp initially the significance of the argument between the two opposing views in theatrical trends, but he was attracted by the noisy processions, games, and festivities in the play.

On his arrival in San Francisco, Sergei Prokofiev was not allowed to go ashore because, he said later, " 'Russia was being ruled by the Bolsheviks—a strange people and, most probably, very dangerous.' For three days I was kept on White Island as if I were a Bolshevik agent. There I was constantly interrogated by the authorities. I was asked, among other questions, 'Have you ever been in prison?'

" 'Yes, I have.'

" 'That's bad. Where?'

" 'On your island.'

" 'Oh! ... Are you trying to be funny?' "

Sergei Prokofiev was finally allowed to enter the United States. He had very little money left, but fortunately, some of his traveling companions who had taken an interest in him lent him three hundred dollars, which helped him to reach New York at the beginning of September, 1918.

"I had hoped that my musical activities in the United States would be as easy as they were during past years in Russia," Prokofiev said. "Actually, however, here I was faced with a musical world, excellently organized, but from a different aspect. In Russia, during the whole past century, the public was accustomed to deal with composers who, having written something, posed before it problems which the public discussed pro and con. The results of these discussions were varied: sometimes the composers wrote utter drivel, and were later forgotten, and sometimes the public talked utter drivel, and the composers survived. These discussions of musical novelties, new trends and styles, as well as the composers' personalities were an important manifestation of our musical life. In the United States, on the other hand, there were no composers 'discovering America,' if one does not count those who had arrived from Europe with an already established reputation, and the whole accent in musical life was concentrated on the art of performing. In this domain one must be very careful: carelessness which would have been overlooked in Russia would not be tolerated here."

Since the average American was interested only in hearing famous performers and preferably presenting programs devoid of "experiments" and "novelties," Prokofiev soon realized that he would have to compete with artists like Sergei Rachmaninoff, who was expected to arrive in New York at the end of the year—for Prokofiev, such competition offered a hopeless prospect.

His first appearance went almost unnoticed. On October 29, at the Brooklyn Museum, he participated in a Russian concert given in connection with the opening of the exposition of works by the Petersburg painter Boris Anisfeld, at one time connected with the Maryinsky Theatre. On a program that included numbers sung by several Russian artists and Prokofiev's *Fugitive Visions* (Op. 22), choreographed by Adolf Bolm—well known for his work with Diaghilev— Prokofiev played his Toccata (Op. 11), and the Prelude, Gavotte, and Scherzo (Op. 12).

The critics who expected "modern excesses" obviously were disappointed: "Perhaps Prokofiev is the lion of the musical revolutionaries, but last night this lion roared gently, like a charming dove. In vain we were waiting from him a demonstration of musical extremes." (*Brooklyn Eagle*, October 30, 1918).

Their initial impression, however, soon changed when Prokofiev had his own first recital in the Aeolian Hall on November 20. This time he played four Études (Op. 2), Second Sonata (Op. 14), Prelude, Gavotte, and Scherzo (Op. 12), and Diabolic Suggestion (Op. 4), and, in order "not to frighten his audience," he included two Scriabin Études and three Rachmaninoff Preludes.

Prokofiev felt that his concert was successful as he read on the following day in the *Evening World* (November 21, 1918): "That very audience which filled Aeolian Hall to the brim shows the respect which Prokofiev's name commands among the most eminent musicians of New York." And he was not at all upset by the glaring headlines of the reviews that, using such adjectives as "savage," "furious," "weird," and "very Russian," spoke of him as a "Piano Titan," and of his compositions as "Russian chaos in music," "Godless Russia," "Bolshevism in art, a carnival of cacophony."

They compared his fantastic imagination to that of Edgar Allan Poe, his virile rendition, his primitive forcefulness to Jack London's, saying that his fingers were made of steel, as were his wrists and muscles.

"The critics who ventured to analyze my music," Prokofiev smiled, "spoke utter nonsense. They discovered influences of Chopin, Wagner, and Beethoven, traced its origin to Scriabin, and even to 'Mendelssohn played on wrong notes.' And one prominent critic said that the finale of the Second Sonata 'reminded one of a herd of mammoths charging across an Asiatic plateau . . .' and that, 'when a dinosaur's daughter graduated from the Conservatory of that epoch her repertory must have included Prokofiev.'"

And as if to try Sergei's tolerance still further, the reviewer of *Musical America* added this profound observation (November 30, 1918): "Take one Schoenberg, two Ornsteins, add a little of Satie, mix all these with Medtner, put in a drop of Schumann, add some Scriabin and Stravinsky, and the result will be something like Prokofiev."

The recital did not cover Sergei's expenses, but at least it brought his name to the attention of a firm manufacturing player pianos—he was asked to record some of his piano compositions—and to two music publishers who commissioned him to write several new piano pieces. To show that the "New World atmosphere" had not taken hold of him sufficiently to influence his work, while in bustling New York he wrote such typically Russian pieces as *Tales of the Old Grandmother* (Op. 31) and Danse, Minuet, Gavotte, and Waltz (Op. 32). Although he was now penniless, he refused to sell these compositions because of the "unacceptable conditions of the contract" offered him. (They were later published by Gutheil and Koussevitzky.)

"Suddenly," Prokofiev observed later, "I found myself involved in a whole system of contracts, agreements, and promises, mostly unfulfilled. One manager offered me a contract for two years of concerts. 'I know,' he said, 'that I am going to lose money on you during the first year, but I hope to make some during the following.'" But Prokofiev was so convinced he would return home before long that he would not listen to talk of "long-term servitude."

Meanwhile, he was gradually introduced to the musical life of New York. He attended concerts, and met Walter Damrosch, the dean of American conductors. "Don't show him the Scythian Suite," Prokofiev was advised. "He won't understand it anyway."

"Even when I played for him my First Concerto," Sergei complained, "he turned the pages in the wrong places. And after he heard my Classical Symphony he remarked, 'It is charming, just like Kalinikov.'* Indignant, I left him, but later discovered that he had meant it as a sincere compliment—Damrosch had been playing Kalinikov's symphony with great success all over the United States."

Finally, on December 10, Prokofiev made his debut at a symphonic concert under the direction of the Russian-born Modest Altschuler.

* Vasily Kalinikov (b. 1866, d. 1900), a nineteenth-century Russian composer, not notable for originality.

Under the auspices of the Czarist government's Russian Embassy in Washington, Altschuler had organized a Russian symphony orchestra in New York. "He was a good musician, but a very bad conductor," Prokofiev said, "and his orchestra was going from bad to worse. New Yorkers could not understand why they should have a 'Russian orchestra,' especially because the majority of the musicians of the orchestra were Americans, and it was led by a bad conductor. The press unanimously tore our performance to pieces—the orchestra, Altschuler, and myself as well."

"The composer played havoc with the keyboard. The duel between his steel fingers and the keys led to the slaughter of harmony," said the reviewer in *The New York Times* on December 11, and James Huneker deemed him "the Cossack Chopin of the future generation. A musical agitator."

Prokofiev fared better in Chicago. He got in touch with Cyrus McCormick, who introduced him to Frederick Stock, the conductor of the Chicago Symphony, and to Cleofonte Campanini, who was connected with the Chicago Opera Association. Stock was not afraid to have the Scythian Suite on his program, and Prokofiev made his Chicago debut with his First Piano Concerto. These works created a sensation, and Prokofiev, by now used to them, read the controversial reviews. Identifying the Bolshevik ideas with anarchy and the annihilation of all traditions, most critics spoke of the Bolshevik character of the Scythian Suite.

"The red flag of musical anarchy waved tempestuously over the old Orchestra Hall yesterday as Bolshevist melodies floated over the waves of a sea of sound in breathtaking cacophony," said the Chicago *Herald and Examiner* on December 7, 1918. Still, taking into consideration the more liberal point of view of the leading Chicago musicians, some critics had ventured to appraise the historical mission of Prokofiev's music. "Russia, it appears, is giving us the long-awaited antidote to French musical Impressionism, to a fragrant delicate twilight that pervades the French music of prewar Europe" (Chicago *Daily News*, December 7, 1918), and the Chicago *Evening American* hailed Prokofiev as "an incarnation of the spiritual greatness of the Russian nation, and the brilliant hope for the future Russia." *

The directors of the Chicago Opera who had attended the concerts suggested producing *The Gambler*, but since he had brought with him only the vocal score (the orchestral score was in the Maryinsky

* This passage is as translated in Nestyev, *op. cit.*

Theatre library and therefore not easily accessible), Sergei spoke to Campanini about *The Love for Three Oranges.*

"Oh . . . Gozzi! Our darling beloved Gozzi!" exclaimed the Italian conductor. "Why, this is marvelous. Wonderful!" It was stipulated that the opera be ready for rehearsals in the autumn, and the contract was signed in January, 1919.

After the none too enthusiastic reception in New York, Prokofiev gave up the idea of further concertizing. He realized that in addition to the purely financial problems involved in launching a career as a pianist, he would have to enrich his repertory with other composers' works, and the mere thought of practicing them bored him. The advance he received for the opera relieved him from immediate financial worry, so that he could devote himself entirely to his score, which he began with exceptional enthusiasm.

He was particularly attracted by the characters in the scenic action: the fairy-tale Prince, Truffaldino, the subterranean forces on whom their actions depended, Mag Chely and Fata Morgana, and all those who represent the public, authors, and the theatrical administration— all this presaged great amusement to his future audiences, and meanwhile it was fun to work on it.

But as bad luck would have it, Prokofiev fell ill in March with scarlet fever, almost immediately followed by diphtheria and a throat abscess that was choking him. Only after seven weeks was he able to resume his work. "Curiously enough," he observed, "my illness refreshed me." Indeed, with incredible energy and speed, he finished the score by June and the orchestration by October 1 as agreed upon.

Campanini was delighted with the score, and the directors of the opera granted a large sum for its production—engaging Anisfeld to do the stage sets—and for the advance publicity, which must have been so successful that the forthcoming performance at the end of December already bore fruit. "Prokofiev's new opera is to be called *The Love for Three Oranges,*" reported the Editor-in-Chief of the *Musical Courier* on February 20, 1919.

Florida and California are engaged in a struggle for the exclusive program rights to advertise their respective, favorite brands. The manufacturers of the California Sunkist oranges offer to supply the singers free with the succulent fruit, and the inventor of the Florida blood orange is willing to present one of them to every auditor every evening at the Chicago Opera if the management will permit him to put up a lobby stand of the Florida bloods and placard it with a sign: "This succulent and healthful brand inspired Prokofiev and is used exclusively by him in this opera and at home."

I shall leave Prokofiev's reaction to this to the reader's imagination. Prokofiev's high hopes, however, were thwarted by the sudden death of Campanini in the first week of December. The directors of the opera were so confused trying to keep to the already scheduled repertory that the new production of Prokofiev's opera had to be postponed until the following season. "Without the opera and with only a few concerts in prospect, I seemed to have run aground," Prokofiev said.

At about that time he met in New York several of his former friends from the St. Petersburg Conservatory. They had formed a chamber music ensemble called Zimro, consisting of a string quartet, clarinet, and a piano. They had come to the United States in the hope of earning funds for a Conservatory in Jerusalem. But the response to their project was so meager that they barely earned enough for their own existence. In their repertory were a number of interesting Jewish compositions for various combinations of instruments—for two violins and for a trio.

"Write us an overture for a sextet that includes us all," they asked Prokofiev, giving him a copybook with a collection of Jewish themes.

At first Prokofiev was reluctant because, as he told them, he composed only with his own material. However, he kept the copybook. Then one evening, sitting in his hotel room, he examined the collection more carefully, and after selecting several themes, began to improvise at the piano. Before long he saw an overture taking shape, and after spending the following day working on it, he finished the composition late in the evening. It took him ten more days to put it in its final form, and although he did not expect it, the composition (Op. 34) enjoyed great success (it had its premiere in New York in January, 1920).

But Prokofiev felt compelled to compose something more "meaty," as he said. Perhaps, he admitted, because of the failure of the plans for the production of *The Love for Three Oranges*, he thought he should start immediately on another opera. It was a frivolous idea to plunge once more into a work of large dimensions without any assurance of its performance, but compose he must; and so in sheer desperation he chose Valery Bryusov's *The Flaming Angel*.

Valery Bryusov (1873–1924) was the founder of Symbolism in Russian literature, the main theoretician of its early phase, and the acknowledged leader of the Moscow Symbolists. A painstaking craftsman with a liking for classical themes, he cultivated and sometimes achieved a majestic but rather cold brilliance in his works. Unlike his other colleagues in the Symbolist movement who had left Russia after the Revolution, Bryusov remained in the country and served the new Soviet regime.

Prokofiev, looking for a suitable subject, came across Bryusov's novel, which was originally published in Russia during 1907–1908 in a Symbolist magazine. This novel, according to Sergei, was among the few truly artistic Russian books available in Russian bookstores in the United States.

Whereas in *The Love for Three Oranges* the predominant characteristic was irony combined with an amusing fairy-tale plot, in *The Flaming Angel* it was tragic frenzy and the frightening and cruel aspects of life. With exceptionally realistic expressiveness, Prokofiev's music depicted the Bryusov story in all its subtle imitation of the German humanistic art of the sixteenth century, the epoch of Dürer and the Counter-Reformation. There are bloodcurdling scenes of Inquisition, of religious mania and hysteria, and the interweaving of sober historical narrative with gloomy and powerful fantasy. This time Prokofiev discarded grotesquerie and humor to depict dramatic emotions. He presented two opposing worlds: that of a clear and sober rationalism and religiously erotic ecstasy.

"The production of this opera was seriously hampered by its excess of musical and dramatic material," Prokofiev said, "by its pathological effects, and the few but rather serious violations of the rules of dramaturgy." As much as he had enjoyed describing the medieval background, with archbishops damning everything everywhere, Prokofiev had finally realized that the subject did not fit the libretto. This is the usual problem with any story told in the first person—the narrator remains constantly on stage, while there is little information about the other characters, their relationships and actions.

Prolonged negotiations with a number of American and European theatres for the production of *The Flaming Angel* ended in failure.

Prokofiev was slowly reaching the conclusion that he had nothing to offer the United States. Often, walking in Central Park and admiring the skyline of New York, he was disturbed by the thought that the excellent American orchestras had no interest in his music, that the critics who pompously announced again and again that Beethoven was a genius, vulgarly kicked everything new, and that the concert managers organized long tours for artists who played time after time the same old programs of well-known compositions.

"I came to the United States much too early, to a mere child who has not yet grown up to new music. But what am I to do? Return to Russia? It would hardly be flattering to return 'on a shield,' " Prokofiev reflected.

But at the beginning of 1920 he made his final choice of where to go next when he went to Canada to give recitals in Montreal and Quebec. As he was leaving for his trip, Prokofiev's New York manager warned him, "Don't forget to get your fee beforehand, or you'll never see it." Prokofiev followed this cautious advice, and upon his arrival in Canada, asked the manager for his honorarium. The Canadian manager shrugged, saying that everything would be taken care of.

The concert hall was immense, Prokofiev thought, and the tickets were sold at twenty-five cents apiece, mostly to students. Before the beginning of the recital, the manager came into the green room, carrying a small suitcase. "Students are paying for their tickets in silver," he told Prokofiev. "Therefore I have to pay you in silver," and he handed him twenty-five large silver dollars, a hundred in fifty-cent pieces, and a hundred in quarters.

Prokofiev filled his pockets with what he thought was half a ton of silver. "But what if one of my pockets should suddenly tear and a pile of silver fall on the stage?" The terrifying thought flashed through his mind. "I'll be the laughingstock of America."

"During the intermission I'll try to change the rest of the silver into paper money," said the manager. "Neither during the intermission nor after the concert did I see the manager again," Prokofiev related later, "and I returned to New York with one third of my fee."

Thus ended Prokofiev's first and longest visit to the United States. He planned to return in the fall, but for a much shorter period, to fulfill promised concert engagements, and to assist in the production of The Love for Three Oranges, tentatively scheduled for the following season.

There was still another reason, purely personal, for Prokofiev's planning to return to the United States. After the concert in New York under Altschuler's direction, he had met an attractive young woman with beautiful large brown eyes, dark hair, and a graceful figure. Seven years younger than Prokofiev, at twenty-four Carolina Codina lived with her parents, studied singing, attended concerts, and at a time when Prokofiev was more criticized than praised, showed a genuine understanding and liking for his work—all of which led to a rapid development of their friendship.

But there has always been a certain mystery about Carolina's origins. She spoke Russian so well that the Russians who knew her never thought of her except as Russian. No foreigner could ever master the language to such perfection, they said, yet there were some among her acquaintances who thought that she must be at least half Spanish or even American, so excellent were her Spanish and English. No one seemed to know exactly where she was born. I have heard Chicago mentioned as her birthplace, while Lawrence and Elisabeth Hanson, the authors of a recently published biography of Prokofiev,* state that she was born in Havana.

I have before me, however, a photostat of her three-page birth certificate. Its authenticity is unquestionable. It was issued at the municipal registry of births in Madrid in 1897. The serial number of the document is N.O. 630.766 43949.

At that time no one foresaw the Russian Revolution of 1917, nor could it have been predicted that the newborn child would become the wife of Sergei Prokofiev, and that the information contained in this document would be of paramount importance in Madame Prokofiev's fate in Soviet Russia.

Carolina was born on October 20, 1897. On the following day her father, Don Juan Codina, accompanied by three witnesses, made the official declaration of the birth of his daughter, and supplied the following information at the registry in Madrid. Identifying himself with a passport issued by the Spanish Consul in Genoa on February 11, 1897, he stated that both his father, Don Juan Codina, and his mother, Dona Isabela Codina, nee Llubera, were Spanish, born in Barcelona.

The background of the child's mother, Olga, was more complicated. Olga's father Ladislas Niemysky was born in Vilna, Poland, and her mother, Irma Carolina Wehrle, came from Colmar, in Alsace. Most of the Niemysky families belonged to the Polish nobility; their coat-of-arms carried the image of a falcon (*Jastrzębiec*), and since 1674 they had held important posts in the government, the army, and the ministry of justice. But not every Romanoff was related to the ruling dynasty in Russia, nor was Ladislas Niemysky necessarily a member of the Polish nobility. He may have been either a merchant or an industrialist.

Jean Roman, at one time a member of the board of the Wehrle textile concern in Colmar, told me that in the past century the firm used to send their men to Russia on business as well as to study Russian textile methods, which explains why Ladislas and Irma Carolina Nie-

* *Prokofiev: A Biography in Three Movements* (New York: Random House, 1964).

mysky went to Voronesh, a small town about four hundred kilometers south of Moscow. There, Olga, the future mother of Madame Prokofiev, was born.

There is no accurate information as to when and where Olga, born in the heart of Russia, in Voronesh, met and married Juan Codina of Barcelona. He is identified in his daughter's birth certificate as an *artista*. But there they were at the end of the last century, living in Madrid at 4 Doña Bárbara de Braganza Street in an apartment on the third floor "to the left," where Carolina was born at six o'clock in the morning on October 20, 1897.

She learned Russian from her mother, Spanish from her father and at school; later, when the family moved to New York, she attended high school in Brooklyn, where she learned English.

This background alone would have been sufficient to intrigue Prokofiev, but since Carolina's parents were, according to her, musicians, he enjoyed visiting them. In the short span of time he knew Carolina, he made her his confidante—that is, he shared with her his future plans and asked her advice in his business negotiations, until gradually she became well informed about him and his life. She enjoyed his company, his charm and wit, and was more impressed than shocked by his "fits of temper" whenever something went wrong with his plans.

That Prokofiev felt toward Carolina, or Lina, more than a passing casual affection could be seen from the fact that he changed "Violetta," one of the princesses in his *The Love for Three Oranges*, to "Linetta."

15

Shortly after his arrival in Paris in April, 1920, Prokofiev had a pleasant surprise: his mother came from Russia. During the two years in which Prokofiev had not seen her, Maria had aged visibly. She was suffering from rheumatism and her eyesight was rapidly failing. The privations she had suffered during the past few years in Russia had taken their toll of her health, and some time was to pass before she felt well again. Upon the doctors' advice Prokofiev immediately placed her in a hospital where she was also to undergo observation before the doctors could decide whether an operation on her eyes would improve her sight.

Sometime later Lina also arrived in Paris and was very helpful by being with Maria much of the time, visiting her daily and keeping her entertained with all she knew about Prokofiev's life after he had left Russia. The old lady, Lina said, was extremely alert to everything that was going on in the world and in the arts, but above all she wanted to hear the details of her Sergusya's life.

Prokofiev had already told her everything that he had not written in his letters to her, but Maria still had many unanswered questions, and Prokofiev was sometimes too busy to describe everything in minute detail. Besides, many of his evenings were occupied, for he had again met Diaghilev and Stravinsky, both of whom happened to be in Paris.

After a long interruption because of World War I, Diaghilev had resumed his ballet seasons, and Prokofiev was pleasantly surprised not only because Diaghilev had had the score of *The Buffoon* which Sergei had sent him five years before beautifully bound, but because the impresario was ready to produce the ballet if Prokofiev was willing to do some additional work on it.

As Prokofiev said himself, during the preceding five years he had learned to differentiate more critically between the more successful parts of his score and those in which his music failed to fulfill his original intent. He readily agreed with Diaghilev, who once again impressed him with his unusual knowledge and understanding, as well as with the weight of his arguments, when the subject concerned ballet production. Diaghilev suggested rewriting the weak parts of the score, composing five symphonic entr'actes so that the six scenes of the ballet could be given without interruption, completely rewriting the final dance, and orchestrating the whole score anew. But the very beginning of the ballet was to be left intact, with all its whistling and rattling sounds, as if someone were "dusting the orchestra" before the beginning of the spectacle.

Very much encouraged, Prokofiev rented a small house near Mantes-la-Jolie (a charming village an hour away from Paris, immortalized by Paul Cezanne) in order to be undisturbed in the work he had to do that summer and at the same time to take care of his mother. The operation on Maria's eyes had succeeded merely in preventing complete blindness, but Lina often visited the Prokofievs, and with her assistance Maria set out to learn Braille.

Occasionally Lina was able to persuade Prokofiev to interrupt his work while Maria was resting, to take a long walk in the neighboring woods, although he still paid little attention to her warnings against overwork. In addition to the ballet, he was making several transcriptions for the piano, since his American concert manager insisted on his playing more compositions by other composers during his future concert tours and keeping his own to a minimum.

He made a piano arrangement of Buxtehude's Prelude and Fugue in D-minor, and at Stravinsky's suggestion he selected a series of Schubert waltzes and Ländler and made them into an orchestral suite. When he was not at his desk working on one of these compositions, he was at the piano "grinding out," as he put it, the pieces that he was going to play at his next American recitals, because, he complained, they were no longer "in his fingers."

Lina, having had enough of Scriabin's D-sharp minor Étude (Op. 57), Medtner's *Fairy Tale* (Op. 8), and Schumann's *Novelettes*, would come to him with a request he could hardly refuse: to teach her some of his songs. She had a pleasant soprano voice, and since she dreamed of having a concert career, it was then that Prokofiev suggested that she take a stage name. "We chose the maiden name of my grand-

*In the garden at Sontsovka: Sergei Prokofiev at the age of one,
with his parents*

The composer's father, Sergei Prokofiev

Prokofiev at nine, with the manuscript of his opera The Giant

Prokofiev in 1910

Prokofiev and his wife, Lina Llubera

Prokofiev and Myra Mendelson

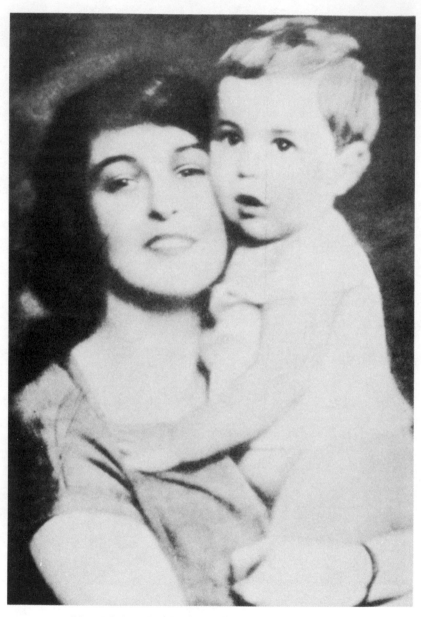

Lina Llubera Prokofieva with her son Svyatoslav

Prokofiev with his sons Svyatoslav and Oleg, Summer 1930

Maria G. Prokofieva, the composer's mother

Caricature of Prokofiev by Nikolai Radlov

Prokofiev and Sergei Eisenstein

Prokofiev and Nikolai Miaskovsky, Moscow 1941

V. Muradelli, J. Solodukho, M. Dvoyrin, D. Kabalevsky, R. Glière, and Prokofiev

mother on my father's side. He was a Spaniard," Lina said. "And since that time I have used Llubera as my last name."

While Prokofiev was working on *The Buffoon*, he often consulted Stravinsky, who, far from showing any professional jealousy, was so interested in Sergei's score that he was very helpful with suggestions, particularly in regard to orchestration. In the autumn of 1920, after completing the ballet, which Diaghilev scheduled for the following season, Prokofiev went once more to the United States. Upon his arrival he was faced immediately with a battle with the directors of the Chicago Opera Company. They were willing to produce *The Love for Three Oranges*, but unwilling to pay any compensation for a year's delay in the performance.

Arguing his points in what he believed was "legal language," Prokofiev told them that he would not agree to the performance: "Your delay in production has spoiled my whole season."

"In that case, we shall be forced to go ahead with our plans without your consent," the directors retorted.

"And I shall be forced to stop the performance by legal means," Sergei stubbornly insisted.

On this point the terms of the contract were not clear, and all Prokofiev could do was be unpleasant about it. Still, he remained adamant: "I preferred to sacrifice the production of the opera rather than let them make mincemeat out of me," while the directors of the opera decided to lose the eighty thousand dollars already spent on stage sets rather than let Prokofiev have any additional money.

On this note, negotiations were suspended. "The opera was not given," Prokofiev said later, "and to be honest—I was to blame."

In December, 1920, he started his concert tour in California. The concerts brought him little satisfaction in themselves, but he enjoyed the beautiful countryside so much that the month and a half he spent there was, he believed, the best possible recuperative period after his unpleasant wrangle in Chicago. His programs—including Beethoven's Sonata in A-major (Op. 101), Chopin's Études, short pieces by Lyadov and Rimsky-Korsakov, and his Schubert transcriptions—he considered rather trivial.

Since he did not find suitable texts, he wrote five Vocalises: songs without words for voice and piano (Op. 35). These were first performed by the late Nina Koshets, the well-known Russian soprano who lived in Los Angeles. But the sharing of his success with the singers on the programs did not bolster his enthusiasm for his concert tour. The reviewers mentioned him merely as a pianist, forgetting him as a composer. The caption of one photograph in the *Musical Courier* said, "Composer Stravinsky and Pianist Prokofiev," which hardly mellowed his state of mind.

But upon his return to New York, he heard at last a bit of good news: Mary Garden, famous for her original creation of the role of Mélisande in Debussy's *Pélléas et Mélisande,* had taken over the management of the Chicago Opera Company. Very soon thereafter she signed a contract with Prokofiev to produce *The Love for Three Oranges* during the following season.

Feeling much more encouraged about his chances in the United States, Prokofiev now went back to France, arriving just in time for the rehearsals of his ballet *The Buffoon.*

Diaghilev was doing everything to make the premiere of Prokofiev's ballet a brilliant event. Among other things, he commissioned Henri Matisse to make a pencil sketch of Prokofiev for the program's cover. Later, when Prokofiev asked Matisse why he had drawn his portrait with such a long face, Matisse replied, "Why, to give the feeling of your being very tall."

Although he presented his ballet seasons elsewhere, Diaghilev saw to it that the premières were given in Paris, for he believed that Paris was *the* city that gave the leading tone to Western cultural life. No wonder, then, that he was much disturbed when he heard that Sergei Koussevitzky, who had recently arrived in Paris, was going to play Prokofiev's Scythian Suite at one of his concerts. The question was, which of the two popularizers of Russian art was going to present Sergei Prokofiev first to a Parisian audience? Sharply worded telegrams were exchanged between Diaghilev and his adversary, but Koussevitzky stood firm, and under his direction, the Scythian Suite was performed on April 29, 1921.

The composition was received with enthusiasm. "It is impossible to resist such a happy combination of skill and freshness," the reviewers commented. Even the concert managers, who called the Scythian Suite the "most expensive work" because of its unusual demands for extra instruments in the orchestra (eight hunting horns, five trumpets, and a number of different percussion instruments), had to admit that the sumptuous sound of the orchestra was fully justified by the subject of the work.

Shortly afterward, on May 17, Diaghilev opened his season with the première of *The Buffoon.* Prokofiev conducted the performance. It was well received, and Roland-Manuel wrote in *L'Éclaire:*

Without any doubt *The Buffoon* places the young composer Prokofiev in

the first rank among the musicians of our time. One is amazed by the auda-
cious élan and melodic character of this music, by its inexhaustible wealth
of ingenuity and orchestral coloring. . . . *The Buffoon*, at least as far as its
music is concerned, is the most important work the Russians have offered
us besides Stravinsky's admirable *Nightingale*.

"The Parisians," Prokofiev observed, "are sharp critics and well
know when to turn a page in a score, and when to turn a page in
musical history." However, Prokofiev found working with French
orchestras less pleasant than with American. The badly paid French
musicians were allowed to find substitutes for themselves in the orchestra when they were offered higher fees elsewhere.

To illustrate this rather unusual procedure, it is sufficient to tell an
anecdote about a purported experience of Koussevitzky. Koussevitzky, in despair because of the constant changes of the members of
his orchestra at each rehearsal, finally said to the piccolo player at the
dress rehearsal, "I am so glad to see that at least you have remained
with me all the time."

"*Ah, monsieur*," the man replied, "but I shall not be here tomorrow
for the performance."

During the rehearsals and the four performances of his ballet Prokofiev saw three different concertmasters in his orchestra.

But this was merely "trouble in the kitchen" as far as Diaghilev was
concerned. To him the most important was the over-all impression of
a production. Prokofiev learned this at the dress rehearsal in London,
where the Diaghilev troupe moved for their performances. As was
customary with Diaghilev, a select audience was present. Noticing
that something had gone wrong in the orchestra, Prokofiev stopped
his men. But before he could resume conducting, Diaghilev was already at his elbow, buzzing into his ear, "I have gathered for you the
cream of London society and you with your nonsense befoul the
whole impression. Please continue without any further interruptions,
no matter what happens."

The ballet was successful with the audience, but the press was bad
and "rough," Prokofiev said. "The English have a reputation for being
one of the best-mannered nations, but this notion does not apply to
their music critics. They are the least polite, except for the Americans."

Nearly all the newspapers attacked the contributors to the ballet,
saying that the audience "should stop their ears in order not to hear
the music," and Ernest Newman wrote in the *Sunday Times*, "Few
composers would venture to write long scores so poor in ideas or so
primitive in technique as Prokofiev has done in *The Buffoon*."

Accustomed to much worse, Prokofiev accepted these criticisms as evidence of the challenging character of his music. "The London musical world," he reflected philosophically, "is more conservative than the Parisians; the English are apt to be slow in accepting the new, but once having accepted, they remain faithful."

In Soviet Russia the ballet was given once (in Kiev, January, 1928). A previous endeavor (1925) on the part of Prokofiev's friends to present *The Buffoon* at the Maryinsky Theatre had failed. The critic Boris Asafiev, an old friend of Prokofiev, tried to add an antireligious element to the ballet to make it more palatable to the authorities, but was rebuffed by Prokofiev: "What anti-religious action are you talking about? Naturally, I cannot permit any such addition or misrepresentation of the ballet," Prokofiev informed Asafiev. But the orchestral suite, which Prokofiev drew later from the score of the ballet, was often performed at symphonic concerts in Soviet Russia.

To return to Prokofiev's stay in London—to get away from the tumultuous atmosphere caused by his ballet, Prokofiev went for the summer to Etretât in Britanny. There, in a picturesque village on the Atlantic coast, he finally wrote the Third Piano Concerto, the material for which he had been collecting for several years.

As early as 1911 his mind was drawn to the idea of composing a concerto in a true virtuoso style. It was characteristic of Prokofiev to work on several compositions simultaneously, making plans, sketching themes, as well as indicating harmonies and even ideas for orchestrations for future reference. These he carefully preserved and often used later in works he had not planned at the time. But with the Third Concerto the problem turned out to be too difficult. Afraid of monotony, he therefore incorporated into this new concerto some of the themes dating back to 1913, 1916, and 1917.

During that summer in Etretât he often visited Konstantin Balmont, who lived only a few miles away from him. Balmont had emigrated to France, but he had enjoyed a considerable vogue in Russia in the early years of the century, mainly due to what the Russian called "the mellifluous character of his verse." Prokofiev was among his admirers. His early works "The Swan" and "The Wave" (Op. 7), "There Are Other Planets" (Op. 9), and "In My Garden" (Op. 23) were all composed after poems by Balmont; Prokofiev had used the text from Balmont's poem for his cantata "Seven, They Are Seven" (Op. 30), and he had borrowed the title "Fugitive Vision" from a quotation in a Balmont verse for his Op. 22. Now their friendship inspired Prokofiev to compose five songs to the poet's verse (Op. 36). Some of the poems were already written, others, like "The Butterfly," Balmont wrote at the time. Prokofiev dedicated this new opus to Lina.

But when at the end of the summer Balmont turned his pen, as he said, "against his suffering homeland," their friendship gradually cooled. For it would have been most imprudent for Prokofiev to break his slender ties with Russia and risk being regarded as a friend of an enemy of the Soviet government. Indeed, it did not take long for the Russian critics to turn their wrath on Balmont, and as late as 1942, and even posthumously in 1957, they were still looking for an alibi for Prokofiev's admiration of Balmont's poetry and his personal relationship with him.

"Evidently this decadent cult of Symbolism with its passive contemplation and morbid revelations had an influence on the young Prokofiev," they said. "This made itself felt also in his interest in Balmont, the whole mood and style of whose poetry might have been expected to be utterly alien to the healthy, realistic outlook of Prokofiev. Yet for a long time Prokofiev was enchanted by the musical poetry of Balmont's language and by certain "cosmic and barbarous exotic images," referring no doubt to "Seven, They Are Seven."

Since the quality of Prokofiev's music written in connection with Balmont's poetry must obviously be severely criticized, the critics concluded their analytical comments with, "This 'illicit liaison' with poetry of a trend so alien to his nature was undoubtedly one manifestation of the conflicting tendencies in Prokofiev's musical language."

At the end of the summer of 1921 Prokofiev saw less and less of Balmont. It was time for Prokofiev to start on his third journey to the United States, which he anticipated with pleasure: the production of *The Love for Three Oranges* was definitely decided upon, he had several engagements for appearances as a pianist in prospect, and above all, he was taking along the new concerto, which he had completed before leaving Etretât.

When at the end of October he arrived in Chicago, the rehearsals of the opera had already begun. "The singers were good, the stage sets excellent, but Maestro Jack Conni, the stage director, was exceptionally uninteresting," Prokofiev said. "He was the kind of professional stage director who knows by heart how to stage a hundred operas, but he himself lacks the imagination to do something original, something on his own."

At first Prokofiev was annoyed; then he tried to call on Mary Garden for help, but in vain. Miss Garden was always too preoccupied with her own roles in the repertory and was never available. Finally, Prokofiev went backstage to explain their roles to the singers and even direct the chorus on the stage himself.

"Once," Prokofiev recounted later, "I became so excited that I got all mixed up in my inadequate English, when one of the members of the chorus stopped the torrent of my senseless speech by saying, 'Why are you struggling with your English when half of the chorus are Russian refugees?' 'But first of all,' Conni interrupted, 'who is the boss here on the stage? You or I?'

"You," Prokofiev said firmly in his best English, "but merely to carry out my instructions."

At long last, on December 30, the curtain rose for the première; Prokofiev conducted the performance to a sold-out house.

"The Chicago audience was both proud and bewildered," he remarked later. "Proud of having first produced a 'modern opera,' and bewildered by the unusual music and by the fact that this enterprise should have cost some two hundred and fifty thousand dollars, as was reported in the newspapers; someone said, 'Those three oranges were the most expensive in the world!' "

Two weeks later, after participating in a concert organized by the "Friends of Soviet Russia," in which he played Moussorgsky's "Pictures at an Exhibition," Prokofiev left for New York. Soon afterwards, the Chicago Opera Company arrived for a performance of *The Love for Three Oranges*.

The date of the performance was changed so often that the final date fell on the day of Prokofiev's own recital. Following the advice of Capablanca, his chess friend, Prokofiev spent the few hours after his recital sitting in a hot bath and resting in bed before going to conduct the opera that evening.

New Yorkers received the opera warmly, but . . . "Lord above, what reviews!" exclaimed Prokofiev as he scanned the newspapers. "I felt as if a pack of mad hounds had been let loose and torn my pants to shreds."

The Third Concerto, one of the composer's finest works, had a similar fate. Prokofiev's performance in Chicago, under the direction of Stock (December 16 and 17) was treated favorably by the press; in New York, with Coates conducting (January 26 and 27, 1922), it was a complete failure.

Once again Prokofiev had to face an unpleasant reality: the promising beginning of his American season had ended in a fiasco. His last hope, that Mary Garden singing the principal role would produce *The Flaming Angel*, remained only a daydream. Mary Garden soon resigned her post and left Chicago.

"I was left with one thousand dollars in my pocket and a throbbing pain in my head from all the bustle and fuss, and one fervent desire to get away to some place where I could work in peace," Prokofiev said.

One of the main reasons for the failure of *The Love for Three Or-anges* was the libretto, which Prokofiev had written in French. Since this particular opera has not only to be heard but seen, the music should not be divorced from the scenic action and the text, or vice versa, in order to appreciate Sergei's cardinal intent fully. Although it might have been expected that one of the American opera companies would suggest to Prokofiev that he have his libretto translated into English, and also make it more palatable to the Western audiences, nothing was done until 1949, when the late Theodor Komissarjevsky, the well-known stage director, proposed to Laslo Halasz, then the director of the New York City Opera Company, that he produce *The Love for Three Oranges.*

Having previously worked with Komissarjevsky on a new dramatic version (in English) of Borodin's *Prince Igor,* I was asked by Halasz and Komissarjevsky to do an adaptation, not a translation, in English of Prokofiev's libretto. While the English text had to adhere closely to Prokofiev's libretto, I had to consult Gozzi's play, for Prokofiev's libretto was based on Gozzi's, which had been adapted by Meyerhold to suit Russian audiences. In it were witticisms and jokes utterly meaningless to any other audience.

And the opera was too long; it had to be tightened, and some cuts made, including two scenes. Although Halasz was skeptical about its success, ever since its first performance, on November 1, 1949, it has been one of the more successful operas performed by the New York City Opera Company, and at least six performances are given almost every year.

The March from the opera has become so popular that from No-vember 1944 to November 1958 it was used as the theme on the CBS radio program *Your FBI in Peace and War.*

16

Accompanied by his old friend Boris Verin, a Russian poet and then an émigré living in Paris, Prokofiev and his mother, Maria, arrived in Bavaria in March, 1922. Verin—a pen name—was of the Bashkirov family, whose large fortune came from flour mills in Russia. It was at their home in St. Petersburg shortly before the Revolution, Prokofiev had often taken part in the literary and musical evenings organized by Boris Verin.

At the beginning of the Revolution Vladimir Bashkirov, the head of the family firm, had emigrated to New York and later had his brother Boris join him. "But my brother was a poet," Bashkirov told me, "and preferred living in Europe. He wanted to be independent and lead his own life." Boris had then settled in Paris where he again met Prokofiev. There can be no doubt that whenever Prokofiev found himself short of funds, both Bashkirov brothers came to his assistance.

Upon their arrival in Bavaria, Prokofiev rented a small villa in a hamlet near the monastery of Ettal, which later became his first home after four years of nomadic living on two continents.

It was three miles from Oberammergau, well known for its performances of the medieval Passion play, probably the most significant survival of the miracle plays that were popular from the thirteenth to the sixteenth century. The play, representing the last days of Christ on earth, originated in 1634 as an expression of gratitude for the cessation of the Black Plague, which had stricken the village. It had been given once in the first year of every decade after its first performance, but because of the unsettled conditions after World War I the performances had been postponed to 1922, two months after Verin brought the Prokofievs to Ettal.

Prokofiev, who almost immediately plunged into work on *The Flaming Angel*, felt that the Witches' Sabbath described in Bryusov's story could have taken place somewhere in the neighborhood of Oberammergau. But the ghostly atmosphere did not prevent him from appreciating the beautiful environment and the quiet so ideally suited to his work. He also had a personal preference for making Ettal his headquarters for the following year and a half. His romance with Lina seemed to progress toward its natural solution, and the secluded, romantic surroundings of the hamlet on the slopes of the Bavarian Alps provided the necessary impetus. Lina, meanwhile, was studying opera in Milan, and the relatively short distance to Ettal made it easy for them to see each other often. And Lina enjoyed her visits there. She always found something pleasant awaiting her, which showed how much her suitor missed her.

When she arrived for the first time, it was late in the evening, and Sergei asked her not to look out of her window until the following day. Although mystified, she agreed. Lina was deeply touched and delighted when, awaking the next morning, she walked over to the window to get her first breath of the fresh mountain air and saw facing her a large flower bed of forget-me-nots arranged in an *L*. Prokofiev was an attentive and romantic lover, but the record of his courtship of Lina was so intimate that it has always remained their private property.

That summer Lina made her debut in Milan as Gilda in *Rigoletto*, and Prokofiev gave a piano recital there, following it by a joint concert with Lina singing some of his songs. Afterward they returned to Ettal via the Austrian Tyrol. According to Lina's discreet and overcautious memoir published in Soviet Russia in 1961, by the time they arrived in Ettal, they were already married. In this memoir, which she wrote at the age of sixty-three, she deliberately omitted all the information about her background, even the date and place of such an important event as her marriage to Sergei Prokofiev.

The matter was not as simple as one might have expected. They could not have had a religious ceremony, since Prokofiev was of the Greek Orthodox faith and Carolina Lutheran, as attested in her passport issued at the Spanish Consulate in Milan on May 18, 1923. But in order to have even a civil ceremony, Prokofiev and Lina had to repair to Germany, for in Italy—where it would have been logical for them to marry in Milan—nonreligious ceremonies had no legal status.

On September 14, 1923, then, they applied for a marriage license at the Municipal Office at Ettal, and after the customary two-week waiting period, were married on September 29. Their marriage certificate (numbered B-5) shows, in addition to Prokofiev's and Lina's signatures, those of the witnesses to the ceremony: Boris Bashkirov (Verin), and Prokofiev's mother, Maria. (Maria's signature clearly indicates the difficulty she had in writing because of her almost total blindness.)

The permit from the Department of Justice in Munich for the civil ceremony to be performed at Ettal cost Prokofiev one million inflation marks (as is shown by Receipt No. 43946).*

Now Prokofiev was willing to take off more time from his work. He and Lina often made excursions into the mountains or went to Garmisch-Patenkirchen, where Richard Strauss was living, and of course, they did not miss the Passion play at Oberammergau. For two months in advance of the performances they had been watching the local "actors"—tradesman, veterinarian, butcher, or tavernkeeper—who, preparing themselves for the forthcoming production, were letting their hair and beards grow long to give their appearance authenticity, for neither wigs nor facial make-up was permitted.

Both Prokofiev and Lina were much impressed by the performance, which began at eight in the morning and lasted eight hours, with a short intermission at noon. Before an audience of several thousand, with some seven hundred participants, including a fifty-piece orchestra and as numerous a chorus, these performances were enacted on a large open-air stage. Prokofiev learned that the original text of the play, slightly revised every ten years, was most probably written in 1633 (a year before its first performance) by the monks of Ettal monastery, the very monastery that had attracted him while he was choosing a place to make his home. The music had been composed much later, in 1814, by Bochus Dedler, a schoolmaster in the parish.

Fascinated by this extraordinary production, Prokofiev also discovered that the participants were chosen only from among the natives of the village who were of impeccable moral character and dramatically qualified, and that they were trained in various classical plays during the years between the performances of the Passion play. Prokofiev and Lina were moved by the religious devotion with which the participants regarded their roles and by the deep reverence in their acting.

They attended several performances, since after the first production on the first Sunday in May, the play was repeated on each following Sunday and sometimes twice or three times during the week. During that first year the Prokofievs were in Ettal, there were as many as sixty performances at Oberammergau.

It was unfortunate that Maria could share their enthusiasm only

* See Appendix.

from the vivid descriptions they brought home, for by now she was blind and could not attend the spectacles. To distract her and because she loved to tell Lina stories about Sergei's youth, Lina persuaded her to dictate her reminiscences, which she and Verin took down.*

Thus Lina also learned that in addition to music and chess, her husband was often absorbed by other interests, such as botany and astronomy, that dated from his adolescence, when his father had given him books on these subjects.

In turn, Prokofiev shared his discoveries with Lina. But her lessons in astronomy and botany never made her an expert in these fields. And although her initial introduction to chess had fascinated her, further progress in solving chess problems sometimes led to tears. Prokofiev, putting his arm around her, would then suggest leaving it alone: "Come along, my lark, and let's do a little singing instead."

Playing chess, however, was almost as necessary to him as his music, and leaving Lina to take care of his mother, he would often play a few games with Verin, who had moved to Oberammergau, where he lived in the home of Dr. Anton Lang. Lang's fifteen-year-old son, Fritz, was another chess enthusiast, thus providing Prokofiev with an extra opponent.

Lina was a devoted wife and tried to share in her husband's hobbies and amusements. Once, during their stay in Ettal, Prokofiev read in the Munich newspaper about a sale of electric incubators for chickens, and to everybody's surprise he ordered one. As soon as the contraption arrived, he insisted on experimenting with it. Following the directions supplied in a pamphlet, he and Lina placed eggs in the incubator and then waited for them to hatch; Prokofiev often got up in the middle of the night to see if there were cracks in the eggshells. Eventually, all the eggs hatched except one—puzzled, they decided to give it a little more time. When finally it did hatch, it turned out to be a duckling. The Prokofievs were very much amused by this, for they were sure that someone, most probably Boris Verin, had played a joke on them. "Only our duckling did not turn into a beautiful swan," Lina remarked.

Prokofiev was happy and valued particularly those weeks when he could remain with his family, for most of the time his work required trips to Paris and London. With Verin back in France, he had to leave Lina in Ettal to take care of Maria.

In April he had played his Third Piano Concerto in Paris and in

---

* Maria's short memoir was published in *S. S. Prokofiev: Materials, Documents, and Reminiscences,* compiled by Semyon Schlifstein (Moscow: State Music Publishing House, 1961; second edition).

London. It was well received in both cities, and the reviews were less severe than after the performance of *The Buffoon*. The critic of the London *Times* observed that Sergei Prokofiev had a little talent, and one could bear listening to his music for a quarter of an hour.

And in June, Prokofiev was back in Paris, where Diaghilev had revived *The Buffoon* and wanted to hear the score of *The Love for Three Oranges*. Stravinsky was present at this "audition," but was so critical that he refused to listen after Prokofiev had finished playing the first act. "Perhaps he was right," Prokofiev said later. "The first act was indeed the least successful of the opera, but on that day I staunchly defended my composition and the discussion turned into a noisy row."

Prokofiev criticized Stravinsky for his new trend toward what he called "Bach on the wrong notes"—an alien language, which, he said, Stravinsky was assuming in his current composition as his own. Stravinsky in turn reminded Prokofiev of his own Classical Symphony, but to this Prokofiev replied that he wrote it simply "on the side," while with Stravinsky the new trend was becoming the strongest characteristic of his current works.

"After this meeting," Prokofiev said, "for several years Stravinsky adopted not so much a malevolent as a critical attitude toward me, and there was a definite cooling off in our relationship." Influenced by Stravinsky's judgment, Diaghilev was also "disappointed" in *The Love for Three Oranges*.

A year later Prokofiev met Diaghilev in Berlin while spending an evening with Vladimir Mayakovsky, the Russian poet, and they all fell into a passionate discussion of contemporary art. Whether as a result of all these discussions or because of the failure of *The Buffoon* and his disappointment in *The Love for Three Oranges*, Diaghilev was reported to have made one of his many Olympian statements: "Sergei is certainly very talented, a fountain of melody—which Igor [Stravinsky] is not—but Igor is intelligent whereas Prokofiev is an utter imbecile. He always can be counted on to do the wrong thing. Fancy calling a symphony 'Classical!' It's almost as ridiculous as Scriabin labeling his orchestral poem 'Divine.' "

And when Diaghilev was asked to explain how he accounted for this imbecile's Third Piano Concerto, with its fresh, lyrical themes and great charm, he "winced a bit, then grew thoughtful. 'Yes, charm . . . ,' he said quietly, 'that's something impossible to acquire. Stravinsky is the only Slav musician who lacks Slavic charm.' "

Still, Diaghilev preferred Stravinsky, and temporarily lost his interest in Prokofiev.

While in Ettal, besides continuing his work on *The Flaming Angel*, Prokofiev made a symphonic Suite from *The Buffoon* and another from *The Love for Three Oranges*, and wrote his Fifth Piano Sonata. He also resumed his correspondence with his friends in Soviet Russia, and his report on his activities outside Russia was published in Moscow in May, 1923, in the magazine *On to New Shores*. His latest works began to appear on concert programs in Moscow, and the Leningrad Philharmonic wanted to know whether Sergei Prokofiev would consider going there for several concert engagements. This was the first call to come home, and Sergei Prokofiev declined.

Although he was living a short distance from Munich, Prokofiev had failed somehow to make contacts with the German musicians. The March and the Scherzo from *The Love for Three Oranges*, the Overture on Jewish themes, and a few short piano pieces played occasionally by the concertizing pianists were his only works introduced in Germany—not enough to create the kind of climate, as he said, necessary for more diverse activities. Paris, as far as he was concerned, was still his center, and he moved there with his family at the end of October, 1923.

"To be living in Paris did not mean that one automatically became a Parisian or a Frenchman," Prokofiev said. "Victorious France wanted to be the leader in music as well." This accounted, in his opinion, for the special reputation gained by a group of French composers who, imitating the nickname of the Mighty Five called themselves "The Six." Arthur Honegger, Francis Poulenc, Germaine Taileferre, Louis Durey, Darius Milhaud, and Georges Auric carried the banner against the Impressionists, but Prokofiev thought that not all of them succeeded in fulfilling the hope placed in them at their debut in the musical world.

Prokofiev did not agree with The Six in regard to Maurice Ravel, whose music, in the heat of their youthful enthusiasm, they considered dated—maintaining that a new generation brings with it a new musical language. Prokofiev, however, preferred Ravel, whose unassuming personality instantly won his sympathy. They had met two years earlier at a "musical tea" attended by Stravinsky and the conductor Ernest Ansermet, among others. "A man about five feet tall with unusually sharp features and a large mop of graying hair walked into the room," Prokofiev said later, describing his first impression of the French composer which remained with him for the rest of his life. "When we were introduced, and I expressed my delight in shaking the hand of such a great composer and addressed him as *Maître*, a customary way in France when speaking to an eminent artist, Ravel suddenly pulled his hand away, as if he were afraid I was going to kiss it, saying,

'Oh, no, please, don't call me *Maître*.' " Modesty was certainly one of Ravel's chief characteristics. Prokofiev said that he never doubted that Ravel was aware of the significance of his talent, but he shrank from all manifestations of personal admiration, a rare characteristic indeed among contemporary musicians.

Prokofiev felt gratified that Ravel, like Debussy, was not only passionately interested in Russian music, but was influenced by it, especially by the work of Moussorgsky and Rimsky-Korsakov. For example, he cited Ravel's admirable orchestral transcription of Moussorgsky's "Pictures at an Exhibition," his orchestration of "Khovantchina," and his own "Scheherazade," although Ravel had treated the subject differently than Rimsky-Korsakov.

Later, after his return to Soviet Russia, when in their unreasonable fervor his compatriots condemned everything in Western art, Prokofiev publicly expressed his regret* that Ravel, "due to a wrong conception that his music was alien to contemporary Russian art," was seldom performed. "I believe that such an assumption is utterly baseless," he said. Analyzing Ravel's works and pointing to "Bolero" as a miracle in mastery of composition, he spoke of the charm of Ravel's string quartet as well and his extraordinary art in using national French and Spanish songs. Prokofiev said, "If some of Ravel's compositions are marked by extreme fineness of style, which we oppose here with more virile, buoyant, and joyous emotions, still, we can and should learn a great deal from his works both in virtuoso orchestration and harmony."

And referring once more to the general French attitude toward Ravel, as if to confirm his early impressions, he added, "Years have passed, the Six have acquired their proper place in French music, but Ravel, as before, remains among the extraordinary French composers and the most significant in contemporary art."

But when Prokofiev first settled in Paris, the general opinion of the French, who were not afraid of complicated and dissonant scores, sanctioned his own way of writing rather than discouraged it. In May, 1924, he played for the first time in Paris his completely revised Second Piano Concerto, while Koussevitzky presented the Seven, They are Seven at one of his symphonic concerts. Both compositions were favorably received, but the audience was rather offended by Koussevitzky's placing the cantata twice on the same program for "further perspicuity," as the conductor noted.

Apparently, the audience misunderstood Koussevitzky's intentions.

---

* In the magazine *Soviet Art*, January 4, 1938.

The word "perspicuity" was not concerned with the clarity of the interpretation of Prokofiev's composition, but was in reference to the cantata's ominous content, the terrible picture of the situation in Soviet Russia under the leadership of the Communist commissars—a situation to which Koussevitzky personally could hardly have been expected to remain indifferent. He had lost most of his fortune in Soviet Russia.

Although he had left the country with a passport similar to Prokofiev's—"for health and business reasons"—Koussevitzky had no intentions of returning, whereas for Prokofiev's work to be used as a demonstration against the Soviets was rather hazardous. Hadn't Prokofiev been told before he left Russia, "You are running away from events, and these events will never forgive you when you return; you will not be understood"? But apparently he was anxious to have Koussevitzky perform his works, regardless of the possible cost in Russia. He felt that performance was of paramount importance to his career in the Western world, and he was willing to risk it.

And who, except the Soviet authorities, would blame him for it? Sergei Prokofiev was a talented musician devoted to his art, a man of complete integrity, whose honesty and outspoken ways won fewer friends than enemies, but who, endowed with all these admirable qualities, was still only human. He was now married and, in addition, had to support his ailing, blind mother. Because of the insufficient funds, they could afford only a small, modestly furnished apartment in Paris; shortly before Koussevitzky's concert, the household was enlarged by a new family member: at the end of February, Lina gave birth to a son, Svyatoslav—a joyous event, no doubt, but also emphasizing once more the desperate need to improve their financial situation.

"Sergei had just finished revising his Second Piano Concerto and he was preparing himself for the concert," Lina recalled. "He was practicing the piano so much, 'cramming,' as he always referred to his practicing, that the two-month-old Svyatoslav had to be taken to a far corner of the apartment so as not to upset the child's nerves."

It was not an apartment suited for a concert pianist. No sooner had Sergei begun practicing than the neighbors protested by banging on the walls. In desperation, to give them a taste of a different "music" to which they could not legally object, Sergei equipped himself with large pieces of lumber and nails, and pretending that he was building book shelves, kept hammering so long that his neighbors were rather relieved when he went back to practicing the piano.

It is also not surprising that at this time—when he was solely preoccupied with trying to gain a firm foothold as an artist in the Western world—he again declined the Leningrad Philharmonic's tentative invitation to return to Soviet Russia. Many years later, when he did return to Russia, in giving an account of this refusal to the Soviet authorities, he said, "I believe that the decisive reason was the fact that at that time I still did not comprehend the magnitude of events taking place in Soviet Russia—events which demanded the cooperation of every citizen, not only of those in political life, as I had thought, but of men in the arts as well. Also, the postponement of my return was caused by an established rhythm in my life: the publishing of my works [Gutheil, his publisher, had moved to Paris] involved corrections of proofs; and there were many concert engagements in France, England, and Italy, as well as a desire to prove my 'stand' toward 'modern music' against other contemporary trends. And finally, there were purely personal reasons: the illness of my mother, my marriage, and the birth of my son."

Such was, at least in retrospect, Prokofiev's official reasoning for not returning to Russia at that time. And once in Russia, what else could he do but speak in well-coached words.

Although he was satisfied with the reception in Paris of his Second Piano Concerto and his cantata, he did not overlook the accusation of some critics that based his success on his "old compositions," a reproach he was often to hear afterward. It led him immediately to start working on a symphony of large dimensions "to be built of iron and steel," as he said, for which he already had a general scheme in mind. Its structure was to be akin to that of Beethoven's last piano sonata (Op. 111). As in the Beethoven sonata's second movement, Prokofiev planned to have what he called a "safety-valve," at least at the beginning of the symphony's second movement. He chose a quiet theme, composed as long ago as during his stay in Japan, on which to write the variations.

"But a whole avalanche of ideas flows through my mind," he said, almost complaining. "I do not need a comb, but a large rake to sort out what will be useful." He worked on this symphony all that autumn and winter, and perhaps for the first time, he was struggling with a composition.

The Prokofievs were still living in the same apartment. His mother was visibly failing, and there were domestic problems that bothered and often interrupted him. "If he were annoyed, he would go to his desk to compose," Lina said later, "but if he sat at the piano and played Beethoven sonatas, then I knew that he was worried about something." At times, seeking a distraction, he would even try to write

short stories in Chekhovian style, but he never showed them to anybody. "He thought they were not good enough," Lina said.

Maria died in December, 1924, with Sergei and Lina at her bedside.
Prokofiev felt this loss very deeply. He had not been attached to anyone as much as to his mother. And it took him some time to return to
concentrated work on his symphony. "If The Classical Symphony was
not much of one, but was nevertheless a symphony, then the Second
Symphony turned out to be a long and complicated work," he said.

On June 6, 1925, at a Koussevitzky concert in Paris, the Second
Symphony was given its première. The audience was just as bewildered as the composer himself. The work was so overloaded with
complex themes superimposed on each other that Prokofiev himself
could not comprehend what was essential and what was not in his
work.

"And if I could not make head or tail of it," he wrote his old friend
Miaskovsky in Moscow (August 4, 1925), what could you expect
from the audience. *Schluss!* It will be a long while before they hear another complicated work from me.

"And yet," he wrote in the same letter, "somewhere deep in my
heart I nurse a hope that in a few years it will suddenly become clear
that the symphony is well constructed. Could it be possible that in
my old age [he was thirty-four] and equipped with my technique in
composition I have made such a mess of it, and this after nine months
of the most grueling labor?"

The critics unanimously disapproved of the Second Symphony and
even expressed their disappointment in Prokofiev's "exceptional gifts."
For the first, and perhaps the only time in his life, Prokofiev's faith in
himself was shaken. "What if I am destined, after all, to become a
second-rate composer?" The disturbing thought droned in his mind.

In desperation he blamed the fickle Parisian audience. "Paris is the
undisputed leader in women's chic, and the same necessity of creating a vogue is felt in other fields, including the arts. After they show
an interest in one composer, they look for the sensational discovery of
another. Even Diaghilev turned his back on me after my discussion
with Stravinsky," Prokofiev brooded.

Prokofiev remembered Romain Rolland's *Jean Christophe:* "The
vogue does not last long and the idol invariably awakes one fine morning to find himself on the rubbish heap."

17

At this crucial time, in the summer of 1925, soon after the performance of the Second Symphony, Diaghilev called on Prokofiev. He spoke of another "new" ballet.

"But I cannot write in the style you like," Prokofiev told him, alluding to works written for Diaghilev by Milhaud and Auric that he considered banal and trivial.

"You should write in your own style," Diaghilev said, explaining to Prokofiev that he wanted a ballet on a "Soviet subject," something reflecting life in Soviet Russia.

Prokofiev could not believe his ears—to hear this from Diaghilev, of all people. Or was Diaghilev prompted more by a "good business sense," than by an artistic one? At that time several Western countries had recognized the Soviet government and there was ever-growing interest in the lives of Russians under the new regime.

At first Ilya Ehrenburg, the Soviet author then living in Paris, was considered as the librettist, but later Diaghilev asked Sergei Yakulov, "the Soviet theatrical constructivist artist"—that is, a painter who was also a designer of stage sets. Yakulov happened to be in Paris, where his work had won him an honorable diploma at the International Exposition of Decorative Arts.

Sitting in a small café on the banks of the Seine half an hour away from Paris, Yakulov and Prokofiev made a few tentative sketches for the future scenario. They agreed the ballet should not be devoted to an "interesting" plot, but to a demonstration of the accomplishments in the industrial upsurge taking place in Soviet Russia.

"We imagined on the stage," Prokofiev said, "men working with hammers and axes, revolving flywheels and transmissions, and flashing light signals. With this as a background there were going to be a number of scenes from the period of the Revolution to the present. The first part of the ballet would show the breakdown of the Czarist regime: meetings of workers, speeches by commissars, trains full of black-market goods, a former duchess bartering her gowns for food, a revolutionary sailor, and homeless waifs. The second part would present a picture of socialist reconstruction, the building of new plants and factories, yesterday's sailor-turned-worker, and so on."

The entire subject, Prokofiev admitted, belonged to Yakulov, who had spent these years in the Soviet Union and who colorfully described to him all the characters. One could see at once, Prokofiev added, that the whole scenario was thought out not by a dramatist, but by a painter who visualized the spectacle.

As soon as the scenario was worked out and Diaghilev had more or less approved it, Prokofiev began to compose with great enthusiasm. This time his musical language was to differ from that of *The Buffoon:* it would reflect contemporary Russia.

For some reason, Diaghilev named the ballet *Le Pas d'acier*, and although he had definitely accepted it for production, he scheduled it for his 1927 season, a year and a half later. Now that he had it in his hands, he was fearful of being accused of contributing to Soviet propaganda.

Meanwhile, Prokofiev left for a long concert tour in the United States. He was accompanied by Lina, with whom he planned to give several joint recitals. He brought with him the piano score of *Le Pas d'acier*, and in order to continue his work on its orchestration, he devised a system that permitted him not to lose time on the long trips across the country.

Because the vibration of the train made it impossible to write the orchestral score, he did all his preparatory work by marking in his piano score which of the instruments was to play this or that melody or passage, including the indications for accents and dynamics, so that when he left the train and found himself even for a short time on "firm ground," all he had to do was to copy automatically his indications into the orchestral score.

At first it seemed impossible to write into the piano score the names of the instruments, particularly when the chords occupied all the staffs, but with practice he succeeded. When absolutely necessary, he used a separate piece of music paper that he attached to the piano score. He was pleased with having perfected this method, for it allowed him to turn over the piano score to a capable musician who could then easily transcribe it into the orchestral score. It saved both time and energy, which Prokofiev hated to waste on purely mechanical work. After that, all his scores, with the exception of *Alexander Nevsky*, were written this way.

Four years had passed since his last visit to the United States. Now he was better received, no doubt due to the frequent reports, which sometimes bordered on the sensational, of his many activities in Europe. He played his Third Piano Concerto seven times in Boston and in five other cities with the Boston Symphony Orchestra under the direction of his old friend Koussevitzky, who fervently furthered his works. Six other concerts were organized by the Pro Musica. At these Lina sang, in addition to Prokofiev's, the songs of Miaskovsky and Taneyev. Judgments of Lina's talent vary, but the fact that she appeared in joint programs with her husband—who was notoriously uncompromising in musical matters—amply testifies to her vocal ability.

PRO MUSICA, INC.
Recital of Modern Russian Music
Residence of Mrs. Charles Robinson Smith 24 West 69 Street N.Y.
January 26, 1926

Serge Prokofiev assisted by *Lina Llubera Vocalist*

I	Third Sonata Op. 28	Prokofiev
	Serge Prokofiev	
II	Three Gavottes Op. 12, 25 and 32	Prokofiev
	Serge Prokofiev	
III	Le hanneton	Moussorgsky
	Berceuse	Rimsky-Korsakov
	Menuet	Taneyev
	"Think of me!" (A Chaldean Incantation) Op. 36	Prokofiev
	Lina Llubera	
IV	Four Bizarreries Op. 25	Prokofiev
	Serge Prokofiev	
V	Les Circles Op. 4	Miaskovsky
	Myosotis	Stravinsky
	Le Pigeon	Stravinsky
	La Rosée Sainte Op. 6	Stravinsky
	Lina Llubera	
VI	Two Marches Op. 12 and 33	Prokofiev
	Scherzo from "The Love for Three Oranges"	Prokofiev
	Prelude Op. 12	Prokofiev
	Toccata Op. 11	Prokofiev
	Serge Prokofiev	

Well satisfied with this tour, though he had enjoyed only a *succès d'estime*, Prokofiev returned to Europe for a tour in Italy in the spring of 1926. After a recital in Naples, Maxim Gorky went to see Prokofiev in the green room, and then took him and Lina to dine at his home in Sorrento. This was one of Prokofiev's few meetings with the author since 1917, when Gorky's intervention had relieved him of military duty, and he was again particularly impressed by Gorky's humanitarian views as he spoke of the complex problems facing the world and, of course, Russia. Gorky was in good spirits, and their discussion lasted into the early-morning hours. Not without obvious national pride, Gorky told Prokofiev that Russian music and, generally speaking, the whole of Russian art were very popular in Italy and constantly gaining more and more of a foothold in Italian life. "You can hear bands playing Tchaikovsky, Moussorgsky, Borodin, and Rimsky-Korsakov in their public squares, and on the programs of their symphonic concerts Scriabin is *de rigueur*. Stravinsky is played often . . . and now— Prokofiev," Gorky smiled.

Remembering their previous discussions of music in Russia in which Gorky had surprised him with an intuitive feeling for and ana- lytical attitude toward music, Prokofiev was now anxious to hear his views of the trend fostered by the building of a socialist state. Gorky smiled, and said to the Prokofievs, "This you must know as well as I do."

"Everybody says that in accordance with our new life we should first of all compose joyous and energetic music," Prokofiev pursued the subject.

"But tender and soulful music as well," Gorky added.

As they were parting, Prokofiev took a last look at Gorky's home, a large *palazzo*-style villa, damp and lacking coziness. As if guessing his thoughts, Gorky, who for years had been suffering from tuberculosis, said, "One of my lungs is completely gone, and only half of the other is left."

The next time Prokofiev saw Gorky's face, quiet in its spiritual beauty, was on June 19, 1936, when, as one of the honorary pallbear- ers, he stood by the open coffin.

There is no doubt that his long discussion with Gorky in Sorrento never left Prokofiev's memory, and perhaps even played no small part in his decision to return to Russia, a thought which had occurred to him more often since he had heard about the frequent performances there of his works.

While he was on tour in the United States, *The Love for Three Oranges* was performed in Leningrad, on February 18, 1926. It was successful with the audience, but the reviewers opinions varied. "Some of them made no sense," Prokofiev thought, while "others tried to establish whom I was ridiculing: the public, Gozzi, the form of an opera, or those who are incapable of laughter. Still others 'discovered' an irony, challenge, and grotesque characterization, while all I had done was to compose a gay and amusing spectacle."

Prokofiev was far more gratified to hear that Persimfans, the first symphony orchestra without a conductor, made up of the leading Moscow muscians (1922–1932) had given several concerts devoted to his compositions. Persimfans, the Leningrad Philharmonia, Miaskovsky, Asafiev, Glière, and other friends with whom he had resumed correspondence all urged him to return to Russia. And in addition to these he saw in the articles published in Soviet magazines frequent quotations from Lunacharsky's speeches. The Minister of Education and Arts—who in 1917 had said that he would not stand in Prokofiev's way when it came to his going to the United States and had kept his word—said among other things, "Prokofiev's characteristic freshness and wealth of invention show his exceptional gifts. He has youth and energy—the juice of the earth. . . . He is alien to the West because his music reflects the attitude of his country, which does not want to become a mere toy of American politics. Stravinsky has already fallen to a certain extent into the ways of cunning tricks. But Prokofiev, in order to develop to the full stature of his ability, had best return to us. Before the evil spirit of Americanization crushes him, he should, like Anteus, touch the earth again."

Prokofiev, however, could not make up his mind.

What did it matter if, in Berlin on October 9, 1926, there was a performance of *The Love for Three Oranges* that Prokofiev attended? As he was examining the stage sets shortly before the dress rehearsal, he heard a stagehand say, "Look at it. . . . How much German money was spent on the designing of these sets—all a waste. This opera will be given a few times and then you can throw it all out."

Prokofiev did not like the stage director, and he thought that Leo Blech (1871–1958), the conductor, was irreproachable—so irreproachable, in fact, that the score under his direction lost all its vitality. "Why don't you speed up this passage?" Prokofiev suggested to Blech as he stood near the conductor during the dress rehearsal.

"Impossible!" Blech answered. "The orchestra would mess it up."

"Well, let them mess it up. What of it?" Prokofiev persisted.

"*Ach* . . . What of it?" And Blech gave Prokofiev such a look that he thought the conductor had lost what little respect he might have had for him forever.

And what of it, if Bruno Walter, then head of the Berlin Opera, was interested in producing *The Flaming Angel?* Prokofiev had spent the entire summer of 1926 rewriting the libretto and adding new material to the score that he had then reorchestrated.

And what difference did it make if the American Pianola company commissioned him to write an overture for the opening of a new concert hall they were planning in New York? "It is far more pleasant to compose for this company than to record my own playing," Prokofiev said as he wrote the overture. Since the hall was not going to be large, Prokofiev decided on a piece with two pianos leading an ensemble of fourteen other musicians; a seventeenth performer was to play on several percussion instruments. Thus, he remarked, it was an overture for seventeen musicians and not for seventeen instruments, as it was erroneously referred to. (Later, seeing the impractical side of such a composition, he made another version of it—for symphony orchestra.)

And what of it, if Diaghilev spoke of further collaboration, of plans for still another ballet? And what if Koussevitzky was always ready to publish his works and present them at his concerts?

What was all of this compared with his growing desire to return to Russia, if only for a visit?

18

"On January 18, 1927, at Bigosov, I put my foot on Soviet terri-
tory," Prokofiev wrote with a triumphant air. He had finally taken the
decisive step of returning to Russia; he was anxious about the forthcoming meetings with his friends, excited over seeing everything with
his own eyes: the progress claimed by the Soviets and the frightening
conditions of which he had been forewarned in the Western countries.

Despite the sincere urging by his old friends to return that he had
received during the years of his absence, he still remembered the parting words he had heard when, in 1917, he left Russia to go to the
United States: "You are running away from events, and these events
will never forgive you when you return; you will not be understood."
It was a disturbing warning that had never left his mind. But he also
remembered Lunacharsky's words, and after all Lunacharsky was Minister of Education and the Arts, not just anybody.

On January 19 he and Lina arrived in Moscow. They were met by
the director of the Persimfans who drove the Prokofievs to the Metropol, the hotel reserved for important foreign visitors. For the moment
Prokofiev forgot everything except that at last he saw a real winter
through the car's frosty windows—a Russian winter, which he had
sorely missed during all the years he had spent abroad.

At the hotel they were joined by Miaskovsky, Asafiev, and other
friends, and Lev Zetlin, the violinist, a pupil of Leopold Auer, who
had founded the Persimfans and was impatient to show off the "five-
year-old child." Despite the Prokofievs' need for rest after the long
journey, Zetlin took them straight away to the orchestra's rehearsal.

As they entered the concert hall, Prokofiev heard the March from

The Love for Three Oranges. Imagining that the orchestra was rehearsing, Prokofiev whispered to Zetlin, "The tempo is a bit too slow." But then, deeply moved, he realized that the slow pace had been taken intentionally to signify the orchestra's triumphal welcome.

Prokofiev was amazed by the facility with which the orchestra had mastered a difficult program and, without a leader, was even able to accompany a soloist. This unity had not been achieved without strenuous rehearsing, of course, particularly in those passages of the score that demanded sudden changes in tempo, for then the ensemble of the musicians had to "feel like one man."

The first concert entirely devoted to Prokofiev's compositions took place on January 24, five days after his return to Moscow. The large Conservatory Hall was packed to the last inch of standing room, and the atmosphere was unusually elated and festive before the beginning of the program. It opened with the ten pieces from *The Buffoon.* The orchestra, stimulated by the composer's presence, tried to display its best qualities. Then Prokofiev, who was to perform his Third Piano Concerto, made his appearance. He was welcomed by a standing ovation, while the orchestra played "Toush" (a sort of Russian "For He's a Jolly Good Fellow") and there was tumultuous applause that did not abate until he took his place at the piano.

Prokofiev's playing of the concerto, as well as the orchestral suite from *The Love for Three Oranges,* which closed the program, only further excited the already feverish enthusiasm of the public. As his first encore Prokofiev played one of Miaskovsky's *Whimsies* (Op. 5).

In an evening devoted entirely to his own compositions, Prokofiev chose this piece as an homage to Miaskovsky and their long friendship. But aware of the composer's presence in the hall, Prokofiev became so nervous that he "muddled" his friend's composition with its *jeux perlée* to such a degree that Miaskovsky failed to recognize it. Before he had reached the end of it, Prokofiev suddenly repeated the beginning, then jumped back again to the end, and finally in an utter confusion of sound, ended with a weird combination of chords.

Many years later the Soviet composer Dmitri Kabalevsky reminded him of the incident. Prokofiev laughed. "You know how much I love and admire Miaskovsky. To be honest, sometimes I am even afraid of him. . . . Well, on that night, when I had almost reached the end of the piece, I suddenly remembered that Miaskovsky was sitting in the hall and was listening to me, and then—I don't know why—I became so terrified that the music just flew out of my head. It was fortunate that I managed to finish playing as well as I did."

Prokofiev, however, was more successful when he followed this "tribute" with his own transcription of the Gavotte from the Classical Symphony, and his Toccata.

Referring to two symphonic programs at which Prokofiev played his Second Piano Concerto and to his two piano recitals, *Sovremenaya Muzyka* (*Contemporary Music*, No. 20, 1927) commented, "There was a sort of peculiar magic in these performances, and, indeed, the composer himself played with an élan that was quite natural, considering that he was playing for an audience that could not but be particularly near and dear to him."

Those who looked askance because of his ten-year absence, who were ready to criticize and pick out with glee the lost qualities of his piano-playing, were surprised that the brilliance of his technique and the clarity of accents, the inflexible rhythm, the unyielding masculine energy, and the dominating persuasiveness of his phrasing were now even more in evidence than before. What used to be considered daring, and even youthful arrogance, had given way to incontestably great art based on constructively thought-out conviction. What he had lost was his youthful carelessness in execution, thanks to the trials during his years of concertizing in the United States. His playing was mature, more masterful.

His physical appearance was also in sharp contrast to that of his Moscow colleagues, who had suffered privations in food and clothing during the years of revolution and civil war. Prokofiev looked cheerful and extremely healthy, younger than his thirty-six years. Among the drably dressed Muskovites, his checkered tweeds, bright-colored neckties, and light-brown shoes drew attention. And he also surprised them with his brisk, businesslike manner.

It was Rachmaninoff who once told me that Sergei Taneyev's pupils were so much under the influence of their master that they even learned to speak as he did—expressing laconically what they had to say, disregarding a tone that often could have been taken as ill-mannered. Sergei Prokofiev, whose chief motto was brevity and avoidance of everything superfluous in his compositions, had also followed this precept in his conversation. But now, or so it seemed to his countrymen, he had acquired from his association with American businessmen an even more pronounced businesslike tone in his speech and matter-of-fact behavior.

When he had first gone to the United States, Prokofiev could not get over the fact that the much-talked-about smile and politeness of an American businessman vanished as soon as he was no longer interested "businesswise." Yet the manner must have been so contagious that the traces of these characteristics were still in evidence in Prokofiev's behavior with strangers.

The brusqueness was particularly shocking to musicians and intellectuals who had heard about him, admired him, but were meeting him for the first time. Vladimir Vlassov, later the director of the Moscow Philharmonia, was still a student at the Conservatory at the time of Prokofiev's return to Russia in 1927. Somehow, he managed to be at Prokofiev's first rehearsal with the Persimfans, and he noticed Prokofiev's slightly haughty way of speaking, which left an unpleasant impression, as well as his businesslike manner in conducting the rehearsal and abrupt departure from the hall as if he were in a hurry, afraid to be late for his next appointment.

Nevertheless, in his enthusiasm Vlassov wanted so much to have Prokofiev's autograph that he bought his photograph in a bookstore and, before the concert, went with Lev Zetlin to Prokofiev's hotel. Timidly, he approached Prokofiev with his request.

"I don't sign autographs," Prokofiev said firmly, "and certainly not before a concert! I don't know you and you have not yet heard me!"

Embarrassed, Zetlin mumbled something about enthusiastic youth: "Our student . . . my pupil, who loves modern music very much. . . ."

"What nonsense!" Prokofiev said. "No, no! I have already said I won't sign it! Come after the concert. Good-by!"

But Prokofiev's principles must have weakened after the concert, for when Vlassov greeted him in the green room, he signed the photograph, saying just as matter-of-factly, "It seems you are a violinist. Then let me write for you the first measures from my concerto," and under his signature, Prkfv (his own abbreviation of his last name), Prokofiev wrote the first theme of his D-major Violin Concerto.

Working with the orchestra at rehearsals, Prokofiev, although pleased with the ensemble's enthusiasm, noticed that his American Overture (in B-major, Op. 42)—commissioned by the pianola firm and which he had reorchestrated for a large symphony orchestra—was not understood either by the members of the orchestra or, when it was performed, by the public.

What was wrong with it? The question bothered him as well as puzzled him whenever one of his compositions failed to "reach an audience." In fact, he noticed that beginning with this overture, a whole series of his works had suffered a similar fate. After having abstractly and carefully analyzed each of the works in question, he came to the following conclusion.

He admitted that he had been searching for novelties in intonation;

but, he said, intonation is something that the average listener misses or lets pass unnoticed. The same is true about a melody. If it is not based on usual turns and intonation, it is not considered melodious. But if the composer is right, then it shows that he has succeeded in widening the diapason of the melodic possibilities, and the listener will follow him, even though at a respectable distance.

"It has often happened to me," Prokofiev continued to explain, "that I would completely forget one of these compositions. . . . Then, playing it again, I would wonder, What is the matter with it? I myself couldn't fathom why I had written it the way I had. But after playing it over and over, two, three, four times, suddenly, as if the image were slowly appearing from the darkness, everything became clear, everything was in its proper place, and I could see that it could not have been written any other way.

"Obviously, if I myself sometimes cannot understand something that I have already known, what can I expect from an average listener and particularly if he is not as musically sensitive? I could wish, of course, that he would have a little more faith in the firm, instead of complaining that the firm that used to offer decent products has now apparently lost its mind. Also, perhaps he should remember that it is not necessarily true that every composition that is easily acceptable to our ears is therefore good. History proves the contrary. If the listener would adopt a more receptive attitude to my 'incomprehensible' compositions, then I am convinced we would quickly come to terms."

From Moscow, Prokofiev and Lina went to Leningrad, where he was received with even greater enthusiasm, for it was here that he had been educated, had later enjoyed his first success, and had gained his first devoted followers. He spent the leisure time between concerts and rehearsals (the same programs were given) introducing Lina to the streets, the harbor, the parks, where so many years of his youth had been passed. They met Leningrad's young composers, who showed Prokofiev their work, among them the twenty-one-year-old Dmitri Shostakovich.

At a performance of *The Love for Three Oranges* Prokofiev sat next to Lunacharsky, who told him that the Scythian Suite was "elemental music" and that *The Love for Three Oranges* was a "glass of champagne." The performance was brilliant, and Prokofiev said it was the best he had heard so far.

After Leningrad he gave two piano recitals in three of the chief cities of the provinces—Kiev, Kharkov, and Odessa. All three had legitimate claim to be considered music centers, since each had a conservatory, a concert hall, an opera house, and a symphony orchestra, yet they were still provincial, and Prokofiev was known to them mostly by hearsay: visiting musicians from Moscow and Leningrad had spoken of the Classical Symphony—some finding it good and others not— and of the March from *The Love for Three Oranges*. And they had not failed to point out that he had left Russia "years and years ago and lives somewhere abroad, in Paris or in the United States."

At his first concert in Odessa, Prokofiev had in his audience three boys who have since become world-famous artists: Emil Gilels, David Oistrakh, and Svyatoslav Richter.

I first met Richter in Prague in 1956, when the Soviet government's restrictions against his traveling outside Russia were beginning to be re- laxed. By then he was already considered one of the most brilliant virtu- osos in the Soviet Union, and since he was singled out particularly as the exponent of Prokofiev's piano works, our conversation naturally led to his reminiscing about his first impressions of the composer.

"I was twelve years old," Richter said. "Papa was teaching at the Conservatory, and I liked to spend days reading the opera scores at sight from beginning to end. One day Papa took Mama and me to the Conservatory—Prokofiev was going to play there. It was one of these dark winter days, and it was like twilight in the hall. A tall, slender young man with long arms came out on the stage. He was dressed in a Western-style suit, with much too short sleeves and trousers. This, perhaps, was why he gave us the impression of having outgrown his costume. Everything he wore was as checkered as the paper cover of his March from the opera, the March which everyone thought was marvelous. It was issued in a yellow paper cover adorned with little circles and squares to give it an air of novelty and Futurism!

"I remember that I thought the way he took a bow was very funny. He looked as if he were splitting in two—*chik!* His eyes never changed their expression—he looked straight ahead of him, and then, as he straightened up, he looked at the ceiling. His face remained expressionless.

"Then he played. I still remember that I was particularly impressed by his playing practically everything without a pedal, and with such perfection. He played many of his short pieces, and each one was of- fered like the sweet on a well-chosen menu. For me it was very un- usual, and very different from anything I had heard before. Because of my ignorance and childishness, it seemed to me that each piece played resembled the other. But then, at that time I felt the same way about the works of Bach.

"The audience seemed to like his playing, but, of course, they were anxiously awaiting the March. Then everybody was happy, and so was Prokofiev. He took his bows with a satisfied air, resembling either a circus magician, or a character from *The Tales of Hoffman*—it was hard to tell." *

Richter told me that he did not hear Prokofiev again until ten years later.

Emil Gilels, a year younger than Richter, retained only vague impressions of that concert, but Oistrakh, who was eighteen and had already been graduated from the Odessa Musical Institute during the previous year, had more to say about his first impressions of Prokofiev's music, as well as of the composer himself.

At that time, like the rest of the Odessa musicians, Oistrakh knew very little about Prokofiev. He had heard of the production of *The Love for Three Oranges* in Leningrad and of Joseph Szigeti's first performance of Prokofiev's Violin Concerto, which evoked a controversial reaction. Some praised the work, while others were critical and spoke of it with annoyance.

Preparing for his final examination, Oistrakh was eager to play something new. When, among the scores he received from Moscow bookstores, he found Prokofiev's concerto, he began to work on it. "I couldn't say," Oistrakh later related, "that I was immediately fascinated by the music—according to our taste at that time, there was much too much that was unusual in the character of the material, as well as in the way the composition was written."

But the more he penetrated the work, the more he was captivated by the melodious themes, the imaginative harmonizations, and the novelty of the technique. "It seemed to me," Oistrakh said, "like a landscape full of sunshine—as if the composer were inspired by the fresh breath of nature."

Oistrakh played the concerto at his graduation, and as had happened when Joseph Szigeti had played it, some of his listeners liked it and others found the music much too "invented," suffering from "musical nihilism" and a false conception of "novelty," an opinion that continued to plague most of Prokofiev's future works. Nevertheless, it did provoke unusual interest.

Now, almost a year later, Oistrakh attended Prokofiev's recital in Odessa. In the packed hall, among all the music enthusiasts in the audience, Oistrakh felt, as he said, as if it were his own birthday that was

---

* The foregoing account of this first view of Prokofiev appears almost verbatim in Richter's memoir, published in *S. S. Prokofiev: Materials, Documents, Reminiscences, op. cit.*

being celebrated. Meanwhile, he had an opportunity to hear the Classical Symphony, two fragments from *The Love for Three Oranges*, including the famous March, and several piano compositions. In addition to these, he himself played the Violin Concerto, all of which combined made him a connoisseur of Prokofiev's music.

After this concert the Odessa musical circles had organized a banquet in Prokofiev's honor at which several of his compositions were to be performed by local musicians. Oistrakh was chosen to play the Scherzo from the Violin Concerto.

At the Home of Science, where the event was held, Prokofiev was given an honorary place near the stage so that Oistrakh could not miss seeing Prokofiev's expression as he listened to Oistrakh's playing.

"The longer I played, the more grave his face became," Oistrakh said. "And when I finished, Prokofiev did not join in the applause. Paying no attention to the excitement of the audience, he walked toward the stage and asked my accompanist to let him have his place at the piano. Then turning to me, he said, 'Young man, you don't play it as it should be played,' and right then and there he began to explain and to show me the character of his composition."

That it was causing Oistrakh terrible embarrassment apparently meant nothing to Prokofiev, for the integrity of his music was challenged. Once before, in Paris, he was even less concerned with the feelings of a well-known soprano. After hearing her sing some of his songs, he said that she did not understand anything about his music and had better stop singing it. And he did not wait to make this remark until they were alone, but told her in front of a group of her admirers in a green room. When he saw that his reprimand had brought tears to her eyes, Prokofiev, sincerely amazed at her reaction, added, "There you go—all of you take refuge in tears instead of learning how to correct your faults."

Many years later, when Oistrakh, already known as a brilliant performer, played the concerto with Prokofiev at the conductor's desk to the composer's complete satisfaction, he reminded Prokofiev of his first visit to Odessa. To his surprise, Prokofiev remembered everything in minute detail: the programs of his recitals, how many encores he had played, and the "unfortunate young man" whom he scolded.

"Do you know who that young man was?" Oistrakh asked. And when Oistrakh told him, Prokofiev was very embarrassed. "You don't really mean it. . . ." he said. "You can't mean it."

After his short stay in Odessa, Prokofiev returned to Moscow for three final concerts, and then, with Lina, he returned to Paris, where Diaghilev had already begun rehearsals of *Le Pas d'acier*.

19

Sergei Prokofiev was not yet ready to return to Soviet Russia for good, since it would mean giving up his activities in the Western world. Although he was still allowed to leave the country, he knew well enough that in the future such permission could easily be denied him—depending on the whim of government authorities—and then he would be isolated from the rest of the world, a world where he had high hopes of realizing many of his projects.

The première of *Le Pas d'acier* on June 7, 1927, was one of Diaghilev's usual brilliant affairs. It was quite successful, although one spectator, Igor Stravinsky, was revolted by the noise of hammers and sickles on the stage. The young people in the audience, pleased with everything advanced and contrary to classical traditions, were naturally ecstatic—but not so the Parisian press.

"Of all Diaghilev's other productions this spectacle is the least pleasing to the eye," Pierre Lalo, the distinguished critic, wrote in *Commedia*. "The magnificence of Rimsky-Korsakov's Scheherazade, and Stravinsky's Nightingale were certainly missing in the performance. Against a bare background there were two elevated platforms on stage. Was this to remind us of the forced privations suffered by the people of the Soviet Union during the chaos and destruction left by the civil war? Do you think the public was disgusted? Not in the least. Snobs, rolling their eyes, sighed: charming, fascinating, amusing; and after the end of the performance the composer received seven curtain calls."

"It is a weird work beginning with its title and ending with its music and choreography," commented the daily papers, wondering whether it was the latest product of Diaghilev's limitless inventive talent or simply Bolshevik propaganda. "Was it perhaps meant to replace Glinka's opera *A Life for the Czar?*"

A month later, despite the Russian émigrés' crying "anathema" and accusing Diaghilev of being a tool of Soviet propaganda, he risked presenting the ballet to his admiring audience in London. "All the lords and ladies, led by the Prince of Wales, packed the house and applauded enthusiastically," Prokofiev said. "The flashing of diamonds hurt one's eyes."

The press, showing with bravado their sympathy for a "Bolshevik ballet," said, "For those acquainted with the Diaghilev productions, the performance of Prokofiev's Bolshevik ballet came somewhat as a shock. . . . But, if the 'red' composer writes better music than Stravinsky, then, of course, let us hear it" (*Daily Telegraph*, July 5, 1927).

"For years authors and orators have been telling us about it, and yet, Prokofiev's ballet expresses better the state of mind of contemporary Russia than all their endeavors put together" (*Empire News*).

"Prokofiev deserves fame," echoed other dailies. "As an apostle of Bolshevism he knows no equal." But the *Daily Mail* commented, "Prokofiev travels in a civilized world but he refuses to adhere to its way of thinking."

This reaction was actually prompted more by the choreography than by Prokofiev's music. Children selling cigarettes and candies, a grotesque-looking sailor with tattoos all over his body wearing one earring and one boot, a former countess in a torn dress bartering her jewelry for food, and dancers trying to portray the work of new machines to the accompaniment of the deafening noise of steam engines —this was a picture that would have startled any audience.

The character of Prokofiev's music was closer to Stravinsky's *Sacre du Printemps* and *Les Noces* than to that reflecting any Soviet influence, for the simple reason that he had written the ballet before he visited Russia. In fact, Soviet critics accused him later of a lack of knowledge of the contemporary Russian spirit and of disfiguring some of the old national themes with peculiar harmonies and his own "weird" treatment just to *épater les bourgeois*.

During the summer Prokofiev revised the score of *The Flaming Angel*. He had gained in experience and now saw more clearly the defects in the original version of the opera. He omitted everything that now appeared to him mere *remplissage* and simplified the orchestration. Several fragments from *The Flaming Angel* performed in concert form in Paris during the following spring (1928) were well received, thus making Prokofiev regret that the opera was still on the shelf, awaiting production. While considering the possibility of making an orchestral suite out of some parts of the score, he suddenly realized that he could make far better use of the material.

He discovered a sufficient wealth of themes for a symphony, his Third, which he regarded later as one of his more significant works. "I don't like it," he said, "when sometimes it is called "The Flaming Angel" Symphony. Naturally, in the opera the music was colored by the subject, but the symphonic music *per se*, at least in my opinion, loses this coloring, and therefore I wish the listener would accept the Third Symphony as a symphony, without any kind of programmatic subject."

He dedicated this work to Miaskovsky, and several years later he repeated what he had said all along: "I should not want the Soviet audience to judge me solely by the March from *The Love for Three Oranges* and the Gavotte from the Classical Symphony."

Besides the new Third Symphony, he was also planning the revision of his Second Symphony. After eight rehearsals, it was played in Paris on February 16, 1928, under the direction of Walther Straram (1876–1933), leader of the well-known Straram Concerts in Paris, at which Straram had performed the compositions written since 1910 of both French and foreign origin. Though this time Prokofiev thought that the symphony's intent was clearer than at its première in 1925, he still believed that he should find a way to express his ideas more simply. For the rest of his life he did not abandon this idea, and as late as 1953, shortly before his death, he finally decided to make three movements of the two in the symphony's original score.

In the spring of 1928 Diaghilev commissioned Prokofiev to write another ballet—this time on a Biblical theme—a big jump, Prokofiev thought, from the "Bolshevist exoticism" of the *Le Pas d'acier*. With his collaborators Diaghilev carved from the Gospel According to Saint Luke a scenario about the prodigal son who deserts his home: he squanders his money on drinking bouts with friends, is seduced by a "beautiful girl," but eventually, beaten and humiliated, returns to his father, who forgives him.

This simple subject caught Prokofiev's imagination, and he found working on the score both interesting and relatively easy, so easy, in fact, that in November, when Diaghilev inquired about his progress, he was able to say that he had already completed the rough draft of the piano score.

"What? Already? . . ." Diaghilev said in surprise. "If you have written it so quickly, then most probably . . . it is very bad." But when Prokofiev played it for him, Diaghilev was very pleased with it, and immediately engaged Georges Rouault, a French painter who belonged to Matisse's circle—the *"Fauves"*—to do the stage sets.

Prokofiev was in high spirits, not only because his composition pleased Diaghilev, but because on December 14, 1928, Lina had given birth to their second son, Oleg, an event Sergei had anxiously awaited.

Speaking of her husband as a parent, Lina said later that Prokofiev did not in the least resemble those sentimental fathers who upon every occasion show photographs of their children and, transported with joy, imitate their first incoherent sounds. Actually, she said, after the birth of Svyatoslav, their first son, Prokofiev was even jealous of Lina's attention to him and called him an "oyster"; but when he managed to be alone with the child, he would sit for hours by his crib and carefully study him. When Svyatoslav began to walk, his father loved to take him into the garden and watch his reactions to these new surroundings, laughing with utter delight when the boy stumbled or fell or suddenly sat down on the ground. Later, when the boys grew up, he enjoyed playing with them and helping them with their stamp collections. "During our long trips we used to leave the children with my parents," Lina said, "usually in the south of France, and after my father's death, with my mother in Paris." While on tour, Prokofiev wrote them amusing letters and sent them postcards of trains, boats, and planes.

Diaghilev planned the first performance of *The Prodigal Son* for his spring season in May of 1929, and Prokofiev had little time left to prepare the final version and to orchestrate the score, particularly since Pierre Monteux had already announced the first performance of the Third Symphony, as well as the Overture (Op. 42). The failure of the latter still disturbed Prokofiev and he wanted to re-examine the two scores carefully, for he felt the importance of both compositions in "reaching" the Parisian public. He was anxious about the Monteux performance because the conductor had set the date of the concert as May 17, only four days before Diaghilev's première of *The Prodigal Son*, which was scheduled for May 21. Prokofiev needed more time than he was allowed for this work.

In addition, he had to spend some time in Brussels, where *The Gambler* was at last premièred, on April 29, 1929, at the Opera Theatre. Although the theatre had at its disposal rather modest means for staging, the production was carefully prepared; the opera was so successful that it remained in the repertory for two years. Prokofiev was especially pleased with the dramatic intensity of the spectacle, which rose to a sustained climax at the end of the opera. He said that on the whole the press was rather kind, and that some critics even went a bit too far in their praise: "As one listens to *The Gambler*, one receives a pleasure similar to that derived from Mozart, except that it is written in a contemporary medium."

"*The Gambler*," Prokofiev said, "is the least 'Dostoyevskyan' of all Dostoyevsky's novels. Nevertheless, some actions of the characters in the story of the opera would have been understood differently in Russia than in Brussels. There, in Brussels, certain actions were considered as examples of the bewildering foolishness of the Slavic soul."

Prokofiev returned to Paris just in time for Monteux's and Diaghilev's rehearsals. Of the two, he had to give more attention to Monteux's forthcoming concert. Between rehearsals he was busy with the Scherzo of the Third Symphony, cutting or adding new material, and trying to find a proper proportion for the composition.

When finally the symphony was performed it gave rise, as all Prokofiev's works usually did, to controversial opinions, but generally speaking, the audience and the press received it respectfully, remarking that despite the various influences to which the composer had been exposed in Paris, he continued thinking in his own way—something that deserved praise. Prokofiev was amused as he read in one of the critics' columns that "The Scythian has at last descended to southern shores and become more human."

Because the rehearsals and the additional work on the symphony had taken most of his time, his own supervision of Diaghilev's production came too late. He was far from satisfied with the choreography, which in places did not follow the music, but there was no time left for any substantial change. To make things worse, a typical backstage intrigue among the performers was now about to sabotage the performance. Brewing for some time, it was based on personal as well as professional jealousies, the antics involving Diaghilev and Sergei Lifar, who was chosen for the leading role of *The Prodigal Son*. Their actions were purely hysterical, and it was fortunate that Prokofiev was wise enough to keep out of it.

After having heard the score again and again, Diaghilev told Lifar in December, "Much of it is very good. The last scene, the Prodigal's return, is beautiful. Your version, the awakening after the orgy, is new stuff for Prokofiev."

But when the company began the rehearsals on May 13, Diaghilev, for personal reasons, was in both a lethargic and a difficult mood. It soon became clear that he was losing his initial enthusiasm for *The*

Prodigal Son. Somehow the ballet refused to take shape and progressed slowly, according to Lifar, who was the most indolent of all, seldom attending rehearsals. Distressed, Diaghilev pleaded with him: "Don't you think it might be possible to put more life into the way the Prodigal is being interpreted?" or "Don't be afraid to put more feeling into your part. And don't be afraid to dramatize it, either, if you see it that way."

To add to their troubles, the preceding months, which Rouault had spent with the company in Monte Carlo, where the initial rehearsals had started, were wasted on general discussions of art, with the result that the painter had done nothing about the stage sets. Fortunately, Diaghilev gained access to Rouault's apartment in Paris, and from his sketches was able to contrive the necessary décor and costumes. All this caused conflicts between Prokofiev and Diaghilev.

After the dress rehearsal Diaghilev implored Lifar to save the performance: "Never before have I had a failure, but this time I feel we might," he said, "if you go on refusing to treat the Prodigal more dramatically, as it should be treated, instead of in your cold academic manner."

Later in the day Diaghilev telephoned Lifar, saying that he would not return to the hotel before the performance and asking him to send his dress clothes to the apartment of one of his friends. This was apparently more than the delicate Lifar could bear, for it meant to him that for the first time Diaghilev was dispensing with their solemn ritual of preparing for each première: as if leaving for a long, hazardous journey, according to an old Russian custom, the two would sit down in silence for a few last minutes before going to the theatre. Then Diaghilev would be the first to rise, and making the sign of the cross over Lifar, wish them both Godspeed.

Now Lifar, sulking, took to his bed, telling Diaghilev's cousin, who followed him everywhere like a duenna, that he refused to go to the theatre. "I don't feel I'm in symphathy with the part of the Prodigal Son, and I'm afraid I may turn it into a failure. I can't understand how they want me to treat the part. Let them act it themselves. I can't and I don't want to, and prefer to stay at home."

Although mute with terror, Diaghilev's cousin fortunately remained with Lifar, occasionally glancing nervously at his watch. He pleaded with him, but to no avail. Lifar would not get out of bed, not even when he was told that it was ten minutes past eight, just a few minutes before curtain time.

Then, according to Lifar, in a flash he saw his own life, starting—as any good psychiatric patient does—long before he had left Russia; his life with Diaghilev, who "lavished on him love, tenderness, and care, becoming his spiritual father"; and still later, his growing into an artist through this association, etc., until suddenly he saw himself as the Prodigal Son. Lifar leapt out of bed to run to the theatre in order not to desert his "spiritual father."

Prokofiev, completely unaware of all these shenanigans, had calmly taken his place at the conductor's desk and waited in silence for the extra fifteen minutes caused by Lifar's delay before he raised his baton for the beginning of his ballet.

The Prodigal Son was a success in Paris, and later in Berlin and London as well. But Prokofiev's relationship with Diaghilev was, like Stravinsky's, strained. That such inane behavior could occur in a responsible organization was incomprehensible to both musicians, whose disciplined natures could not tolerate it.

Two months later Diaghilev died in Venice, thus putting an end to Prokofiev's connection with the company, and at the same time deepening his relationship with Stravinsky.

20

It was characteristic of Prokofiev never to let anything he had written go to waste. Sooner or later he would either revise the whole composition or use some fragments in a new work. He firmly believed in this kind of "building" of the composition. Yet he was very critical of the material already written and particularly watchful not to repeat himself. Certainly he never "borrowed" from other composers, and above all, he avoided the beaten path, always searching for something new.

Many years later, Aram Khachaturian showed Prokofiev his piano concerto. Prokofiev scanned it and said, "It is not easy to write a concerto—you must always invent something. . . . I would advise you to note down all your own discoveries in the way you would like to execute your ideas before the subject itself has come to full fruition in your mind. Write down separate passages, and fragments, and the most interesting 'morsels'; these do not necessarily have to come in any preconceived order. Later, from these 'bricks' you will build the whole."

Now, during the summer of 1929, Prokofiev said that he had decided to clean house, "to pay his debt" to some of the accumulated musical material in his possession. He began with the Divertimento for Orchestra (Op. 43), a composition born of four different pieces written at various times. The first and third had been composed in 1925 for the roving ballet company of Boris Romanoff, Mikhail Fokine's pupil, who used to work at the Maryinsky Theatre in St. Petersburg. The music for a short ballet, *Trapeze*, did not particularly interest Prokofiev, but the first piece was so successful that Diaghilev had insisted on including it as an extra dance number between two scenes in

Le Pas d'acier. The fourth piece was originally written for *The Prodigal Son* but was not used. Now Prokofiev put all this material in order and orchestrated the new composition, whose title, *Divertimento*, was misleading, he said, because it could be applied only to the first piece, not to the composition as a whole.

He tried to create a rather subdued sound in the orchestra, and he admitted here to a certain influence of Stravinsky, whom he now saw quite often, and who suggested a more ascetic orchestration of the score. "Is it possible to expect me," Stravinsky asked, "to be fascinated by the 'festive dressing' of Rimsky-Korsakov?"

Prokofiev even went back to his youthful compositions, the Sinfonietta written in 1914. Never satisfied with its original version, he now took the whole composition apart to reassemble it after adding some new material. This time, he felt, he had succeeded in composing a rather charming piece, but to his chagrin it was relatively seldom performed, although in character it was close to the Classical Symphony.

At about this time, both he and Stravinsky were each commissioned by Koussevitzky to write a symphony for the fiftieth anniversary of the Boston Symphony Orchestra. At first, Prokofiev thought of using the material from *The Prodigal Son*, but on closer examination he discovered that it would be impractical to treat symphonically material already written for a ballet. Besides, he could already hear some critics say, "Aren't you beginning to turn dramatic music into symphonic a bit too often?" For that reason, he gave up the idea and made use instead, of music that had never been incorporated into *The Prodigal Son*. He worked on this symphony, his fourth, with several interruptions during the autumn of 1929 and the first part of 1930.

One interruption was caused by an accident that occurred in October, 1929. A year earlier, after long deliberation as to the choice of make, Prokofiev had bought a car—a small four-passenger Renault—and had learned to drive. To own a car was a long-cherished dream of his, and he behaved as if this new acquisition was his favorite toy. Almost daily he would bring home some kind of gadget: an extra taillight, a spotlight, a horn with an unusual combination of sounds, or a leather cushion for the driver's seat. As soon as his work permitted him to take time off, he would start on a trip with Lina—eventually, they crisscrossed the whole of France—or he would invite one or two friends to join them, and they would go on "gastronomic tours" of the country during which their on-the-road lunches and dinners were far more important than sightseeing in the towns through which they passed.

As a little boy, Sergei had had a passion for train schedules, and whenever he went with his mother to St. Petersburg or Moscow, he always kept a record of the mileage, the speed of the train, the delays, and so on. It gave him a particular pleasure to "compute" the timetable for Glière's journey to and from Sontsovka to Moscow. Now, after carefully studying the maps of France and constantly consulting the *Guide Michelin*—which, aside from indicating the noteworthy sights of each town, also stars the best hotels and restaurants—he would make a detailed itinerary, according to which travel time was divided into arrival, departure, meals, and stops for the night.

Nothing could possibly sway him from this schedule. Not even Lina—when, attracted by a "cozy" inn in picturesque surroundings, she expressed her preference for it over the three-star restaurant on her husband's list, or when she and their guests wished to visit old châteaux, churches, museums, or any other historical monuments of great interest to most tourists—could persuade him to stop unless they were scheduled to do so. The mere suggestion of such a frivolous attitude toward his plans and timetable irritated Prokofiev, and with a bored expression, he would brush the suggestion aside as a "phony, gravedigging ritual." The only comment he made as he looked at the cathedral at Chartres was, "I wonder how they got those statues up so high without dropping them."

Prokofiev, an enthusiastic but not a good driver, drove either too cautiously, at a speed of twenty miles per hour, or pushed the car almost to its full capacity, which finally caused an accident that could have been serious if not fatal, for him and his family.

It occurred when they were returning to Paris from one of their pleasure trips. Lina was sitting next to her husband, who was driving while their two boys were in the back with their Dutch nurse, Elsa. Lina called Prokofiev's attention to something that was wrong with a rear wheel, and they stopped at the nearest town, leaving the car in a garage for repairs. But on the following day, while Prokofiev was driving at full speed to make up for lost time, the car suddenly lurched to one side, and there was a terrible crash.

It happened so quickly that this was all Lina could remember when she came to: they had lost one wheel, the car was lying on its side, and the children were crying. Fortunately, the boys and their nurse were merely bruised, but Prokofiev lay semiconscious in his seat. He had suffered a slight concussion and could not use his hands for two months. Lina had narrowly escaped a serious injury to one eye, which, even so, was badly bruised.

Another interruption to the composition of his Fourth Symphony was his second journey to Russia in November. This time, because of the injuries to his hands, he had to cancel all concerts, and he was glad because, he said, his concertizing during the previous trip had given him little opportunity to see life in Soviet Russia. It also gave him a chance to attend a performance of *The Love for Three Oranges* at the Bolshoi Theatre in Moscow on November 13.

The production was far more lavish than that given in Leningrad, but the elaborate stage sets required so much time for changes in scenes that the entr'actes turned out to be longer than the acts. "It is 'The Love for Three Entr'actes'—that's what it is," grumbled the audience, forced into nomadic pastimes in the opera house lobby.

But Prokofiev refrained from criticizing the production since something else, far more important, was in the offing: he had heard that the directors of the Bolshoi had asked Meyerhold to direct a production of his ballet, *Le Pas d'acier*.

Prokofiev's friendship with Vsyevolod Meyerhold was of long standing. It was Meyerhold who had suggested to Prokofiev that he write an opera on Gozzi's *The Love for Three Oranges*, and who had given him a copy of the magazine he was editing in which Gozzi's play was published.

While Prokofiev had been abroad, Meyerhold's theatrical productions had become very popular, and as early as 1923 he was awarded the highest honorary title, People's Artist of the Republic. Born in 1874, Meyerhold had been a student at the Moscow University Law School and later in the drama class at the Musical-Dramatic School of the Moscow Philharmonic Society. After his graduation he worked for four years (1898–1902) as an actor at the Moscow Art Theatre, and later, as a talented director, he experimented in theatrical productions in Moscow and St. Petersburg. After the Revolution, from 1920 on, he was in charge of the U.S.S.R. Theatre, which later bore his name: the Meyerhold Theatre. When Prokofiev was leaving Russia in 1918 to seek his fortune abroad, Meyerhold was already a member of the Communist Party, thus enhancing and strengthening his position as the leading Soviet theatrical figure.

Meyerhold followed Prokofiev's activities abroad with great interest, and in his discussion of the reforms in opera-writing that he delivered for the members of the theatres on January 1, 1925, he brought Prokofiev's name to their attention. "Prokofiev wrote an opera based on a novel by Dostoyevsky—*The Gambler*," he said. "The opera has not been published anywhere. It is not the subject but the method of construction of the composition that is interesting for the development of a new art in opera-writing. Prokofiev has excluded from his score the arias and endless melodies à la Wagner. Also, in this new dra-

matic composition, the text has not been put into verse. The whole
opera is a continuation of Moussorgsky's art as exemplified in *The
Marriage* and *Boris Godunov*."

Later, during the summer of 1928, Meyerhold came to Paris, where,
with a select group of actors from his theatre, he presented several
performances of Gogol's *The Inspector General* and of Ostrovsky's
The Storm. He spent several months in France, often visited Prokofiev, and upon his return to Russia, sought to produce *The Gambler*.
To ward off any objections based on possible prejudices against Prokofiev, Meyerhold declared, "I am taking this opportunity to express
my indignation toward those irresponsible comrades who assail Prokofiev as an *immigrant*, and the kind of immigrant that should be boycotted. I would suggest that, before attacking Prokofiev, these comrades
take the trouble to read some Western reviews of his ballet *Le Pas
d'acier*, in which he is branded an Apostle of Bolshevism."

But nothing came of Meyerhold's endeavors to produce *The Gambler*. Determined to promote Prokofiev's works in Soviet Russia, he
telegraphed Prokofiev in Paris in January, 1929, and asked if he would
consider writing an opera based on Mayakovsky's *The Bedbug*. Because of his lack of free time, Prokofiev had to decline this suggestion,
and Meyerhold turned the idea over to Dmitri Shostakovich. Now in
the autumn of 1929 the directors of Bolshoi offered Meyerhold the direction of Prokofiev's *Le Pas d'acier* on the same program with Shostakovich's recently completed three-act opera *The Nose*, based on
Gogol's satire on the epoch of Nicholas I.

Well aware of the critical attitude of certain groups in musical and
theatrical circles toward Prokofiev, Meyerhold once more, in his report
of October 9, warned the directors of the Bolshoi against the "over-
simplified" position toward creative artists. "Because of certain personal circumstances, Prokofiev lives in Paris and not in Moscow," he
said. "But we should not say that he is not *one of us* on account of it.
Although he lives in Paris, he can still agree with *us* because, in his
inner feelings, he is with us. A street address does not mean anything.
The language and the subject of his writing are far more important."

On the day after Prokofiev had attended the production of *The
Love for Three Oranges* at the Bolshoi, he was asked to come to Beethoven Hall, where an audition of *Le Pas d'acier* was to be given for
the directors of the Bolshoi and the members of Russia's Association
of Proletarian Musicians (RAPM). Such auditions amounted to critical examinations of a composer's work, followed by "comradely discussions" of the composition's merits which in Soviet Russia determined
the fate of the work. At that time the notorious RAPM's was the

leading voice in such matters, and in its ruthless way it dictated its own "left trend" to those composers who did not sympathize with its ideas. For the first time in his life Sergei Prokofiev was given a taste of these "comradely discussions."

In published articles, as well as in oral declarations, RAPM had already branded Sergei Prokofiev an enemy of Soviet culture, insisting that there was no hope of leading him to the path of "realism." These attacks were hardly conducive to gaining his favor, but since the directors of the Bolshoi were supported by the magazine *Contemporary Music*, which, referring to *Le Pas d'acier* as a "revolution in ballet," had predicted its success all over Soviet Russia, Prokofiev decided to attend the session.

The "comradely discussions" turned out to be rather stormy. The leaders of RAPM, showing off their decisive role in the matter, were responsible for the tenor of this conference: they greeted Prokofiev with open antagonism. Prokofiev tried to defend his work and himself, but in vain. Not even Meyerhold's courageous attitude could save Prokofiev's ballet.

Nevertheless, three days later at Prokofiev's recital in the Radio Theatre—the only one he agreed to give during this visit to Russia—Meyerhold made an introductory speech in which he said, "It is Prokofiev's fate that, despite being drawn toward us, he is compelled at present to remain abroad for a while because of his concert engagements and the contracts he must fulfill. Still, I repeat that although he lives in the West, his creative tendencies are entirely directed toward a harmonious relationship with the great work of our epoch. . . . Prokofiev is an active fighter against the diffuse, precious music nursed in the hothouses of so-called modernism. It is understandable that as early as 1915, he was attacked by the decadent middle classes. The basic tenor of his music reflects our epoch. His art pours like a powerful stream into Russian contemporary music, which is in principle different from Western European music. Does the West attract Prokofiev? To this question you can find an answer in his *Le Pas d'acier* and the attitude that the West had taken toward him. And to realize the propaganda value of his ballet, it is sufficient to read the Paris and London press. Prokofiev does our job in the West. He is our musical advance guard."

But even the championing by such an eminent personality in Soviet theatrical and cultural matters as Meyerhold made not the slightest impression on RAPM's stand against Prokofiev. Shortly afterward, "commissioned by the Plenum and Soviet of RAPM," two articles appeared in the magazine *Proletarian Music* (No. 6, 1929) in which, in no uncertain terms, Sergei Prokofiev was completely "annihilated" and his ballet stigmatized as a "flat and vulgar anti-Soviet anecdote, a counter-revolutionary composition bordering on Fascism."

Those who disagreed with the all-powerful verdict nevertheless called off the preparations for the production of the ballet, and kowtowed to the "legitimate decision." "Prokofiev's intentions to turn toward Soviet subjects indisputably deserve support," the composer's bootlicking comrades would babble. "We should help him in a comradely way to find the true path in solving this problem."

But such remarks were not uttered at the time; they were recorded almost thirty years later, after Stalin's death, when in a short breathing spell of freedom of expression everyone felt it necessary to echo the "brave" critics of the past with their "I told you so."

Thus, when in Western countries Sergei Prokofiev was regarded as a "red" composer, an "apostle of Bolshevism," "a tool of Soviet propaganda," he was branded in the Soviet Union as an enemy of Soviet culture, his latest work "bordering on Fascism."

On this occasion Prokofiev's visit to Russia was short. In December he was on his way back to Paris to conduct the first performance of the Divertimento, and I wonder whether, on his long train journey to France, Anton Rubinstein's remark of some fifty years before did not come to his mind.

"Composers say I am a pianist and pianists say I am a composer," Rubinstein had said. "Some say that I am the author of advanced ideas in music, while others prove that I am the apostle of everything old-fashioned and dull. The Germans say I am a Russian, and the Russians say I am a German; the Jews say I am a gentile, and gentiles say I am a Jew—now, Who the hell am I?"

Both musicians needed no answer. But if, with his sense of humor, Rubinstein could brush off such inane accusations, Sergei Prokofiev needed more than merely a sense of humor in dealing with the Soviet decisions. It must have taken all his stamina and self-control not to say what Mikhail Glinka, the "Father of Russian National Music," had said some seventy years before as he was leaving the country following severe criticism of his work. Glinka had stepped out of the carriage that was taking him to Germany to have a last look at St. Petersburg; and he exclaimed, "Cursed be this land that I hope never to see again."

21

At the beginning of 1930 the Prokofievs returned to the United States. Prokofiev was to take part in twelve concerts and in eleven recitals in which Lina was to participate as a singer.

This time he was received with even more respect by both the public and the press—they had become used to his name, he said. The twelve years that had passed since his first visit to this country showed the remarkable progress America had made in musical matters, Prokofiev observed.

"Although Americans like to have their own independent judgment—'we, the richest country in the world, have a right to invite and to choose and judge whom we wish'—still, from pure caution Americans keep one eye on European opinions," Prokofiev remarked.

This concert tour, which took Prokofiev and Lina all the way across the country and to Canada and Cuba, he found most pleasant. For a while the Metropolitan Opera House carried on negotiations for a production of *The Flaming Angel*, but nothing came of it. Prokofiev blamed an American woman, who, he said, was sponsoring the Metropolitan with a large sum and whose remark had sealed the verdict: "Our theatre is so large that our boxes are a whole block away from the singers on the stage. How then do you expect all your finest points to reach us?"

Prokofiev did understand that *The Flaming Angel* was not sufficiently alive dramatically—there were many "stagnant" places in the score. One of the stage designers at the Metropolitan offered a suggestion about refreshing such places visually if it were impossible to do it dramatically—that is, to divide an act that was particularly slow in its development into several scenes with different stage sets, thus creating a new impression and accelerating the pace of action. Prokofiev liked the idea and even sketched a new plan that did not demand radical changes in the opera, but because of the failure in negotiations for a production at the Metropolitan, he hoped to return to it later. But he never did.

Instead, upon his return from the United States, he began a string quartet (Op. 50), commissioned by the Library of Congress. To prepare himself for this task, he studied Beethoven's quartets, usually on trains going from one city to another during his tours. This study, he explained, led to a sort of classical character of the first movement.

The quartet's first performance was given in Washington on April 15 of the following year (1931), and later in the same year Ferenc Roth's string quartet was sent by the Library of Congress to Europe to perform the compositions, including Prokofiev's, that it had commissioned. Prokofiev's quartet was introduced by Roth's ensemble in Moscow on October 5, 1931.

During the summer the Paris Grand Opera commissioned from Prokofiev a ballet entitled *Sur le Borysthène*—an ancient name for the Dnieper River in the Ukraine. "We in Russia like long ballets," Prokofiev said, "but in the Western countries they prefer them to be short so that in one evening three ballets or one ballet and a short opera can be given. This preference stems from the fact that *we* consider the subject and its development in the ballet important, while in the Western countries the subject plays a secondary role—three one-act ballets performed in one evening offer much more entertainment when provided by three choreographers, three stage directors, and three composers." Therefore, the subject of the ballet that Prokofiev composed with his collaborators was not so much their aim as it was the means to achieve a kind of musico-choreographical composition.

The story of the ballet was extremely simple: A soldier falls in love with a peasant girl, but her father wants her to marry someone else. The engagement feast is interrupted by the soldier, who challenges the fiancé—the culminating dramatic point of the ballet—but who is overpowered by other guests and tied to a tree. In the last scene, to the accompaniment of quiet and "pensive" music, the girl frees her beloved soldier.

Planning the ballet with Sergei Lifar from purely choreographic structure, Prokofiev composed abstract music without any specific idea for a basis of the ballet. The locale of the action and the type of characters the heroes were to represent were utterly unimportant. Thus, the title had no direct relation to the ballet—except for the stage sets and costumes designed by Mikhail Larionov and Natalie Goncharova, the Russian painters who were living in Paris. In Prokofiev's score there was not the slightest trace of Ukrainian national color.

The ballet was approved by the Grand Opera, but it was not performed until the end of 1932. This time the postponement of the première resulted from the general economic depression in France. The government subsidy was not sufficient for a new production, and the director of the opera, who previously had come to its rescue with his own funds, had resigned.

In its style the ballet was close to *The Prodigal Son*, but it had a different fate: whereas the latter was immediately successful in Paris, the première of *Sur le Borysthène* at the Grand Opera on December 16, 1932, just passed muster. Despite the well-mounted production, Prokofiev's lyricism "did not reach" the public, and the ballet survived only a few performances.

In Prokofiev's own opinion it was not due to a lack of lyricism—"the lyricism of my youthful period was understood only ten years later; let's hope that *Borysthène* will have its turn too. Original invention in a composition is even more important than its integral content," Prokofiev claimed further. "The great classicists were great 'original inventors.' If a composer happens to 'invent' something without sufficient content, someone else will use his invention, and adding to it a good subject, will become known to posterity. But if a composer is either unwilling or incapable of the original invention, then sooner or later he would be relegated to the archives."

A year later Prokofiev made an orchestral suite out of the ballet, using the best material from the score.

He also wrote what he called his Fourth Piano Concerto, a concerto for the left hand alone commissioned by Paul Wittgenstein. Serving as a dragoon officer in the Austrian Army during World War I, Wittgenstein had been wounded and taken prisoner by the Russians. Although he had lost his right arm, his former piano teacher in Vienna offered to write for him a concerto for the left hand.

Through his family connections Wittgenstein was exchanged for another Russian prisoner of war in Austria and returned to Vienna long before the end of the war. There, he first devoted himself to acquiring the necessary technique for playing with the left hand alone, and later, since the original piano literature provided a rather small repertory for "one hand," Wittgenstein began to commission piano concertos from the well-known contemporary composers, including

Richard Strauss, Franz Schmidt, Erik Korngold, Paul Hindemith, and Maurice Ravel.

Upon receiving Prokofiev's concerto, Wittgenstein wrote to him, "Thank you for your concerto, but I do not understand a single note of it, and shall not play it." Actually, it was not Prokofiev's fault. Wittgenstein admitted to me on several occasions that his taste and even understanding of music was limited and did not go further than the period of Brahms. Thus, Prokofiev's composition was alien to him.

I believe that he had never even tried to learn its content, but, discouraged, left it on a shelf in his library. Shortly before Wittgenstein's death I introduced to him Yuri Bukov, the Bulgarian pianist, who was anxious to see the concerto; and I could not ignore Wittgenstein's surprise and even sudden interest in the composition when Bukov brilliantly sight-read Prokofiev's manuscript. It is also possible that the thirty years that had passed since Wittgenstein had first looked at the concerto had something to do with his awakened interest. In the interim, he had heard a great deal of contemporary music, and his ear must have become more attuned to such a medium.

A young German pianist, Siegfried Rapp, who, like Wittgenstein in World War I, lost the use of his right arm in World War II, also like Wittgenstein wanted to continue his career. To enlarge his repertory he obtained the score of Prokofiev's concerto, and gave its first performance in the Conservatory Hall in West Berlin on September 5, 1956, almost twenty-five years after Prokofiev had completed the composition.

But Prokofiev was no longer alive, and at the time of Wittgenstein's refusal to play it, Prokofiev had said, "I myself am not sure about this concerto: at times I like it, and then again—I don't. I should find time to make a new version, but for two hands." This intention, however, was never fulfilled.

Instead, Prokofiev wrote his Fifth Piano Concerto. In the ten years that had passed since he had composed his Third Piano Concerto, he had acquired a new conception of how to treat this form of composition, as well as some purely technical "innovations," that intrigued him, and he was anxious to experiment with them: a passage of a run across the whole keyboard, in which the left hand overtakes the right, or a succession of chords with the piano and orchestra constantly interrupting each other.

At first he planned a simple and easily performed composition—he even intended to name it "Music for Piano with Orchestra," so that one would not be confused by the order of concertos' numbers, since to all intents and purposes the fourth was no longer there. But in the end the composition turned out to be complicated, "a fatal occurrence," Prokofiev said, "pursuing me in several of my works at that time." He admitted that while he was seeking "simplicity," he was afraid that this "simplicity" would turn into a repetition of old forms, into the "old simplicity" that certainly would have been out of place in a new composition.

In experimenting with a "new simplicity," he often discovered that with "new technique" and particularly with "new intonations" the simplicity would not be acceptable. "Sometimes I could not succeed in writing this or that passage simply," Prokofiev said, "but I never lost hope that with time one's ear would become better attuned to these ways of phrasing." This concerto was his last composition before he went once again to Russia.

On October 31, 1932, he introduced the concerto in Berlin, with the Berlin Philharmonic under Wilhelm Furtwängler's direction, and on November 25 he performed it in Moscow. Late in December of 1932 Prokofiev returned to the United States for a series of performances with orchestras in which he played both the Third and Fifth Concertos. "In Chicago," he said, "in the middle of the fourth movement of the Fifth Concerto, I fumbled and had to begin the passage all over again, but Frederick Stock did not flinch and caught me in time." And in New York he heard Bruno Walter in a Suite from *The Gambler*.*

After completing his tour in the United States, exhausted by living in trains between his concert appearances, Prokofiev returned to Europe to fulfill the remaining concert engagements. Then he went back to Moscow, and this time for good.

Then, and ever since, musicians all over the Western world have been puzzled by the question: What prompted Sergei Prokofiev to make this final decision, a step that would obviously isolate him, even if only in a physical sense, from the Western world?

I have always felt that it is futile to read anything into his decision. He made several "preliminary" trips to the Soviet Union, and therefore by then was well acquainted with the political, economic, and cultural conditions in Russia. He knew what he was doing. He had weighed carefully all the pros and cons.

If in 1929 he still believed that "music and politics are incompatible, even mutually rejecting each other" and that "a dedicated musician can exist with a sole interest in his art as a thing in itself," now he had come to the conclusion that the musical life in the Western world had limited ideas. "In fact," he said, "there are no ideas. I am not interested

---

* This concert is described earlier.

in my ancestors, and I am losing interest in the future of European [Western] music.

"Darius Milhaud has presented his opera *Maximilian* at the Grand Opera in Paris," Prokofiev commented. "His hero—the only Mexican Emperor who perished during the Revolution in Mexico. Milhaud is capable of writing large national scenes, but his tendency toward lyricism has limited the subject to a personal tragedy of the unsuccessful Emperor." Prokofiev had undoubtedly expected Milhaud to treat the subject as Moussorgsky had done in his *Boris Godunov*. (Moussorgsky had portrayed the drama of the Russian people and not the Czar Boris' personal tragedy, as it appears in Rimsky-Korsakov's well-known "rearranged" version.)

"Another French composer, Roussell, has offered his ballet *Vakh* on an ancient Greek theme, and his latest opera, *Padmavati*, on a subject from Indian life, again a turn toward history, toward archaic subjects, or toward the erotic, which no longer interest me."

Prokofiev saw what had happened to those Russian composers who had left Russia: Medtner, Rachmaninoff, Stravinsky. "Medtner's former fascinating individual technique is reduced to chewing over and over again old means of expression," Prokofiev said, accurately judging Medtner's work. After leaving Russia, Medtner had not written anything of importance. "And Stravinsky," Prokofiev added, "has lately turned away completely from program music. After his Violin Concerto he wrote duets for piano and violin." "Rachmaninoff, whose talent for melodies I have always admired," Prokofiev said, "now is solely preoccupied with concertizing, playing his old compositions. He has written nothing new. Or if he does compose, it is in most cases a work based on somebody else's material—for example his Variations on a Theme by Corelli."

Medtner, in my opinion, had written himself out even before he left Russia, and therefore I doubt that if he had remained or returned to Russia, he would have shown any radical change in his compositions. Of all Russian composers, Stravinsky is a cosmopolitan, for as Asafiev had pointed out as early as 1914, "in all varied cultures he is at home."

Rachmaninoff, more than the other two, had definitely suffered from living in self-imposed exile. He never tried to suppress his nostalgia, and the older he became, the more pronounced it was. He had spent twenty-five years in the United States and Europe, but "in all varied [non-Russian] cultures he was never at home," he never mastered the English language well enough to be able to attend a single theatrical performance or to wish to read anything besides Sinclair Lewis' *Main Street*.

He missed just the kind of musical life in Russia that Prokofiev had spoken of so often, with its discussions of the latest works by their colleagues, and as late as 1943, he said to me, "With whom in America, I ask you, should I talk about my work?"

He had lost his native soil—"the air smells different here," he said. He had lost *his* audience—his people, his sounding board, as he said. And this was the core of Prokofiev's nostalgia. Rachmaninoff wept when, during the last war he heard the recordings of Russian songs, and Prokofiev most probably feared facing a similar fate.

"He is tremendously proud of being a Russian (an attitude not too common among Russians)," Nicolas Nabokov, who knew him well, wrote in an article about Prokofiev.* "He considers his people superior in gifts, particularly as far as music is concerned, to many other peoples in Europe. He is proud of Russian history, Russian literature, Russian art, and there never has been a doubt in his mind about the great destiny and future of his country. When the Revolution occurred and most of the intelligentsia and bourgeoisie fled from Russia, Prokofiev did a very rare thing for those days. He went to the Soviet Government, took out a passport, and left Russia in a perfectly legitimate manner. He saw that it would not be wise to become an outlaw.

"Later in Paris, when people were doubting and worrying over Russia's future, he was continuously repeating in words and acts that the Revolution for him was an inescapable, positive event of Russia's national history, and he did not see in it, as so many of his compatriots did at that time, a desperate and fatal calamity. He believed that the Russian Revolution was teaching a lesson to the West and would ultimately lead to a regeneration of European society."

To his friends in Paris who were anxious about his decision to return to Russia, Prokofiev said:

Foreign air does not suit my inspiration, because I'm Russian, and that is to say the least suited of men to be an exile, to remain in a psychological climate that isn't that of my race. My compatriots and I carry our country about with us. Not all of it, to be sure, but a little bit, just enough for it to be faintly painful at first, then increasingly so, until at last it breaks us down altogether. You can't altogether understand, because you don't know my native soil, but look at those compatriots of mine who are living abroad. They are drugged with the air of their country. There's nothing to be done about it. They'll never get it out of their systems. I've got to go back. I've got to live myself back into the atmosphere of my native soil. I've got to see real winter again, and spring that bursts into being from one moment to the next. I've got to hear the Russian language echoing in my

* *Atlantic Monthly,* July, 1943.

ears, I've got to talk to people who are my own flesh and blood, so that they can give me back something I lack here—their songs—my songs. Here I'm getting enervated. I risk dying of academism. Yes, my friends! I'm going back.*

And was he not repeating what Chopin had said—Chopin, who also went into exile for political reasons, an exile that was the principal motive for the drama in his life, and who, shortly before his death, wished to return to his native Poland, despite the Russian occupation? He wanted to hear once again the songs of Poland—his native songs.

Perhaps I should add to all this what Sergei Prokofiev told me when we walked on the barren Champs de Mars in Paris in 1932, when he had already made up his mind to return to Russia. "First of all," he said, "I have two sons who speak French like Russians and Russian like Frenchmen. And I want them to speak at least their own language properly. I also want them to be educated in Russia. And then, here I have to kowtow to publishers, managers, all sorts of committees, sponsors of productions, patronesses of art, and conductors each time I wish my work to be performed. A composer doesn't have to do that in Russia. And as for 'politics,' they don't concern me. It is none of my business."

* Serge Moreux: "Prokofiev—An Intimate Portrait," *Tempo*, London, Spring, 1949.

PART THREE
1936-1953

22

At first it was not easy for Prokofiev to gain the favor of his audiences or, for that matter, even to make contact with his public. The Fifth Concerto, the "Portraits" from *The Gambler,* the Sonata for Two Violins, and the String Quartet (Op. 50) were criticized for lacking "actuality of subject matter" and the natural joyous character that had been so seductive in his youthful compositions. Even his old friend Miaskovsky found these works of the "Parisian period" somewhat strange—interesting, but dry.

Prokofiev took this negative attitude in Moscow and Leningrad as a warning not to overload his programs with his latest compositions when he concertized in small musical centers. "It is dangerous," he said. "Neither the orchestras nor the audiences are apt to be receptive." And yet he kept repeating to himself that he did not wish to be known solely for the March from *The Love for Three Oranges,* and the Gavotte from the Classical Symphony. Because of the singular popularity in the United States of his Prelude in C-Sharp Minor, Sergei Rachmaninoff was nicknamed "Mister C-Sharp Minor." Prokofiev did not want a similar thing to happen to him, even if only in jest.

Again and again he was asked: What sort of music did *he* believe a Soviet composer should write?

". . . Music should be written in a grand style—that is, both the subject matter and the technique of its delivery should reflect the large scope of the development of a new era in Soviet Russia," Prokofiev had written in an article published in *Izvestia* (November 16, 1934). "Such music would guide us to new musical forms, and would show abroad our 'true image.' In the Soviet Union music exists for the millions who formerly had to live without it or who rarely came into direct contact with it. It is those new millions whom the contemporary Soviet composer must serve."

In these two remarks his critics had detected "echoes of his former modernistic view of art, a tendency to divide music into two categories: a higher—for the 'connoisseurs,' and a lower—for everyone else." But apparently to pacify those who prescribed the stringent principles for artists, Prokofiev went on to say that it is not so simple to write this kind of music, and that the danger of Soviet composers falling into provincialism was only too real.

"It is not an easy task to find the necessary language for this sort of music," he said again and again. "First of all, it has to be melodious, and the melody should be simple and easily understood without being imitative or trivial. Many composers find it difficult to compose a melody of any kind; therefore, it is even more difficult to compose a melody with a definite purpose. The same idea should apply to the technique of writing: it should be clear and simple, but not commonplace. And its simplicity should not be old-fashioned but contemporary."

That Prokofiev firmly believed in these principles can be seen from the fact that years later he repeated that they were still as valid as they had been before, and that his views had already forecast those that developed later.

But actually Prokofiev himself was not quite ready to test his theories. "I didn't feel like risking being wrong," he said. "Therefore I was very happy when Belgoskino asked me to write music for the film *Lieutenant Kijé*. This gave me an opportunity to experiment even though not with a Soviet subject—nevertheless, with music for a Soviet audience, and a very large one."

Prokofiev always considered motion pictures to be one of the vital contemporary arts, but accused the "uneducated" directors of "unmusicality." "Perhaps because of the early stage of development of this art, we in Russia have not learned to value the other 'member' in the structure of the film, and are apt to regard music as something of a 'sideline,' not deserving much attention," he said. He firmly believed that music should have as important a dramatic function in the structure of the film.

Lieutenant Kijé was based on a novella of the same name by Yuri Tynyanov, and its satirical plot suited Prokofiev's sense of humor perfectly. The problems and tribulations of Lieutenant Kijé stem from a mistake committed by a military clerk who inscribed the nonexisting lieutenant into the military register. The mythical lieutenant becomes

a victim of the all-powerful bureaucratic machine: He receives a
commission, marries, and dies.

The story takes place at the beginning of the nineteenth century
during the reign of the Czar Paul, whose mania for military discipline,
uniforms, and parades in strict Prussian style bordered on insanity. It
has been said that after reviewing one of his interminable parades,
Paul remarked to his aide-de-camp, "It is a pity that you can still see
them breathe."

In his score Prokofiev succeeded not only in illustrating sarcastically
the ridiculous situation of the story, but also in vividly re-creating the
ludicrous barrackslike atmosphere of Czar Paul's St. Petersburg.

Unfortunately, the dénouement of the film was often changed, over-
burdening and confusing its end to such an extent that a year later
Prokofiev preferred to make an orchestral suite out of his original
score. "It's a devil of a work," he said, "but then how gay and amusing the music is!" And indeed, the Lieutenant Kijé Suite has become
one of his popular works, while the film has been completely forgotten.

Almost at the same time as he was still working on the score for
Lieutenant Kijé, Prokofiev was commissioned to write the incidental
music for a dramatic play The Egyptian Nights, which was to be given
at the Kamerny Theatre in Moscow. The play was a curious combination of a monologue from Pushkin's The Egyptian Nights, Bernard
Shaw's Caesar and Cleopatra (with its portrayal of Cleopatra's youth),
and Shakespeare's Antony and Cleopatra (depicting Cleopatra's last
days).

"Despite Bernard Shaw's charming wit, the old man Shakespeare appeared such a titan that he was awarded a bigger part in the play,"
Prokofiev said. "Having been ruthlessly cut, Shaw lost in stature and
became an unimportant addition in the beginning of the spectacle."

The première did not take place until a year and a half later. Alexander Tairov (1885–1950), the stage director, and the conductor Alexander Medtner (the composer's brother) did the best they could with
it, but the play turned out to be much too artificial to be successful.
Nevertheless, this was Prokofiev's first experiment with Shakespeare's
drama, and it ignited his interest in the English dramatist's powerful,
passionate characters. As usual he made an orchestral Suite out of
those parts of the score that were not merely serving as accompaniment to the action on the stage.

In fact, after long deliberation, with a nota bene for conductors to
omit it à piacere, he even included one of those "purely accompani-

ment" numbers, "The Alarum," written for percussion instruments alone: bass, side drum, and kettledrum. "Surprisingly enough," Prokofiev remarked later, "this number won the audiences wherever the suite was played." But he felt that the best part of the score was "The Eclipse of Cleopatra."

Needless to say, while surprised by his return to the Soviet Union, France did not forget Prokofiev. A group of admirers of Robert Soetens, the violinist, commissioned Prokofiev to write a violin concerto, stipulating that the violinist would have the exclusive rights to perform it for one year.

"As with my previous concertos," Prokofiev said, "at first I looked for another title, something like 'a concert sonata for violin and orchestra,' but in the end I called it simply Violin Concerto No. 2." With this concerto was associated a long concert tour through Spain, Portugal, Morocco, Algeria, and Tunis during which, besides the concerto, Soetens performed with Prokofiev Debussy's sonata and one of Beethoven's.

The concerto was introduced in Madrid on December 1, 1935. As Prokofiev mounted the podium, he was given a standing ovation by the orchestra and the audience, who greeted him as the first eminent Soviet artist to visit Spain. The Spaniards were very proud that the première was given in their capital, and a special delegation called on the composer to express their gratitude.

On his tour through the country Prokofiev was impressed by a remarkable interest in music in Madrid, Barcelona, and San Sebastian, and particularly by the Spaniards' curiosity about Soviet Russia and the cultural life there. "No matter where I played," he recalled later, "always after a concert, either in a café or at a supper, I was asked thousands of questions about life in the Soviet Union. The Spaniards were especially interested in our unions of creative artists, our system of contracting the works, and the centralization of our symphonic orchestras and concerts."

During these travels abroad, Prokofiev also became active in promoting in England, France, and Italy the works of his musical colleagues and carried on long negotiations with the West European composers and conductors. On his recommendation Dmitri Mitropoulos was invited as both conductor and pianist for a concert tour in Soviet Russia.

In turn, the European musicians followed with keen interest Prokofiev's latest accomplishments, and at the beginning of 1934 he was awarded an honorary membership in the Academy of Saint Cecilia in Rome.

"The Roman Academy made me an honorary member," Prokofiev wrote to his friends in Russia, "so much the worse for me. The cycle is completed—I used to tear things down, and now I am inscribed as an academician."

Meanwhile, the Leningrad Opera and Ballet Company was planning a new production. Their choice was Shakespeare's *Romeo and Juliet,* but influenced by the general criticism of such a project, they soon gave up the idea. The project was taken over by the Bolshoi Theatre in Moscow, and Prokofiev was asked to write the music.

During the spring of 1935 Prokofiev worked out a scenario in collaboration with Sergei Radlov (1892–1958)—the stage director who was well-known for his productions of *Hamlet, King Lear,* and *Othello*—often consulting with a choreographer on all the technical problems.

One of the main reasons for the Leningrad's refusal was the question of whether it would be possible to express in a ballet the delicate psychological content of the tragedy without the poet's words. Some critics maintained that to produce Shakespeare's drama in a ballet would be a sacrilege, while others insisted that the previous experiments had proven that the transfer of Shakespeare's plays to ballet was not feasible. They spoke of the well-known early-nineteenth-century production of *Othello* by Salvatore Viganò, the Milanese choreographer. Even earlier several ballets had been performed in Venice on the subjects of *Hamlet, Midsummer Night's Dream,* and *Macbeth.* But in all of these the music was commonplace. The subject of *Romeo and Juliet,* however, served as librettos for some fourteen operas and inspired Tchaikovsky's overture, as well as Berlioz's dramatic symphony with chorus.

"Whenever I am asked to write music for a dramatic spectacle or a film," Prokofiev said, "I almost never agree immediately, even though I may know the text of the play, but I take five or ten days to watch the play—that is, to see the characterization of the roles, illustration of their emotions, and their action. Thus observing it, I get my best ideas."

In this undertaking Prokofiev certainly was faced with no small competition, but a short excerpt from his scenario indicates how carefully he thought out every emotion of the characters and how, in writing the scenario, he was as much a dramatist as he was a composer.

In the description of the ball at the Capulets', Prokofiev laconically marked the score: "Juliet is dancing ceremoniously and indifferently with Paris, her partner. —Romeo is watching her, enchanted. . . . —Madrigal. —Romeo—with love, Juliet—playfully. —Romeo—with more love than before, Juliet—still playfully. —Both pleasant. —Juliet frees herself and playfully runs away. —Juliet, dressed in white, an emblem of virginity, comes to see Father Lorenzo. —The encounter between Tybalt and Mercutio: they look at each other like two fighting bulls; blood is boiling. —The encounter between Romeo and Tybalt should be different in spirit from that of the fight between Tybalt and Mercutio. The latter fought from pure bravado, but Romeo and Tybalt fight wildly, to the death."

During the summer Prokofiev completed the score of the ballet, but the directors of the Bolshoi Theatre, finding it not suited for dancing, canceled the contract. "In the last act," Prokofiev said later, "Romeo comes a minute too soon and finds Juliet alive. The reason for taking such barbarous liberty with Shakespeare's play was purely choreographic: live people can dance, but the dying can hardly be expected to dance in bed."

"To justify our taking such liberty," Prokofiev said, "we pointed to the fact that Shakespeare himself vacillated about the final dénouement in *King Lear*, and while writing *Romeo and Juliet*, wrote also *Two Gentlemen of Verona*, in which everything ended well.

"It is interesting to note," Prokofiev continued, "that while in London they limited themselves simply to stating that Sergei Prokofiev is writing a ballet *Romeo and Juliet* with a 'happy ending,' our Shakespeare-scholars turned out to be more catholic than the Pope, and stormed in defense of the maltreated Shakespeare.

"Actually I was affected by something else—someone had remarked that at the end my music did not sound like 'true happiness,' and this was true. Therefore, after discussing the whole problem with choreographers, we found a way of ending according to the original play, and I have rewritten the music."

Since the project was rejected, Prokofiev made two separate orchestral suites from his score, each containing seven parts and not intended to be performed consecutively. The first suite was performed on November 24, 1936, in Moscow under the direction of George Sebastian; the second on April 15, 1937, in Leningrad with Evgeni Mravinsky conducting the Leningrad Philharmonic.

Prokofiev, however, had no luck with the ballet itself. In 1937 the Leningrad choreographic school proposed its production to commemorate the school's two hundredth anniversary, but later canceled their plans. The first performance of the ballet took place at the opera house in Brno, Czechoslovakia, in December of 1938. But Prokofiev had to wait until 1940, when the Kirov Theatre in Leningrad finally agreed to produce the ballet in Russia.

Before the beginning of rehearsals L. Lavrovsky, the ballet master, went from Leningrad to see Prokofiev in Moscow and to get acquainted with the score of the ballet. Having heard so much about the tribulations in connection with the previously canceled production, Lavrovsky later admitted that he went to see Prokofiev with mixed feelings—"To be, or not to be," he thought of the project.

Prokofiev greeted him in a gracious, disarming manner, and for a moment the two men studied each other. Prokofiev spoke first. "Undoubtedly you have your own plans for the performance," Prokofiev said, and invited Lavrovsky to an easy chair near the piano. Lavrovsky did not miss Prokofiev's emphasis on "*your own*," and said that he had none, but wished to hear the music. Prokofiev went to the piano.

Lavrovsky was immediately fascinated by the music, and the more he heard of it, the more interested he became. Noticing his enthusiasm, Prokofiev himself became excited: he played, sang, whistled, and even tapped out the rhythm on the music rack, announcing the entrances of various instruments of the orchestra. When he reached the scene of Tybalt's death, Prokofiev struck one and the same chord fifteen times. Surprised, Lavrovsky asked Prokofiev what he pictured for this scene and how one should interpret the meaning of this repeated chord.

"None, none! . . ." Prokofiev replied, turning to Lavrovsky with a challenging look.

"But what am I supposed to do on the stage?" Lavrovsky asked.

"To do? Do what ever you like," Prokofiev said, and went on playing.

Thus, with an occasional question from Lavrovsky and similarly curt replies from Prokofiev, they went through the score. Lavrovsky, nevertheless very much impressed, told Prokofiev that he would produce the ballet. This pleased Prokofiev, but he made a wry face when Lavrovsky told him that for a ballet there were still some numbers missing, and some had to be reworked, rewritten, cut, or enlarged upon.

"And what makes you think that your corrections are going to improve it?" Prokofiev asked, annoyed. Lavrovsky did not reply. After a pause, Prokofiev asked where he would have to add music and how much. Lavrovsky explained that he would have to think about it, and that he would like to discuss it again after he had made his plan for the spectacle. "But are you going to produce it?" Prokofiev asked. Lavrovsky noticed a tinge of doubt in his voice and hastened to reassure him.

With this first meeting, their work together on the ballet began. Lavrovsky acknowledged that all his suggestions dictated not by his own whim but by the plan for the production were met with difficulty and in most cases stubbornness on Prokofiev's part.

"I have written the exact amount of music that is necessary. And I am not going to do anything more. It is done. The piece is ready. If you want to produce it—there it is, if not—then not," was Prokofiev's inevitable reply; but as Lavrovsky learned, it was not final in every case.

In the very first scene there was not a single dance number in Prokofiev's score. In addition to the fact that in a choreographed performance this could hardly be admissible, Lavrovsky argued, it was contrary to his plan for the first scene—he wanted the *dance* to introduce the nucleus of the story and to give the exposition of its historical and social background.

Prokofiev brushed aside Lavrovsky's suggestion of writing an additional dance number by saying, "Try to manage with the music that is there. I'm not going to add another line."

Thereupon Lavrovsky, not saying a word to Prokofiev, went to a music store, where, after looking through several Prokofiev compositions, he chose the scherzo from the Second Piano Sonata. Using some material from this, Lavrovsky created the first scene: in a small bar on a square in Verona a young girl working in the bar meets the Capulets' servants—it develops into a lively folk dance (in the score this number is called "The Morning Dance").

When Prokofiev happened to go to a rehearsal at which this scene was being studied, he turned on Lavrovsky. "You have no right to do this! I shall not orchestrate this number."

"I am sorry," said Lavrovsky. "Then we'll be forced to have it played on two pianos, and you won't like it." Prokofiev got up from his seat and stalked out of the rehearsal.

A few days of tense silence followed. Lavrovsky and Prokofiev neither saw nor telephoned each other. Then Prokofiev went to another rehearsal. This time Lavrovsky was working on the scene called "Juliet—The Little Girl." Prokofiev liked the scene and made several observations, particularly about the action not always following his music accurately.

Galina Ulanova, then twenty-nine, was given the part of Juliet. Like the rest of the cast, Ulanova was afraid of Prokofiev: all she saw in him was a tall, gloomy man who scowled at everybody and particularly at the dancers. Speaking for the dancers, Ulanova said, "We simply did not understand his music. We were disturbed by his weird orchestration, the frequent changes in rhythm, which made it difficult to dance. We were not used to such music and we were afraid of it. It seemed to us while we rehearsed for instance the andante in the first act that it was better to hum to ourselves some other melodies, more melodious music, and thus create our dances to our own music. But, of course, no one dared to say this directly to Prokofiev. He was much too severe, much too haughty-looking, and all our complaints were transmitted through Lavrovsky."

And Lavrovsky tried to pacify Prokofiev by saying that although his remarks were sensible, the problems were all caused by the fact that the dancers had not been used to his music.

"But what have you done with that dance number from my scherzo?" Prokofiev changed the subject in a more pleasant tone.

"I'm still working on it. It will soon be ready."

"Let me see it," Prokofiev said, and in a few minutes he noted down for himself the form of the scene and the orchestral coloring Lavrovsky wanted. On the following day he sent Lavrovsky the completed dance number.

Romeo's parting with Juliet at the beginning of the third act caused even more arguments. Ulanova (Juliet), sitting on her bed was to caress Romeo's (Konstantin Sergeyev's) face as he bent toward her. The bed was at some distance from the orchestra; therefore, the two dancers could barely hear the music, which Prokofiev expressly wrote in subdued tones.

"Why aren't you doing anything," shouted Lavrovsky, who, sitting next to Prokofiev, was watching the rehearsal from the hall.

"We cannot. . .we cannot hear the music."

"Why not?" Prokofiev shouted at the dancers. "I know what you need—you need drums, not music!"

Not used to such language, Ulanova and Sergeyev asked Prokofiev to come up on stage and hear it for himself.

"They simply cannot hear the orchestra," Lavrovsky intervened.

"Utter nonsense," Prokofiev retorted. "And why do we hear it, why do I hear it?"

Lavrovsky patiently explained that they were sitting near the orchestra, but the dancers were far away from it, and that when they moved on the stage, they had to think about their own action in addition to "listening" to the orchestra. "Your orchestration is so light that while they 'act,' they simply cannot hear it!"

But Prokofiev was not convinced. He climbed up on the stage and sat in a chair near the footlights. "I hear everything," he said.

"You are still sitting close to the orchestra; go further back, try to hear it from the bed where they are sitting, or better still, while walking on the stage."

Prokofiev obediently followed his directions, occasionally stopping on his way to listen carefully to the orchestra. "All right," Prokofiev said with annoyance, as he walked out of the rehearsal. "I shall add, and perhaps reorchestrate some of it."

What Prokofiev seemed to have failed to understand was that his harmonically complicated musical language and the sharpness of his rhythm simply did not "reach" the dancers, did not inspire them. Even such an artist as Galina Ulanova at first did not understand the music of his *Romeo and Juliet*. Whenever she was asked how she felt about it, she invariably replied, "Why don't you ask Lavrovsky—he has ordered me to love this music."

This lack of understanding naturally influenced the dancers' interpretation, and Prokofiev, irritated, would turn to Lavrovsky. "Is it really possible that you don't hear or see that they move not with but against the music?"

"Give them time, please be patient," Lavrovsky would reply, himself on the verge of losing patience with Prokofiev. "Give them time to understand and learn your music."

Prokofiev would raise his eyebrows; he did not feel that his ballet music was unusual and needed time to be "digested."

Lavrovsky went on to explain that for decades ballet dancers had dealt with powerfully orchestrated music, and it was firmly imbedded in their technique. The art of ballet at the end of the nineteenth century and the beginning of the twentieth has been demonstrated in a whole series of productions typical of Marius Petipas' creations. They were a sort of ballet-concerts, performances in which a rather meager story bound together a series of danced numbers entirely unrelated in their genre and form. Each solo dancer performed his own independent dance: a variation, *pas de deux*, or character dance. The ballet consisted of a variety of separate numbers, which pleased the audience because of the dancers' purely technical mastery. The performer, therefore, was not concerned with expressing the thoughts and emotions of a character through the musical image, but with following the well-accentuated rhythm to show off his technical mastery and disciplined body. He did not need music that developed symphonically. Moreover, such music merely complicated and even disturbed his performance.

These were the difficulties that dancers faced in the Tchaikovsky ballets. The realism of his ballet images, their poetic significance, and the symphonic unity of the dramaturgy all demanded new forms and methods in performers' technique. The dancers were faced with the creation of a unified-by-one-subject performance—a symphonic problem.

Prokofiev developed further Tchaikovsky's art of writing ballet music. He was one of the first composers to introduce to ballet full-blooded musical images, a freedom in solving musical problems, finely chiseled characterizations, and the variety of complicated rhythms. The third act of *Romeo and Juliet* could serve as an example: Romeo has just left Juliet's bedroom. Juliet, desolate, stands near the balcony and watches Romeo's disappearing figure. Suddenly the doors are flung open and, accompanied by music from the ballroom, her father, mother, and Paris, her fiancé, enter.

All the dancers were perplexed; they expected, for the entrance of her parents and the fiancé, music powerfully orchestrated, but they heard instead a fragment from the ball music, subdued and barely audible. It had to be explained that according to Prokofiev's score, Juliet was not yet "alone"; she was still preoccupied with her love and thoughts of Romeo. She was still "with him"; the very air of the room was still filled with his presence. And Juliet's parents and Paris were intruders into her intimate life. Therefore, the music appeared as if hesitating to speak in full voice, trying to preserve Juliet's emotions, and at the same time magnifying the drama of the situation.

To "mark" Paris' entrance would destroy the atmosphere of the scene, the whole plot and character, which were the basis for further development of the episode. It was not accidental that Prokofiev orchestrated the whole scene in subdued tones. Only when Juliet runs in desperation toward Father Lorenzo does the orchestra suddenly burst into powerful, passionate sounds and carry the audience with Juliet.

But the dramaturgy, the solution of the problem, the taste and the finesse of the orchestration were appreciated by the dancers much later.

Two weeks before the scheduled première of the ballet, at a conference of the members of the orchestra and the dancers, it was decided to cancel the performance to avoid complete confusion and a fiasco. Paraphrasing a line from Shakespeare, the performers went about saying, "There is no duller narration in the world than Prokofiev's music in the ballet."

Nevertheless, the ballet, premièred on January 10, 1940, was received enthusiastically.

23

Five years earlier, during the summer of 1935, while he was working on the score of *Romeo and Juliet*, Prokofiev had written short piano pieces for children. By autumn he had completed twelve compositions (Op. 65), which were published in an album entitled *Music for Children*. These pieces carried program titles: "Morning," "Rain and the Rainbow," "Evening," and "The Moon Goes over the Meadows"—the summer landscapes, "Little Fairy Tale," "Grasshoppers' Parade," and "Promenade," "Tag," and "Regrets"—pictures of the children's world, and "Waltz," "Tarantelle," and "March"—character dances.

The last piece in this collection, "The Moon Goes over the Meadows," was written not on a folk theme, as has been erroneously stated, but was Prokofiev's own. "During that summer I was living in an isolated peasant hut in Polenovo," Prokofiev said. "In the evenings, sitting on the balcony, I often enjoyed the charming view of the River Oka, and watched the moon 'walking over the fields'."

The year 1936 was very difficult and confusing for composers in Soviet Russia. Almost four years had passed since the disbanding of the RAPM, but new theories for a true Soviet music, trying to fit into the Communist "Party Line" pattern, were contradicting each other and still made very little sense. The term "formalism" hung like a Damocles sword over composers' heads.

Prokofiev, who had already tasted the dictatorial attitude of the RAPM when his ballet *Le Pas d'acier* was rejected as bordering on Fascism and he himself was branded as an enemy of Soviet culture, now like the rest of the Soviet composers was warned about "formalism in his works."

Since the arts in Soviet Russia are closely bound with the national life, the fortunes of the artists and their works are entirely dependent on the concurrent political situation. Thus, the complexity of the position of Russian artists cannot be fully understood without the knowledge of certain events that had taken place in the country several years before the outbreak of World War II.

Dmitri Shostakovich, then in his late twenties, for some time had been considered a composer who could be placed at a level second to Prokofiev, despite occasional ups and downs in his early career. And his latest work, the opera *Lady Macbeth of the Mzensk District*, written in 1932, became more famous and more notorious, even far beyond the borders of Soviet Russia, than any other artistic work since the Revolution.

It was Shostakovich's long-cherished project to compose a major work dealing with the freedom of the Russian woman. Russia had never had an organized suffragette movement: the Russian men of letters had always been responsible for women's emancipation. Nekrassov's poem "Who Can Live Free and Happy in Russia?" written about the middle of the nineteenth century, Ostrovsky's Katerina in his play *The Storm*, Dostoyevsky's Sonya Marmeladova in *Crime and Punishment*, and his Grushenka in *The Brothers Karamazov*, Tolstoy's Katyusha Maslova in *Resurrection* and his Anna Karenina, and the heroine of Chekhov's story "The Darling" all were milestones in the history of this emancipation. The appearance of each of these works and their characters caused a great stir and interminable debates within Russia. In the case of Tolstoy's Katyusha Maslova, popular feeling ran so high that mock trials to determine her innocence or guilt were held every year, with the cream of the Russian intelligentsia participating. Tolstoy himself challenged the critics of Chekhov's "The Darling," and upheld the story as one of the most significant ever written on this subject.

"I want to write a Soviet *Ring of the Nibelung*," Shostakovich said, speaking of his project. "This will be the first operatic tetralogy about Women, one in which Lady Macbeth will be the Rheingold. It will be followed by an opera about the heroine of the People's Will Movement, Sofia Perovskaya, the daughter of the Governor-General of St. Petersburg, who organized the assassination of Czar Alexander II and was hanged with the rest of the "First of March Men." The third will be about a woman of our century, and finally I will create a Soviet heroine, who will combine in her character all the qualities of the woman of today and tomorrow. This theme is the leitmotif of my daily thoughts and will be for the next ten years." *

For the first part of his project Shostakovich chose Nikolai Leskov's novel *Lady Macbeth of the Mzensk District* (or *Katerina Ismailova* as it is now called, after the name of its heroine). He could not have chosen a more dramatic plot, with the utterly corrupt society of a small town in the 1840s as a background.

Shostakovich had scored a major success when his three-act opera *The Nose* was produced in January, 1930. The praise he received for solving the problem of "opera-dialogue" was certainly the result of Meyerhold's close collaboration. But when the criticism of Meyerhold's innovations began steadily to gain in momentum, Shostakovich wisely following the current trend of the official opinion, changed his view about the true image of contemporary opera, and casting to the winds the successful results of his recent experiment with new ideas for reforms, returned to a conventional operatic form.

In "About My Opera," an article published in the libretto of *Lady Macbeth*, Shostakovich wrote:

> . . . I have tried to make the musical language of the opera very simple and expressive. I cannot agree with the theory, at one time very popular with us, that modern opera should not have any sustained vocal line, and that the vocal parts are nothing more than conversation in which the intonation should be marked. Opera, first of all, is a vocal composition; the singers should discharge their prime duty—to sing, not to talk or declaim or intone.

The opera was a success, playing to packed houses in Leningrad and Moscow. The Nemirovich-Danchenko Theatre in Moscow offered its patrons a handsomely bound libretto containing pictures of the production and including ten glowing articles contributed by members of the theatre and a well-known critic, Alexander Ostretsov. In detailed commentary on the music Ostretsov wrote that only under the conditions prevailing in Soviet Russia could a composer criticize the old clichés and traditions. Although he was using the most bewildering phraseology, he could not disguise the fact that he did know what he was talking about. "With a sure hand," he wrote, "Shostakovich has torn off the masks and exposed the false and lying methods of the composers of a bourgeois society. . . . Shostakovich brings to us a new genre of tragic satire. His opera is a victory and is an expression

* This passage and the account that follows is based on my book *Dmitri Shostakovich* (New York: Alfred A. Knopf, 1943).

of the great creative upsurge that characterises our musical front."

Nemirovich-Danchenko considered the opera "rich in dramatic, social, and psychological content"; he said that they "were witnessing the birth of a most important work of art" and that *Katerina Ismailova* was the beginning of the Soviet *Ring of the Nibelung*.

The opera was considered important enough to be exported to the United States. In addition to being a bona-fide Soviet composer, Shostakovich now, for the first time, had produced a work worthy of being used as propaganda by his government. He was not unknown in the United States as a symphonic composer, but *Lady Macbeth* was traveling in a different class. For in November, 1933, the United States had formally recognized the Union of Soviet Socialist Republics. In April, 1934, Amtorg, in its chamber of commerce capacity, announced a "trade promotion tour to sponsor feelings of friendship between the two countries." Troyanovsky, the Soviet Ambassador, made a short speech on the radio, and the strains of the "Internationale" were heard for the first time on the air in the United States. And it was given a grand "send off" by William C. Bullitt, the American Ambassador to Russia, to stimulate American interest in the Soviet Union. *Lady Macbeth* was an integral part of this "campaign of Soviet-American understanding."

Arthur Rodzinski, the conductor, had gathered an all-Russian cast and presented four performances of the opera in the United States in February, 1935—two in Cleveland, one in Philadelphia, and one at the Metropolitan Opera House in New York City—and the production drew more comment than any music to come out of Soviet Russia to date. A sold-out house greeted the New York performance, where the "raised eyebrow brigade turned out *en flamme* for its bitter bite into the Soviet culture," said the New York *World-Telegram*. The performance "fluttered the dowagers and disappointed the debutantes" in Philadelphia, and brought a capacity audience in "bright array with red color predominating" in Cleveland. The opera obviously was a success, although the critics were divided. Some thought that the writing was "scarcely up to the permanent repertory quality," and that it was "melodrama of a rather juvenile sort," while others found it "rich in melodic content, poignant and expressive."

Shostakovich's idea of portraying the development of the freedom of Russian women was not sufficiently explained to the American public and was drowned in an attitude of "Soviet Composer Gives Hot Stuff."

Lady Macbeth had been running for two years to sold-out houses in Russia when on the morning of January 29, 1936, lightning struck from a blue sky: *Pravda,* the political organ of the Soviet government, carried an editorial titled "Confusion Instead of Music" and subtitled "About the Opera *Lady Macbeth of the District of Mzensk.*"* *Pravda's* article addressed itself to Shostakovich, but actually concerned all Soviet composers—and Prokofiev as well.

On February 6 *Pravda* ran a second editorial, as prominently displayed as the first, titled "Falsehood in Ballet." Written in the same vein as the first, it denounced Shostakovich's ballet *The Limpid Stream* as vulgar and stylized. It resented the portrayal by the librettists and the composer of the collective farmers of the Kuban region—which is in the northern part of the Caucasus, and inhabited chiefly by Cossacks—as "painted peasants on the lid of a candy box." "The music is without character, it jangles, it means nothing. The composer apparently has only contempt for the national songs. . . . The authors of this ballet, the composer, and the producers obviously must imagine that our public will accept everything concocted by opportunists and high-handed men. In reality, it is only our music and art critics who are not discriminating. They will often praise undeserving works."

Before *Pravda's* editorials, any critical bickering would have been considered by the average reader as merely a sort of "domestic quarrel," not really significant, however important musicians thought it. But when the State became involved in it, it took on a different aspect. In utter confusion the Moscow Union of Composers summoned all its members, as well as critics and musicologists, to a series of "creative discussions." They were to attend a trial; but it turned out to be only a hearing, since the verdict had already been handed down.

For three days—February 10, 13, and 15—the hall of the Moscow Union of Composers could not accommodate all those who wanted to participate in the heated denunciations of Shostakovich and his work, and the list of men who had asked to be heard was not completed even in these three conferences. It was Shostakovich's public court-martial, but emotions ran so high that in confusion the speakers brought up subjects in no way related to Shostakovich, and in a frenzy of self-criticism, denounced everything and even turned on one another.

Technically speaking, Prokofiev was not yet considered a Soviet composer. He was accepted into their family later; therefore, the quality and the "tendencies" of his works were at first referred to without mentioning his name. But when criticism of Shostakovich's work

* The text of the editorial can be found in the Appendix (pp. 319–320).

turned to an additional variant—Who was to blame for influencing Shostakovich?—Tikhon Khrenikov, a mediocre composer, took the floor. At that time Khrenikov was still called "Tishka," a humiliating nickname given to him by the actors of the Vakhtangov Theatre, where he was working as a composer of incidental music. He had recently married Clara Waks, whose chief attributes were neither her looks nor her feminine charms, but an ardent ambition to make her husbands—she had had three before Tishka—important workers in the Communist Party. A member of the Communist Party, she had just completed promoting Tarasenkov, her third spouse, who through intrigues and timely denunciations became a literary critic, a master at wielding Communist Party cudgels and at bludgeoning poets and writers. She then turned her benevolent attention to another field— music.

After marrying Tishka—whom she called "Tishinka," a most endearing diminutive—she quickly managed to put some veneer on that uncouth country lad of "proletarian background" by doing away with the moral scruples with which so many simple-minded people unnecessarily burden their consciousness. Having taught him a "deliberate and dignified manner," she sent the twenty-three-year old Tishka to his debut at the "creative discussions," which eventually led to his becoming, some twelve years later, the General Secretary of the Organization Committee of the Union of the Soviet Composers and executioner of the "insubordinate composers and their works."

From the start of his infamous career the most sinister character in the history of Russian music, Khrenikov made Sergei Prokofiev his prime target. Since he had been too late in denouncing Shostakovich, a task already thoroughly accomplished by *Pravda*, Khrenikov was anxious to be the *first* to assail Sergei Prokofiev, thus showing his foresight, a quality very much appreciated by suspicious members of the Communist Party. He indignantly declared that "at the time we were growing up, when our social consciousness was developing, and we were striving to be the true Soviet composers, the true sons of our epoch, Prokofiev arrived with a declaration that Soviet music was provincial and that the only worthy contemporary Soviet composer was Shostakovich. . . . Prokofiev has tremendous influence over our young composers, and it is the same Prokofiev who made the statement only a year ago that he writes two kinds of music: one for the masses, and the other . . . may I ask, is it perhaps for posterity?" Complaining, Khrenikov continued, "I told Miaskovsky that Prokofiev considers Soviet music provincial. 'Pay no attention,' Miaskovsky said."

Khrenikov was too immature, too provincial to understand that Miaskovsky had no desire to discuss with him his old friend Prokofiev.

But after Khrenikov's speech, other composers repeatedly mentioned Prokofiev as the man responsible for all the evils.

The *Pravda* editorials were taken as historical documents of unprecedented importance in the musical life of the Soviet Union, and the leading tone in the discussions was set by *Pravda*'s attitude, which made it clear that Shostakovich's talent and ability should not be assailed, but that all criticism should be directed at his "formalistic" *tendencies.*

"Formalistic," that most elastic of terms, came into general use in Russia in 1932, when the Central Committee of the Communist Party advocated more self-criticism. Everything could become "formalistic," and the critics who were to guide not only the public but the artists as well never knew which way to use the term. The fateful word hung over the heads of the men who were desperately trying to keep their positions by following *Pravda*'s comradely "advice or . . . else."

In his opening speech Nikolai Chelyapov, the president of the Union of Soviet Composers, explained "formalistic" as follows: "Every composition should be considered formalistic in which the composer fundamentally does not have as his aim the presenting of new social meaning, but focuses his interest only on inventing new combinations of sounds that have not been used before. Formalism is the sacrifice of the ideological and emotional content of a musical composition to a search for new tricks in the realm of musical elements—rhythm, timbre, harmonic combinations, etc." And like a rooster who is frightened of his own crowing, Chelyapov quickly added, "This is only a general definition that must be fitted to each individual composition," thus making his own exposé even more confusing than the term itself.

According to this precept, most of Prokofiev's works obviously should have been scrapped as formalistic because of his constant "search for new tricks in the realm of musical elements—rhythm, timbre, harmonic combinations, etc."

Later, in summarizing the "creative discussions" and while condemning Ostretsov for his erroneous analyses and his praising of *Lady Macbeth*, Chelyapov paid tribute to Ostretsov's penetrating critical evaluation of the formalism in Prokofiev's Second and Third Symphonies. "Prokofiev," Chelyapov observed, "has some good compositions . . . for instance the Songs, which he sent to the competition held by *Pravda*, but there is no denying that he is guilty of formalism."

Had these discussions taken place outside of Russia, we would have heard of Prokofiev's naturally contemptuous reaction to such an inane evaluation of his works. He could have referred Chelyapov to Ivan Krylov's (1769–1844) fable "Jackass and Nightingale," known to every Russian schoolboy, in which a jackass prefers the crowing of a cock to the singing of the nightingale. But Prokofiev said nothing and let this comment remain as proof of the critical competence shown by the president of the Composers Union.

Still believing in the prestige of his name, Prokofiev courageously defended Shostakovich, and in his articles in *Pravda* and the magazine *Sovietskaya Musica* said, "In our country everything that is not understood at the first hearing is condemned as 'formalistic.' " His artistic pride would not allow him to bow to the ridiculous dictates of a "Party Line" pattern, and he condemned the cheap bootlicking indulged in to please the common taste of the masses. Prokofiev asked, "Am I expected to compose symphonies in the vein of 'Marusya has taken poison and is lying in a mortuary?' "* (an old popular Russian Song).

Since the criticisms were directed not only to Shostakovich but to all musicians and to Prokofiev in particular, the blunt warning in *Pravda* that "the game of clever ingenuity may end very badly" could hardly have added much to Prokofiev's "happy" permanent return to Russia. Although his personal life was not yet affected, Prokofiev saw what was happening to Shostakovich as a result of this chastisement. There was a lack of elementary decency among his fellow composers, his friends among the music critics, and even his former teachers—all turned their backs on him. Conductors removed his works from their programs, pianists asked to be excused from playing his piano concerto, and the critics, who had formerly praised his works, now ripped them apart and linked his name with that of Meyerhold, who was already in disgrace. Although *Pravda's* editorials were not an official ban on Shostakovich's music, comments on his work ceased to appear, and there was no mention of his name in *Sovietskaya Musica* for the rest of 1936 or during 1937, except for a few belated knocks in the form of adverse reviews from abroad which normally would not have been reprinted. For those musicians in the far-flung corners of the Soviet Union who received their information only through *Sovietskaya Musica*, Dmitri Shostakovich ceased to exist.

There was not even a "musical obituary" by Ostretsov, who on the day of *Pravda's* first editorial asked the Moscow Union to allow him to change the theme of his already scheduled discussion from *Lady*

* A line from a popular Russian song of the genre of "Roll Out the Barrel."

Macbeth to *Quiet Flows the Don,* an opera by Ivan Dzerzhinsky. Ostretsov knew which way the wind was blowing, for on January 20, a
week before the blow that was to fall on *Lady Macbeth,* the news
agency Tass published the following:

CONVERSATIONS OF COMRADES STALIN AND MOLOTOV

WITH THE AUTHORS OF THE OPERA PRODUCTION

"QUIET FLOWS THE DON"

On January 17 in Moscow a last guest performance was given by the
Leningrad Academic Government's Little Opera Theatre. Dzerzhinsky's
opera "Quiet Flows the Don" was performed. Comrades Stalin and Molotov were present and also Comrade Akulov, the Secretary of the Central
Committee of the U.S.S.R., and Comrade Bubnov, the People's Commissar
of Education. After the third act, Comrades Stalin and Molotov had a talk
with the authors of the opera, with the composer I. Dzerzhinsky, conductor S. A. Samosud, and M. A. Terezhkovich, the stage director. During the
conversation Comrades Stalin and Molotov gave positive appraisal to the
work of the theatre in the realm of creation of Soviet opera, and remarked
on the ideological and political value of the production of *Quiet Flows the
Don.*
At the conclusion of the talk Comrades Stalin and Molotov expressed the
necessity of remedying certain shortcomings in the production and expressed also their best wishes for further success in the work on Soviet
Opera.

This unprecedented interest on the part of Comrade Stalin in music
and particularly in opera was part of the posthumously termed "personality cult." Stalin was the supreme judge of all matters, and no one
was to doubt his competence, even in such a special field as music in
which a more sensitive ear than his was required. It is not unusual to
find that a predominant part of our concert and opera audiences'
appreciation of music does not go further than Brahms and the Roman-
tics, but Stalin's standard was absolutely primitive.

According to those who were able to observe him at official gatherings in which musical programs were performed, Stalin never enjoyed
the beauty of serious music. Describing the room in which Stalin died,
the room in which "he had spent all his last years, nearly twenty of
them," his daughter Svetlana wrote: "In one corner there was a record
player. My father had a good collection of Russian, Georgian and
Ukrainian folk songs and didn't recognize the existence of any other
kind of music." * Stalin liked vocal music because he could follow the
text, and he preferred to the concert hall a more intimate atmosphere
in which the music was an accompaniment to eating and wine-

* Svetlana Alliluyeva: *Twenty Letters to a Friend* (New York: Harper & Row,
1967).

drinking. He was bored by symphonic and chamber music. He disapproved of such long compositions for solo instruments as concertos and sonatas, so that these particular forms of compositions were designated as being "anti-democratic." He was against "modern music" in all its forms, including popular music that originated in the West, Viennese operettas, American jazz, French songs, and Argentine tangos.

There was no reason why anyone should have objected to his taste, actually, except that it was rather obvious that Stalin was no music critic and that his omnipotent opinion could bring only disaster to the development of a Soviet musical culture; his influence was far more dangerous than Prokofiev's.

The story was current in Moscow that Stalin had attended the *Lady Macbeth* production and he did not like it, that he walked out before the end of it, and that this took place a few days before the *Pravda* bombshell.

There was obviously nothing bourgeois in the story of the opera (it can be taken for granted that he understood nothing of the music) that could have ruffled Stalin's feathers: *Lady Macbeth* portrays the nineteenth-century merchant class in most unfavorable colors, and both the text and the music clearly show the downtrodden servants ridiculing their masters. The monumental symphonic music depicts the drab atmosphere and the moral sufferings of the "oppressed" as well as the idle and corrupt existence of the merchant class with bitter sarcasm and irony.

The two editorials could hardly have been prompted solely by one man's reaction, no matter how important this man's position might have been; "personality cult" notwithstanding, Stalin's personal displeasure could have had about the same degree of influence on the fate of *Lady Macbeth* as Lenin's enthusiasm for Beethoven's "Appassionata" Sonata ever had in fostering that composer's popularity. That *Pravda* took a hand in it showed that the matter was far more important than mere criticism of a musical score, which, after all, could have been revised, improved, or cut. *Pravda's* concern in the affair signified that it was of a vital importance to the State itself. *Pravda* is a political organ that usually does not review musical events, and Stalin had never before appeared in the role of music critic. It would have been ridiculous in the eyes of the Western nations and even a bit presumptuous to the most "faithful" in the Soviet Union.

The bitter proof that the Soviet arts are closely bound with the affairs of state was shown when one of the works acclaimed as a great achievement and pride of Soviet culture fell beneath the pressure of events.

The truth of the matter was that the Soviet government had been anxiously watching the spread of Fascism and the complete failure of the Western powers to check its growth. It was also aware that all was not as it should be on the "home front." As early as 1933 Stalin had spoken of Communist blunders, of their failure to foresee the methods of hostile forces boring from within. Collectivization was facing great difficulties in obtaining the vital seed supplies, for the peasants were hiding them. Sporadic sabotage and looting finally led to the death penalty being imposed on those actively hindering the spring planting, and "stern methods" were to be used against the Cossacks who resisted collectivization.

Then on December 1, 1934, Sergei Kirov, a high official of the Leningrad Soviet and a close friend of Stalin, was assassinated, and a wave of suspicion and fear of treason swept the country. The official communiqué reported that a conspiracy to assassinate all the Soviet leaders simultaneously had been discovered within the Communist Party in Leningrad. Thousands of arrests were made, and about four hundred suicides were reported within the following days.

This so called "purge" was directed not merely toward government employees, Communist Party members, peasants, and workers; it was turned also against men and women in every walk of life. In what sort of hornet's nest Sergei Prokofiev found himself upon his final return to Russia can be seen from a belated report of the general situation written by Ilya Ehrenburg (1891–1967) in his memoirs over twenty-five years later, when he felt safe enough to speak of it.

Ilya Ehrenburg, who for the past two years (1935–1937) had been reporting in *Izvestia* on the Civil War in Spain, had decided to return to Moscow. "I had to know what was going on there," he wrote in his memoirs:

The bourgeois newspapers alleged that there had been many arrests, but that had been said before; they were probably exaggerating. . . I would see Irina [his daughter], Lapin [his son-in-law], Babel [the writer], Meyerhold, all my friends.
. . . We [Ehrenburg and his wife] arrived in Moscow on 24th of December. Irina met us at the station. We were happy, we laughed; a taxi took us to Lavrushensky lane [the location of Ehrenburg's apartment]. In the lift my eyes fell on a handwritten notice: "It is prohibited to put books down the lavatory. Anyone contravening this order will be pursued and punished." *

As if Ehrenburg were a naive tourist from the West and did not immediately understand that every house, every apartment was under

* Ilya Ehrenburg: *Memoirs, 1921–1941* (Cleveland and New York: World, 1963).

suspicion and surveillance, he asked his daughter, "What does that mean?"

She replied, with a sidelong glance at the lift-girl, "I am so glad you've come." Inside the flat, Irina came up close to me and said in a low voice: "Don't you know anything?" Throughout half the night she and Lapin told us about all that had happened: an avalanche of names, and after each the single neologism: "taken."

Ehrenburg follows his account with the names of men and women well-known in Russia who were arrested: one because he had been in Spain, another because he drank and talked too much, one woman who had just arrived from France, another because she was too popular in Armenia—and all the Polish Communists because they were Poles.

Ehrenburg continued:

Irina answered my questions each time, "How can I know? Nobody knows." Lapin advised me with a rueful smile: "Don't ask anyone. And if someone starts talking about it, just shut up." Irina was rather angry: "Why did you ask me over the telephone about Mirova? Don't you understand? They took her husband, then she got back here, and they arrested her too." Lapin added: "They often arrest the wives and put the children in homes!" [He meant a home for orphans.]
  . . . The life we led in those days was quite exceptional. Whole books could be written about it. There was no one in the circle of my acquaintances who could be sure about the morrow: many of them kept a small suitcase with two changes of warm underwear permanently in readiness.
  On the surface, life seemed to go on as usual. It was decided to organize a Writer's Club and to have club days. I once met Sergei Prokofiev at the club—he played some of his compositions. He was unhappy, even grim, and said to me, "Today one must work; work's the only thing, the only salvation."

What else could Prokofiev have said to Ehrenburg, since at that time in Russia people used to say, "Today a man talks frankly only with his wife . . . at night, with a blanket pulled over their heads"?

Living in Moscow, Sergei Prokofiev knew as much as Ehrenburg had learned and much more, but so far the two executioners, Henrich Yagoda and Nikolai Yezhov, were more preoccupied with the Soviet writers—"the engineers of the citizens' souls," Stalin had named them—than with musicians. The date for the musicians' turn had not yet been determined.

Henrich Yagoda, who as early as 1920, at the age of thirty, began his career at the notorious Cheka (Soviet Secret Service), later to become the head of NKVD (People's Commissariat of Internal Affairs, but actually the same secret service under a different name), was the man empowered to conduct purges. But in 1937 he himself was arrested, tried, and executed (1938) on charges of being a foreign spy working for a conspiratorial group called the "Anti-Soviet Bloc of Rights and Trotskyites."

He was succeeded by Nikolai Yezhov, who was four years younger than he, and who for the following three years carried on his duties during the period of witch hunts, purges, and spy trials.

Up to Lavrenti Beria's time, musicians were not executed, but were dealt with by measures stern enough to bring them to despair. They were considered "specialists" in their field, and since the government provided them with certain privileges accorded only to "specialists," it was demanded that in return they do their duty as faithful citizens.

Those who were under slight suspicion of being "security risks" were assigned to remote parts of Russia as teachers, supervisors in music schools, or organizers of musical activities (among the natives of these regions there was neither the possibility of nor the necessity for "musical activities"). A refusal to obey such an assignment would have meant trial and a certain "guilty" verdict, with deportation to similarly distant regions but in a different capacity.

Sergei Prokofiev had every reason to be grim. He did not even have Lina with whom to share the daily gruesome news. She was still in Paris with their children, and there was no possibility of his getting a passport to leave Russia to join them. All he could do was to write meaningless postcards (all letters were censored) and keep telephoning her, urging her to come to him. He was virtually a prisoner of the State. The question of why all this was going on was as puzzling to Prokofiev as it was to Irina, Ehrenburg's daughter, who said "Nobody knows," and to the supposedly well-informed journalists.

According to verbatim reports of the trials that were held in Moscow between 1936 and 1938 (published in English by the People's Commissariat of Justice of the U.S.S.R.), a most fantastic plot to wrest the power from the Soviet leaders through assassination had been in the process of preparation for the past few years by members of the Communist Party in high official positions under the direction of Leon Trotsky, who was in exile.

The government explained, in the words of the accused men, how the conspirators—who had accomplices in all the key positions in industry and communications as well as in the army and in the Kremlin itself—had sabotaged and "wrecked" the country's economy during the early 1930s. To achieve their final goal, they had planned their country's defeat in the event of war. Germany was to attack Russia, which, after the work of sabotage had been thoroughly accomplished, would have been unable even to put through the mobilization of her armed forces. Meanwhile, groups of terrorists had been assigned the task of "removing" the heads of the government.

The arrest of about fifty of the most prominent members of the Communist Party—men whom the Russian people had known as the leaders of the Revolution and therefore had always regarded as above suspicion—confused and frightened the populace. Men on the streets became suspicious of one another, and distorted rumors shattered the nation's confidence. The Russian people avoided any contact with foreigners and even refrained from corresponding with friends outside Russia. Foreign musicians were informed that their contracts would not be renewed, and it was politely suggested that they leave the country when their work was completed.

"Let's fight with gentle words/Till time lend friends and friends their helpful swords" was the attitude of the European powers toward the growing menace of Fascism. But Soviet Russia had to rely on her own strength, for whom could she call her friend in 1935? The government realized that a thorough housecleaning was necessary, and quickly.

One need only remember the years that followed the Revolution to realize that the problem of welding the "home front" into a strong and self-confident body was not so simple. There was a time when marriages and divorces were practically nonexistent. If a man lived openly with a woman for some time, she was considered by the State to be his wife, and it did not matter if he was not meticulous enough to register at the marriage office. If he had been married with the greatest pomp the State could provide and then after a few days decided that he had had enough of matrimony, he could casually drop a postcard in the mailbox stating his desire for a divorce, and thereby automatically terminate his marriage, thus legally relieving himself of all responsibilities. The housing problem, which forced more than one family into crowded communal quarters, presented an unlimited field for free love and adultery, and lack of moral and social standards as we know them in Western society.

Antagonism within the family was prompted by the government's encouragement of the younger generation's criticism of the old. This criticism by the children of their parents, accompanied at times by denunciations based on theories of "Party Lines," produced disastrous consequences: disrespect of parental authority created a fertile field for this extreme split in family relations. In any new revolutionary country, youth has the upper hand—youth born and brought up on the streets during the revolution and civil war with the "order of the day" as their only moral guide.

In addition, by 1932–33 the government, proud of its accomplishments—the completion of the First Five-Year Plan—was urging more freedom by dissolving the Cheka. To raise the morale of those who had suffered from privations and even hunger during the Civil War, Stalin recommended light music—dances and gay, rousing popular songs—with an Olympian utterance: "Life is better, Life is gayer."

But with the assassination of Kirov and the switch from a Marxist to a national policy, all this came to an end. In Moscow one often heard it said that 1936 began on December 1, 1934, when Kirov was murdered in his Leningrad office. Lectures, newspapers, but even more, theatres, motion pictures, and music are the tools that a government can use to strengthen and even, when necessary, reverse the attitude of the people. And this the Soviet government proceeded to do.

The threat of a brutal foreign invasion apparently loomed larger by the hour, and there was no time to lose in preparing to meet it. The first and the most important task, in the government's opinion, was already begun with the arrests that were to eradicate the most gigantic "fifth column" the world had ever known, if the reports of the confessions by those brought to trial were true. The authenticity of these reports may have to be examined still further by historians, but at that time the Kremlin treated them as established facts and acted accordingly.

It was imperative, in any case, to rebuild the self-confidence and the solidarity of the Russian people. The love of children for their parents and for their homes—which they were to defend as precious possessions and not regard merely as another place provided by the government in which they might rest their heads—and the respect for lawful marriage all had to be restored to their former position and respectability, whether bourgeois or not. And finally, love for their "rodina"—a proud name for fatherland—this was the spirit that the government of the U.S.S.R. had now to build up for the attacking nations to face and dare to destroy.

While calling the citizens to their duties as patriots, whipping up their fervor with the spirit of "my country right or wrong," the Soviet government could not afford to have in the people's favorite theatres plays that depicted the Russian character with criticism and sarcasm, leaving the audiences in gloom and pessimism. The building up of self-confidence, even if it might be based on undue optimism, was of the utmost importance in order to avoid any sense of inferiority.

Shostakovich's *Lady Macbeth*, with not a single note of optimism in it, left its audience in deep gloom. All the characters, from peasants to merchants, were depicted as base and immoral, and in view of the new policy, Shostakovich had even failed to make a noble character of his heroine.

What the audiences needed was a heroic subject, one that was close to the memories and the lives of the people. Mikhail Sholokhov's novel *And Quiet Flows the Don*, whose scope was considered akin to Tolstoy's *War and Peace*, fulfilled the demands. Sholokhov had dedicated his book to "The Socialist Village" and in it described the life of the Don Cossacks before and during the First World War and through the Revolution. The traditional Cossack heroism was built up in the minds of every Russian to a legend representing the strength and the backbone of the Russian Army, whether Czarist or Red. The Cossacks as a unit, however, always true to their origins, have never cared to take orders from Moscow, and the Soviet government tried unsuccessfully to disband them and mix them with the peasants and workers.

By 1934, when Shostakovich wrote *The Limpid Stream*, the Soviet government had ordered "stern measures" to be used against the Cossacks whenever they resisted. In Shostakovich's ballet, therefore, the Cossacks of the Kuban region were depicted not in their own tribal dress, singing and dancing their own folk songs and dances. But now, in 1936, when the cooperation of the Cossacks was becoming increasingly necessary and they had to be re-established as a military unit, they were given back the right to wear their glamorous uniforms and to stand apart from peasantry. It was most opportune that Dzerzhinsky had written an opera based on Sholokhov's novel, which was appearing in serial form in *Pravda*.

Although this opera was far below the caliber of Shostakovich's music, it was immediately brought before the public, for it was more in the character of Cossack folklore, "closer to the soil," and fulfilled far better the needs of the time, in the government's opinion. The final touch to the *Lady Macbeth* affair was the awarding of the Stalin Prize to Dzerzhinsky's opera—an opera dedicated to Shostakovich and written, as Dzerzhinsky clearly emphasized during the "creative discussions," with Shostakovich's most cooperative help.

As early as January 11, 1936, Soviet Premier Molotov quoted from Hitler's *Mein Kampf* Germany's aims for expansion at the expense of the Soviet Union. In February the Soviet press again quoted from the book, pointing out Hitler's intentions toward France. The Soviet government felt that war was inevitable, and the opening wedge in the campaign on the "home front" was the banning of *Lady Macbeth*. *Pravda*'s editorials, blasting the opera, coincided, with only a few weeks to spare, with the Nazi march into the Rhineland—the Wehr-macht's first blow against the Treaty of Versailles, which had terminated World War I, and the first steps leading to World War II.

But neither the average man nor the intelligentsia in the Soviet Union were even remotely aware of the "why" of the purges, the blood bath in which countless innocent victims perished.

I came to the above conclusion when, in 1942, I was writing Dmitri Shostakovich's biography and trying to explain the case of *Lady Macbeth*. Anxious to have if not a confirmation at least some support to my theory, I called on Maxim Litvinov, the Russian Ambassador to the United States, and had a talk with him on this subject.

Naturally, I did not expect Litvinov to endorse my exposé for publication. All I hoped for was to draw from his reaction some idea of how near I was to the truth. In fact, I asked him just that.

"You are close [to the truth] . . ." Litvinov replied, "but why do you want to write about it?"

"Because I am writing about the *Lady Macbeth* incident and it is an important part of Shostakovich's career." Today I can add that it was important, not only to Shostakovich's career, but to all the composers in Soviet Russia and certainly in Prokofiev's life.

But at the time of the trials and purges, who in Soviet Russia dared to raise his voice against the preposterous measures taken by the government against the population, even if there was a legitimate excuse such as the Kremlin claimed to have had? And as if to pacify a terri-fied population, a new Constitution, Stalin's Constitution, was announced.

To draw a veil over the guillotine, which never ceased to function, the New Constitution claimed to grant more freedom than previously enjoyed since the Revolution. It was to give equal rights to all classes (not only to the proletariat), including the former bourgeoisie; indirect elections were to be replaced by direct, open ballot by secret, etc. But the constitution had one paragraph that made all the rest meaningless. It provided for a constitutional ban on any opposition. "Freedom for several parties," Stalin explained, "can exist only in a society in which there are antagonistic classes whose interests are mutually hostile and irreconcilable. Since this is not the case in the U.S.S.R., here there is ground only for one party."

But the Russians, who longed for at least some kind of breathing spell, were ready to accept the Constitution as the greatest expression in history of the rights of man. Among the many other prominent members of Soviet society called upon to comment on the Constitution, Sergei Prokofiev headed the list representing the musicians.

"The new Constitution," Prokofiev was quoted in *Sovietskaya Musika* (No. 10, 1936) from an article in *Pravda*, "was an act of great faith in the Soviet citizen. There is no better way to lift the morale of a human being than to give him your confidence. I have no doubt that the New Constitution will help to foster further general liberation of the Soviet citizen's consciousness from the ideologically bad and outdated past. It is no secret that we do not always do our work as we should, that we do not always respect our own word, and are not sufficiently eager to raise the standards of our qualifications. . . ." Here, with several dots suggesting that he had more to say on this subject, Prokofiev was taking advantage of promised freedom of expression. But what he did say was sufficient to remind his colleagues and the critics to be more open-minded in their appraisals, and to stick to their opinion once they had recognized the worth of a work. "A great deal has already been accomplished," Prokofiev went on, "but there is still a great deal that needs to be worked on. Thus, when the number of such advanced citizens multiplies, our country will proceed even faster on the road of its further progress.

Was Sergei Prokofiev, the man who had fought against conformity all his life, now going to conform?

24

Because his family had not yet joined him in Russia, Prokofiev was not allocated an apartment and was forced to stay at the Hotel Metropol.

After his return from a concert tour with Soetens, to avoid any new embroilment in "comradely" or "creative" discussions of his next work, he greeted with joy a suggestion for writing something for children—safe ground.

Prokofiev's first acquaintance with the theatre for children dated back to 1935, when, accompanied by Lina and their two sons (Svyatoslav, eleven; Oleg, seven), he attended the performance of Leonid Polovinkin's opera for children, *Fisherman and Goldfish*, based on Pushkin's poem. The performance was very poor: the first clarinet player was ill and the young man who substituted for him sight-read, playing many wrong notes. And thirty-year-old Natalie Satz, a talented actress and a member of the theatre administration, ran backstage to tell the young performers that Sergei Prokofiev was in the audience. This was a mistake, she realized after the intermission: some of the young artists began to show off an unnecessary verve in their "art." Because of the excitement, the *Fisherman* while taking a high note produced a whistling sound, and several girls missed their cues, adding unexpected pauses to the score.

After the performance, when Natalie Satz was introduced to the Prokofievs, she tried to apologize, but Prokofiev would barely speak to her. He unwillingly answered her questions, and the poor young woman, who had never met him before and was not familiar with his brusque manner, would have been even more frightened if it were not for Lina and their children, who were kind and seemed pleased by the performance. She would have never dared invite him to come again.

A week later, when the Prokofievs went to see another spectacle, *About Dzuba*, Satz sat with them in a box and could observe Sergei Prokofiev's reactions. Her first impression of him as a haughty man changed when she saw him react far more acutely than his children: he laughed aloud, praised or criticized everything spontaneously, and showed a very keen interest in the theatre as he spoke to her.

"One has to get used to him," Satz said later. "Even his haughty manner is nothing more than a 'toga' in which he wraps himself when he is in a bad humor or wants to be left in peace. His unusual appearance in a foreign-made suit of a sandy-red color, his sparse reddish-blond hair, rosy cheeks, rimless eyeglasses, and rare smile led one of the young actresses to remark: 'He looks like the fourth from his *Three Oranges.*' "

Prokofiev told Satz that he was delighted that there was a "musical theatre for children," but he criticized the orchestra and the vocalists. "In your production," he said, "I liked the melodeclamatic delivery of the story, but I didn't like the singing. Why do you have to stage opera?" he asked as if he were thinking aloud. "On the other hand, if you are not going to create children's operas, who else would do it? Bolshoi does not seem to have any particular interest in this very important field."

Satz knew Prokofiev's compositions based on fairy tales—"The Ugly Duckling," "The Grandmother's Fairy Tales," and the short piano pieces—but she did not dare ask for his collaboration.

In February of 1936 the Moscow Theatre for Children was allocated another building. Instead of the former motion-pictures house not properly suited to theatrical productions, the Children's Theatre was transferred to the Nezlobin's Theatre, where Koussevitzky had given his symphonic concerts and Sergei Rachmaninoff had often participated in programs. Rechristened The Children's Theatre Center, it was opened on March 5, 1936, and besides theatrical productions, symphonic concerts were planned.

At the first concert Tchaikovsky's orchestral suite from his ballet *The Nutcracker* and the finale of his Second Symphony were performed, as well as several new compositions written especially by Soviet composers.

Prokofiev obviously was pleased by the sight of a hall filled with children who behaved as if they were at home, though a little more restrained than if they had been on their playgrounds. They were intrigued by the musical instruments lying on the floor or propped up against the walls of the stage before the beginning of the concert. For a moment Prokofiev watched their outstretched hands pointing at the instruments while they discussed their names, until a blond curly-headed boy ran to the footlights and, turning to his friends, shouted, "Do you see all these instruments? Today they are all going to play only for *us*."

It was an unusual sight, for before the Revolution there were no concerts for children in Russia. The performance was received with great enthusiasm, and Prokofiev warmly congratulated all the participants. This, thought Natalie Satz, was the moment to ask Prokofiev to compose something for the theatre.

The company had planned to devote one of the scheduled concerts to explaining the musical instruments to the children. They listened eagerly to songs—words with music. What would it be like, she thought, if the words could be combined with symphonic music, but in a way that would fascinate the children? She thought of a symphonic fairy tale that would help them become acquainted with the instruments.

On the following day she summoned her courage and went to see Prokofiev. She was nervous about everything: she was afraid of Prokofiev, afraid to suggest a theme for his composition, afraid to ask him how much he would expect to be paid, if he agreed.

"I like the realistic way in which you speak about it," Prokofiev said matter-of-factly, and told her he would think about it. Two days later he asked her to come and discuss the project in more detail.

"We would have to find some 'images' that will be easily associated with the characteristic sounds of the instruments," Prokofiev said.

"How about . . . the flute as a little bird," Satz suggested, and almost choked with the fear that Prokofiev would become angry with such a commonplace idea.

"Absolutely," Prokofiev smiled. "We should not be afraid of the most elementary childish fantasy. The most important thing is to find with them a common language."

"Perhaps it would be good," Satz said, gaining courage, "to have a number of animals and birds in the composition, and at least one person."

Prokofiev nodded. "But if we designate one instrument to the role of each animal, then the 'image' of a person should be performed by, let's say, a string quartet." Prokofiev was growing enthusiastic. "Of course, of course, we have to start with something concrete, something with contrasts easily understood by a child: a wolf—a bird, good—evil, something big—something small. And each one should have its leitmotif."

Finally they decided that the subject should have a fascinating plot and unexpected action, otherwise even a twenty-five-minute symphonic work would not hold the children's attention.

Having succeeded thus far, Natalie Satz asked Prokofiev if they could have a written agreement, since she still expected other problems: his refusal or an exorbitant price for the theatre's budget.

"An agreement never hurt anyone," Prokofiev said calmly, "but I'm going to write this fairy tale anyway. You can pay me whatever you can."

As if walking on air with her success, Natalie Satz, to speed the "tempo" of Prokofiev's work, asked Nadezhda Sakonskaya, a poet, to work out a scenario for the future symphonic fairy tale. She gave her the notes she had taken while discussing it with Prokofiev and asked Sokonskaya to deliver the text to him as soon as possible.

A great admirer of Prokofiev, Sakonskaya worked day and night and within a few days brought the fruits of her literary creation to him.

Satz happened to go to see Prokofiev at the end of his interview with Sakonskaya—the poet was backing toward the door, and as Satz entered the room, she made a quick exit. "I saw fire in the composer's eyes," Satz related later, "and he scolded me for Sakonskaya's unrequested visit."

"Far too many, far too many rhymes," Prokofiev shook his head. "The correlation of the words and music in such a work should be very delicate—every word should have its place. The word can help the music, but it can also take you away from it. No, no, I have to try to do it myself, and if . . . if I should fail, then. . . ."

Four days later Prokofiev brought Satz the vocal score, which he called "Petya Fooled the Wolf."* He went to the piano and gave her the first performance of it. In the adjoining room at the theatre a group of children who took an active part in productions were having one of their regular discussions of their work. Satz persuaded Prokofiev to play the piece for them. They listened with absorbed interest and made Prokofiev repeat the closing march three times.

But no sooner had Prokofiev finished, when they broke into a lively discussion:

"What sort of a bird was it?"

* A diminutive of Peter.

"Ah . . . just an ordinary kind of a bird . . . a gay bird."

"But what was it? A sparrow, a magpie?"

"No-o-o-o, a singing bird. And she was the one who sang when Petya came."

"It doesn't matter—every bird has a name—a nightingale, a robin redbreast, a lark."

Prokofiev was very amused and laughed at their desire for something "absolutely concrete." It was a good lesson for him, he thought.

He completed the score a week later, and on May 5, 1936, it was given its first performance at the Children's Theatre Center. Before the performance, the children were shown the instruments that were used in the score, and they were introduced to the sounds of each separately and in groups. Each performer was then presented to the audience, each playing his leitmotif on a given instrument.

The program also included a short piece, "The Chatterer," written by Prokofiev for the theatre and based on the verse of Agini Barto. It was accompanied by a symphony orchestra under the direction of Leonid Polovinkin. And finally Prokofiev played "Morning," "Rain," and "March" from his *Music for Children*.

The enthusiastic applause did not limit itself to Prokofiev's audience. The administration received an avalanche of letters of the following type. Master Volodya Dobuszinsky wrote:

I like the music about Petya, the wolf, and the little bird. As I listened, I recognized them all. The cat was beautiful, she walked so lightly that no one could hear her, she was a sly one. The duck was lopsided, awkward, and stupid. When the wolf ate her, I felt sorry for her. I was glad to hear her voice again at the end of the piece. I liked best of all when Petya fought with the wolf and when all the instruments played as they caught the wolf and were taking him off to the Zoo. I drew a picture of this. I also had tried to pick out the music on the piano, but it is more interesting when the orchestra plays it. Please write me when you are going to give another concert.

Peter and the Wolf became a permanent number in the symphonic concert repertory, but it had a special meaning when it was performed in July, 1936, for the invited foreign guests at a festival in the "Center House of Pioneers." In the audience were Prokofiev's wife and children, who had recently come from abroad— this time to stay.

"*Peter and the Wolf*," Prokofiev said, "is a present not only to the children of Moscow, but also to my own."

At that time Anastas Mikoyan, the Commissar of Supplies in Soviet Russia, was imitating the American way of promoting goods. The theatre was offered, at his suggestion, the opportunity to participate in popularizing children's songs, poems, and fairy tales by using them on attractive wrappings of chocolates, children's toys, and sweets. Many artists, including Barto, the famous caricaturists of the magazine *Krokodil*, the painter V. Ryidin, and the composer J. Rauchberger, offered their services. Prokofiev was asked to join in.

At first he vacillated, not certain as to whether this was advisable, but eventually he agreed to write a short "sweet little song" for the wrapper of chocolates, his favorite childhood sweet.

"As for the text," he added good-humoredly, "please ask Nadezhda Sakonskaya, the poet who unsuccessfully tried to write *Petya Fooled the Wolf*, and whom I so upbraided then. She would do very well with the 'sweet little song.'"

Prokofiev seemed to have been completely satisfied with the success of *Peter and the Wolf*, except for one thing that had marred the happy event: Tatyana Bobrova rather than Natalie Satz was the narrator. Natalie Satz, who had suggested the composition to Prokofiev and who was his close collaborator in this work, was "no longer available." Several months later, Natalie Satz was arrested and sent to a concentration camp because she happened to have been the wife of Marshal Mikhail Tukhachevsky, the prime target of the trials, who was convicted of treason and executed.

25

While the controversy of establishing a definite program for composers that would adhere to the "Party Line" was still in progress among the musicians, Prokofiev did not limit himself to writing pieces for children which, having an educational aspect, placed them on safe ground, so to speak. His more important project—writing music on Pushkin's texts—was just as safe, and there was a perfectly legitimate reason for it: the forthcoming centennial commemoration of the poet's death.

Prokofiev agreed to write incidental music for the dramatic productions of *Evgeni Onegin* and *Boris Godunov*, and for the motion picture *The Queen of Spades*. It was a daring undertaking to challenge the Russian classics—the works of Moussorgsky and Tchaikovsky—and Prokofiev had deliberated at length before making his decision. A year earlier the painter Peter Konchalovsky, Prokofiev's old friend, suggested he should compose new music to *Evgeni Onegin*. "No," Prokofiev had said. "After Tchaikovsky it is, somehow, not quite right."

But now, having seen the new S. D. Kriszanovsky production, which stressed particularly the episodes omitted in Tchaikovsky's opera, Prokofiev felt justified in undertaking this project by including several such scenes. "I think it would be interesting," he said, "to see Lensky arguing heatedly over a bottle of wine with Onegin, or Tatyana visiting Onegin's abandoned home, or Onegin on 'the banks of Neva.'"

Although Tchaikovsky's opera has been accepted without question, there were some, including Prokofiev, who believed that Tchaikovsky had deprived Pushkin of his inner rebellion and instead had imparted to the score his own characteristic pessimism. Prokofiev's aim was to adhere more closely to the poet's spirit. "The idea of writing music to *Evgeni Onegin* is as seductive as it is unrewarding," Prokofiev said. "No matter how well I may succeed, our audiences love Tchaikovsky's music too much to refute his musical images."

The further Prokofiev penetrated into Pushkin's works, the more he felt the poet's reticence to express emotions akin to his own, and it is not surprising that he chose the following lines for his first "song" on the Pushkin text:

> Ten years have passed since then—and much
> Has changed in life for me,
> I, too, obedient to life's laws,
> Have altered—but here again
> The past enfolds me in its arms
> And lo, it seems but yesterday
> I roamed these woods. . . . *

Among some forty-four musical numbers, he had composed three lyrical themes reflecting Tatyana's slowly growing love for Onegin and several themes portraying Onegin. Prokofiev believed that he had succeeded best in the episodes depicting the serene rural atmosphere of the Larin estate, and in some fragments of dances at the ball: Waltz and Polka, played on two pianos.

His scores for *Boris Godunov* and *The Queen of Spades*, each consisting of twenty-four musical numbers, as well as the score of *Evgeni Onegin*, remained in manuscript and were never used for production. Only three songs—"Pine Trees," "Roseate Dawn" (based on Pushkin's "Cherry"), and "In Your Chamber"—were true "echoes of the Pushkin centennial," Prokofiev said. The first performance of the second and third songs was given over the Moscow Radio on April 29, 1937, by Lina with Prokofiev at the piano. These three large scores remained for a long time in Prokofiev's desk, but eventually he used some of the material in his later compositions.

As if to prove that he was not lackadaisical in his work, he undertook still another project, one of far greater magnitude. Like his Soviet colleagues, he worked on a composition for another jubilee: the twentieth anniversary of the October Revolution.

Some years previously, when he had decided to return to Russia, he had often been asked in France what kind of subject he contemplated for his music. "Not a caricature of our failings," Prokofiev replied,

* Translated by Rose Prokofieva, *loc. cit.*

"which mock the negative aspects of our present life in Soviet Russia. I am looking for a theme that will confirm a positive beginning—the heroism of building up a socialist society, a 'new' man, his struggles and his surmounting of obstacles. I would like to fill my musical canvas with such emotions." But this was merely a precept, for he admitted that the musical language in which Soviet life should be depicted was not yet clear to him. "It was not yet clear to anybody," he added.

Now, in 1937, Prokofiev thought he had discovered at last the "right language," and in an article published in *Pravda* (December 31, 1937) under the title "The Blossoming of the Arts," he wrote:

It is not easy to find a musical language which would be harmonious with a socialistic epoch—a difficult but rewarding problem for a composer. In our country music had become available to large masses. Their artistic taste, the demands which they put to the arts increase with incredible speed indeed. Therefore, the composer should keep this in mind while writing any new work.

There is, I believe, a certain similarity with shooting at moving targets—only by taking aim ahead of the moving objects, of taking aim at "tomorrow," so to speak, will you not remain behind, remain with demands of "yesterday." This is why I consider it a mistake for a composer to "simplify" his methods. Each venture to "please" the listener conceals not only the composer's underestimation of his listener's cultural maturity and the quality of his developed taste, but such an attempt contains an element of insincerity. And music written insincerely is lifeless.

It is no longer the time when music was written for a small group of esthetes. Today, large crowds of people are interested in serious music, and are waiting. . . .

Prokofiev addressed his colleagues:

Composers, you should consider seriously this moment: if you repulse people they will turn to Jazz or to "Marusya Has Taken Poison and Is Lying in a Mortuary." If, on the other hand, you succeed in keeping your listeners, you shall have an audience the like of which has never existed anywhere or at any time. The masses want great music, monumental events, great love, and beautiful and gay dances. They understand far more than you grant them and they need you in their progress.

But Prokofiev also made it clear that although he strove in his compositions for clarity and melodic expression, he was in no way willing to refute the well-known methods of harmony and melody. "There is the main difficulty in writing 'clear music,' " he said, "and this clarity should be 'new'—not conventional."

He planned a cantata for two choruses (professional and amateur) and four orchestras (symphonic, military brass band, jazz band, and accordion). There were to be five hundred performers. The principal themes of his work were: "the great October Revolution, the Victory, the Industrialization of the country, and Stalin's Constitution."

For his texts he used excerpts from the speeches and writings of Lenin, Marx, and Stalin. "Lenin," Prokofiev said, "wrote with such imagery, in such clear and convincing language that I did not want to turn his words into verse. I preferred to go straight to the original source and use verbatim the leader's words."

Using these texts in a chronological order, he divided the cantata into ten parts:

1. Orchestral introduction (the epigraph to this is a quote from the Communist Manifesto: "A specter is haunting Europe—the specter of Communism")
2. Philosophers (chorus to the text taken from Marx's theses on Ludwig Feuerbach: "The philosophers have interpreted the world's situation in various ways; the main point, however, is to change it")
3. Orchestral interlude
4. "We are marching in closely knit groups along a precipitous and difficult path . . ." (chorus on Lenin's words from Chernyshevsky's *What Is To Be Done?*)
5. Orchestral interlude
6. Revolution (chorus to texts from Lenin's speeches and articles, October 1917)
7. Victory (orchestra and chorus on Lenin's texts)
8. Stalin's Pledge (chorus on text from Stalin's speech at Lenin's bier)
9. Symphony (symphony and accordion orchestras; theme: socialist reconstruction)
10. The Stalin Constitution (chorus on text from Stalin's speech at the Eighth Extraordinary Congress of Soviets)

The score called for such "realistic" effects as shots from light and heavy artillery, machine-gun fire, a tocsin, and sirens.

"I wrote the cantata with great enthusiasm," Prokofiev said. "The complicated events that are narrated in it demanded a complicated language. But I hope that the spontaneity and the sincerity of this music will reach my listeners."

Sergei Prokofiev was mistaken. Although this, his second cantata on a political theme, was a far cry from his first, "Seven, They Are Seven," it suffered the same fate.

The Soviet critics had bitterly denounced several previous attempts to give a musical documentation of the Communist movement: an oratorio by the Czech composer Irving Schulhoff on the text of the Communist Manifesto, some works by the German composer Hans Eisler, and Alexander Krein's symphonic dithyramb "The Soviet Union—the Shock-Brigade of the World's Proletariat," in which the musical episodes were united by excerpts from Stalin's speeches.

Now, Prokofiev's cantata was added to this list, for in it the critics discovered his "tendency to leftist deviation and vulgarity which is predominant in the works of some so-called revolutionary artists in the West."

Since the cantata remained in manuscript, we have to accept the critics' words, showing their resentment, which was based mainly on the following:

No matter how artistically clear and vivid the speeches are of the leaders of the Revolution, they are not intended to be sung. When they are transposed to singing, they not only encumber the melodic idiom itself, but lose much of their convincing oratorical power.

Needless to say, the cantata was never performed.

Not in the least discouraged, Prokofiev joined with his colleagues in another venture in connection with the approaching anniversary of the October Revolution.

For the past few years, on Gorky's initiative, several expeditions had been organized to collect "songs" and "tales" from the folklore of different parts of the Soviet Union—Russia, the Ukraine, Byelorussia, and the Caucasus. From some of this material, which dealt with such themes as "devotion to the motherland, the Communist Party, and socialism," the best "songs" and "tales" were selected and published in one volume by *Pravda*.

Prokofiev used the texts from these works for several of his compositions, written in the folk style, and grouped them into a suite for chorus, soloists, and orchestra, which he named Songs of Our Days. The suite consisted of an orchestral introduction, a march, and eight songs: "Over the Bridge," "Be Well," "Golden Ukraine," "Brother for Brother," "Girls," "The Twenty-Year-Old," "Lullaby," and "From End to End."

It was performed on January 5, 1938, at the Grand Hall of the Moscow Conservatory under the direction of Alexander Gauk, but this composition did not fare any better than his cantata. The critics found that his sincere desire to achieve a "new" simplicity unfortunately did not always fit the vivid images he attempted to reproduce. And speaking on behalf of the average listener as well, they unanimously agreed with Vera Vasina-Grossman, who wrote in her article on the Soviet musical art:

To be simple and at the same time remain true to himself appeared to be much too difficult a problem for the composer—a great deal in the suite is pale and lacking in individuality.

No wonder that after a long year of extraordinary productivity—though, as far as his general public was concerned, utterly in vain—Prokofiev welcomed an invitation from his friends in the United States, and at the beginning of the following year arrived there on his last journey outside of Russia.

26

The Russian music critics glossed over Prokofiev's journey to the United States in 1939. In his biography of Prokofiev (published in Moscow in 1945, and in New York in 1946), Nestyev failed to mention whether the composer was accompanied by his wife and children, whether they had left the children with Lina's mother in Paris, or whether they had left them in Moscow to assure Prokofiev's return to Russia. Nestyev left Lina out of this trip, as he had left Lina's name out of his biography, for reasons that I shall explain in the next chapter, when I deal with the general method of supplying information in Soviet Russia.

In his second biography of Sergei Prokofiev (published in Moscow in 1957, and in California in 1960), Nestyev substituted for "Americans welcomed Prokofiev as an old friend" (as it appears in the first biography) the phrase "Progressive circles welcomed. . . ." He used this term in freely interpreting Prokofiev's own words, "My friends in America." Nestyev obviously tried to indicate for the benefit of his Soviet readers that Prokofiev's friends were not Russian refugees or the American bourgeoisie. In communist parlance "progressive circles" is usually applied to those whom we call "fellow travelers."

Actually, during this last visit to the United States, Prokofiev avoided his former close friends, at least in New York. And if by chance he happened to meet one of them on the street, he made a quick sign with his eyes indicating that he was being watched. As for his visit to Hollywood, there he saw among others Rouben Mamoulian, Marlene Dietrich, and Walt Disney, who did not belong to the "progressive circles," any more than did Sergei Koussevitzky in Boston, where Prokofiev conducted a performance of *Peter and the Wolf*.

Prokofiev was scheduled to return to New York as a guest conductor with the New York Philharmonic in 1940, but the engagement was cancelled because he could not obtain the necessary visas.

Upon his return to Russia from the United States, Prokofiev shared his impressions with his countrymen in an article published in *International Literature* (No. 7–8, 1939).

Contrary to the assumption of some insufficiently informed Europeans, Americans are really sincerely interested in music, and many actually love music. A desire to know music and to make it their own is growing remarkably in the United States. The famous American motto—to have nothing but the best—makes them spend a great deal of money on importing everything that has already been successful in Europe. Therefore, the most talented performers come to the United States and organize excellent orchestras for which they engage musicians from various countries: France supplies them with woodwind instrumentalists, Germany with brass, and so on. Such orchestras as the Boston Symphony, the New York Philharmonic, and the Philadelphia Orchestra are without a doubt the best in the world.

The concert life in the United States is a regular festival for visiting Europeans, who are given an opportunity to hear the famous soloists and to feast on the remarkable ensembles.

As to what concerns the Americans, they have learned to evaluate and demand good performances, and I have noticed that many artists who arrive from Europe have to "pull themselves together," or their failings will be pointed out.

The business of composing their own music, on the other hand, is somewhat different. They may be able to import performers, but they cannot create their own composers in that way. It is true that many European composers have gone to live and work in the United States, but their works can never be considered as authentically American. The American composers themselves have not yet developed satisfactorily.

In connection with this, the American music lover has acquired a psychology that is somehow different from ours. While we have had an unbroken chain of eminent composers during the past hundred years whose works have presented problems of understanding for our audiences, the composers who arrive in the United States come from Europe with well-established names, and works already appraised and accepted by the public.

In Russia, in France, and in Central European countries the public is accustomed to evaluating the quality of the music offered to them by "new" composers. I would even say that the public "loves" to hear a performance of a new work, to argue about it, praise or scorn it. It is true, they often criticize good works and loudly praise the mediocre. But these misjudgments sooner or later are cleared up: a "true" composition triumphs, even if not immediately. But, after all, this is the pulse of a true musical life. And there is no such practice in the United States, not yet, or perhaps very little of it.

Therefore it is very hard for a young composer to make his way. The music critics seem to argue in this way: "From one hundred compositions perhaps only one remains for posterity. Therefore, if I don't understand the new composition and write that it is mediocre, I have ninety-nine chances in a hundred to be right." The critics forget, somehow, that their aim is to discover and to "promote" this "one" from the hundred.

For the past twenty years I have been going on concert tours in the United States and have noticed that American criticism and appreciation of the art of performing are far more accurate than their understanding of a "new language" in a new composition. This, however, does not mean that the Americans do not have respect and love for composers. Unfortunately, it takes a very long time to develop either.

Thus, Brahms, whose music lacks external effects but is rich in its inner content, is held there in great esteem. And again, the Americans understood his music and learned to love him only long after his death.

At the present time one feels in the United States a great desire to create a music of their own. I might add that there is a true longing for a native composer. And if this desire has not yet found complete fulfillment, still one senses a partial manifestation of their creative ability.

In this respect it is interesting to analyze the role which Jazz could play in the development of their art: on one side Jazz is a typical American product, and on the other it remains somehow removed from serious music. Jazz was formed from several different elements. It has the rich syncopated rhythm of a Negro origin, but it has also melodic turns of Anglo-American folk songs. There is also an element of the night-club dance tunes, and the sensual wailing of a more common origin that is akin to gypsy music.

Many serious composers are repulsed by Jazz—others are sincerely interested in it. I believe it depends entirely on your choice of elements. Should you choose the vulgar and commonplace, then Jazz is both annoying and revolting, should you try to select the best from the rhythm, melodies, and the orchestration, you would be rewarded with a great deal of wealth.

By the way, one finds in Jazz some extremely interesting orchestral effects, that is, when a work is orchestrated by a capable musician. In addition to this, some Jazz performers such as horn, trombone, clarinet, and percussion instrument players have developed a technique never dreamed of by musicians in symphonic orchestras. It would be worthwhile not only for composers but also for performers to hear them.

We in Russia often maintain that a Jazz orchestra must be something so loud, so noisy that it hurts our eardrums. Actually, the famous American Jazz ensembles are rich in nuance, and "sport" remarkable effects when playing softly. And I believe that the contemporary American composers are trying to found their own national music on these best elements of Jazz, trying to discard the commonplace and retain everything of value.

In this respect, George Gershwin, who died recently, certainly deserves our attention.

Having made a skyrocket career as a composer of light music—Jazz, little songs, musical comedies, and motion pictures—he then tried to "transfer" himself into the field of serious music. His Piano Concerto, as well as other pieces, have been performed by symphonic orchestras, and his opera *Porgy and Bess* has been given at well-known opera houses.

(With charming naïveté we in Russia have translated the Rhapsody in Blue as Blue Rhapsody. *Blue* does not necessarily mean the color blue, but means, colloquially, *sad*. The *blue* Jazz dance pieces are of a sad character, usually on the same theme: "I love you, but you don't love me." Therefore, the Rhapsody is written on sad themes, but is not in the color *blue*.)

Gershwin was undoubtedly endowed with a great talent, but in the development of his serious music the years he had spent in composing "light music" turned out to be a millstone around his neck. To be more specific—he simply could not find criteria for what he was trying to do in the symphonic compositions.

The patriots of American music were ready to proclaim him as a long-awaited star. Gershwin did have definite chances. One could have hoped that after overcoming the burden of his early mediocre musical education, he could spread his wings and soar high. Unfortunately, a premature death claimed this interesting artist. But the very appearance of such a talent gives the hope that there will be other composers who could develop a new style of American music.

I speak of Gershwin because to us, at least, he is the most typical American composer.

In addition to these impressions, Prokofiev brought home with him some technical knowledge in sound-film production, which he had acquired while visiting film studios in Hollywood. It stood him in good stead when, soon after his return, Sergei Eisenstein, the director who had been Meyerhold's pupil and had won worldwide acclaim for *Potemkin* and *Ivan the Terrible*, asked Prokofiev whether he would be interested in writing music for *Alexander Nevsky*, a film he planned to direct.

"I was an old admirer of Eisenstein's films, and was delighted to accept his offer," Prokofiev said. "My pleasure was even greater when, during our work together, I discovered that in addition to being a brilliant director, Eisenstein was a keen musician."

The subject of *Alexander Nevsky* belongs to the twelfth century, and was built on two opposite elements: the Russian on one side and the Teutonic Crusaders on the other. It is understandable that

Prokofiev was initially tempted to use the music of that epoch. But after having studied the twelfth- and thirteenth-century Catholic chants, he realized that the music had lost its meaning during the past seven centuries and had become so alien to us in its emotional expression that it would not be interesting to the film's audience. Therefore, he decided to write the music not as it had sounded at the time of the "Battle of Ice," but in a way in which we could imagine it today. He felt the same way about the Russian songs, and disregarded how they were sung seven centuries earlier.

Having chosen the character of his composition, his curiosity and newly acquired knowledge of sound reproduction brought him in closer contact with the actual sound recording of his own score. Despite the extraordinary progress in sound production, Prokofiev maintained, perfection had not yet been achieved, and the rattling noises in even the best microphones distorted the music. But why not use these negative aspects of the microphones, he asked, and try to draw from them unusual effects? For instance, a powerful stream of sound directed at the microphone during the recording session affects the record to such a degree that during the performance it produces an unpleasant crackling sound. "And since the sound of Teutonic trumpets and horns were no doubt unpleasant to the Russian ear," Prokofiev said, "in order not to miss the dramatic effect, I have insisted that these fanfares be played directly into the microphone.

"Also," he continued, "in our orchestras we have very powerful instruments, such as a trombone, and in comparison the more feeble sound of a bassoon. If we place the bassoon right near the microphone and the trombone some twenty meters away from it, then we will have a powerful bassoon and in the background a barely audible trombone. This practice can offer a completely 'upside-down' means of orchestration, which would have been impossible in compositions for a symphonic orchestra."

Prokofiev also suggested placing the horns and trumpets in one studio and the chorus in another. From each studio there was a direct line that led into the box in which the sound recording was being made and in which, with a simple movement of a switch, the volume of each group's sound could be augmented or diminished, depending on the requirement of the dramatic action. They also used three microphones, which at that time demanded an extraordinary facility in mixing the three streams of sound.

"The motion picture is a young art that offers the composer interesting possibilities," Prokofiev said. "He should develop them, and not limit himself to writing music and then delivering it to a motion-picture factory, as it were, for others to do the recording. Those men may have the best intentions in the world, but they are not as capable in dealing with the music as the composer himself."

Prokofiev admitted, however, that not all his "inventions" were acceptable; still, he found in his collaborators such a sympathetic attitude that he derived a truly unusual pleasure from this work. He was particularly impressed by Eisenstein's respect for music which sometimes led to his willingness to "pull" the dramatic action backward or forward in order not to be destroy the integrity of the music.

Their exceptionally harmonious relationship stemmed from Eisenstein's understanding and knowledge of Prokofiev's works, and of Prokofiev the man.* "He is a perfect composer for the screen," Eisenstein often said, for he believed that Prokofiev's music was "amazingly plastic." "It never remains merely an illustration," he said, "but reveals the movement and the dynamic structure in which are embodied the emotion and meaning of an event. Whether it was the March from *The Love for Three Oranges*, the duel between Mercutio and Tybalt in *Romeo and Juliet*, or the galloping of Teutonic knights in *Alexander Nevsky*, Prokofiev had grasped before anything else the structural secret that conveys the broad meaning of a subject. And having grasped this structural secret, he clothes it in the tonal 'camera-angles' of instrumentation, compelling the whole inflexible structure to blossom into the emotional fullness of his orchestration. The moving graphic outlines of his musical images which thus arise are thrown onto our consciousness just as, through a blinding beam of a projector, moving images are thrown onto the white plane of the screen."

Eisenstein added, "Prokofiev is profoundly nationalistic. But not in the *kvass* and *shchi* manner of the conventionally Russian pseudo-realists. Nor is he nationalistic in the 'holy-water' detail and genre of Vasily Perov's and Ilya Repin's brush. Prokofiev is nationalistic in the strictly traditional sense that dates back to the savage Scythian and the unsurpassed perfection of the thirteenth-century carvings on the walls of the cathedrals in Vladimir and Suzdal. His nationalism stemmed from the very source that had shaped the national consciousness of the Russian people, the source that is reflected in the folk wisdom of our old frescoes or the icon craftsmanship of Andrei Rublev. That is why the antiquity resounds so authentically in Prokofiev's music—not through archaic or stylized means, but through the most extreme and even hazardous twists of ultra-modern musical composition."

* Sergei Eisenstein: *Film Form and the Film Sense*, Jay Leyda, ed. and trans. (New York and Cleveland: Meridian, 1957).

But Eisenstein also saw in Prokofiev's music a paradoxical synchronization, as if an icon had been juxtaposed with a cubist painting: Picasso with the frescoes at the Spaso-Nereditzkaya, the eleventh-century church near Novgorod. Through this true originality in the Hegelian sense, Prokofiev was, Eisenstein maintained, both national and international—just as international and ultra-modern as an icon painted on sandalwood hanging among the canvases in a New York art gallery.

Analyzing Prokofiev's music further, Eisenstein observed that it was also international because of the variety of his musical language. In Prokofiev's musical mentality he saw a certain affinity to that of the Byzantine tradition, which was, he said, always distinguished in every environment—always fresh and unexpected: on Italian soil in the Madonnas of Cimabue, on Spanish soil in the works of El Greco, and in the state of Novgorod in the murals of anonymous masters, murals trampled underfoot by the hordes of invading Teutons. Eisenstein concluded, "Thus the art of Prokofiev has been inspired by more than purely national, historical, or patriotic themes, such as the heroic events of the thirteenth, sixteenth, and nineteenth centuries (the triad of *War and Peace, Ivan the Terrible*, and *Alexander Nevsky*), but also by Shakespearean Italy of the Renaissance in his *Romeo and Juliet* ballet, by the magic phantasmagoria of Gozzi in *The Love for Three Oranges*, and in the nursery of Andersen's *The Ugly Duckling* and *Peter and the Wolf*."

During work on *Alexander Nevsky* every method had been used. There were sequences in which the shots were cut to a previously recorded music track, and there were sequences for which the entire piece of music was written to a final cutting of the film. Eisenstein often watched Prokofiev as he sat in the studio while one of the scenes was shown to him. He could see Prokofiev's hands resting on the arms of the chair, and see how his fingers would suddenly begin to tap as if he were receiving Morse code.

Was he beating the measure of his music? Eisenstein wondered. Later he learned that Prokofiev was marking the structure of the film where the length and the tempi were combined with the action of the characters. And Eisenstein was even more amazed when he learned that Prokofiev could catch the intonation of their speech.

"One such example occurred in the battle scene, where pipes and drums were playing for the victorious Russian soldiers," Eisenstein recalled. "I couldn't find a way to explain to Prokofiev what precise effect should be 'seen' in the music for this joyous moment. I ordered some 'prop' instruments made, and a shot of these being played visually (without a sound) was shown to Prokofiev. Almost immediately he handed me an exact 'musical equivalent' for the visual image of pipers and drummers that I had shown him."

The two collaborators, however, did not always agree. When Prokofiev's score was finally recorded on the soundtrack, Eisenstein asked him to write an overture. Prokofiev refused. "The film begins," he said, "with a tragic episode—'Russia under the Mongolian yoke'—but an overture should be historically victorious." And he said that he could not see the transition from such an overture to the tragic music. He added, however, that he was willing to write any amount of music if the film required it, but from a purely artistic point of view he could not write an overture. But Eisenstein insisted. Well then, Prokofiev said, he would compose the overture on one condition: Eisenstein should start the film with a less tragic episode. Eisenstein did not see how he could change the plan of the film; the overture was never written.

Prokofiev took a very active part in the recording of his score. He studied all the technical possibilities of the Moskfilm studio, and experimented with placing selected groups of musicians of the orchestra at various angles from the microphones in an attempt to produce some sound effects different from those in a concert hall. Finally, he asked that the orchestra be divided into four groups, each facing one of the microphones.

He refused to conduct the orchestra because, he said, he had to be able to judge the sound from the recording box. Because of the unusual seating of the orchestra, it was not an easy task for a conductor to achieve satisfactory results, and it required many rehearsals, for Prokofiev was extremely demanding. He was demanding with the musicians and the men who made the recording, and even critical of his own music. He had written a rather difficult part for the French horn—it had to be played with the horn turned upward and with a *sourdine*—and during the intermission the French horn player told Prokofiev that one particular phrase was awkwardly written. "I was concerned with an artistic effect, not with your comfort," Prokofiev said. "I am afraid I may 'scratch,' " the horn player warned him. With a look that prohibited any further discussion, Prokofiev said, "If you should "scratch," then it shows that you don't play well enough, and it will be necessary to call in someone who can manage your part satisfactorily."

He often criticized the "mixer" and even insisted on taking his place at the mixing desk. During the recording he paid no attention to the indications shown by the recording box, nor did he take into consideration the technical possibilities. He was guided solely by his ear. On one occasion, having recorded two doubles, he announced that he was perfectly satisfied, that the musicians could go home because he, too, was leaving. Saying this, he departed. But the "mixer" remained and asked Eisenstein to let him re-do the recording of the same two doubles. A few days later, when Prokofiev's own recording was played, Prokofiev exclaimed, "This is not worth a damn." And he liked the recording made by the "mixer." "Ah, so it is you who made a fool of me," he said to the man. "Well, it serves me good and right—one should never *mix* oneself into other people's business. Still," he added, "you have swallowed one eighth note in the transition from one group to another."

Sometimes, however, he was willing to take advice when it concerned the orchestration: to give a certain phrase or a part in his score to a different instrument. "You are right," he said, "at the Bolshoi they have a trombone with a piece attached to it—the man could play on it the contrabassoon part. Let's call him in."

And when he heard the rehearsal of "The Field of the Dead" scene—with which everyone was pleased because of the beauty of the music—Prokofiev remarked, "How strange it sounds. The music . . . not a bit like Prokofiev's."

On December 1, 1938, the film was shown to Soviet audiences, and since then has been acclaimed all over the world as one of the masterpieces in the art of motion pictures. It is still occasionally shown in the United States. Its long-lasting success is no doubt partly due to its being one of the most musical films ever produced. In 1941, when Hitler's armies invaded Russia, the film—a purely artistic achievement—gained additional significance: political, and as a timely patriotic manifestation of the Russian people. The Soviet audiences identified the eleventh-century Swedish knights with the Nazis, and the song "Arise, Men of Russia" called on their patriotism to prove once more that For an Enemy There Is No Place on Russian Soil—the leitmotif of Prokofiev's score.

As soon as Prokofiev had completed work on the film, he was busily revising plans he had made in Paris in 1933 for a cello concerto. "I was far from satisfied with the original sketches," he said. "I could see the 'white seams' connecting various sections of the concerto, and besides, I felt that the music was not always good. Now, after a long 'interruption,' I had revised the concerto, adding to it some new material."

He divided the concerto into three parts: Andante, Allegro risoluto in a toccata character, and a Theme with Variations. The young cellist Leonid Berezovsky was entrusted to prepare the concerto for its first performance, and Svyatoslav Richter was closely connected with Berezovsky's initial studies of the concerto.

The twenty-three-year-old Richter was Heinrich Neuhaus' pupil at the Moscow Conservatory, which he had entered during the previous year after deciding to devote himself to a career as a pianist. Since he had heard Prokofiev's recitals in Odessa some ten years before, Richter had seen the composer just once, shortly after Richter arrived in Moscow in 1937. "On a clear sunny day," Richter said, "I saw an unusual looking man walking toward me on the street. He wore bright yellow shoes and a checkered red-orange tie. He seemed to carry a challenging force, and he passed me like a vision. I couldn't help turning to follow his disappearing figure. That was Prokofiev."

Now, in 1938, because Richter was lodging with Heinrich Neuhaus in the same house in which the Prokofievs' apartment was, it was not unusual for him to see them. "These boys, over there, such charming children . . . Those are Prokofiev's sons: the elder looks like him, but the younger is like a doll—simply enchanting!" Richter overheard their neighbors say. He often saw Madame Prokofiev, an elegantly dressed young woman in a dark blue beret, "with an anxious expression." Richter saw the Prokofievs at concerts, but he had not yet met the composer.

When Richter was asked to work with Berezovsky on the cello concerto, he accepted it like any other job, he said, in order to earn his living. I shall let Richter tell the story in his own characteristic way: "For two solid months I used to walk several miles to Berezovsky's apartment on the sixth floor," Richter recalled later. "My attitude was purely businesslike. Although Berezovsky was pleased with the engagement, the music was obviously alien to him. He shrugged, he sighed, and he complained about the difficulties, but he practiced the concerto diligently, and he was very nervous. I cannot say that I myself had liked the concerto, but I felt that it was interesting to work on it."

Later on, when Berezovsky had finally learned the concerto, Richter went with him to play it for Prokofiev. "Prokofiev himself opened the door, and led us into a small canary-yellow room," Richter continued his story. "A few drawings of stage sets from *The Love for Three Oranges* were hanging on the walls. These, if I am not mistaken, were in pencil or India ink. To begin with, Prokofiev said sternly to his sons, 'Children, go away! Don't bother us!' and then he sat down. Berezovsky looked terribly upset. Probably because of this, Prokofiev did not feel like talking to him too much, and went to the piano and began to show him 'this way or that way.' . . . I stood a little way apart, all on my own. Prokofiev was businesslike, and not at all sympathetic. Apparently he was irritated by Berezovsky's questions. But I was very pleased that Prokofiev's demands were similar to my own perception of the piece. Prokofiev wanted to hear only what was written in the score—ah, but all! And Berezovsky had a tendency to be sentimental, and could not find a single spot in the score where he could show off the sound of his playing. Prokofiev never asked me to play a single note, not once, and so . . . we left."

Later, Berezovsky and Richter played the concerto at the Composers' Union, and the composition was acclaimed a "true event, just like the one created by Prokofiev's Second Violin Concerto." A lively discussion followed, but everybody was finally convinced that the composition was going to have great success. From then on, Berezovsky began to work with Melik-Pachayev, the conductor, in preparation for the performance on November 26, 1938, and Richter no longer had anything to do with it.

But Richter naturally came to the première and sat in the dress circle "as if oppressed and terribly nervous." "I was nervous about the composition and, of course, about Berezovsky. Throughout the performance I felt as if the floor were disappearing from under my chair. Melik-Pachayev was taking very 'uncomfortable' tempi, actually, not the right kind anyway. I thought that he had never really understood the composition. The performance was a complete fiasco. Berezovsky and Pachayev managed to take some kind of bow, and with this everything ended."

Prokofiev obviously had tried to enrich the cello technique with some complicated virtuoso passages more suitable to the violin, which added to the general dryness of the composition, causing more criticism than praise. "It lacks that melodic élan, the expressive *cantabile*, which are inherent in compositions for string instruments," noted the critics. Even Miaskovsky sounded disappointed: "Brilliant piece but . . . somehow it does not come off."

For a while Prokofiev was merely irritated by these critical comments. "They are indifferent to the concerto," he said, "because they are silly—it is akin to my Second Violin Concerto." But eventually, giving in to Miaskovsky's arguments in regard to the serious defects in the actual form of the composition, Prokofiev substantially revised the score and even added a cadenza. A year later, in 1940, Gregor Piatigorsky introduced the concerto in the United States.

At the end of 1938, no doubt because Prokofiev was still inspired by the typical Russian character of his recent work, *Alexander*

Nevsky, he sketched his First Violin Sonata (Op. 80), but a far more important project made him lay aside the already written beginning of the first movement and some major themes for the last movement of the sonata. He decided to make a cantata from the material written for the film.

It took him much longer than if he were writing a new composition, Prokofiev said, for now he had to create a large symphonic work from the separate parts of his music for the film. These parts had to be connected, if not at times completely rewritten, and finally the whole had to be reorchestrated to suit a symphonic performance.

The introduction, "Russia Under the Mongolian Yoke," the second part, "The Song about Alexander Nevsky," the fourth part, "Arise, Men of Russia," and the sixth part, "The Field of the Dead," were almost identical to those in the score for the film, but "The Battle on the Ice" and the finale, "Alexander Nevsky's Entrance into Pskov," had to be reconstructed.

On March 17, 1939, Prokofiev himself conducted the Moscow Philharmonic in the first performance of the cantata. Its immediate success spurred him on to planning an opera on a Soviet subject, although he had been making sketches for a cycle of three piano sonatas—the Sixth, Seventh, and Eighth. Following his own long-established method of composing, he had already written some of the major themes, indicating for future reference where to use them. "Themes easily slip away, they come and go, sometimes never to return," he often said and, with a sly wink, he would add, "Some of my critics, no doubt, would say that the more of my themes 'never to return' the better."

Actually, he was working simultaneously on all ten parts of the three sonatas, for, as he said, whenever he "got stuck" on one, he would work on the other in order not to lose time. And as if all this work were not enough to fill his day, he worked at the same time on the four movements of his future Fifth Symphony.

But these projects had to be postponed because in the fall of 1939 he was commissioned by the music department of All-Soviet Union Radio to write a cantata for the forthcoming celebration of Stalin's sixtieth birthday on December 21. In view of all the horrors the people of Soviet Russia had been suffering during the past several years, it is a matter of conjecture how Prokofiev could "sing an ode" to the man responsible for them. And yet it would be hard to condemn him. Obviously he had no choice, for his refusal might have brought down upon him the tragic fate of those who had been accused of being guilty of even lesser offenses.

"The text of the cantata was a successful choice by the composer himself of seven folk songs dedicated to Stalin by various Soviet nationalities: Russian, Ukrainian, Byelorussian, Mordovian, Kurd, Mari, and Kumykian. Russian folk melody predominates in the cantata, which is written in an extremely clear melodic idiom, colored by Prokofiev's own individual style," Israel V. Nestyev wrote in 1945 while Stalin was alive, as befitted the composer's official biographer. ". . . *Zdravitsa* [as the cantata is called] has been justly appraised as one of the best Soviet compositions singing of the love of the people for Stalin."

A few excerpts from the text are sufficient to show the basic tenor of the work.

> Never before was our field so green,
> Never before had our village known such unheard-of happiness,
> Never before was our life so gay,
> Never before had our rye flowered so high,

sang the peasants, expressing their happiness in the "free collective farm work."

> He hears everything, he sees everything in the people's lives,

was another song referring to Stalin, which needs no comment. And the farewell song to Aksinya, a prize worker going off to a reception at the Kremlin, added the final touch to the cantata:

> "If my eyes sparkled as when I was a girl,
> If my cheeks were as red as an apple ripe,
> I would hie me to Moscow, the great city,
> And say 'thank you' to Joseph Stalin."

Ten years later, after Stalin's death, and after Nikita Khrushchev had launched his campaign against the so-called "personality cult," Israel Nestyev had carefully avoided using Stalin's name in his second book on Prokofiev, but still afraid to speak of the true reasons for Prokofiev's most humiliating work, he wrote, "The main virtue of the cantata lies in the sincere and sensitive interpretation of the feelings of the Soviet people, who are so estatic with the fruits of the freedom in their work." And he closes his commentary with the following exclamation: "What complicated evolution Prokofiev's creative thought had to undergo in order to pass from the distorted, urbane, invented Russia of his *Le Pas d'acier* ballet to the truly contemporary Soviet images of Zdravitsa!"

The cantata was hailed as a great success when it was performed by the orchestra and chorus of the All-Soviet Union Radio under the direction of Nikolai Golovanov at the Grand Hall of the Conservatory on Stalin's birthday, and Prokofiev was awarded a second prize for his composition. Nevertheless, he did not oblige his biographer with any comment, nor did Prokofiev mention the cantata in his own commentaries on his work.

27

"To write an opera on a Soviet subject is not a simple problem," Prokofiev often said. "One needs new people, new emotions, new customs, and therefore many methods which were natural in classical operas could be alien and useless. While Lensky's aria in *Evgeni Onegin*, or Prince Igor's aria in *Prince Igor* form an integral part of Tchaikovsky's and Borodin's operas, an aria of, let us say, the president of a district council would bewilder the listener if the composer had committed the slightest error in portraying the character. And a recitative of a commissar trying to dial a telephone number could also cause the raising of eyebrows.

"Personally, for a long time I had wanted to write a 'Soviet opera,' but did not dare start working on one until I had developed a definite way of solving this problem. There was no point in choosing a stilted or commonplace subject, or an edifying kind of plot. I wanted living people, with their true passions, love, hatreds, happiness, and sorrows which were caused naturally by the 'new' events.

"This is how I happened to become interested in Valentin Kataev's novel *I Am a Son of the Working People*," Prokofiev explained.

Six years younger than Prokofiev, Kataev began a literary career in his early youth, when his poems were published in magazines in Odessa and St. Petersburg. During the First World War he was a front-line correspondent; then, after serving two years in the Red Army, he participated in the Civil War in the Ukraine. This novel deals with the struggle of the Ukrainian guerrillas against the German invaders in 1918 as portrayed in the dramatic story of Semyon Kotko, a young soldier who returns to his native village after spending four years in the First World War, and is granted by the Soviet government a piece of land and some cattle. Kotko wants to marry Sophia Tkachenko, but her father, a former noncommissioned officer and now a well-to-do peasant, objects to their marriage. During the celebration of Kotko's engagement to Sophia, a German regiment invades the village and treats the villagers brutally. They burn down Kotko's hut and beat his mother and his little sister. In danger of his life, Kotko leaves the village and joins the partisans who are fighting the invaders. Upon learning that Tkachenko is giving Sophia in marriage to a wealthy landlord, Kotko returns to his village, breaks into the ceremony at the church, and kidnaps the girl. Kotko falls into the hands of the enemy, but is saved from execution by a group of partisans who arrive in time.

"This novel," Prokofiev said, "combines the most opposite elements: there is a young man's love, hatred of the representatives of the old regime, the heroism of a people's struggle and the sorrow over their losses, and there are gay and amusing jokes so characteristic of the Ukrainian people. Kataev's characters are alive, which is very important. They live, enjoy life, grumble, or laugh—and this is the life I wished to portray when I chose Kataev's novel for my opera *Semyon Kotko*, a title derived from the name of the principal character in the story."

But to find the right kind of subject seems to have caused less difficulty than to solve some problems that Prokofiev had posed for himself. At a concert an audience listens to music, he argued, while at an opera the audience does not wish merely to hear the music, but wants to witness the action on the stage. Therefore, it is very important that the dramatic action be *active*, for static moments on stage are very dangerous—the accompanying music might be good, but the audience would be bored if their eyes were not supplied with the necessary "visual food." Thus, Prokofiev's first concern was with uninterrupted action on the stage.

But what should be done about the arias? he asked himself. It was a vital question, for he knew as well as anyone else that arias have a legitimate place in an opera: they offer the composer an opportunity to develop a beautiful melody, and the singer to show off his voice. The problem was what to do if, during an aria, sometimes lasting five minutes (and five minutes can be an eternity on stage), nothing happens except that the singer occasionally lifts one or both hands?

For this reason, Prokofiev said, he divided arias into two groups very different in character from each other. To the first he ascribed Lensky's aria in *Evgeni Onegin*, during which nothing whatsoever happens on stage, and to the second, the scene of Tatyana's letter (also in *Evgeni Onegin*), which is of an entirely different character—a long aria lasting almost as long as the whole scene. "But although during that scene there is no physical action on the stage," Prokofiev said, "the scene is so imbued with emotion that we cannot tear our eyes away and don't even notice the length of the aria. And this is the kind of arias I would like to have in my opera."

He felt the same way about a chorus. To avoid static dramatic action while some eighty or a hundred members of the chorus were singing, he tried to superimpose action on the stage. He also tried to avoid the "dry" recitatives, which he called the most uninteresting element in the operas. In the more expressive moments he made the recitative more singable, more of a melodic-recitative; but in the score's "matter-of-fact" places he used a rhythmical conversation.

The tradition of conversations in an opera is an old one, Prokofiev observed—Mozart's opera arias and ensembles, for example, are always interlaced with scenes of conversations. Nevertheless, Prokofiev felt that a conversation between singing is not always interesting, and therefore he preferred a rhythmical conversation, something akin to an unintoned recitative. In each case he was careful to see that the transition from the singing to the conversational style was natural, so that the audience would be unaware of it.

Having often been accused of having a lack of melody in his compositions, Prokofiev repeated that he had always considered the melody to be the most important element in a composition, but, he explained, "Each melody is easily remembered if its melodic line reminds us of something, if it is built on a familiar musical image. But if the melodic line is 'new,' at first it is not accepted as melodic, and therefore the melody is understood only after several repeated hearings.

"If there are only a few melodies in an opera, but they are often repeated, then an audience easily remembers them. If, on the other hand, there are many melodies in an opera, then the audience at first is lost, does not remember them, and is apt to consider the melodic wealth as a poverty of melodic material. For instance, for a long time audiences were of the opinion that Wagner's *Götterdämmerung* was merely an incoherent noise, only because the unusual quantity of melodies were superimposed on each other. And during the first performance of Tchaikovsky's *Evgeni Onegin* the audience understood and remembered only Gremlin's aria and Triket's amusing couplets."

Prokofiev also pointed out that our "capacity to 'hear' music changes with time. What pleased people a hundred years ago today leaves us indifferent, and the melodies which were not even considered as such today are praised as interesting and beautiful. Beethoven's contemporaries used to criticize him: 'The old man is deaf and does not hear what he is composing.' And yet a hundred years after his death they give us the greatest of joy. The same can be said about Wagner, Liszt, and other remarkable composers."

But despite the advantage of an immediate success in filling an opera with melodies written on well-known melodic lines, Prokofiev preferred to adhere to an opposite system, trying to supply his opera, as much as possible, with new melodies in great quantity.

"Although such music at first, perhaps, would be hard for the ear to retain," Prokofiev reasoned, "a great deal of it would easily be remembered after a second or third hearing. And it is better for an audience to discover something new each time than to say, 'I know all this, and it is not worth listening to again.' A hundred to a hundred and fifty years ago our ancestors enjoyed gay pastorales and music of Mozart and Rameau; last century they admired slow, serious music; in our day, in music as in everything else, it is speed, energy, and drive that are preferred.

"The subject of my opera is 'new,'" Prokofiev concluded in discussing the work. "Therefore the method of composing should be new. The audience should not protest that it will take too much of its attention to understand it."

So far, so good—as far as his precept of treatment of the opera was concerned, but it was different when he tried to put these theories into practice. Although initially he had the impression that Kataev, who had agreed to write the libretto, showed a true understanding of the style of the opera as Prokofiev saw it, their collaboration ran into difficulties almost from the beginning.

Kataev had imagined an opera about the hero of his novel in a typical Ukrainian folk-opera character—both primitive and provincial—abounding in arias and folk songs and dances. Prokofiev emphatically brushed aside such suggestion. This was not the opera in which he was going to experiment with the long arias he had so eloquently talked about in principle. "I need neither arias nor verses," he told Kataev. In fact, ever since he had been working on *The Gambler*, Prokofiev maintained that the use of verse in an opera was an outmoded method, and that Dostoyevsky's prose could be just as effective in an opera as Gogol's was in Moussorgsky's *The Marriage*. He insisted on having a dialogue form in the opera based on conversational prose with a minimum of arioso elements.

But Kataev argued that an opera of this type would never become popular. "Is it possible that you would not want your opera to live on the stage as long as Bizet's *Carmen?*" he asked Prokofiev. "If he would at least let Zarev, the sailor, dance "The Little Apple" [a popular song during the Revolution and Civil War in Russia]. After all, he was a sailor!" Kataev complained to his friends about his uncooperative collaborator. But Prokofiev considered such a commonplace idea utterly unacceptable.

Already experienced in the lackadaisical ways the poet's disregard for time, almost inherent in Russian authors, Prokofiev handed Kataev a detailed schedule for their work and demanded that each part of the libretto be delivered to him on specified dates. It took Prokofiev four months to complete the opera (until June 28, 1939) and two months to orchestrate the score, which he had taken with him to Kislovodsk, where he was spending the summer with his family.

The opera was to be produced at Konstantin Stanislavsky's Opera Studio under the stage direction of Vsyevolod Meyerhold. No contract was signed but, Meyerhold said, Prokofiev had told him that he would not give this opera to anyone else.

The two friends were looking forward to their collaboration on the opera, particularly since the bloody purge that had started in 1936 was even more rampant than before and had caught up with Meyerhold. In January 1937 the Meyerhold Theatre had been shut down as "alien, and hostile to Soviet aims." Ilya Ehrenburg dared to disclose almost thirty years later that "Meyerhold's wife, Zinaida Reich, a talented actress and an exceptionally beautiful young woman, had a nervous breakdown. Meyerhold himself bore it manfully, spoke about painting and poetry, recalled Paris. He went on working, planning a production of *Hamlet*, even though he did not believe that he would be allowed to produce the play."

He was not, but as far as Prokofiev and Meyerhold knew, he was to direct Prokofiev's opera, for it was his old friend and mentor Konstantin Stanislavsky who in those desperate times had offered Meyerhold the position of a director in his opera studio.

"No one will want to see anything I produce—the opera will be a failure," Meyerhold told Stanislavsky.

"You underestimate the Moscow audiences," Stanislavsky reassured him. "There are still hundreds of people who love art and who will appreciate your production."

Prokofiev later learned that on June 15, 1939, Meyerhold had attended the First National Convention of Theatrical Directors, whose purpose was "to summarize the recent accomplishments of the Soviet theatre, to place socialist realism on sound ground and to issue a final condemnation of formalism." The sixty-eight-year-old Meyerhold was greeted with an ovation as he mounted the rostrum to deliver his speech.

He began by saying that he was sincerely ready to admit to many of the mistakes in his work of which he had been accused—almost a traditional introductory phase to a *mea culpa* confession that the presiding jury expected from everyone brought to a "trial." But what he actually did say was that every director must have the right to experiment, "the moral right to test his creative ideas, the right to make mistakes." He brushed aside the accusation of "formalism" in his productions by explaining that his efforts had been directed toward finding an authentic style that suited a given subject. And in turn he asked his audience whether they had a definition for the term "formalism," which by its incoherent interpretations was plaguing every other field in Soviet culture as much as it did the musical. "Is socialist realism an anti-formalism?" Meyerhold asked. This term came into use at about that time, and even today, almost thirty years later, makes about as much sense as the term "formalism."

And since it was not unusual for Meyerhold to forewarn his listeners of each forthcoming production—this time of Prokofiev's opera —he brought to their attention the problem of "socialist realism." He said that he did not know whether it was anti-formalism, or realism, or naturalism, or some other "ism," but that the current works in the theatres were uninspired and bad. "This pitiful and sterile something that aspires to the title of socialist realism has nothing in common with art. Yet the theatre is art, and without art there can be no theatre." He suggested that his listeners should go to the Moscow theatres and look at "the colorless, boring productions which were all alike and had lost their own individual creative signature, so to speak.

"In the very places where only recently a creative life was seething," Meyerhold continued, "where men of art were searching, making mistakes, experimenting, and finding new ways to create productions, of which some were bad and others magnificent, now there is nothing but a depressing, well-meaning, shockingly mediocre and devastating lack of talent." And in concluding his speech, Meyerhold asked, "Was this your aim? If so, you have committed a horrible crime. In your effort to eradicate 'formalism' you have destroyed art."

Then, at the end of the summer, when Prokofiev had finished his work on the opera, he received word that Serafima Birman had been assigned to direct the opera instead of Meyerhold. "It was not Meyerhold's lot to stage the opera"—such is the laconic reference published in "S. S. Prokofiev, Articles and Documentary Material." *

* *Soviet Composer*, Moscow, 1962.

Except for those in the Western world who are familiar with Soviet publications dealing with facts and history, such shameless cynicism must be shocking. Indeed, it was not "Meyerhold's lot to stage the opera." His was to share the lot of countless other innocent victims of the purge.

"For alleged counter-revolutionary activity, Meyerhold was arrested and deported to a labor camp, where he died in 1942," was all that Ilya Ehrenburg was willing to mention about his friend in his memoirs written more than twenty years later. Ehrenburg failed to mention the fate of Meyerhold's wife.

Because of the orders from "higher-up," Meyerhold was not interrupted, and was allowed to have his say at the convention. But on the following night, Lavrenti Beria, who had taken over the uncompleted Yezhov job, had Meyerhold arrested. Meyerhold was sent to Kolyma, a penal region, but was shot in a concentration camp, Magadan, on the shores of the Sea of Okhotsk.

Three weeks after her husband's arrest the body of Zinaida Reich bearing seventeen knife wounds was found in their apartment. The Soviet sealed the premises for a month thereafter.

Prokofiev was not so much surprised by the gruesome news as he was that the outspoken Meyerhold had survived the purge as long as he did.

"Today one must work. Work is the only thing, the only salvation," Prokofiev repeated to himself what he had already said to Ehrenburg two years before. And so he called on Serafima Birman, who also happened to be in Kislovodsk, to discuss with her the forthcoming production of his opera.

Madame Birman's own reminiscences of her association with the composer leave the impression that she did not get along with him. She considered him haughty, and she admitted that she was not particularly interested in discovering the fundamental reasons for his unusual character. But she admired him as a great composer, although she was obviously not a musician and was more impressed by the external aspects of his personality.

She had heard him at a concert in Moscow, and while she did not remember which compositions he had conducted, she did remember well how he looked in his dress suit with its "too long coattails," as she thought, and how, while someone was still talking in the hall, Prokofiev held his raised baton until complete silence permitted him to start the concert. Or how he looked on a tennis court, his face flushed with excitement under a green visor, and his obvious resentment whenever he missed a ball; his quarreling with his partner and his delight over winning a point. Serafima Birman was that kind of young woman. Or was she merely being cautious in her memoir, preferring not to be too closely associated with Prokofiev?

She did not remember the preliminary discussions about the opera with Prokofiev, but remembered the day when he came to show her his composition. She was staying at one of the sanatoria, and her small room contained a bed, two chairs, a table and a wall closet. After greeting her, Prokofiev moved two chairs opposite her bed, which was going to serve as his imaginary piano, and told her to sit down next to him. He sat himself on the end of his chair, as pianists do when they play, and put his hands on the white bedspread as if it were a keyboard.

During the next two hours he "played" and sang the opera, from the overture to the last orchestral chord in the score. He sang the parts of all the characters, the chorus, and the orchestral score so vividly that even Madame Birman was compelled not only to listen to his opera, but even to see the action in it. And Prokofiev, despite his complete absorption in his own performance, was, so Madame Birman thought, aware of his audience even though it consisted of one person.

The first performance of the opera at the Stanislavsky Opera Studio, on June 23, 1940, was not a happy event for either the composer or for those connected with the production—the stage director, the conductor, and the singers. During the rehearsals Madame Birman tried to satisfy Prokofiev with the particular care she was giving to her work on the production, but in vain. "This opera," she said later, "requires an entirely new attitude toward an artistic and vocal performance; it requires a most penetrating understanding of the composer's intentions." In her opinion the opera needed the same enthusiasm and excitement that was so much in evidence at the initial production at the Moscow Art Theatre of Chekhov's *The Sea Gull*. This atmosphere was lacking, apparently, and the opera caused more argument than praise.

Since Prokofiev had not yet succeeded in comprehending the emotions of the people involved in the Revolution and Civil War, those who criticized the opera said, how could he interpret the feelings of the characters in the story? The critics accused him of distorting the realistic aspects of life in Soviet Russia and, in this composition, of returning to the "methods of modernism." However, a few among the critics acclaimed the opera as a definite achievement in Soviet "realistic culture."

For six months the discussions were carried on in the pages of the *Sovietskaya Musika*, often comparing "Prokofiev's unsuccessful experiment" with—of all operas—Tikhon Khrennikov's *Into the Storm*, an opera that made its appearance in the same season and when Khreni-kov's diverse administrative activities as an "Inspector General" of Soviet music and musicians began to be felt more and more acutely. Khrenikov's opera was hailed as an example of Soviet opera because it was by far the most "democratic," whatever that musically ambiguous statement was supposed to convey.

But the musicians who were not influenced by the ideological con-siderations and who judged the opera on its musical and artistic merits seldom missed a performance. "The more I see it, the more I am im-pressed by this opera," Miaskovsky said. "It is an extraordinary work, and has extraordinary music."

"The première of *Semyon Kotko* was an event of major magnitude in my life," Svyatoslav Richter recalled later. "It is one of Prokofiev's works which has actually 'bound me to him.' I believe it is one of his most successful works, and without a doubt one of the best Soviet op-eras. In this opera Prokofiev has continued on Moussorgsky's path in the creation of a People's National Musical Drama [Richter was refer-ring to *Boris Godunov* and *Khovanshchina*.] While listening to it, one begins to experience the life, the period of history which is depicted in this work." And being well aware of the adverse criticism, Richter said that the realization of the values of the opera is entirely depen-dent upon a sincere desire to enjoy the work, and that he was convinced that there always would be such listeners. "When I first heard *Semyon Kotko*, I realized that Prokofiev was a great composer," Richter con-cluded.

Obviously, the fate of the opera was not decided by the number of listeners who desired to enjoy it; it was sealed by those who felt that Prokofiev's new attempt at writing something on a true Soviet subject, while a laudable endeavor, had failed. During the following season the opera was taken off the theatre's program, not to be performed again until twenty years later in Perm (in the Urals) on April 12, 1960, and in Leningrad on June 11, seven years after the composer's death, and at a time when the "Party Line" had taken a new attitude by rehabili-tating works formally condemned.

28

Four years had passed since Sergei Prokofiev settled in Soviet Russia, yet he knew no more of what was expected of him as a composer than he did when he first returned home. He had definitely failed in his sincere endeavor to understand and comply with the prescribed formula for the realistic interpretation of Soviet life. The praise he received from the president of the Musicians' Union for the folk songs he had submitted to the competition organized by *Pravda* and the recent acclaim of *Zdravsya* painfully emphasized the question: Were his compositions on folk songs all he was worth to the Soviet Union?

He had never accepted the official criticism of *Semyon Kotko*, and he was weary of choosing Soviet subjects for operas. He returned to his work on the cycle of three sonatas and on the Fifth Symphony, compositions in which the interpretation of their "programmatic" content could be left to the critics, who were perfectly capable of reading into his works their own imaginings. Even to see at long last *Romeo and Juliet* given by the Kirov Ballet was not much compensation, but he put up a brave front and attended the performances in Leningrad and Moscow.

Although he recognized the artistry of the Kirov dancers, he came away with a feeling that their mastery would have had even more value had the choreography followed the musical score more closely. After returning home from the final rehearsals, in fact, he told Lina that he would neither see it again nor go to the première. But of course he did, for Prokofiev was as excited by every first performance of his works, whether a symphony, a ballet, or an opera, as if he were a young composer beginning his career. And he did not succeed in deceiving anyone with the nonchalant, jovial, indifferent attitude he adopted to cover up his anxiety about the public's reception of his work.

Romeo and Juliet was not his first ballet, yet for the first time he confessed to Ulanova that before the Kirov production he had never believed that a ballet could "impersonate" musical images. It was not easy, Ulanova told him, to create dances to his music, which at first appeared incomprehensible and not suited for dancing, and that it took some time to "dance oneself into it," just as singers often have to sing themselves into their roles in an opera.

Far from being discouraged, Prokofiev asked her what she would like to dance.

"*The Snow Maiden*," Ulanova suggested.

"Oh no!" Prokofiev replied. "How can you say this? Rimsky-Korsakov has written such a beautiful score that I would not dare to attempt writing another on the same theme. . . . But what about *Cinderella?*" he added half in jest.

While Prokofiev did not start immediately on this project, his discussions with Ulanova led to their close friendship. She remembers well how, after the première of *Romeo and Juliet*, happy with its success but exhausted, she returned to her hotel. She had barely recovered when there was a knock on her door. To her surprise, it was Prokofiev.

"Come with me immediately to the Authors' Home. They are waiting for us," he said in a tone that allowed no argument.

"We were greeted with applause, and with this accompaniment were led in grand style to our places at the table," Ulanova recalled later.

But Ulanova was even more surprised when Prokofiev asked her to dance with him. "It was a very simple fox trot," she said, "but Prokofiev began every step not to the rhythm of the music, but retarding it a fraction, as if he were following his own rhythm. I became confused, kept missing steps, and was afraid that I would never catch his rhythm, would step on his feet and, in short, would show that I simply didn't know how to dance." After the second dance, however, Ulanova caught her partner's unusual rhythm, but her opinion of Prokofiev as a ballroom dancer was the same as that of Vera Alpers, with whom Prokofiev had danced in his Conservatory days. "He loves to dance," his friends commented, "but he dances very badly." And this despite all the lessons in ballroom dancing he took while living in Kislovodsk.

This was one of the last times Prokofiev indulged in his favorite pastime. His life was not conducive to dancing or to any other form of gaiety. More than ever before he was faced with the problem of what to compose. He thought of *Cinderella*, and, in fact, shortly after his discussions with Ulanova, he was commissioned to write the ballet by the directors of the Kirov Ballet. He made only tentative plans for it, for he was anxious to get on with the unfinished work of the sonatas.

He laid aside the Seventh and Eighth Sonatas to concentrate on the Sixth, and as soon as he had completed that composition, he decided to play it for his friends before performing it publicly. At the musicales held at the home of Paul Lamm, the well-known musicologist, he was certain to find a sympathetic audience. As if they were following the tradition established in the past century by the Mighty Five, members of Moscow's musical society used to meet regularly every Thursday in Lamm's old-fashioned, typical Moscow apartment, furnished predominately with two grand pianos, books, and countless volumes of music. The composers of the "older generation" formed the core of the audience, although conductors, pianists, and violinists were also often invited. Miaskovsky never missed an evening. Taciturn and discreet, he gave his critical opinion only when he was asked. He spoke with authority, but quietly.

On the particular evening when Neuhaus brought Svyatoslav Richter, little did Richter know that this occasion was to lead to his eventual reputation as *the* exponent of Prokofiev's piano works. Prokofiev walked in just as Richter and three other pianists were finishing Lamm's eight-hand arrangement for two pianos of Miaskovsky's Thirteenth Symphony. "He did not appear like a habitué, but more like a guest of honor," Richter said later. "He looked as if it were his birthday . . . and a bit haughty. He was younger than the rest, and yet one felt that Prokofiev seemed to be saying to himself: 'I may be younger, but I am worth all of you put together.' This impression, however, did not concern Miaskovsky, to whom he showed great respect. 'Well,' he said, 'let's get to work. I am going to play it.' " Prokofiev played the sonata from manuscript, and Richter turned the pages for him.

He played it twice and then left. But even before he had finished, Richter decided to learn the sonata. "I was struck by the extraordinary clarity of the style and the perfection of the construction of the composition. I have never heard anything like it," Richter said. "With singular boldness the composer severed himself from the ideals of Romanticism and included in his music the shattering pulse of the twentieth century."

During his summer vacation Richter assiduously practiced the sonata, despite his father's adverse criticism of the work. A professor in the piano class at the Odessa Conservatory, of the old Vienna school, he found Prokofiev's composition "too exotic and too extravagant." "It is simply terrible," he said to his son. "It sounds as if someone were slapping your face—*slam! bang! Trraaaakh, trraaakh,* and then again . . . as if after he had taken aim—*trrrraaakh!*"

After Prokofiev himself had played the sonata over the Moscow Radio on April 9, 1940, Richter gave its first public performance on November 26 in the Small Hall of the Moscow Conservatory. It was Richter's debut in his pianistic career, and he was so nervous that during the three days preceding the concert he would lock himself in the classroom and practice as much as ten hours a day.

The audience, consisting predominately of musicians, liked the sonata and the way Richter played it, although he was too nervous to have any idea of his own performance. All he remembered was that Prokofiev, smiling, walked through the aisle of the hall to the stage and shook his hand. Later, in the green room, he heard Prokofiev say to Neuhaus, "Perhaps the young musician would consider playing my Fifth Piano Concerto, which has failed and has had no success anywhere. Perhaps if *he* plays it, they'll begin to like it."

Neuhaus preferred Prokofiev's Third Piano Concerto, but the twenty-five-year-old Richter believed it was his fate to play the Fifth. At twenty-two he had decided to become a concert pianist, and now, three years later, Prokofiev himself suggested that he perform the concerto that no one else except the composer dared to play. In less than a month Richter had learned the concerto; Neuhaus arranged for him to play it for Prokofiev.

"Prokofiev came with his wife, and the room became filled with Parisian perfume," Richter recalled. Without any further ado Prokofiev began to tell incredible stories about the American gangsters. He told them in his own individual Prokofiev manner, with a great deal of humor and matter-of-factness. We sat at a small table, too low for the comfort of our legs, drank tea with ham sandwiches, inevitable at the Neuhaus home, and waited for Prokofiev's signal to 'get to work.'"

Richter played the concerto through twice, with his friend Alexander Vedernikov playing the orchestral part on the second piano, while Prokofiev, standing between them, conducted. Evidently Prokofiev was pleased, for he presented each performer with a chocolate bar and immediately made arrangements for Richter to play with him at his own forthcoming symphonic concert.

On the evening of the performance Richter arrived at the Tchaikovsky Hall in time to hear the Scythian Suite before the end of the first part of the program. To his nervous state was now added the

impression of Prokofiev's own interpretation of the suite, which, he
said, sent chills running up and down his back, and disturbed him so
much that he thought, "Well, now I shall come out on the stage and
. . . it will be the end of everything. I won't be able to play a note."

He played "accurately," Richter recounted later, but derived no
pleasure from it. After the first movement there was no applause, as
would have been customary, and after noticing some "sour faces" in
the first row of the audience, Richter was convinced that no one understood anything at all. He felt an icy reaction blowing through an
almost empty hall. But the concerto scored a success. Both Richter
and Prokofiev were recalled many times, and as they mounted the
platform, Prokofiev said to him, "How strange. . . . It seems they like
it. I never thought they would . . ." and then he added sarcastically,
"Oh, I know why they applaud—they expect you to play Chopin's
Nocturne as an encore."

Richter was happy, and yet he had a strange feeling of dissatisfaction, caused perhaps, he said, by the excitement of the performance:
"Go and try to play the Fifth Concerto—then you'd understand me,"
he said; and he had a weird premonition: he would not play the concerto again for a long time. But Prokofiev felt differently. For some
time he had been thinking of giving up concertizing. Even giving the
first performance of his own piano works no longer interested him. He
claimed that they required too much time for practicing. "It would
cost me half a sonata," he said, and though Richter did not know it,
Prokofiev chose him as his favorite interpreter, not only of his piano
works, in fact, but of the orchestral ones as well. But these plans also
had to be postponed for some time.

The general criticism of his Sixth Sonata interrupted his completion
of the two others in his cycle of three sonatas. He began to think
again of an opera that would have a musical entity of its own, and he
asked his friends to search for a suitable subject.

Miaskovsky suggested Shakespeare's *King Lear*, or *Merchant of
Venice*, but Prokofiev said that if he were to write an opera on a
Shakespearean subject, he would prefer *Hamlet*. Another friend,
Elizaveta Telisheva, one of the directors of the Small Art Theatre,
told him about Leskov's novel *The Spendthrift*. The first reading of
the novel left an ambiguous impression on Prokofiev: he was fascinated
by the story's dramatic situation and interesting characters, but he was
confused by the verbose discussions of money. He did believe, however, that "one could carve a powerful theatre piece out of Leskov's
novel," and he wrote down a detailed plan for a libretto in five acts.
Still another suggestion put aside this choice.

Myra Mendelson, of whom I shall be speaking later, mentioned to

Sergei Prokofiev *The Duenna* of Sheridan. Before she had finished explaining the story of the play, whose action takes place in eighteenth-century Seville, Prokofiev exclaimed, "But this is champagne! One can make an opera out of this in the style of Mozart, Rossini!" And he immediately set to work on it.

He wrote the libretto himself, dividing the opera into nine scenes in four acts. "I discovered that I should either emphasize the humorous side of the story or its lyricism," he said. "I chose the second. I felt that I should emphasize the love of two pairs of happy young daydreamers—Louise and Antonio, and Clara and Ferdinand; the obstacles their love encountered, their engagements, the poetry of Seville, and the ancient deserted convent. However, I did not neglect the humorous situations that are so brilliantly depicted by Sheridan: the old Don Xerom, who, blinded by his wrath against the old nurse, drives out of the house his own daughter, who was dressed up in the old nurse's clothes, thus helping her to flee to her lover; the avaricious Mendoza, who is so overwhelmed by the large sum of money that he lets himself be deceived, and instead of charming Louise, marries her old nurse; and finally the passionate Ferdinand, who is so jealous of his beloved girl that he is ready to suspect every young woman he sees with a young man of being his unfaithful Clara. These characters and the comical situations would become even more vivid against a background of lyrical scenes, and especially if the humorous *quid pro quo* is played with serious expressions."

And he went on to say that the interpretation gave him several new opportunities. "Thus, after the comical incidents in the first scene, I tried to give a musical interpretation of the city slowly going to sleep. Since, according to Sheridan, there was a carnival in the city, I composed a large scene for a ballet."

Sheridan's story also gave Prokofiev an opportunity to compose many songs, serenades, ariettas, duets, quartets, and large ensembles. The opera was scheduled for production in 1941, but like his other projects, it had to be postponed.

29

"We were spending the summer of 1941 in the country, in Kratov near Moscow. I was working there on the *Cinderella* ballet," Prokofiev recalled later. "On June 22, a sunny summer day, I was at my desk. Suddenly, our caretaker's wife appeared, very excited: 'Is it true,' she asked, 'that the Germans have attacked us . . . that they are bombing our cities?' We were stunned by the news. We went to Sergei Eisenstein, who lived in the neighborhood, to find out if he had also heard about it. Yes, it was true. The German Fascists had attacked the Soviet Union, and the Soviet people had risen to defend their fatherland.

"Everyone was anxious to do his part immediately in the grave struggle, and the composer's natural response to these events was to write songs and marches of a heroic character, music which could be heard on the fighting front."

Prokofiev wrote several of these, but his thoughts turned more and more to Tolstoy's *War and Peace*. Somehow the pages describing the fight of the Russian people against Napoleon's invasion of 1812 and the lives of the principal characters in Tolstoy's story became closer to him. On learning of his plan to write an opera based on Tolstoy's novel, the Arts Committee offered him a contract that he accepted with enthusiasm.

Actually, while searching for a subject for an opera, Prokofiev had often thought of Tolstoy's novels. His first choice was *Resurrection*. He had imagined some of the scenes so vividly that he had even made a plan for a libretto, but then the idea of writing an opera based on *War and Peace* drew his attention to that novel. Thus, he had been contemplating it long before the outbreak of the war. He reread the novel, and in fact even read some parts of it in English, for he maintained that it was good exercise for improving his knowledge of English to read a translation of a work familiar in his own language. But now, with the invading armies surging toward Moscow, he became even better acquainted with an atmosphere of war as described by Tolstoy.

"Although Kratov, where we lived, was a summer resort an hour away from Moscow and in no way could have been considered a military objective, the German planes with their hideous wail often flew overhead in the middle of the night and illuminated the whole countryside with their skyrockets," Prokofiev related later. "Almost simultaneously the Soviet planes would appear. Sometimes we could hear a German bomber fall somewhere and explode with a terrific roar—apparently it had failed to free itself from the load of bombs it was carrying. The sky was crisscrossed by long strips of light from the projectors somewhere on the ground, while the German planes sent down yellow illuminating 'lamps'—it was a beautiful but terrifying sight."

In the available records of Prokofiev's life there is at this point a wide gap in information. Because of World War II, guns had silenced music and had focused the attention of people in the Western countries on events of far greater magnitude and importance than the personal lives of even famous men. Dmitri Shostakovich's Seventh Symphony (the "Leningrad") was in a way the first to cause, at least in the United States, a renewal of interest in the musical activities of Soviet Russia. The dramatic delivery of the symphony to New York—under the protection of the Russian government and the Western Allies the score on microfilm was flown via Teheran and Cairo—could not have failed to arouse curiosity, even among those to whom music was an alien field, for the symphony had been widely publicized. Long before Arturo Toscanini conducted its first performance in Carnegie Hall on July 19, 1942, the symphony's programmatic story had become known: it was about the war, about the struggle of the Russian people against a ruthless foe who was destroying their peaceful lives, and it was dedicated to those who were willing to fight and die for a freedom to which the Allies were devoting all their strength and resources.

The Soviet government not only proudly considered Shostakovich a product of Soviet culture, but a national hero. Never before had Soviet propagandists reserved so much space in the newspapers and magazines as it had for the detailed accounts of Shostakovich's life and work in besieged Leningrad, composing under fire, in bomb shelters.

Even nearly a year later, when I saw Sergei Rachmaninoff about an article I intended to write to commemorate his seventieth birthday (April 2, 1873–1943),* he was reluctant. "Why write it?" he said. "All of us Russian composers are forgotten; there is only one— Shostakovich."

And indeed, during those initial years of the war, little was known about Prokofiev's work and even less about his personal life. And yet the events that occurred then had radically influenced the course of his life.

It is natural for any student of Prokofiev's life and work to turn first to the Soviet sources of information. Such an opportunity was offered by Prokofiev's own autobiography published in Moscow, and by Israel V. Nestyev's subsequently published biography of the composer.† Although the latter was based on Prokofiev's autobiography, it was freely "interpreted" by Nestyev. In 1957 Nestyev published a second biography of Prokofiev, enlarged to almost three times the size of the first volume.‡

No biography is ever complete without an account of its subject's personal life, and despite the detailed record of Prokofiev's compositions and his role in the history of music, Nestyev omitted information concerning Prokofiev's relationship with Lina and their children.

Neither the first biography, written when the composer was alive, nor the second, written after Prokofiev's death, were authorized by the composer or his next of kin, Lina and their children, as might sometimes be done in the Western world. They were authorized by a much higher authority—the Soviet government.

To show the reaction Nestyev's books caused in the West, it would be sufficient to quote musicologists and those who wrote about Prokofiev. In the preface to *Prokofiev* by Lawrence and Elisabeth Hanson the authors said:

This book is by the Soviet musicologist Israel Nestyev. It is thorough, it analyzes almost everything Prokofiev wrote, it has many merits, yet it remains quite unacceptable as the final, or even interim, word on the subject because it is hopelessly marred by political bias. Nestyev sets out to prove that Prokofiev got harm and nothing but harm from his many years in the West, that everything he wrote in those years was poor music, and that he became a great composer only when he returned to Soviet Russia for the final years of his life.

* *Vogue*, April 1, 1943.
† *Sergei Prokofiev, His Musical Life, op. cit.*
‡ *Prokofiev* (Moscow, 1957).

This is simply not true and makes nonsense of biography, of art, and of the man Nestyev is writing about. The result is a picture of Prokofiev and his music which is riddled with misjudgments deliberately made to support a political creed.

In his review of Nestyev's book, Edward Lockspeiser * wrote:

. . . Nestyev's book on Prokofiev is not without some silly statements; lipservice is obviously paid to dictatorial commands of a political nature. I do not think we need to be over-concerned with such aberrations.

And Kurt List in "The Story of Sergei Prokofiev," † wrote:

. . . According to Nestyev, Sergei Prokofiev came to his own only after his return to Soviet Russia at the age of forty-three. . . . It is quite obvious that this is musical history seen through the pink-colored glasses of a political zealot, especially when we read Mr. Nestyev's various epithets for musicians whose style he dislikes. Then there is no end to the name calling: "bourgeois," "white émigré Scriabinite," and "decadent" are terms that appear on most every page. Conversely, someone less benignly disposed toward the Soviet system could have made quite a case of Prokofiev's musical degeneration after his return to Russia. Such a view, however, would lack as much understanding as Mr. Nestyev's biography lacks scholarly objectivity.

It must be noted that in Soviet Russia all information—whether supplied by radio, television, the theatre, or through newspapers, periodicals, or books—has but one aim and function, to serve the interest of the state. The Communist Party's "line" is its sole judge and censor. But since the "Party Line" has to be extremely flexible to satisfy the Politburo, even the historical facts already published often have to undergo thorough surgery, either to be deleted or completely rewritten, depending on the "demands of the day."

Therefore, it is utterly unimportant whether Prokofiev's biography was written by Nestyev or any other author. It must testify not so much to the qualifications of an aspiring biographer, as to the extent of his lipservice to the high authorities.

In their first lessons of arithmetic, Russian children are taught the axiom, "No matter how you juggle the numbers in an addition, its final sum remains the same."

Since the Soviet government denied the Russian people all unauthorized foreign information, Nestyev became its mouthpiece for supplying the records of Prokofiev's life and work to the Russian people and the history of Russian music.

He was born in 1911 in Kerch, the Crimea, and is supposed to have

* "The Unknown Prokofiev," *The Listener*, October 22, 1953.
† "Reality and Realism," *The Listener*, September, 1946.

studied at the Moscow Conservatory—neither the dates, nor the subjects of his studies, nor records of his graduation have been disclosed. Indeed, we are informed (in his own preface to his first biography of Prokofiev) that he was a war correspondent during World War II. Thus his reputation in the musical field was well protected by the obscurity of his accomplishments.

Unfortunately for Prokofiev, as well as for the history of music and the Russian people, he returned from the war to usurp the role of Prokofiev's biographer. For his compiled, analyzed and interpreted information remains the principal record of Prokofiev as man and composer—a sort of *dossier* not to be overlooked by the authorities in their attitude toward the composer.

Nestyev tried to prove the devastating effect on Prokofiev resulting from the years he had spent in the West, and the United States was his special target: he treated it with derision on every available pretext. But as far as certain facts and aspects of Prokofiev's personal life are concerned, Nestyev, conforming to the prescribed general policy, remained mute.

In Soviet Russia an individual can be evaluated, praised, or severely criticized as long as he remains "at liberty"—that is, neither arrested nor sent to hard labor in one of the concentration camps nor shot—but the day he becomes *persona non grata* he is removed from the roster of the living, and his name, if it has been mentioned in published works, is deleted from further editions. (This practice was adopted in Nazi Germany. I have seen in a school book the name of Henrich Heine, author of the famous ballad "Lorelei," omitted. Instead, it read: " 'Lorelei,' *bei einem unbekannten Dichter*" by an unknown author.)

Such authorized high-handed behavior in Soviet Russia has sometimes led to ludicrous results. I would like to quote at least one example from the Great Soviet Encyclopedia. Shostakovich's opera, *Lady Macbeth of Mzensk*, was based on Nikolai Leskov's novel of the same name. In the article written for the Encyclopedia in 1933, at the height of the opera's popularity in Russia, *Lady Macbeth of Mzensk* was listed as one of Shostakovich's major works. It took five years to compile the Encyclopedia and the articles were not supplied alphabetically, so that by 1938 (after Shostakovich's opera was condemned) Leskov had lost his *Lady Macbeth*. Stalin died on March 5, 1953. In the second printing of the Great Soviet Encyclopedia, cleared for publication on December 8, 1953, *Lady Macbeth* was rehabilitated and restored to Leskov. By 1957, *Lady Macbeth* in the article on Shostakovich was demoted from a major work to a "controversial work."

Nestyev glossed over Prokofiev's marriage to Lina. Lina was already *persona non grata* at the time Nestyev was writing his first biography of Prokofiev, and he avoided mentioning her name in the record of the composer's life. The only reference to this event can be found in his quotation of Prokofiev's statement explaining his reasons for not returning to Russia sooner: ". . . Family affairs, too, played no small part—the long illness of my mother, ending in her death, my marriage, and the birth of my son."

Had Nestyev limited his information to these few words, he would have saved the innocent reader from confusion, for in the index, next to the names of Prokofiev's parents, he had listed "Prokofieva, Myra (Mendelson), composer's wife, page 94" * as well as Prokofiev's son [no first name given], referring also to page 94. At that time Myra Mendelson was about nine years old. Yet according to Nestyev, she was the mother of Prokofiev's son Svyatoslav.

Having been established as an official authority on and biographer of Prokofiev, ten years later, in 1957, Nestyev published his second book. This was four years after Prokofiev's death, and what is more important, four years after Stalin's death and two years after Nikita Khruschchev's well-known denunciation of the "personality cult" which announced "freedom of expression" to writers.

But apparently Nestyev was not going to take chances with the "freedom of expression and criticism" Soviet-style, for his second volume suffers, even more than the first, from such toadying to the Soviet state that it would have embarrassed Stalin himself. To be on the safe side (the number of Stalinists in Soviet Russia was not to be disregarded), far from changing his attitude toward the West, Nestyev gloats the more whenever he has an occasion to quote Prokofiev's mild criticisms of the conditions of American musical life.

And as for Lina, Nestyev granted her his attention in a few inaccurate lines: "The cycle of Songs, opus 36 [on Konstantin Balmont's poems], was dedicated to the young Spanish singer Lina Llubera, whose acquaintance Prokofiev made in the United States. This woman, who spent her childhood in Russia (her mother was half-Russian), soon became the composer's wife and eventually the mother of his two sons." †

And referring to Prokofiev's arrival in Ettal (Bavaria in 1922), Nestyev says: "He [Prokofiev] settles in Ettal with his family—his wife L. Llubera-Prokofieva, and his mother, Maria Grigorievna, who had recently arrived from Russia." (Nestyev omitted mentioning the poet

* American edition
† Russian edition, page 208. In the American edition the derogatory "This woman" has been omitted.

Verin-Bashkirov, a close friend of the family, who was financially responsible for taking Prokofiev and his mother to Ettal before Prokofiev married Lina. For Verin was a "white émigré, and bourgeois," and
earlier in his book Nestyev spoke of him as a representative of "fop-
pish merchant modernism," "feebly aping the symbolist poets," and
his poem "Trust Me," which in 1915 Prokofiev had set to music, as
"written in a cheap drawing room style.")

Nestyev disposed of Lina for good after the last mention of her
name in parenthesis: "after his [Prokofiev's] break with L. Llubera."

Thus ends the Soviet's official information about Sergei Prokofiev's
wife. She was removed from the list of the living, until she was mentioned again in *S. S. Prokofiev: Materials, Documents, Reminiscences,*
compiled by Semyon Schlifstein,* and in *Sergei Prokofiev 1953–1963,*†
which included Lina's short memoir.

Before I try to explain what actually happened in the Prokofievs'
lives and caused Lina to become *persona non grata*, I must complete
my analysis of the official record given through Nestyev's biographies,
which unfortunately, as I have already said, have been serving as the
only source of information for everything written about Prokofiev.

Nestyev states that after his break with Lina, Prokofiev married
Myra Mendelson, and henceforth she is referred to in all Soviet publications as Prokofiev's wife. Although Nestyev knew only too well
what caused Lina to become *persona non grata*, he never said a word
about it. No one can be expected to believe that a mere matrimonial
disagreement between Prokofiev and his wife could have endangered
the state to such a degree that Lina had to be classified as almost a "security risk." Certainly neither Lina's nor Myra Mendelson's Memoirs
about Prokofiev indicate the slightest evidence of matrimonial troubles. Since no official version for this sudden break in their relationship has ever been given, it has left this gap in the Prokofiev history.

But their separation was an established fact. While even its approximate date is nowhere mentioned, it should be ascribed to the year
1941. Lina's memoir ends abruptly with the first half of the year; in
his short note "An Artist and War" Prokofiev still mentions his wife at
the outbreak of the Soviet war with Germany; and in the first paragraph of her memoir Myra Mendelson speaks of twelve years she had
spent near Prokofiev (1941 to 1953, the year of Prokofiev's death).

Myra Mendelson's name appears for the first time in the text of
Nestyev's second biography in connection with Sheridan's play *The*

* *Op. cit.*
† Moscow, 1961.

Duenna. According to Nestyev, Myra Mendelson, who had been helping her classmate at the Literary Institute with the translation of the play, brought *The Duenna* to Prokofiev's attention. (But according to Prokofiev's own statement, he was already acquainted with the play in 1940.) And hence began, Nestyev states, "the fruitful collaboration between Prokofiev and Myra Mendelson for the rest of the composer's life."

Lawrence and Elisabeth Hanson, the authors of *Prokofiev*, say that Prokofiev fell in love with Myra Mendelson; and later in their book they go so far as to allege that Prokofiev loved Myra Mendelson more than he loved Lina. They fail, however, to indicate the source of this rather intimate information. Was it Myra Mendelson who told them? And what did Lina have to say about it?

Ever since Kirov's assassination in 1934, that is, shortly after Prokofiev's return to Russia—the years of purges had kept the Russian people in mortal fear of the reign of terror. First directed by Henrich Yagoda, it was intensified by even more cruel persecutions conducted by Nikolai Yezhov. While this dwarf-sized man was officially referred to as "the people's beloved," his period of inhuman rule was nicknamed by the Russians with the hate-filled "Yezhovshchina." (Yezh means a porcupine, and reminds the Russians of the expression "to squeeze one with porcupine gloves.") It ended with his arrest as an "enemy of the people." It was rumored in Moscow that during his arrest he went insane. He was executed in 1939, a fate similar to that of his predecessor. But the violence of the purges gained a new impetus when Lavrenti Beria, Stalin's old chum, took over Yezhov's incomplete work. If Beria's rule, which ended with his execution immediately after Stalin's death in 1953, did not receive a nickname, it was solely because his infamous deeds had no appropriate word in the language of the Russian people.

Thus the years of 1939 and 1940, and the first half of 1941 were less conducive to romance than they were to survival. Russian men at fifty, *pères de familles*, as a rule do not run after girls of twenty-five, no matter how westernized they may be. Prokofiev's nature, his upbringing, which was imbued with respect for the dignity of family ties, the entire record of his personal life, even if "dated" and "bourgeois" in the eyes of some, make such a supposition just as unlikely as it would be in the case of referring to Rachmaninoff, Medtner, or Glière.

And why, then, was the date of his marriage to Myra Mendelson never mentioned, if indeed such a happy event did occur? And when and on what grounds was he divorced from Lina? Bigamy is not permitted even in Soviet Russia.

Henri Sauguet, the well-known French composer, an old friend of the Prokofievs, who had visited with Lina in Moscow in 1964, wrote to me: *"Prokofiev est toujours resté son mari, car il n'y a jamais eu divorce entre eux. Elle a été seulement éloignée de lui quand il a vécu avec Myra Mendelson qui n'est pas sa deuxième épouse, mais seulement sa maitresse: il n'y a qu'une Madame Prokofiev, la mère de ses garçons, qui j'ai vus, qui sont charmants, très fins et intélligents. . . ."* *

It must be noted that in her memoir Myra Mendelson never speaks of herself as Prokofiev's wife. And she signed the two letters to Sergei Eisenstein so far published not as Prokofieva, but as Myra Mendelson.

Who, then, is Myra Mendelson and how did she happen to enter Prokofiev's life in such a mysterious way?

From the information so far available, one can ascertain that Myra Mendelson at that time (1941) had been graduated from the Literary Institute in Moscow and aspired to become a poet. She was a member of the Communist Party and active in the Communist Young Pioneers. But of more importance, she was the niece of Lazar Kaganovich, then the Minister of Heavy Industry. An old and close friend of Stalin, Kaganovich was credited with coining the expression "we peel them off by layers," when referring to mass-arrests and deportations to forced labor camps.

It was an open secret that Stalin was living with Kaganovich's sister Rosa. ("Soon after Nadia's death [Nadezhda Alliluyeva] we learned that Stalin had married a sister of Kaganovich. Up to now, however, not a word has been published in the Soviet press about this marriage.")†

Thus the significance of Myra Mendelson's relationship to the highest authorities in Soviet Russia could not have been easily underestimated at a time when the persecution of intellectuals "guilty of formalism and deviations from the prescribed Party Line" finally was catching up with Sergei Prokofiev.

His latest effort to please the authorities had failed. His opera *Semyon Kotko* had been severely criticized for its lack of understanding of the Soviet people. He had definitely failed, according to the official

* "Prokofiev was always her husband, because they were never divorced. She was merely estranged from him while he lived with Myra Mendelson, who is not his second wife but simply his mistress. There is only one Madame Prokofiev, the mother of his children, whom I saw and who are charming—quite sensitive and intelligent. . . ."
† Alexander Barmin: *One who survived* (New York: Putnam's, 1945).

judgment, to learn the lesson that had been so emphatically given to all composers when Shostakovich's *Lady Macbeth of Mzensk* was condemned.

For less serious reasons thousands had been deported to forced labor camps by Yagoda and Yezhov, and now Beria was proving his worth as their successor. His hand did not falter at striking Meyerhold. Hadn't Beria sent Andrei Vishinsky to the Actor's Home in Moscow to "assist" the conference of stage directors, attended by three hundred delegates, on June 13, 1939, the last conference for Meyerhold? And didn't Vishinsky's cries of "Shoot the mad dogs" at the close of every verdict he pronounced during the trials of 1934–36 still echo in the ears of the Russian people? Did Prokofiev have to be reminded of Meyerhold's and Meyerhold's wife's fate? Was it not about time for Prokofiev to face Soviet reality?

With the beginning of the war one of the first measures the Soviet government took was to deport all those considered "security risks," whole sections of population who lived close to the borders of the country were immediately transported further inland—as far as Siberia. Foreigners, even those who had become Soviet citizens, were particularly affected. Whether communist or not, the Spaniards who had emigrated to Russia after the Civil War in Spain were exiled with their families to Karaganda, in the Uzbek Republic. Not many of these four hundred survived the inhuman conditions of the camps.

Lina was of Spanish origin. But that was not all. Lina had been corresponding with her old mother (her father had died long ago), who had remained in Nazi-occupied Paris. This would have been sufficient reason for Beria to declare her *persona non grata*—or still worse—"an enemy of the people." Who could save her? What would save the Prokofievs? Appeal to their friends abroad? Where? In occupied France? In bombarded London? Or in the capitalist United States? It would only have worsened their situation. And who in Russia would risk lifting a finger in their behalf?

I will leave to the discretion of my readers the choice of answers to these questions. Was Prokofiev forced to do as he was told, like any other Soviet citizen? Anyone who knew Prokofiev personally or who has studied all the available information on his life would have to admit that at no time in his life had he shown himself to be anything but a man of extreme integrity and dignity, straightforward, and at times brutally honest and courageous. There is not the slightest evidence to contradict these characteristics of his nature. Would it be possible, then, to believe that at the moment of misfortune such a man would desert his wife and children? Or would it not be more likely that they, the Prokofievs, were urged to bow to the only solution for their salvation?

In his letter to me, Henri Sauguet did not say that *"Madame Prokofiev s'est éloignée* (withdrew from her husband while he lived with Myra Mendelson), but advisedly said *elle a été seulement éloignée"* (she was merely estranged). Perhaps the unhappy family was given to understand that Myra Mendelson could protect Sergei Prokofiev. She had the perfect credentials to enable her to act as his shield—she was a Party member, she had been active in the most patriotic organization, the Young Communist Pioneers, and in case of arguments with any extremely aggressive bureaucrat, she still had one extra indisputable charm: she was Kaganovich's niece.

And perhaps this barbarous measure was made more palatable to the Prokofievs by the assurance that it was merely temporary, expedient because of the war.

As if this incredible performance were in need of camouflage, it coincided with the arrangements made by the Soviet government for the evacuation of artists and musicians to a safer region of the country, because the danger of Moscow falling into the hands of the enemy loomed even more clearly. At the beginning of August, 1941, members of the "old guard" with their families—such as Vladimir Nemirovich-Danchenko, Vasily Kachalov, Olga Knipper-Chekhova of the Moscow Art Theatre, Alexander Goldenweiser and Paul Lamm, professors of the Moscow Conservatory, and the composers Dmitri Kabalevsky, Yuri Shaporin, and Sergei Prokofiev—were to be taken in four cars on a three-day journey from Moscow to Nalchik in the northern part of the Caucasus.

Leaving Moscow, Prokofiev took with him several compositions already in work, including the sketches for the Seventh and Eighth Piano Sonatas and the Violin Sonata (Op. 80), two acts of *Cinderella,* and the almost completed libretto of *War and Peace.*

According to the Hansons' biography of Prokofiev, Myra Mendelson accompanied Prokofiev on that "special train." But I am inclined to believe that for the sake of decorum—it would have been too complicated and embarrassing to explain her presence on the train—Myra Mendelson went by herself to Nalchik, where she joined Prokofiev.

Lina and the children remained in Moscow.

30

Prokofiev found the first three months of his two-year "evacuation" very conducive to his work. The "evacuees" were warmly welcomed by the natives of Nalchik, who provided them as best they could with comfort and facilities for working. Although it carries the imposing title of "Capital of the autonomous region of Kabarda," Nalchik is a small provincial town situated at the foot of the Caucasian mountains. Lacking sufficient and adequate living quarters, the town administration had put at their "guests' " disposal one large building of a sanatorium that, in addition to its isolated location, offered a beautiful view of the Elbrus Mountain slopes—the highest in Europe—and the grandiose panorama of the Bezengis snow wall.

The easygoing community of Nalchik, with its sleepy Oriental character, was suddenly awakened by the "invading" artists into a bustle of activity. Never before or since have there been so many theatrical performances and concerts given in the town's theatre by illustrious Russian artists. And the local administration, particularly interested in the work of composers, offered them a collection of their native Kabardian folk songs—among them those written down by Sergei Taneyev, who years earlier had made a study of the folklore of the Kabardians and Tartars living in the mountains.

"Don't you see," the president of the local art administration said to Prokofiev, "we have excellent musical material that has not yet been tapped. If you find it worth your while, you can lay the foundation of our Kabardian music." The material turned out to be fresh and original indeed, and while Miaskovsky had taken some of it for his Twenty-third Symphony, Prokofiev was inspired to write a string quartet,

thus using the heretofore "virginal" Oriental folklore in the most classic form of composition.

But there was a problem that Prokofiev tried to explain to the president of the local art administration: the musical culture of Kabarda
was not yet developed, therefore his quartet would neither be understood nor appreciated.

"Write it any way you feel it," the man said. "If we should fail to
understand it now, we will later on." This was a broadminded statement, the like of which Prokofiev had not heard in a long time.

First, however, he completed the cycle of Seven Songs (Op. 89)
dedicated to the war heroes, natives of Kabarda, and written to the
poems of Myra Mendelson. It was performed in Nalchik, but when it
reached Moscow, it was severely criticized for its "unnecessary elementary quality," and it never gained popularity. Nor was his programmatic orchestral suite, *The Year of 1941*, which he wrote at the
same time, appreciated by the critics when it was performed almost
two years later in Moscow. It was condemned for its "superficial musical material and the discrepancy of its content with the scope and
the significance of the subject." Even Shostakovich, while delivering
his report on the "creative accomplishments of 1943," pointed to its
"immaturity and lack of profound conception." The suite has remained unpublished.

The String Quartet in F major (Op. 92), which he wrote in Nalchik
in November, was Prokofiev's first successful work of the "evacuation" period. Though it is based almost entirely on the folklore of
Kabarda, he managed in this composition to avoid the usual clichés of
musical "Orientalism." A year later, on September 5, 1942, it was performed in Moscow by the Beethoven Quartet and given unanimous
approval by both the public and critics.

This composition marked the end of Prokofiev's stay in Nalchik,
for by the end of November the German Army was approaching the
town; once again the Moscow artists were evacuated, this time further
south, to Tbilisi, formerly Tiflis. Despite the lack of success of most
of the works that he composed in Nalchik, Prokofiev carried away
with him happy memories of his sojourn there. Later, he was visibly
saddened on learning that the president of the art administration, the
man who had inspired him to write the F-major String Quartet and
who had been extremely helpful and sympathetic to their artistic
work, had been killed after he had joined the partisans in attacking the
enemy's communication lines; and that the beautiful park—Nalchik's
scenic pride—had been demolished by the Germans when they captured the town.

Going to Tbilisi was like returning to one of Russia's large musical centers. The arrival of the Moscow group gave an extra impetus to the theatre and concert season already in full swing. The actors of the Moscow Art Theatre were engaged in dramatic performances, and the musicians either conducted the symphonic concerts or gave piano recitals. At the Russian drama theatre Prokofiev heard, along with the operas written by the Georgian composers, several classic European and Russian operas. Every Monday evening was devoted to symphonic concerts, which included in their programs such symphonies as Beethoven's Ninth, Tchaikovsky's Fifth, and Shostakovich's Fifth and Seventh, as well as Scriabin's *Poème de l'exstase*. Miaskovsky's Twenty-second Symphony had its première there, and Prokofiev conducted his own works, including the two suites from *Romeo and Juliet*. In addition to this, he gave piano recitals in Tbilisi, Baku, and Erivan—his last appearances as a pianist. As he had planned to for some time, he put an end to his concert career. Preoccupied solely with composing, he had been neglecting piano practice; he no longer played as well, and he was aware of it. "Let young pianists play my works," he said. "They can do just as well, if not better."

"I have to confess that life in Tbilisi is not easy," Miaskovsky wrote to his friends in Moscow. "We have to tighten our belts—everything here is very expensive, and besides, we are having an unusually severe winter, and yet, although it is difficult, all of us are trying to work."

Prokofiev was in the midst of his score of *War and Peace*. He and Myra Mendelson, with whom he was working on the libretto, tried to preserve Tolstoy's style. When the novel lacked sufficient dialogue, they tried to compose them from Tolstoy's narrative and the specific characteristics of his heroes. They also worked at the Tbilisi library, where they had an opportunity to find books on Russian folklore— proverbs, colloquial expressions, and folk songs composed during the War of 1812, as well as some notes written by Denis Davidov, a poet who had joined the partisans in the pursuit of Napoleon's retreating Grande Armée.

Despite all this work, Prokofiev found time to enjoy the production of Shakespeare's *Othello* at the Georgian Theatre (although he did not understand a word of Georgian), as well as several performances of the dramatic works of local authors. He visited museums and galleries, rich in pictures and objects of ancient Georgian art, and attended Russian-language lectures on their history. And he never missed recitals at the Conservatory and symphonic concerts.

But what was more important, he had completed the Seventh Piano Sonata, which, he admitted—after the initial start, when he was writ-

ing it simultaneously with the Sixth Sonata—presented so many problems that he had laid it aside. "Now, suddenly everything has become
clear to me," he said, and he finished the composition in three days,
just in time to accept Eisenstein's invitation to go to Alma-Ata to collaborate with him on the historic film *Ivan the Terrible.*

Alma-Ata, formerly Vyernyi, the capital of Kazakhstan, situated in
Central Asia near the Chinese border, some thirty-five hundred kilo-
meters from Moscow, was an ideal place for the motion picture
studios. The film industry workers had converted Alma-Ata from a
provincial town of some fifty thousand inhabitants, mostly Kirgiz-
Kazakhs (not to be confused with the Russian Cossacks), into a sort of
Russian Hollywood. When after a long voyage from Tbilisi via Baku,
across the Caspian Sea, and a long trek through Krasnovodsk and the
Turkomen steppe, Prokofiev and Myra Mendelson arrived in Alma-
Ata, they were pleasantly surprised to see against a background of the
mountain range on the horizon a town with wide streets, framed by
two rows of trees in full bloom, several parks, and an opera house.

Prokofiev's collaboration with Eisenstein seemed to the two old
friends as if it were a continuation of the work they had done together on *Alexander Nevsky*. They followed the method previously
worked out: some portion of the music was to be written before the
shooting of a scene so that the scene would be acted to a completed
accompaniment; and some parts of the music were to be written after
Prokofiev had been shown the photographed material.

But, as had happened when they collaborated on *Alexander Nevsky*,
their work did not progress without arguments. One of the first numbers Eisenstein asked Prokofiev to write was the so-called "Oath
Taken by the Boyars"; the scene was to be shot with the prerecorded
music. Prokofiev wrote this part guided solely by his general discussions of the film with Eisenstein. But Eisenstein did not like the music
—it was not at all what he had expected—whereupon, Prokofiev declared that he would not write another note unless he was at least
shown some drawings, which would enable him to understand the nu-
ances of Eisenstein's intentions. Prokofiev called these drawings
"cribs," and he was very much impressed when he discovered that in
addition to being a remarkable director and sensitive musician, Eisenstein was also a very talented painter. After Eisenstein had supplied
him with a whole series of such drawings, the collaboration continued
rather smoothly, except for occasional interruptions when Eisenstein
would say, "Here I would like the music to sound as if someone is
tearing a child away from its mother's arms," or "Do it so that it will
sound like a cork rubbed down a pane of glass." Puzzled at first by

such graphic images, Prokofiev nevertheless eventually succeeded in obliging his friend.

The film, which Eisenstein had planned before the outbreak of the war, was to be in three parts, he told Prokofiev. He said that he intended to show Ivan the Terrible, not according to the traditional, rather simplified portrait of a bloodthirsty despot, but as a brilliant statesman, whose aim was the unification of the Russian state, and as a courageous warrior, who consolidated his country's power, despite the personal greed of the reactionary noblemen.

The first of the three sequences of the film, on which Eisenstein was working at the time of Prokofiev's arrival in Alma-Ata, portrayed Ivan's youth, his coronation, his deep sorrow over the death of his wife, who had been poisoned by the boyars, and his administrative activities toward one goal: "On top of the bones of the dead enemy, and despite disastrous conflagrations, Russia unites into one land." These were the words Prokofiev had the chorus sing in his overture.

All told, Prokofiev wrote some twenty-nine musical numbers for the film, but this work did not distract him from his basic plans. He continued on the score of *War and Peace*, and during those first summer months in Alma-Ata he also wrote a cantata for dramatic tenor, dramatic soprano, chorus, and orchestra—"The Ballad About a Boy Who Remained Unknown."

Prokofiev had been thinking about this composition ever since he had read Paul Antokolsky's poem, which was published in *Literature and Art* while Prokofiev was still in Tbilisi. The fate of a boy whose mother and sister were killed by the Germans served Prokofiev as the basis for his musical interpretation of the story. Having been deprived of a happy childhood, the boy matured early and was eager to act independently. Later, when the Germans were retreating from his town, he threw a hand grenade, blowing up the car that carried the German generals. His name and his fate remained unknown, but the story of his heroism was carried throughout the fighting front, lifting the morale of the desperately struggling men. "When I was writing the cantata, I saw clearly the boy's destroyed childhood, a cruel enemy, the boy's courage, and our faith in an early victory," Prokofiev said.

The fate of the cantata was similar to that of the boy. After its first performance, on February 21, 1944, at the Grand Hall of the Moscow Conservatory, it was never repeated or published. It was severely criticized for its exaggerated expressionism of the "barbarous invasion," which, while resembling similar episodes in *Alexander Nevsky, Semyon Kotko*, and "Seven, They Are Seven," lacked heroic themes depicting the Soviet people's bravery, offering instead soft, almost feminine contemplative melodies. Prokofiev never agreed with this sort of criticism, and regretfully remarked, "It is a pity 'The Boy' was trampled down."

Just as he had been anxious to learn the Kabardian folklore in Nalchik, so now in Alma-Ata he listened to the Kazakhs' national music at concerts and on broadcasts over the local radio station. He saw the Kazakh's operas, such as they were, and the dramatic performances. He made an arrangement of five songs for piano and voice from Alexander Zataevich's collection of One Thousand Songs of the Kirgiz People, and since Eisenstein's work on the film proceeded much too slowly for him and left him plenty of free time, he decided to write an opera on the Kazakh material he had collected.

"After my experiment with the Kabardian quartet, which was appreciated by the natives who recognized their own melodies and even by my severe critics," Prokofiev reasoned, "I wanted to write a lyrico-comical opera based on Kazakh's folklore." From the various fables and legends he chose the one concerning a young shah who had grown horns on his brow—a symbol of His Majesty's greatness, of which the Shah was both proud and a bit ashamed.

At first Prokofiev thought of calling the opera *Ah, But the Shah Has Horns*, but later changed the title to *Khan Busay*, derived from the name of one of the principal characters in the story. Dzhuman's love for the beautiful Aizhgan and the poetry of their feelings were to be the main theme of the opera and were to be developed against a background of several comical situations. But the libretto, which he was writing in collaboration with Myra Mendelson, progressed slowly because of several interruptions; yet four years later Prokofiev again included this project in his plans. Unfortunately, despite all the preliminary work, the opera remained unwritten.

In December of 1942 Prokofiev returned to Moscow, where he was going to introduce the two major works he had completed in his absence from the capital: *War and Peace* and the Seventh Piano Sonata. As might have been expected, he sent the score of the sonata to Richter, asking him to give its first public performance. Richter's playing of the sonata on January 18, 1943, at the Hall of the Home of the Unions proved a great success, although utterly unexpected, since most of Prokofiev's compositions had recently been more criticized than praised. At long last Prokofiev had written a piece that pleased everybody. He was called several times to take a bow, and in fact the sonata was so much appreciated by the critics and even by those in power that two months later the government awarded him no less an honor than Second Prize. But what was infinitely more important, it was considered good enough to be "exported" to the United States, thus giving the composition an opportunity to be heard in the Allied countries.

However, Prokofiev had no "program" in mind for this sonata, for the Sixth or for the future Eighth—the cycle of three sonatas. If he did have any specific intention, it was to get away from the programmatic compositions with which he obviously had not succeeded in pleasing the critics. Furthermore, since he had originally sketched most of the major themes in 1939, two years before the war, if the critics insisted on reading into his score a descriptive element, they could just as well have turned to the horrifying events caused by the purges that were still rampant in 1939.

Besides, Prokofiev was always anxious to have the intentions of his compositions understood to the full extent in every detail—each section, each phrase. Would this attitude, then, have been compatible with his having said nothing to Richter about the intended "program subject" of his sonata? Upon receiving the manuscript, Richter became so enthusiastic about the sonata and the opportunity to give its first performance that after learning it in four days, he went to play it for Prokofiev, who was staying at the Hotel National.

"He was alone," said Richter, who remembered his visit with the composer well. "There was a grand piano in his room, but . . . everything started with our discovery that one of the pedals was not functioning. 'Well, it is too bad,' Prokofiev said. 'Let's repair it. . . .' We both were crawling under the piano and were 'repairing' something, until we bumped our heads together with such a blow that I saw stars.

"Our meeting was purely businesslike," Richter continued. "We both were preoccupied with the sonata. We spoke little. I must say that I never did have long conversations with Prokofiev. They were always limited to a few remarks. It is true that except for this visit we had never been alone. And when there was a third person, it was always the third person who did the talking."

The audiences, however, affected by the concurrent events, had, *a priori*, their own interpretation of the works that were to be presented to them. "They perceived the spirit of the composition as if it were reflecting everything with which they lived, just as they did when they heard Shostakovich's Seventh Symphony for the first time," Richter commented later. "Right from the start the sonata projects you into an alarming atmosphere of a world that has lost its balance, so to speak. Disorder and uncertainty reign supreme. Man is observing the havoc of destructive forces. But life, which the man has

lived, does not cease to exist for him. He still senses it, he is still capable of love. And with these emotions he addresses himself to everybody. He joins everyone in their protests and common suffering.
Then comes a sudden stiffness of will and desire for victory which
sweeps away everything in its path. Man gains strength in his struggle
and achieves gigantic powers which assert life itself."

In addition to the sonata, Prokofiev had played for his colleagues the
finished parts in a vocal score for *War and Peace*, and this work was
bolstered particularly by Shostakovich's enthusiasm. Thus, reassured
of an eventual production of the opera at the Bolshoi and encouraged
by the success of the sonata, he returned to Alma-Ata.

Because of Eisenstein's always slow progress on the film, Prokofiev
had more leisure than he wished. Ever since his years in Paris, where
he was fascinated by the artistry of the French woodwind players, he
had wanted to write something for the flute. He had never forgotten
the "heavenly sound" of the instrument when played by Georges Barère, the famous flutist. Prokofiev thought that a sonata for flute and
piano would offer him an opportunity to display not only lyrical daydreaming melodies, but also the light and humorous sides to which
this instrument lends itself so well. He succeeded in composing a de-
lightful piece in four movements, but because it was rarely performed
by flutists, in collaboration with David Oistrakh a year later he rearranged the sonata for violin, and it became known as his Second Violin Sonata.

The rest of his stay in Alma-Ata was influenced by the Red Army's
sudden change of fortune, and the corresponding change in the
mood of the government and the people. While the German armies
were at the gates of Moscow and Leningrad in the North, had reached
Stalingrad and the Volga in the East, and were threatening to capture
the Caucasus in the South, the pessimism of the Russian people about
the fate of their country was at its lowest ebb. But since the German
offensive near Stalingrad had ended disastrously, with more men killed
and taken prisoner than in their whole war campaign in Europe, and
since, pursued by the Russians, the Germans were stampeding back to
where they had come from, the faith of the Russians in their victory
led to a nationwide confidence in their power. With it, nationalism
rose to its highest degree.

Because they had been despondent over the postponement of the
"opening of the second front" by the Western Allies, and because the
bulk of the Allies' supplies of war materials had begun to reach Russia
after the battle of Stalingrad had been won, the Russians justifiably felt
that so far they had not only carried the brunt of the war single-

handed, but had turned the tide against their own and their Allies' enemy.

The Soviet government chose this moment to support the rising morale and national pride by several gestures, which could not fail to impress the people with the government's gratitude for their sacrifices and valor. Abolishing "socialist competition" in the army, *Pravda* bluntly stated that the soldier had no socialist obligations whatsoever and that his job was to serve his fatherland as his forebears had done. Epaulets and other insignia that had been banned as marks of a reactionary caste system in the army, were reintroduced. Nearly four hundred commanders were promoted to the rank of general, and the most brilliant commanders were handed marshals' batons. But the military were not alone in receiving the highest prizes and medals; the artists also were awarded honorary degrees.

No longer discriminating between *Soviet* composers and *Russian* composers, the government first of all bestowed the Order of the Red Banner on the "eldest" group of composers: S. N. Vasilenko, N. Y. Miaskovsky, A. H. Alexandrov, Y. A. Shaporin, V. V. Scherbachev, and the youngest of them, Sergei Prokofiev. And as if to show that the war had practically been won and that temporary measures for their safety were no longer required, the government suggested an immediate return to Moscow of the evacuated artists, so that they could participate in the cultural activities scheduled for the following season.

Prokofiev was invited to conduct a concert of his compositions, and after having been awarded high honorary distinctions, he returned to Moscow, accompanied by Myra Mendelson, in December, 1943.

31

The general optimism of the Russian people, stimulated by the constant improvement in the war situation, had also affected Prokofiev's
state of mind. That his disposition was becoming more mellow was
noticed not only by his close friends but by his colleagues—the composers—members of the Kirov Ballet, the men connected with his
work with Eisenstein, and in fact by all those with whom he came
into contact. One no longer spoke of his haughtiness and his reticence,
but on the contrary, commented on his friendliness, compassion, and
even shyness. While his faith in himself never wavered, criticism of
his compositions led to a longing for an affectionate and encouraging
attitude toward his work. He sought out company and well-meaning
friends. The composers, more than anyone else, could speak of this
change, since they had had the opportunity of observing him when,
during the summer of 1944, they all lived in close quarters at the
"Composers' Home," near the town of Ivanovo, some fifty miles west
of Moscow.

The Soviet government had turned over to the Composers' Union a
large estate with a typical Russian landscape: fields of rye as far as the
eye could see and on the horizon a dark forest that seemed endless.
The large farm had 66 cows, 8000 chickens and ducks, and 135
pigs. The one-story stone mansion, formerly the home of a wealthy
landlord, with its newly added five cottages, each equipped with a
piano, was converted into headquarters for the composers. Here, away
from the bustle of the large cities, sometimes as many as twenty composers and their families spent the summer months: Glière, Shostakovich, Shaporin, Khachaturian, Kabalevsky; even Miaskovsky, who had

always zealously guarded his privacy, lived there for months at a time.

During that summer Prokofiev was working on his Fifth Symphony and Eighth Sonata. His methodical work habits and his hourly divisions of the day, each devoted to a special assignment, surprised everyone except Glière—it was reminiscent of the strictly regulated life of the Prokofievs' home in Sontsovka. The early-morning swims, however, could not be repeated, because the small river that ran through the estate was drying up as the summer wore on.

Prokofiev and Myra Mendelson lived in the large house, and every morning after breakfast in the dining room Prokofiev, carrying a large briefcase under his arm, walked over to the nearby village, where rooms were rented by the government for the composers' work. Since Prokofiev's room was in a small wooden house on the far side of the village, he had an opportunity for his morning walk. Dmitri Kabalevsky, the young composer, by chance had a "working room" near Prokofiev's, and he almost invariably kept Prokofiev company on their way there.

Kabalevsky had soon learned that there was a kindergarten for the children of the factory workers at Ivanovo not far from their destination, and that the children's promenade under the supervison of their instructress coincided with his and Prokofiev's approach to the edge of the village. Prokofiev was the first to strike up a friendship with these children. "He won their hearts," Kabalevsky said, "by giving them some kind of colored cigarette boxes, candy, and lollipops, but even more by his affectionate and kind manner." No sooner did they see Prokofiev on the small path leading toward them than all fifty of them rushed toward him shouting in a chorus of lively sonorous voices, "Here comes our uncle!"

Kabalevsky was included in this friendship, for, being tall, he was made the principal object of their games. He had to stand with his legs wide apart while the children ceremoniously marched, one after another, through the "gates." To this amusement was added an extra variant: holding on to his legs they took a special delight in "taking a ride" on what they called "a swing," while Prokofiev stood by to see that the boys would not "steal an extra ride" out of turn. Kabalevsky never was quite sure whether one of the boys successfully managed on his own to outwit him or Prokofiev, as he said, it was hard to tell who derived the greater pleasure from this game—the children or Prokofiev. "For we usually reached our working rooms in an excellent humor," Kabalevsky remarked, "and if the children were kept indoors because of bad weather, we confessed to each other that for our good work there was something missing."

After the midday dinner in the large house Prokofiev seldom returned to his working room, but remained "at home," either going over the work he had done during the morning or making plans for the next day. But before the end of the dinner he would go around the table with a deep dish in his hand, asking everyone to contribute something from their plates for Zmeika, a homeless little white dog who could claim a distant relationship to a Spitz. Zmeika was devoted to Prokofiev and followed him everywhere as if he were her master. Later, when she was run over by a car, Prokofiev felt as if a major tragedy had befallen him.

On the dot of five o'clock Prokofiev knocked on the door of Kabalevsky's room, always repeating the same phrase in English: "It is time to go for a walk." Kabalevsky had begun to study English, and while Prokofiev's own knowledge of the language was far from perfect, he insisted that Kabalevsky practice it with him. Depending on the weather, their promenade developed into what Prokofiev called "a large tour around the world" or a "small one." Prokofiev derived a special pleasure from these walks in the country—he loved the fields and the forest; he could become ecstatic over the color of a sunset, the unusual design of a cloud, the songs of the birds. He would never pick up a mushroom without calling his companion's attention to the mushroom's beauty against the background of the moss. Even on the route that he took daily and knew thoroughly he would find some interesting new detail: a picturesque side path, a weird-looking tree trunk, or a large anthill. "On our route," Kabalevsky related later, "he had several of 'his own' anthills, whose growth he liked to observe." Prokofiev spoke to Kabalevsky at length about the ants, admiring the sensible organization of their lives and work, and he insisted that Kabalevsky read books about them. Once in the forest he found an old, torn slipper, and took it to one of "his own" anthills. Then for several days he returned to watch the ants working in it. He was convinced that he had helped them in constructing their home. "Can you imagine," he said, "the luxurious halls they are going to build for themselves in that old slipper."

Returning from such afternoon walks, he often joined the rest of his colleagues in volleyball. But he was much too near-sighted and awkward to be an interesting partner in the game, which the composers took seriously with an almost professional ardor and not merely as a "summer pastime." He was far more respected at a chessboard to which each passing day inevitably led.

And at the end of the day, during the supper, as if following his mother's practice at Sontsovka when he was still a boy, he would ask each member of the small community "what they had accomplished during the day, and whether they were satisfied with their day's work." Obviously, with this sort of "corporal" on the premises, his younger colleagues had to pull themselves together in their work. Later, reminiscing about their stay at Ivanovo, they were grateful to Prokofiev for those summer months, and they held him up as a model of the well-organized, creative artist.

Prokofiev returned to the Moscow concert season of 1944–1945 with the completed Fifth Symphony, the Eighth Piano Sonata—the last in the cycle of three begun in 1939—and six piano pieces from *Cinderella*. Although he had given up public appearances as a concert pianist, he had diligently practiced the sonata so that he could play it at the Composers' Union before its first public performance.

He played it twice. "After the first hearing," said Richter, who was present, "it was evident that it was an extraordinary composition but when I was asked whether I would perform the work, I did not yet know what to say." According to Richter, it was difficult for Prokofiev to play; his former self-confidence was no longer there: "He seemed to throw his hands about aimlessly with slapping sounds."

Prokofiev turned the composition over to the twenty-eight-year-old Emil Gilels. Like Richter and Oistrakh, who were then in their teens, Gilels at the age of twelve had heard Prokofiev for the first time at his piano recital in Odessa in 1927, and had become interested in the composer's work. Since then, Gilels had developed into a first-class virtuoso, second only to Richter, had captured prizes at the international competitions for pianists held in Vienna and Brussels, and was well launched on his career in the Soviet Union. He worked enthusiastically on each of Prokofiev's new major piano compositions, learned the Seventh Sonata while it was still available only in proof sheets, and now was flattered by the composer's suggestion that he give the Eighth Sonata its first public performance.

While learning it from a manuscript, he often played the sonata for Prokofiev, who would make some alteration in the composition, and occasionally would go to the piano to show Gilels what he expected to hear from a performer, although Prokofiev himself played for Gilels only sections of the sonata, never the whole composition.

On December 30, 1944, at a Grand Hall at the Moscow Conservatory, Gilels gave a brilliant performance, and a year later the composition was awarded the First Prize. A zenith in Prokofiev's pianistic virtuosity, rich in its inner content and variety of lyrical episodes, the sonata was nevertheless too complicated for the average listener and did not gain in popularity.

Two weeks later, on January 13, 1944, at the same Grand Hall of the Moscow Conservatory, Prokofiev conducted the first performance of his Fifth Symphony. The audience was in a particularly festive mood, for shortly before the beginning of the concert, the victory of the Red Army on the banks of the Vistula was announced. The hall was illuminated as usual, but when Prokofiev mounted the conductor's stand, the audience felt as if the light were directed on him. He seemed to stand there like a monument on a pedestal.

There was dead silence as Prokofiev raised his baton for the opening bars of the symphony. Suddenly, a roar from the heavy artillery shook the hall—a salute to the Red Army, which was crossing the Vistula into Germany. Prokofiev remained with upraised baton until the guns became silent. There was something significant in it, something symbolic, the audience felt, as if a new life were beginning for all of them, and for Prokofiev as well.

The composition was deemed one of his best works, as if in it he had raised himself to the full stature of his talent and revealed everything he had lived through: his country's past history, its misfortunes and sorrow, war, patriotism, and victory. But for Prokofiev himself the Fifth Symphony had a special significance. "This work was very important to me," he said, "for after a long interruption [sixteen years] I have returned to a symphonic form of composition. It was the culminating point of my creative life. I imagined the symphony as an expression of the greatness of the human spirit."

The symphony had an overwhelming success. But in the green room crowded with admirers Prokofiev spoke in an aside to Boris Volsky, the "mixer" with whom he had worked on the recording of the music for *Alexander Nevsky*, and asked him about the balance in some orchestral registers. Volsky thought that he had unnecessarily toned down some parts in the bass. And Miaskovsky, Prokofiev replied, had said just the contrary at the rehearsal, had said that he brought these parts out too much in the bass, and that was why he tried to subdue them at the performance. "Next time I shall adhere to the golden mean," Prokofiev said.

But there was no "next time" for Prokofiev. This was the last time he was at the conducting desk. A few days after the concert, while visiting friends, he fell down and suffered a brain concussion. It was the beginning of an illness from which he suffered for the rest of his life.

32

For days Prokofiev lay prostrate in his bed, sometimes unconscious, failing to recognize anxious friends who came to visit him. For some unaccountable reason the Soviet musicologists and his biographer have refrained from naming his illness and have referred to it merely as "a grave illness"; the doctors diagnosed it at the time as an extreme case of hypertension that led the excessive flow of blood to his brain and caused his fall. Nor can the reason, given by the Soviet sources as "overwork," be accepted as satisfactory. It is much more likely that the constant "disappointment," to put it mildly, in the "existing conditions under the Soviet regime," the struggle to survive through the years of the purges, the tragedy of his family life, and his failure to "please" the critics and those in power, had taken a heavy toll on his nervous system.

Of strong physical constitution, Prokofiev could not easily resign himself to permanent invalidism, and was willing to accept the regime of complete rest prescribed by the doctors, who promised him a recovery. He was placed in one of the sanatoria at Podlipki near Moscow. Strictly forbidden to do any work, he remained most of the time "in a horizontal position," except for occasional short walks, as he reported to his friends.

The spring of 1945 was slow in arriving; nature was just awakening after a bitterly cold winter, but because of good news from the fighting front, promising a foreseeable successful end to the war, the Russian people looked proud and content, and Prokofiev was visibly affected by the general mood. He was in an unusually happy frame of mind, anxiously listening to all the news and full of plans for future work. "Secretly" from his doctors he kept on composing—in his mind only—an "Ode on the End of the War," and "secretly" he conferred with the visitors from the Bolshoi who were preparing a production of *Cinderella*. "They don't seem to have enough basses in my score; it is not loud enough for them," Prokofiev grumbled jestingly. And because he was forbidden even to read, Myra Mendelson read to him Leskov's *Spendthrift*, which he was still interested in using as a basis for an opera.

The medical care, and in no small way the generally jubilant atmosphere surrounding him, lifted his spirits so much that by the beginning of June (the seventh) he was allowed to attend the first performance in concert form of his *War and Peace*, and ten days later a festive gathering to receive a gold medal presented to him by the British Ambassador in the name of the British Philharmonic Society.

He again spent the rest of the summer at the Composers' Home at Ivanovo, and as during the previous summer, he tried to follow his own daily schedule, working on the ode and his Sixth Symphony, but the strict regime curtailed his working hours. He no longer smoked, and had to refrain from drinking even a glass of light wine or from joining his colleagues in volleyball. Chess, his favorite occupation next to composing, was also forbidden.

But nothing could daunt his love of competition. In addition to his work on the ode and the Sixth Symphony he had joined a competition organized by the Radio Committee in Moscow for the best arrangement of some Russian folk songs. He urged Kabalevsky, who was also at Ivanovo, to take part in the contest. "Do it, as I have done," he advised him. "Take the folk melodies and develop them as if they were your own," he said, as he played for Kabalevsky the arrangements he had made of two Russian folk songs.

Later, when Kabalevsky showed him his arrangements of two folk songs, Prokofiev approved particularly the one in a ballad form: "How a Husband Destroyed his Wife." "This is wonderful," he remarked half in jest, half seriously. "I will receive the first prize, and you the second. And then we will celebrate together." But Kabalevsky received the first prize and Prokofiev the second. For a long time, Kabalevsky recalled later, he would pretend to be seriously annoyed as he repeated, "Aren't you ashamed of yourself? I was the one who urged you to join the competition, and I was the one who taught you how to do such arrangements, and you . . . without any further ado, snatched the first prize right from under my nose!"

According to Kabalevsky, who had become closer to Prokofiev than other composers, after his accident at the beginning of the year

Prokofiev's whole being turned to a constant struggle for life and creative activity, for there were long periods during which he was not allowed to work at all, or at most no more than two hours a day. "Nevertheless, Prokofiev did not give up, did not lose his optimism, his joy of life, his courage and youthful cheerfulness, and a phenomenal capacity for concentration on his work," Kabalevsky said. "He took to heart every criticism and constantly strove toward even more profound content in his compositions and perfection in their form. He was seldom discouraged by his failures, for at the time of the performance of his latest composition he was already 'living' in his future plans, new works."

Such, at least, was the outward impression Prokofiev gave to his friends. But Myra Mendelson, whose devotion and wise care no doubt relieved him from some of his suffering, well knew that the repeated occurrence of terrible headaches was a constant reminder that Prokofiev was a very sick man. Nevertheless, he insisted on following the old schedule of working and was extremely annoyed when anyone tried to interfere with it. During that summer he completed the "Ode on the End of the War," made several sketches for the Sixth Symphony, and was planning the Ninth Piano Sonata.

On November 12, 1945, Samuel Samosud, leading the U.S.S.R. State Symphony Orchestra in Tchaikovsky Hall, introduced the ode to a Moscow audience. But the symphonic poem in one movement with an ear-splitting Finale, which Prokofiev marked "Ring the bells and strike the tympani!" required an extremely enlarged orchestra not yet available in the country so soon after the war. The composition, though brilliant in form, unfortunately was overshadowed by the descriptive element rather than by the significant depths of its content, and it failed to "reach" the average listener. As a purely experimental work, it remained in manuscript and has not been performed since.

Nine days later, on November 21, his *Cinderella* was given its première at the Bolshoi. Obedient to doctors' orders, Prokofiev showed remarkable self-control by refraining from attending the rehearsals and by seeing the production in "three doses"—one act at each of the three performances. Although he had begun work on *Cinderella* in 1941, because of interruptions during the war he completed the score only in 1944.

"The poetic love between Cinderella and the Prince—its beginning and development, the obstacles in its path, and the realization of their dream—was the main theme that I wanted to portray in the music of *Cinderella*," Prokofiev said. "It presented to me as a composer several interesting problems: the mysterious fey-grandmother, the fairylike twelve dwarfs jumping out of a clock and, by doing a tap dance, reminding Cinderella of the hour to return home; the quick succession of countries through which the Prince passes on his search for Cinderella. But the authors of the ballet wanted the spectator of the production to see living people in this fairylike frame. Therefore, in order not to leave the audience indifferent to the sorrow and happiness of the characters in the story, I strove to express in music the characters of the sweet, daydreaming Cinderella, her shy father, nagging stepmother, the self-willed and arrogant sisters, and the passionate youthful Prince. Also, in addition to the dramatic construction of the piece, it was important to me that the ballet be suited for dancing: that the dances stemmed from the subject, that they were varied in form and character, and that the dancers were given an opportunity to show off their artistry. I wrote the score in the tradition of the old classical ballet: pas de deux, adagio, gavotte, several waltzes, pavane, passe-pied, bourrée, mazurka, and a gallop. And each character had its own leit-motif."

Galina Ulanova, whom Prokofiev had asked before the war what she would like to dance and who had suggested *Cinderella*, naturally was chosen for the leading role. But not even his friendship with the ballerina could make him give to Cinderella the enchanting melody he had written for the beggar-woman: all of Ulanova's arguments were in vain. "Prokofiev," she said, "was incapable of any compromise in his sacred work. Since he saw and heard the particular melody as designated for the beggar-woman, no power on earth could have made him waver or convinced him to give that theme to Cinderella or any other character in the ballet."

Speaking for herself and the rest of the ballet cast, Ulanova said that it was much easier to understand Prokofiev's intentions, "to get used" to his music while working on *Cinderella*, because a great deal of the score pleased them "at first sight," so to speak, and had become clear to them much faster than was true when they had first worked on *Romeo and Juliet*. "And yet," she added her personal opinion, "it would perhaps be unjust to admit that *Cinderella* was a sort of letdown after the Shakespearean ballet. For these two ballets are in the same "correlation of significance" as the immortal Shakespearean masterpiece is with *Cinderella*."

The ballet was acclaimed as one of the best Prokofiev had written. But Prokofiev, while delighted with Ulanova's artistry, was critical of the arbitrary changes in his score made by the theatre directors, who considered his orchestration much too "transparent" and lacking in the traditional "fuller sound" in the orchestra—the same objections he had heard about his score for *Romeo and Juliet*.

Five months later, on April 6, 1946, *Cinderella* was produced in Leningrad by the Kirov Ballet, this time adhering to the original score. The Leningraders justifiably considered *Cinderella* as their own "child" since it was the Kirov Ballet that had originally commissioned the work. It was a different production, in no way repeating that of the Bolshoi. Its success kept the ballet permanently in the repertories of Moscow and Leningrad theatres, and it was later produced in Poland and Czechoslovakia as well.

During the winter of 1945–1946, despite the state of his health—he was hospitalized during this period—Prokofiev made three orchestral suites from the ballet, and was in constant contact with Samosud, who was preparing the first production of *War and Peace* at the Malyi Opera House in Leningrad. Of all his projects, the production of *War and Peace* was the closest to Prokofiev's heart. He kept working on the score, stealing extra time by cheating his doctors. Lying in the Kremlin hospital, he would ask one of his visiting friends to stand guard outside his room in case of a doctor's unexpected visit, while he would quickly write down new themes into his notebook, which he kept under his pillow, or on paper napkins he had kept from his meals. "I can't understand these doctors," he complained. "Can't they see that it is much easier for me to write down the themes that come to my mind than to keep them in my head, repeating them to myself . . . and sometimes losing them forever. . . ."

Prokofiev's *War and Peace* had to pass along a thorny road before it was given a full production. Four years previously, in 1942, after he had finished what was later referred to as his first version of the score, it was introduced to a small group of musicians by Richter and Vedernikov playing it four-hands. At that time the subject as treated by Prokofiev could not have been more appropriate to the patriotic feelings with which the Soviet people were living through those hard war years. When Shostakovich was lent the vocal score for a few hours, he kept playing several scenes over and over again—the one before the battle of Borodino, and the death of Andrey Volkonsky—and was so ecstatic about the music that he wrote immediately to Prokofiev: "Who else except the Bolshoi should assume the mission of presenting the new 'People's Musical Drama'?" The letter, which missed Prokofiev in Tbilisi, eventually caught up with him in Alma-Ata. "When it comes to the production, we'll work on it, and then we will talk about it," Prokofiev answered.

When, in December of 1942, Prokofiev went to Moscow, the preliminary discussions took place. First of all, Prokofiev had to listen to
the objections in principle of musically interpreting Tolstoy's novel.
Tolstoy's ironic remark in regard to opera was pointed out. In the
words of Natasha Rostova, in *War and Peace*, "People behave as they
do in everyday life, so why instead of talking should they suddenly
begin to sing?" And Miaskovsky, more concerned with Prokofiev's
score itself, said, "While the music is no doubt extremely interesting,
it will not make an opera—again it is always the same, one scene after
another, as if it were a dramatic play, spoken words and barely any
singing. And besides, there are far too many unnecessary episodes."

But Samuel Samosud, the conductor, liked the score and insisted
that it was up to the theatre to prove its worth. Before it was officially
accepted he had several conferences with Prokofiev. The score called
for eleven scenes, the first five dealing with Peace and the rest with
War. Prokofiev argued that the subtitle should not be a "Musical
Drama," or "Opera," but that he preferred to speak of it as a series of
lyrico-dramatic scenes, similar to the original subtitle given by
Tchaikovsky to his *Evgeni Onegin*. Prokofiev also refused to call it
Natasha Rostova because that seemed to him to lack significance. But
he agreed with Samosud about the necessity of reworking a great
many episodes in the score, and on his second visit to Moscow in January 1943, Samosud organized a "hearing" of the score at the Bolshoi,
with Prokofiev playing the score on the piano and singing the parts.

At the same time, taking advantage of his presence in Moscow, his
Duenna was given an audition and was accepted for the following season at the Bolshoi, while *War and Peace* was also tentatively marked
for an eventual production; it was even announced in the papers.
Promising to make the necessary revisions, Prokofiev returned to
Alma-Ata. But during the spring of 1943 the members of the Bolshoi
were evacuated to Kuibishev, and therefore the rehearsals could not
begin until late in October of that year.

Eisenstein was chosen as stage director for the opera, and Prokofiev
was delighted. Because of their close friendship, and their most pleasant collaboration on the production of *Alexander Nevsky* and on the
score for *Ivan the Terrible*, he could not wish for anyone better. In
fact, when Meyerhold, who was scheduled to stage his *Semyon Kotko*,
was no longer "available" because he had been killed for alleged anti-
Soviet activities, Prokofiev asked Eisenstein to take his place, but
Eisenstein did not then have sufficient free time from his own work.

Samosud, also a great admirer of Eisenstein's, voted for him. Once
before Samosud had asked Eisenstein to stage the *Valkyrie*. At first,

Eisenstein admitted that this proposition frightened him, but later he agreed. (Over a dozen sketches for the planned *Valkyrie* production remain in the Eisenstein archives.) This time Eisenstein gladly accepted the Samosud-Prokofiev offer and had had several discussions with Prokofiev about the opera, when suddenly Samosud was relieved of his post at the Bolshoi. With his departure *War and Peace* was dropped from the Bolshoi's scheduled program, but interest in the opera did not die.

During the spring of 1944, at a conference devoted to works composed during the war, Shostakovich spoke about the opera, and in the fall of the same year the Soviet Opera Ensemble gave a performance of it to a piano accompaniment at the Actors' Home in Moscow. But all this was not what Prokofiev had hoped for, and when in January of 1945 he received an ovation after conducting the Fifth Symphony, he wistfully said, "And now . . . if only *War and Peace* would be produced. . . ."

But he became ill, and was incapable of assisting the Malyi Opera Theatre in the preparation of their production. Although at the rehearsals the opera made a favorable impression, plans for its performance were momentarily suspended, due to the "most unexpected circumstance," as the Russians even in retrospect some twenty years later dare to refer to the "omnipowerful dictates" of those in power. Samosud wrote in 1961:

Despite the authenticity of the events as depicted in the opera, "some people" found that they were not historically accurate. Therefore, although not officially, but in a manner allowing no argument, the directors of the opera were told to eliminate several important scenes. Without the scene at Napoleon's headquarters, and the one portraying the burning Moscow captured by the enemy, the production was made senseless. Prokofiev was too ill to attend this dress rehearsal. It is not necessary to say to what degree Prokofiev was chagrined by the sudden turn of fate in the production of his opera.

Still, the fully prepared production was divided into two performances: the first part of it, eight scenes from *Peace*, was given its première at the Grand Hall of the Moscow Conservatory. Prokofiev went to see it twice. Barely able to stand on his feet, he bowed to the ovation given him, but his doctor was extremely annoyed.

"What in God's name were you doing there? You should have been at home, in bed, and not getting excited over trifles."

Quoting Ostrovsky, Prokofiev said, "One does not die from happiness."

What he was not aware of, although his doctors were, was that his emotional upsets over losing his close collaborators (Meyerhold, Eisenstein, and now Samosud) had further impaired his health. He was advised to live in the country. With Myra Mendelson at his side, he moved to Nikolina Gora, a small settlement near Zvenigorod, sixty kilometers west of Moscow. It meant not only leaving his new apartment, where he had just arranged everything for their comfort and his work, but also foregoing the interesting literary evenings, current art expositions, occasional visits to a chess club "with its dimmed lights and quiet, where men forgot their daily worries and temporarily were transported into another world full of its own special interests," as Prokofiev said, reminding him of the evenings in his youth when he was not reduced as he was now to the mere role of silent observer. It meant giving up his close contact with a large circle of friends, musicians, writers, and actors, and the occasional friendly chats at suppers, and above all attending the theatres, operas, and concerts. And this at the time when, ever since the celebration of his fifty-fifth birthday, his compositions were being performed more frequently than ever before.

At a recital in his honor Richter played the Sixth, Seventh, and Eighth Sonatas, and at another concert of Prokofiev's works Yakov Zak gave a brilliant performance of his first three piano concertos, while pianists all over Russia were playing his piano compositions and conductors were presenting his orchestral works.

Leaving Moscow also meant a sudden change from life in a bustling metropolis—the kind he had enjoyed all his life—to that of the quiet of a country home. But since this retirement was his only opportunity to continue to work, Prokofiev, at last realizing the gravity and permanence of his illness, bowed to his doctors' advice.

33

The country house, with a large garden in picturesque surroundings, differed from a *dacha*—as Russian summer homes are called—because it was well appointed for living all year round. It became Prokofiev's home, which he rarely left from 1946 to 1950, and to which he anxiously returned each spring from 1950 to 1953.

In his youth, while in Sontsovka, he had not particularly enjoyed country life, for he was fascinated by the lively pulse of large cities. But as he grew older he was more and more attracted by the beauty and mystery of nature, by the changes of the seasons. He often spoke of it, and he told Myra Mendelson how he particularly loved the Russian villages, with their gravel and dirt roads, dilapidated peasant huts and courtyards, where dogs and cats lived in relative peace, and chickens, geese, cows, and pigs were one large family. "I love the rooster's crow," he said, "and the smell of smoke coming out of a peasant hut, and the horses' odor mixed with the smell of cheap tobacco."

Extremely disciplined, Prokofiev accepted his retirement with good humor, and far from complaining about his fate, strove to derive as much pleasure out of his imposed country-squire life as he could. "I am not the son of an agronomist for nothing," he told Myra Mendelson, who watched him supervising and participating in planting flowers, bushes, and trees (maples were his favorite). He started a fruit garden and carefully watched it grow. He was as intently interested in all stages of vegetation, as he was in listening to the chirping of the fledgelings in their nests and "the woodpecker's incessant drumming, as if he had lost his mind," as he said. "Do woodpeckers ever suffer from hypertension?" he asked Myra Mendelson.

Early in the morning, or when forced to interrupt his work, or in the evenings before going to bed, he made the rounds of the narrow paths of the garden, occasionally stopping at the fence surrounding the property to chat with neighbors. He missed the intercourse with people that was now denied him. But he substituted for the lack of human relationships the pleasure he derived from the domestic animals.

He had always loved dogs, and one of the neighbors had a young cocker spaniel; Prokofiev was never too tired to walk the extra distance to "chat" with him. He would call him, and when the little barking puppy would reach the fence, Prokofiev would bend down to pat him and ask why at so early an age he had such a sonorous bass voice and such sad eyes.

This uneventful country life also lacked any reason for competing, which was one of the characteristics of his nature. All his life, whether he was playing chess, bridge, tennis, or volleyball, he was not contented with them merely as pleasant pastimes and organized regular "matches" with his partners. He had even worked very hard on his piano technique in order to win the Rubinstein Prize at his graduation from the Conservatory, not so much for the honor as the competitive spirit of the contest with his fellow students. And he never missed joining his colleagues whenever a competition for the best composition was announced in Soviet Russia. It was sad to see him now reduced to organizing "chicken races," which, with his typical sense of humor, he christened in Italian: *"Corsi."*

As soon as he appeared in the courtyard carrying their feed in a large pot, the chickens rushed toward him from all corners. Then, having them all "lined up for the start," he would throw the choice pieces of bread as far as he could and with childish delight watch them race after their "prize." The Queen chicken, as he referred to her, was a bit too heavy to compete in those races, and so he fed her separately in accordance with her dignified position in the community.

The white rooster, whom he named "the Boiler," because of his irritable disposition, was usually the champion. But he also was the showpiece of Prokofiev's chicken kingdom because of his rose-colored tailfeathers. Claiming to have been an eye witness, Prokofiev enjoyed describing to his friends the singular event when the rooster inadvertently dipped his tailfeathers into a large pot of cranberry juice that had been left to cool in the courtyard.

Spring was Prokofiev's favorite season. He took long walks along the banks of the Moscow River, where he savored the fragrance of the new-mown grass, or visited the neighboring villages and the Nikolina forest. He never liked the somber, dense forests, but preferred the more "transparent" ones, where he could suddenly find himself in a sun-flooded green grove. He diligently gathered mushrooms, a pastime to which he was introduced by Miaskovsky, to whom he had to concede the title "master of the mushroom sport."

Prokofiev left the arrangement of their living quarters to the care of Myra Mendelson. He was indifferent to antique or expensive furniture. It was useless to ask him to describe an apartment of any of their friends. All he remembered were the books or the shelves with music. And when upon occasion they expected a visitor, and Myra Mendelson was busy with putting the house in order, he would advise her not to tire herself, saying that nobody pays any attention to such trifles.

But three objects, all in his working room, were of paramount importance: his piano, his writing desk, and an easy chair in which he liked to relax and think over his work. Before starting his day, he found one more diversion: their cat chose the easy chair as her sleeping accommodation, and often, completely disregarding the eminence and the social position of her master, she assumed most frivolous postures. For her "edification," pretending not to see her, but careful not to hurt her, Prokofiev would ease himself into the chair, thus sending the frightened cat flying out of the room.

Myra Mendelson saw to it that in his working room, close at hand, were his favorite books: not only the musical literature, but books on the origin of our planet, a geographical atlas, the current issues of the literary and art magazines, books on history and on the theory of chess.

Although leaving the management of their home to Myra Mendelson, Prokofiev nevertheless took an interest in acquiring the objects necessary for their household, enjoying shopping, not because of the value and usefulness of the items, but because of the pure fun of purchasing them. He was especially pleased with the installation of two round electric lanterns on either side of the porch, which he lighted himself whenever they received friends.

Prokofiev tried to be an obedient patient but seldom succeeded. He was allowed to work only a few hours a day, but how could he stop thinking? he asked—and his thoughts were always on music. In his pockets he carried notebooks in which he wrote down the melodies that came to his mind, and even while he was chatting with friends, one could occasionally notice the sudden change in his expression and the rapid motion of his fingers as if he were trying out a passage on a piano. He never seemed to be bored or lacking occupation; *dolce far niente* would have been for him the worst of calamities. And in the evenings he still insisted on giving an account of his accomplishments during the day. Everything in the progress of education, science, and even astronomy, as well as in the arts, and the solutions to economic problems and the international relations of various countries fascinated him, and he followed the information on maps, sometimes consulting books on the history of different nations.

But he left to Myra Mendelson the reading aloud of literature, listening attentively, occasionally writing down in his notebooks the ideas, expressions, and even separate words that caught his imagination. Myra Mendelson recalled later that since Prokofiev was unusually impressionable, he felt as if he himself were a part of the story she was reading to him. The characters' problems became his own, as those in his operas or ballets had. Just as during work on *Duenna* he laughed heartily at the comic situations, so his eyes were full of tears when, in reading *War and Peace* to him, Myra Mendelson reached the meeting scene between Natasha Rostova and Andrey Volkonsky.

When he was asked to write a ballet based on *Othello*, he refused, saying, "It would mean to live in an atmosphere of ill feeling, and I don't want to have anything to do with Iago." Prokofiev was particularly sensitive to the moral implications of the character of Iago, having, in his own person and Lina's, been victimized by treachery and deceit. He was mainly attracted by the varied works of those classical and contemporary authors in which he found depth of ideas, humanitarian attitudes, keen humor, and clear images that portrayed the spiritual beauty and strength of man and his striving for good and justice.

He was bored by "edifying" and verbose works, and thought that falsehood in any form was contemptible. And he was weary of sentimentality and what he called "the digging into painful feelings." He loved to hear about man's true happiness, and he was deeply touched by a common misfortune. Although as a musician he lived in an imaginary world, in literature he liked memoirs, diaries, and the letters of artists, composers, and authors as well as fiction. It goes without saying that he made Myra Mendelson read the Russian classics to him, but he also cherished Shakespeare, and enjoyed Thackeray and Theodore Dreiser.

Among Russian authors, Chekhov stood apart: Prokofiev could hear his short stories over and over again. And one can easily imagine the unforgettable impression Vasily Kachalov, the eminent actor of the Moscow Art Theatre, had contributed to Prokofiev's love for this author. Kachalov frequently visited Prokofiev often reciting the poems of Pushkin, Lermontov, Mayakovsky, Blok, Essenin, and Pasternak, but it was a real treat when he read Chekhov's *Uncle Vanya*. For two successive evenings Kachalov read the whole play, the parts of all the characters.

Besides Kachalov and other actors with whom Prokofiev had become friendly during the evacuation period in Nalchik and Tbilisi, he was occasionally visited by musicians who brought him the latest "musical news" from the capital. He was eager to know "who was composing what" and to get first-hand impressions of new works being performed.

When Richter came to see him, he took him to his working room, saying, "And I? I have something interesting for you," and he showed him the beginning of his Ninth Sonata. "This will be your sonata," he said. "Only don't imagine it will be just for an effect. . . . No, no, not to startle the Grand Hall of the Conservatory."

The sonata was to be in four movements in sonatina form, a style that ever since his youth had a special attraction for Prokofiev. It had no complicated technical effects, but was rather pastoral, with an intimate, lyrical character predominating the first and third movements; the other two were scherzando. It appeared a bit "too simple" to Richter, and he was a little disappointed. Prokofiev dedicated the sonata to him, but Richter did not perform it until several years later.

"Ah . . . one works well in the peace of the country," Prokofiev remarked as, during the first year of living away from Moscow, he completed his Sixth Symphony (February 18, 1947), wrote an additional scene for the *War and Peace* score, made sketches for a future cello sonata, composed a short violin sonata that was to be played in unison by several violins unaccompanied, and again began to look for a subject for an opera or a ballet.

Prokofiev intended to dedicate the Sixth Symphony to Beethoven (its opus number, 111, was the same as that of Beethoven's last sonata, one of Prokofiev's favorites). But the opus number was purely coincidental. Again Prokofiev intended no program for the symphony, although he admitted that since the major themes were written down during 1944–1945, they were inspired in a way by the war. "Now we are celebrating the victory," he said, "but everyone of us still has unhealed wounds: some lost their dear ones, others their health. . . . We should not forget this."

Evgeni Mravinsky, the leader of the Leningrad Philharmonic, gave the symphony its first performance on October 11, 1947. In Prokofiev's presence, one of the rare occasions on which he left his country home, it was performed on two successive evenings. Well received, it was later often performed abroad.

"The Soviet press, *Soviet Art,* and *Leningrad Evening* hailed the new symphony as an extraordinary event, but missed certain contradictions in the symphony," Nestyev noted in his book on Prokofiev. And always ready to pay lip service to those in power, he coyly

added, "But soon life brought substantial corrections to that evaluation."

Life in Soviet Russia did indeed. But Prokofiev was not yet aware of
it. For the jubilant celebration marking the beginning of the October
Revolution's fourth decade Prokofiev composed the Festive Poem for
Symphonic Orchestra (A major, Op. 113) and a cantata, "Blossom,
the Powerful Land" (D-flat major, Op. 114). The former was performed on October 3, 1947, but disappointed the audience, while the
latter, with its fresh and gay character, fared a little better with the
critics. On the eve of the celebration the Soviet government bestowed
on Prokofiev its highest honor, naming him People's Artist of the
U.S.S.R.

Prokofiev was not given much time to rejoice. Perhaps through her
relationship to Rosa Kaganovich, Myra Mendelson was instrumental in
this sudden gesture of magnanimity. Such an assumption would be
more gratifying than the suspicion of a sadistic policy on the part of
the authorities. For during the purges, the more important the man,
the more severe his punishment. Or was this awarded distinction only
one of the executioners' wiles—the condemned man being served the
menu of his choice for his last repast?

Prokofiev was completely unaware of what was in store for him.

The opening gong for the turbulent events that were to follow was
not another controversial work by Prokofiev or Shostakovich, but an
"exclusive" première of Vano Muradelli's opera *The Great Fellowship*
at the Bolshoi shortly after January 1, 1948.

Muradelli was a mediocre composer and his opera could not interest
anyone, but Stalin with his retinue, including Andrei Zhdanov, were
in the audience and did not like the work. After the performance
Stalin and Zhdanov went backstage to express their feelings to the
composer and to Leontyev, the director of the Bolshoi, who had provided them with the evening's entertainment.

After their visit Leontyev had a heart attack, and a few days later
the Moscow press casually mentioned his death. Several musicians
were arrested, and some were urged to reconsider their choice of
programs for their performances.

In the first week of February 1948 the three-day discussions about
Soviet music took place in Moscow at the Central Committee of All-
Union Communist Party. Andrei Zhdanov, General Zhdanov since the
battle of Leningrad, heading a number of members of the the Central
Committee of the Communist Party, including Mikhail Suslov, pre-
sided over this extraordinary "conclave."

No "outsiders," no spectators, and no reporters—certainly no foreign reporters—were allowed to attend such conferences. But Mr. Alexander Werth, then the British correspondent in Moscow, was able to obtain the 176 small pages of the published report, and gave a résumé of the conference in his book *Musical Uproar in Moscow.* *

Full summaries of Zhdanov's speeches were published in the press, but little else. Was it because the "opposition," polite though they were, had still made out a very good case against the Party line? Was it feared that their arguments, if widely known, might weaken the effectiveness of the speeches made by the new pundits of the Composers' Union and by Zhdanov himself?

To give the necessary prestige to Zhdanov's role as a judge of music and musical matters, the Party, Mr. Werth reported, had used at that time its technique of rumor-launching.

All kinds of people started saying, nobody knew on what basis, that Zhdanov was a most accomplished musician [a pianist], and a graduate of the Leningrad Conservatory. This "fact" had never been recorded in any official biography of Zhdanov, and the suddenness with which this now became common knowledge was peculiar. Later inquiries showed that there was not a word of truth in the story; but the public nevertheless acquired the idea that Zhdanov was a great musical expert.

For several hours Zhdanov told his audience that "it had all been a dreadful mistake, a terrible racket, and that the great composers of Soviet symphonic music were little more than a bunch of artistic spivs, un-Soviet and even anti-Soviet in their activities, 'anti-People,' formalist, divorced from reality, and, in short, unwanted by the people of the Soviet Union." And referring once more to the *Pravda* article,† written at the time of Shostakovich's *Lady Macbeth of Mzensk* affair in 1936, in which the Communist Party with its "fatherly directness and care" had pointed to their errors, he urged the composers to repent and "become more conscious of their duties to the Soviet people."

Echoing Zhdanov, Khrenikov was more specific in his address to his fellow composers: "Composers have become infatuated with formalistic innovations, artificially inflated and impracticable orchestral compositions, such as the inclusion of twenty-four trumpets in Khachaturian's *Symphonie Poème*, or the incredible scoring of sixteen doublebasses, six harps, and four pianos, and the exclusion of the rest of the string instruments in Prokofiev's 'Ode on the End of the War.' "

On February 10 the Central Committee of the Communist Party issued a decree severely criticizing the "wrong path" taken by the

* London, 1949: Turnstile Press, Ltd.
† See Appendix.

composers and, branding "formalism" as a dangerous trend against the people of Soviet Russia, condemned the best-known composers, including Sergei Prokofiev. A number of critical observations pointing out the deficiencies in Soviet Music were duly echoed throughout the Soviet press.

A week later, on February 17, at the All-Moscow Composers meeting, Prokofiev's Sixth Symphony, "Ode on the End of the War," and the recent *Festive Poème* were branded as worthless and even evil. Listed chronologically, but in reverse order, the next group contained the Sixth Sonata (successfully performed by Richter at the debut of his concert career), the Seventh Sonata (which had been awarded a prize in the Soviet Union and was considered good enough to serve during the war as a propaganda piece to be flown on a microfilm to the United States. Since then it had become a showpiece not only on Vladimir Horowitz' programs but on those of most of the concertizing virtuosos all over the world), and the Eighth Sonata (which had been introduced by Gilels and was also a prizewinner in the Soviet Union).

To these works were added some of Prokofiev's arrangements of Russian folk songs and all the ballets he had written while living abroad which had already been discarded as "evil products of bourgeois tendencies": *The Buffoon, The Prodigal Son, On the Boristhène,* and *Le Pas d'acier*, as well as his opera *The Flaming Angel*. And finally, the Third and Fourth Symphonies, and the Fifth Piano Concerto, the performance of which by Richter had made Prokofiev choose him as his favorite interpreter of his works.

Prokofiev had faced a similar "comradely conference" once before in 1927 when he went to Moscow on his first trial return to Russia and the Russian Proletarian Musician's Organization branded him an enemy of Soviet culture and his *Le Pas d'acier* as bordering on Fascism. But Prokofiev was young at that time, endowed with universally envied good health, and relatively independent. He could return, as he did, to France and stay away from Soviet Russia—his mother was dead and therefore there could not be threat of reprisals—or he could choose his fate and return to Russia for good, as he did in 1933. Also at that time there were Meyerhold, then at the height of his popularity, who stood by him, Lunacharsky and Gorky, who held him in high esteem, and many musicians who, although helpless, were far from agreeing with the Russian Proletarian Musician Organization's opinions, and hoped for better times to come when the organization would be disbanded and their verdicts nullified.

Now, in 1948, Prokofiev was summoned from his peaceful recuperation in the country to appear not before the members of merely another musicians' union, however powerful, but before a group of commissars—all musical illiterates but endowed with the power of the highest offices in the Soviet Union.

This was not an impromptu conference, for the following excerpt from Nestyev's book—he was on the spot and was well informed about it—shows that while the highest honor, People's Artist of the U.S.S.R., was being bestowed upon Prokofiev, a thorough and complete dossier on him had been in preparation for months.

Nestyev duly recorded the case:

During 1947–1948 Prokofiev's creative ability showed definite symptoms of his discord with the Soviet audiences. It was apparent in the failure of his Festive Poeme and the extremely cool reception of his Sixth Symphony, because of the difficulty of being understood by an average listener, his last three piano sonatas, and other compositions. The critics seemed to miss the deficiencies in these works and at that time praised everything composed by Soviet masters.* A serious critical evaluation of the activities of the Soviet composers became imperative; it was necessary and urgent to help the talented artists overcome their delusions and to bring their creations into accord with the demands of the people.

To General Zhdanov, who had his own way of judging such ticklish matters, Prokofiev was a typical representative of the bourgeoisie, a typical sample of a man who, as a boy, had known no privation and had been raised by governesses and "attended" by a staff of "downtrodden" servants. In the record of his youth there was no mention of his joining the peasants in their work on the farm, of helping them at harvest time, but it showed that he played the piano instead, even before his future profession had been decided upon, thus wasting his time and energy on bourgeois pleasures.

He had deserted his country when it had needed the cooperation of every citizen; and abroad, as a composer, he had served under the command of Sergei Diaghilev in titillating the taste of a decadent Western society. And when he had returned to Soviet Russia, like some sort of visiting foreign dandy, he had the nerve to accuse his Soviet colleagues of provincialism in their work and dared to suggest that instead of sneering and condemning Western culture, they should try to learn something from it, thus advocating disobedience to the Communist Party's directives.

Despite the hard years of struggle and privation during the war, his appearance remained that of a bourgeois. He wore foreign-made clothes, even double-breasted jackets, which were identified with the

---

* In his speeches Zhdanov repeatedly said: "Their reputation was built by sycophantic, boot-licking critics."

Western Ambassadors, bright ties, tweeds, and instead of a cap of non-descript shape or color, he "sported" soft felt hats, which in the communist countries even as late as 1956 epitomized Western bourgeois headgear.

Furthermore, he apparently could still not rid himself of the bourgeois way of living (Zhdanov was well informed about that). Even while living a country life, he appeared at breakfast with his colleagues in the dining room at Ivanovo, or later, alone with Myra Mendelson at Nicolina Gora, always impeccably and elegantly dressed, wearing clean linen, freshly shaved—with, of all things, an electric shaver acquired in the United States—and even scented with French perfume. His soft white hands showed no trace of callouses from hard work; they were well kept, the nails manicured.

And if with all this he still claimed to be, like his parents, a member of the intellectual class, then so much the worse for him, for was not the intelligentsia Zhdanov's pet hatred? Was not the intelligentsia at the bottom of all evil? During the purges Zhdanov distinguished himself in taking an active part in "liquidating" the intellectuals, and at the time of Shostakovich's *Lady Macbeth* affair he gave the composers fair warning. But since this went unheeded, he was back to uproot and destroy the evil once and for all.

There is more than one way to destroy a human being. It would be naïve to presume that in building his case against Prokofiev, Zhdanov had not taken into special consideration that Lina was already considered persona non grata. And it would be equally naïve to presume that with all the data on Prokofiev before him, Zhdanov was not aware of his victim's physical condition. Only a year earlier, when Prokofiev had been given an ovation after the première of the first part of his *War and Peace* at the Grand Hall of the Moscow Conservatory, his doctor was beside himself because of the excitement, but had to agree with Prokofiev that one does not die of happiness. Calls to appear before the Central Committee of the Communist Party seldom promise to be entertaining or pleasurable, and they are issued without medical consultation. Prokofiev's summons to appear sounded a fateful chord in a life which, under Myra Mendelson's incessant care, he had tried to make harmonious for his work during the few years left to him. But if General Zhdanov ever had a conscience, it had long since been buried under the medals decorating his chest conferred in recognition for his sinister deeds.

I was not present at those "three-day discussions" at the Central Committee of the Communist Party in Moscow. But I have attended an exact replica of such a discussion, held shortly afterward in

Prague,* and since, to the best of my knowledge—except for Mr. Werth's report, derived from the official published minutes—an actual account of the proceedings of these "conferences" has never been given, I feel compelled to describe them, for I believe it would contribute to the understanding of Prokofiev's state of mind and his behavior, and the natural consequences that led to the further deterioration of his health.

As a music critic and a reporter for American magazines I happened to be present at the music and drama festivals during 1946, 1947, and 1948 which had taken place in Prague. I witnessed the glorious birth and ignominious death of the so-called International Music Festivals there, and I also saw the two pitiful attempts, in 1947 and 1948, to have an International Congress of Composers and Music Critics run parallel to the music festivals, as a sort of companion for the brilliant performances.

In 1947 there was still hope that Prague could become a forum for these gatherings. There, it was believed, opinions as well as information on the life and work of musicians from all over the world could be freely exchanged and discussed. I remember how a few hundred musicians—some from such distant parts of the globe as India, China, what was then Palestine, and South America—came to the large hall at the Narodni Club and eagerly listened to their confrères from the United States, England, and the Continent.

I remember how, after listening to the papers read by the American Carlton Sprague Smith, and the Englishman Gerald Abraham, they were "agog" waiting for Dmitri Shostakovich's "lecture" about "The Life and Work of the Soviet Composer." This was Shostakovich's debut among the musicians outside of his homeland; this was the first time since he grew to manhood that he had crossed the Western borders of Soviet Russia. And I remember the sad disappointment of his audience, for he read to us the facts and figures from a paper he had brought from Moscow—a paper, obviously approved by the powers, a copy of which had been circulated by the Soviet Embassies' cultural attachés through nearly all the European countries some six months before Shostakovich appeared at the Congress.

And I remember well how his extreme nervousness prevented asking him questions or starting the discussion that was planned and announced by the organizers of the congress. Yet, apparently there were enough musicians at this first congress who sincerely and anxiously believed that given a chance, things might improve, that eventually we would get better acquainted with each other and there would be less

* My report was published in *Etude* (January 1949) and reprinted in *The Catholic Digest.*

suspicion to obstruct our work, for the organizers of the first congress held on to their idea of a Second International Congress, this despite the Communist coup in Prague in February of 1948 which had alienated Czechoslovakia from the Western countries.

To my surprise, while the music festival was boycotted, officially by some and unofficially by others, the Second International Congress of Composers and Music Critics again opened its sessions at the Narodni Club in Prague. But, as in the festival's concert halls, one did not see a large number of Western musicians at the congress. There were a few from France and Italy, Gerald Abraham from England, and a few from Austria, East Germany, and the Scandinavian countries.

Since the majority of musicians had come from Eastern Europe—Poles, Yugoslavs, Bulgarians, Rumanians, and Hungarians—they and their Czech hosts were primarily interested in discussing "new items," items similar to those which had brought about the "purge" of the best-known Soviet composers by the decree of the Central Committee of the Communist Party. To the composers and critics it seemed imperative and most urgent to find some kind of definition for that ugly word "formalism" on which, it seemed, not only their work, but life itself depended. For days each group of musicians tried in vain to give its own interpretation of this term, which had been so elastic that it appeared to fit any situation, or any "party line," at any time. "For God's sake!" Gerald Abraham cried out at the end of a week's debate, "Can't any of you explain it?" But no one seemed to be able to.

The organizers of the congress, in their naïve way, had invited Sergei Prokofiev to it, but they received a curt telegraphed message of regret—the composer's health prevented him from joining the congress—and instead, it was announced that a Russian delegation headed by the composers Tikhon Khrenikov and Yuri Shaporin had arrived, and that Khrenikov would explain everything once and for all. And, indeed, who else in the world had at his command the recent interpretation of a term that he had been juggling in all its versions ever since the beginning of the Russian purges in 1936.

Certainly no one could have been better qualified—he had risen, as mentioned, not by virtue of his musical talent, to the official position of General Secretary of the Committee of the Soviet Composers' Organization. After his well-remembered debut at the "comradely discussions" in 1936, when he attacked Prokofiev, he had apparently gained sufficient experience in ten years to be chosen by Zhdanov to deliver his lethal message to the musicians outside of Russia.

To those who had never heard of Khrenikov as a composer it was whispered that he had written an opera, *Into the Storm*, which was

held up as a model to composers like Prokofiev and Dmitri Shostakovich, who had "attempted to write an opera on a Soviet subject."
"Khrenikov's heroes are healthy, red-blooded Soviet citizens, who are
fighting for the happiness of their people, their country . . . ," his
official biographer, Martinov, was quoted. "You will never hear in
Khrenikov's music any sentimental, slushy cries. . . ." But Martinov
admitted that "of course not all of his compositions were interesting,"
and that "he was better known for his army songs, written during the
war." Khrenikov did better as a sort of Lavrenti Beria, who had succeeded Yagoda and Yeshov as chief of the secret police. In a similar
"musical" capacity Khrenikov's record is far more impressive.

Small of frame, with cold, shifty eyes, Tishka—as he had been
called before the start of his odious career—never smiled but looked
extremely preoccupied, no doubt to give an air of importance to his
none too prepossessing appearance. He was accompanied by the second in command, Yuri Shaporin, a fifty-nine-year-old composer who
was at least a head taller.

Gaunt, with a shaved head, impassively silent, Shaporin gave the
impression that he would have liked to be excused for being mixed up
in this sordid business. Shaporin belonged to the "old guard," which
now included Miaskovsky and Prokofiev, men who kept away from
intrigues, from denunciations and accusations of their colleagues. He
was little known outside Russia since his music was seldom performed
outside of his country, except for his symphony, the cantata "On the
Field of Kulikovo" (1939), and the oratorio "Legend of the Battle for
Russian Soil" (1944). It was known too that for years he had been
working on an opera, *The Decembrists*, about the thwarted uprising
led by a group of noblemen against the Czar Nicolas I in December
1825, an opera referred to in Soviet Russia as an "optimistic tragedy"
when it was finally performed in 1953.

Sitting on the stage with Shaporin and a few other members of the
Russian delegation, Khrenikov read for two hours the paper that he
had brought from Moscow. If the audience had to learn from his lecture something about the definition of "formalism," it was quickly dis-
illusioned, for he never mentioned the meaning of the term. Instead,
he told his confrères what would be expected from them in the future
if they wished to remain composers. Most of his speech consisted of
banalities about duties to one's country, but he was merely warming
up for what he was to say later.

He attacked the American press, particularly Olin Downes, then the
chief music critic of *The New York Times*, for misrepresenting facts
concerning Soviet musicians. Actually, Downes had often bent over
backward to excuse the Soviets' behavior toward their musicians, and

he had even been accused of being a "leftist" by not too well-informed Americans.

Echoing Nestyev's attack on the United States at the Moscow conference, Khrenikov abused the American composers for their bourgeois tendencies and told the audience to beware of the dangerous American influence. He spoke of Henry Cowell as *the* exponent of the American piano school, referring to his unconventional treatment of the keyboard, known as "clustering," of which Khrenikov's audience was totally ignorant, and he spoke of the threat of American jazz and its deadly influence in France. He advised the French composers—there were a few French Communist musicians in the hall—to go home and form a "front" against the American domination of music in France. He denounced Honegger, Poulenc, and Messiaen, branding them as decadent; and apparently overestimating his audience's naïveté, he praised Beethoven and Schubert.

He warned the Czechs, above all, to accept the recent "new look" in the "Party Line" and told them to compose "closer to their soil." The speech left no doubt in the listeners' minds that the dreaded "Party Line" was being dictated, and during the short intermission, in the corridors of the Narodni Club, the musicians, nervously smoking their thin cigarettes, exchanged frightened glances that spoke more eloquently than any comments they could have dared to make. This was only the beginning.

Following the usual program of Moscow proceedings, Khrenikov announced the three days of "comradely discussions." The audience was offered a free examination of the subject, to have a "free, brotherly, friendly debate," with "tovarich-like" criticisms. But nothing of the kind happened. When several members of the audience asked Khrenikov to tell us of the fates of Shostakovich, Prokofiev, and Khachaturian, and pressed him for details of the recent "purge" of these musicians, Khrenikov jumped to his feet. In the manner of Andrei Vishinsky, he called a lie all the information that we had assumed to be true, since the reports were published throughout the world under a Moscow dateline. "It is all a lie," he repeated several times, "all invented by the capitalist press." Brushing aside any further discussion of the question, he suggested that each one in the audience who wished to participate in the debate send in a list of questions he would like to discuss.

While Khrenikov was busily sorting the papers with questions at his large table on the stage, he was occasionally interrupted by two or three Dostoyevsky-type men who, kowtowing, kept bringing to his august attention long pages containing, as it shortly became obvious, denunciations against the record of this or that composer. Having sufficiently consulted these "musical police files," Khrenikov first accused

Alois Haba, the venerable Czech composer of quarter-tone music, of writing "unproletarian music."

By the way he conducted the interrogation, it soon became evident that he was using against Haba his own list of questions, and realizing that they were trapped, those who had sent in their questions to the presiding group now were frantically, but hopelessly, trying to retrieve them, for they saw only too clearly that by exposing their views, they were getting themselves into worse positions than they were already in.

Haba, at first unaware of what had happened, stood up firmly before his accuser and defended his right to his own way of thinking and composing. A mild and unpretentious man, he refrained from self-praise, did not mention that his opera *Matka* was constantly played in Prague, that his Octet and other compositions had won favor with audiences, but spoke instead of the importance of his endeavors in the general development of music, if from no other standpoint than a purely experimental one.

But when Haba began to explain his tonal discoveries, Khrenikov, whose musical erudition went no deeper than the most elementary aspects of composition, had to call on Shaporin for help. It did not take long for Haba to receive his sentence: he was to lose his positions as professor at the Prague Conservatory and as one of the directors of the opera. It mattered little that he was the sole support of his ailing wife and a consumptive young daughter.

I have seen men being called in one after another, for an accounting, men who had recently been released from German concentration camps in which they had stoically endured inhuman treatment, proud men, who confessed, trembling, and apologized for their "mistakes"—crimes against the proletariat. I saw one composer, over six feet tall and of herculean constitution, who, I was told, was of proletarian background, but whose latest compositions showed signs of foreign, bourgeois influence. This man originally received recognition for writing a symphony with a title no less dramatic than "Stalin's Order Number One," which referred to Stalin's "scorched earth" policy at the beginning of World War II. I saw him break down like a child—confessing his "crimes," he begged for mercy.

While the "brotherly" discussions were being held at the Narodni Club, the Russians saw to it that the audiences in the festival concert halls were given samples of the best artistry of their music performers. They had sent to Prague David Oistrakh, Evgeni Mravinsky, Lev Oborin, and Emil Gilels, as well as whole choral and dance companies in the popular field whose dazzling performances were to support subtly the righteousness of the Soviets' attitude toward music.

So far, the performers had been spared criticism, for not even Khrenikov could have been accused of having made so disastrous a demand that Oistrakh fiddle in a more proletarian way or of having forced Gilels to reflect "socialist realism" in his playing of a Chopin sonata.

Having finished with haranguing the composers, Khrenikov called on all the musicians present at the discussions to draft a "resolution," without which no "discussions" have ever been complete in Moscow. But by now his audience was so confused and bewildered, limp with exhaustion and plainly terrified, that nothing intelligible would have been accomplished had Khrenikov not dictated the "resolution." It was unanimously accepted on the spot. And instead of a "resolution"—a summary of all the problems resolved at the Congress—the composers and critics were actually given a manifesto, a sort of decree, an "order of the day," with a handsome headline: All Progressive Musicians Unite! According to this manifesto, every musician in the audience, upon his return to his native country, was to organize into unions the "progressive musicians," and then, two months later, return to Prague and the next session of the congress to receive further instruction. In short, the International Congress of Composers and Music Critics had become a sort of musicians' Cominform, and only those who subscribed to the manifesto's principles were eligible to join.

The headquarters of this organization were in Moscow, where Khrenikov had been kowtowing before Zhdanov as he supplied him with "musical dossiers." It was in such an atmosphere that the ailing Prokofiev was shamelessly abused. Shostakovich, Khachaturian, and Shebalin, who with Prokofiev headed the list of the guilty, immediately bowed down, confessing and apologizing just as the other musicians had done in Prague. Miaskovsky, who did not attend the "conference," ignored the reprimand; he was stripped of his professorship at the Moscow Conservatory. Shostakovich and Shebalin were "relieved" of their duties as professors at the Conservatory, and Khachaturian of his post as the secretary of the Musicians Union. Prokofiev did not take part in the discussion: he held no official post, and the humiliation could strike only at his health.

With gleeful satisfaction Prokofiev's official Soviet biographer notes that at a subsequent meeting of the Central Committee of the Communist Party, Prokofiev's letter was read:

To THE GENERAL SECRETARY OF THE UNION OF SOVIET COMPOSERS TIKHON NIKOLAEVICH KHRENIKOV.

The state of my health does not permit me to attend the general assembly of Soviet composers, and therefore I wish to express my ideas in regard to the Resolution of the Central Committee of the All-Union Communist Party of February 10, 1948 in the present letter, which I request be made public at the assembly should you deem it necessary.

The Resolution of the Central Committee of the All-Union Communist Party of February 10, 1948, has separated decayed tissues in composers' creative production from the healthy part. No matter how painful for a number of composers, myself included, it may be, I welcome the Resolution of the Central Committee of the All-Union Communist Party, which creates the prerequisites for the return to health of the entire organism of Soviet music.

The Resolution is all the more important because it has demonstrated that the formalist trend is alien to the Soviet people, that it leads to impoverishment and decline in music, and has pointed out to us with definite clarity the aim which we must strive to achieve as the best way to serve the Soviet people.

In his long description of his former mistakes Prokofiev blamed the Western influence and promised not to regard the decree as merely another "prescription," but actually to endeavor to fulfill it in his future work. He closed his apologia with a cliché: "I would like to express my gratitude to our Communist Party for the concrete directives of its decree which are helpful in my search for a musical language clear and close to our people, a language worthy of our people and of our great country."

Shocked by the chastisement of Prokofiev, everyone who ever heard of him in the Western world was even more bewildered by his apologia, which the Soviets published for everyone to see. Several theories have been advanced to interpret or at least explain his action. Some like Samosud, the conductor—who was "relieved" of his post at the Bolshoi but who was in contact with Prokofiev because of the composer's continued work on *War and Peace*—thought that Prokofiev believed that the accusation would eventually be recalled. In the Western countries some have attributed his reply to his sarcastic attitude toward the whole farce. I am inclined to believe that he had never looked upon it as a laughing matter, but this is a conjecture, for he said nothing, and one can only guess what went through his mind. He had before him countless examples of what had happened to those who dared to disobey or merely voice their right to think and work in their own way, including the tragic fate of Satz, of Meyerhold, of countless others.

It would not be too farfetched to presume that under the circumstances Myra Mendelson, through her family relationship with Stalin, had managed to wrangle a promise of rehabilitation for an ill man whose years were numbered. She might have been assured that he

would be awarded the Stalin Prize if he would publicly acknowledge
his "mistakes" and promise to "behave" according to the wisdom of
the decree. (Actually, such an award would serve the government's
needs by silencing the criticism and condemnation of Prokofiev, and
also as proof of its unprejudiced attitude toward the composer.) But
for that a certain amount of time had to pass, and Prokofiev had to be
given a chance to compose a new work, which, regardless of its merit,
could be used as a pretext for such an award. And indeed, a year later
Prokofiev was awarded the Stalin Prize.

Prokofiev realized only too well that not merely was he being
handed a criticism, which in Soviet Russia does not necessarily hold
up indefinitely, but that this time, by one stroke from the Communist
Party, most of his lifelong work was being condemned to oblivion. He
was also well aware that he was not as young as Shostakovich, Khachaturian, Kabalevsky, all of whom would have to weather many storms
but whose lives were still ahead of them. His was over: nearing sixty,
he was hopelessly ill and restricted in his work. But there was still one
desire that never left his mind: ". . . if only my *War and Peace* could
be produced." And for which no sacrifice would be too great.

Still, for a proud man like Sergei Prokofiev, it must have been terribly humiliating to sign a letter like the one he had written,
unless. . . . And the following is my own guess.

One does not need a keen imagination to suggest that the entire
"hearing" at the Central Committee of the Communist Party could
have reminded Prokofiev of the last pages of the chapter seven in
Pushkin's *Captain's Daughter*. Prokofiev could easily have seen General Zhdanov as Emilian Pugachev, a runaway Cossack, who had
staged an uprising during the reign of Catherine the Great, and who,
in the scene to which I am referring, is sitting on an easy chair, as if it
were the throne, and with a wave of his white handkerchief sends
men who refuse allegiance to him to the gallows.

Peter Grinev, an officer and the principal character in the story, had
been saved from the noose through the intervention of an old servant,
who begged Pugachev for his pardon. And when Grinev was brought
to kneel in front of Pugachev and everyone around urged him to
kiss the Cossack's hand, the old servant whispered to the reluctant
officer, "Dearest Master, don't persist. . . . What do you care? . . .
Spit! . . . but kiss the hand of the. . . ."

Pushkin's words—"Spit! . . . but kiss . . ."—have become a Russian saying, and it could have been Miaskovsky who had reminded
Prokofiev of it. Prokofiev spat . . . and wrote a letter. And that was
that as far as Sergei Prokofiev, the composer, was concerned. But two

months later Prokofiev, the man, suffered another severe attack of his grave illness.

The year 1948 was one of the worst in Sergei Prokofiev's life. And yet, before it ended, he had to bear up under one more disaster. It was the last chapter of his marriage to Lina.

There is no reliable record as to whether Prokofiev ever saw Lina and their children on his visits to Moscow during the war, and it must have been most humiliating for Lina not to have been seen at her husband's side in the concert halls—her place having been taken by Myra Mendelson. But after the war, when Lina realized that the "temporary" separation from her husband was still in force and, especially after Soviet citizens were forbidden to marry foreigners by the decree of February 15, 1937—a decree that was retroactive, thus making her marriage illegal and their children illegitimate—Lina must have become desperate. Now Prokofiev no longer needed a divorce from her; he was free to marry Myra Mendelson if he so wished.

Although Lina was aware that the Soviets did not recognize the right of expatriation for their citizens, and was also well aware of the methods the police were using against those who applied for permission to go abroad, she still decided to try to leave Russia with her two boys.

"She devoted her efforts to getting out of Russia, where she no longer had friends or roots, and rejoining her mother in Paris," Edmund Stevens wrote in his book *This is Russia, Uncensored.*

Whenever we [Mr. and Mrs. Stevens] saw her, she assured us that exit visas would soon be issued to herself and the two boys, that she had talked to a very important person who had promised to assist her. One day, not having seen Linette [Lina] for months, we phoned her. A frightened voice on the other end told us she no longer lived there. Soon we had confirmation that Linette had been arrested and the boys were in the care of the State.

The following few lines in Edmund Stevens' report suggest the approximate date of Lina's arrest. "By then Prokofiev was completely immersed in his own troubles. His opera *Tale of a Real Man* [of which I will speak in the next chapter] about a Soviet hero, on which he had pinned his hopes of a come-back, had been given in Leningrad in a concert form." [December 3, 1948.]

With this ends Mr. Stevens' report on Lina's fate.

Thus Lina must have been arrested in 1948 (spring or summer). She was detained on charges of "espionage." The trials for high treason usually were held not by civil but military courts, and the guilty were shot by a firing squad.

Only Lina could supply the record of her survival, something she most probably would never do, or could not do, because in most cases, if and when they were given their freedom, the once condemned had to sign a sworn statement not to disclose the treatment they had received after their arrest. Failure to comply with such a ruling would bring even more severe punishment. However, the routine of all proceedings in such cases is well-known—proceedings which included solitary confinement in either of the most infamous of prisons, Lublyanka or Butyrki, sometimes lasting for months, with the endless nightly interrogations often accompanied by torture, deprivation of an already insufficient prison diet, banishment for days and nights to an underground "punishment cell" (four to five days and nights at a time is considered the maximum of human endurance)—all in order to force signing confessions to imaginary crimes, which frequently included a written denunciation of others presumably involved in the same deeds. The humiliating mockery of these performances varied in their degrees—before 1937 only men were beaten during these interrogations, but Yezhov's ruling included women as well. And turning a hose with icy water on a prisoner was not the last measure in breaking down his resistance.

The truest idea of the treatment Lina must have received before her verdict was pronounced can be learned from Erica Wallach's *Light at Midnight*, and Evgenia Ginsburg's *Krutoy Marshrout*,* two recently published books, which for the first time to my knowledge give an account of the fate of *women*, arrested and condemned on trumped-up charges of guilt, commuted from the death penalty to deportation for years to forced labor camps.

Although fundamentally the descriptions of the horrifying personal experiences of both these authors are in many ways similar, they differ, nevertheless, in one respect. German by origin, though married to an American, but not yet an American citizen at the time of her arrest in East Berlin, Erica Wallach was a foreigner and therefore was treated with less brutality, than Evgenia Ginsburg—a Russian. Also, Mme. Ginsburg was banished to Kolyma, the farthest part of the penal region in Northern Siberia's *taiga*, while Mrs. Wallach was sent to Vorkuta in the arctic region, "facing Novaya Zemlya," as she said.

The Russian prisoners managed to sing, "Siberia? Siberia is also a land of Russia," but of Vorkuta no song has as yet been composed, for as Mrs. Wallach had been told by the prisoners who already had experienced Siberia, Vorkuta was much worse. Only the worst criminals

---

* Both books were published in New York in 1967, the latter under the title *Journey into the Whirlwind*.

and "dangerous enemies of the people" were deported to this "end of the world."

Past the tree line, Vorkuta's winters last for nine to ten months a year, with temperatures falling to 65° below zero. There, under the frozen soil large deposits of coal had been discovered, and thousands of hard labor male prisoners are shipped there to work in the coal mines, the women to build a railroad leading to the foot of the Ural mountains. Lina's death sentence was commuted to banishment for fifteen years in one of the many labor camps in Vorkuta.

When the years of solitary confinement with all its degrading horrors, physical, moral, and mental, were followed by deportation—a month long trek to Siberia among some seventy-six women jammed into one box-car of a train—Evgenia Ginsburg heaved a sigh of relief by quoting Pasternak, "Hard Labor! What bliss!" Lina must have felt the same way after the months of suspense pending her verdict—to be shot by a firing squad, or to be deported via several prisons—transit camps—at Gorki, Kirov, and Kotlas to one of Vorkuta's three labor camps lodging about one thousand women.

The charges against Lina could have been based on her Spanish origin, on her correspondence with her mother in Paris during the Nazi occupation, on her attendance at parties of the foreign embassies— American, British, or French—on her knowing personally some members of the foreign diplomatic corps, on almost any conceivable fact, action, or even word, which could have been interpreted as evidence of espionage.

Harrison Salisbury of *The New York Times*, who often saw her in Moscow in 1944, told me: "She was constantly in and out of the American Embassy. She was, as you know, a flamboyant person, very outspoken, and always very chic; she was just the kind the Soviets would arrest at that time."

In 1955, when Erica Wallach was transferred to Abez labor camp, some sixty miles south of Vorkuta, she was told of Mme. Prokofieva, the composer's wife, being in one of the barracks of the women's camp. But although it was already two years after Stalin's death, when the severe regime of the camp had been somewhat relaxed, Lina was still too cautious to want to associate with Mrs. Wallach, a foreigner. Mrs. Wallach described to me her first meeting with Lina, illustrating how Lina looked around to make sure she was not being overheard before she finally spoke to her. As a rule, the prisoners never dwelt on the reasons for their sentences. They were in Vorkuta for an obvious reason—article 58 of the Soviet Penal Code, the most dreaded in Soviet jurisprudence. "According to her story," Mrs. Wallach wrote in her book, "it was her contact with U. S. Ambassador Steinhardt that had led to her arrest and conviction of espionage." And to me Mrs. Wallach explained this contact: Lina had tried through the ambassador to send some money to her mother in Paris. This, however, could have happened during the years 1939 to 1941 when Laurence Steinhardt was Ambassador to Russia, or by correspondence with him after Steinhardt left Russia to assume his post as Ambassador to Turkey from 1942 to 1945, and to Czechoslovakia from 1945 to 1948.

Such retrospective accusations were, and still are, not unusual. Weren't the charges of "espionage" for the Germans brought against Svyatoslav Richter's father based on the fact that some twenty years before the last war he had been giving piano lessons to the children of the German Consul then stationed in Odessa? As the German armies were approaching the city in 1941 he was shot by a firing squad.

"Prokofieva was a very pretty woman even then, in her fifties, and after seven years of camp life," Mrs. Wallach wrote in her book.

In her youth, she must have been exquisite. She was small and well rounded with tiny hands and feet. Her hair was still thick and coal black; the round black eyes in a smooth, round face were lively and fiery as those of a young girl. Seven years is a long time, and I marveled at her looks. She smiled gratefully. "I have tried so hard not to go to pieces. It's difficult under the circumstances."

But this was in 1955, when, after Stalin's death, the regime in the camps was less rigorous. How did Lina survive all those previous years, I asked Mrs. Wallach, how did she live through the "hard labor" such as Mrs. Wallach herself had to endure when she was first brought to Vorkuta in 1953—the building of an embankment for the railroad while *purga*, the blinding arctic snowstorms, raged over the icy plains? For, as if Beria's regime in the labor camps were too soft, already in 1939 Stalin's personal directives were issued to the administrations of all labor camps "to make sure that the inmates did not get any fancy ideas that they had been sent to a health-resort."

Upon a prisoner's arrival in Vorkuta, she was given a medical examination, which decided her status: healthy, semi-invalid, or invalid. Women over fifty-five belonged to the third category. When Mrs. Wallach saw Lina, she was an "invalid," and thus exempt from work in the field, but assigned to work in the barracks. After Lina's return to Moscow, she told a friend confidentially that if she survived at all, it was only because she was fortunate enough to have often been in hospitals, either as a patient (having had a nervous breakdown), or because she was kept by the medical staff—prisoners like herself—on the pretext of some work as a nurse, or in a clerical job.

After Stalin's death, although it took years, gradually the prisoners were sent back to Moscow as "free men and women," and some of them were eventually rehabilitated. Lina's turn came in 1957, after nine years of imprisonment. She was finally released from the labor camp because "they" (as Russians referred to the authorities in Moscow) had at last arrived at the conclusion that she had been condemned on unproven charges. She had been, as it was officially stated, the victim of a "breach of Socialist jurisprudence."

Upon her return to Moscow, she rejoined her two sons—Svyatoslav, an architect, and Oleg, an engineer. Both were already married and had children. The prisoners were not allowed to send letters to their relatives except twice a year, but they managed occasionally to communicate with them surreptitiously; receiving letters was permitted, and Lina's boys had kept in touch with her and sent her food packages.

To this day, Lina is still struggling to assert her rights as Prokofiev's widow. When in 1966, a representative of an English music publishing firm went to Moscow to arrange for the payment of accrued royalties due Sergei Prokofiev, he was unable to obtain Lina's address or that of her sons.

"We have quite a bit of money in his account," he told me after his return from Russia. Instead of being given Lina's address, he was advised in Moscow to contact Tikhon Khrenikov, now President of the Musicians' Union. This meant that "quite a bit of money" would have to be paid to the Musicians Union, and never reach Prokofiev's legal heirs. Since in addition other large sums of money have accumulated in other countries besides England, Khrenikov's sudden special attention to Lina can be easily understood.

34

When Danton was brought before the Revolutionary Tribunal to answer for his "crimes" against the people of France, he did not plead. "I have lived solely for my country," he said. And on the following day, just before he was guillotined, he turned to his executioner with these words: "*Et toi, tu montrera ma tête au peuple: elle en vaut bien la peine*" ("And you, you will show my head to the people; it's well worth showing.")

Prokofiev's "executioners" showed the Russian people not the true Prokofiev but their own concocted image of him. They, who prided themselves on being the masters of the only country in which artists are treated as aristocratic members of society, had robbed their most eminent member of his wife and two sons, and were slowly destroying him. Prokofiev's only "crime" against the people of Soviet Russia was that, like Danton, he had advocated all his life in music, "*Il nous faut de l'audace, encore de l'audace, et toujours de l'audace*" ("We must dare, and dare again, and always dare"). And like Danton, he was less influenced by the accepted formulas of what is *right*, than he was guided by a sense of *justice*.

Still, Prokofiev was not simply a victim of the commissars but also the victim of a servile Soviet society. There was no sound of protest —either then or later.

Lunacharsky, the first Minister of Education and Arts, who on the eve of Prokofiev's departure for the United States in 1918 had said to him, "You are a revolutionary in music, and we, we are revolutionary in life; we should be working together," and had later urged him to return to Russia, was dead. Meyerhold's voice had been silenced in a concentration camp. And Maxim Gorky, who to relieve the young Prokofiev of the obligation of military service had written to the War Ministry, "We are not so rich that we can afford to sole soldiers' boots with nails of gold," had died "mysteriously" during the purges.

It would have been naïve to expect Prokofiev's colleagues, the Soviet musicians, to rise to his defense. Despite all the honors bestowed upon them and the economic privileges granted them, these members of "the aristocracy of Soviet society" are even more dependent for their lives and work than the average Soviet citizen on the prevalent policies of those in power. They had been subject for so long to a fear of Stalin, dead or alive, that even today they do not dare communicate freely with an outsider without first receiving from their embassies approval of the subject to be discussed.

During the years 1946 to 1948 and later, in the fifties, I met most of the Soviet performing artists—pianists, violinists, conductors, and singers. They left me with the impression of being what the Russians call *remesleniki*, craftsmen, excellent performers in their various fields, but lacking in character and civic courage. Neither Prokofiev nor we should have been surprised that although at one time they had benefited by their association with the composer, at the time of crisis they deserted him. They shirked voicing their individual convictions by hiding behind, "We are small men to speak about so great a composer as Sergei Prokofiev."

They had behaved in a similar way toward Shostakovich at the time of the *Lady Macbeth* affair, and even today, almost thirty years later, they are reluctant to speak about it. And this despite their glamorous roles as Soviet cultural ambassadors to the Western world, roles to which only those who are "trusted" by the Soviet government—trusted to behave according to Soviet propaganda and trusted to return home—are eligible. And in case they should fall prey to "frivolous and decadent" capitalistic notions of freedom of choice, members of their families are held as hostages, although unofficially. What could they have said then, or even now in Russia where the Khrenikovs of Soviet cultural life keep a watchful eye on them?

Today, in 1967, speaking as the President of the Composers Union, Khrenikov still maintains:

The experience of the Soviet Union shows that the state's support does not require from the artist that he surrender his individuality. A sensible government is interested in the maximum development of each artist so that his individuality will rise. If he is dominated, he cannot prosper. Shostakovich and Khachaturian would only have developed in an atmosphere of state support. Each is supported by the state, but none of them will admit to any interference in his art.*

The Prokofiev case certainly substantiates Khrenikov's authoritative pronouncement.

Yezhov had spared some of the performing artists, but Beria included them in his list of the "enemies of the people." Boris Dyakov, author of *Povest o perezhitom* † (*The Story of Personal Experience*), who had been exiled to forced labor camps in the depth of the Siberian *taiga*, gives a long list of prominent men—doctors, professors, scholars, writers, and artists—whose fate he shared. He speaks of Moscow-born Vsevolod Topilin, David Oistrakh's former accompanist, whom he met in one of the camp's hospitals. Topilin was operated on for appendicitis, and, as sometimes happened, thanks to the more humanitarian attitude on the part of the medical staff (also prisoners), was subsequently kept at the hospital on the pretext of some sort of assistantship to the doctors.

Topilin used to tell us about the international competitions for violinists which had been held in Warsaw and in Brussels, where he accompanied Oistrakh, who won the prizes. He also told us about their concerts in the Grand Hall at the Moscow Conservatory. With a resigned smile he would remark: "If I should die here, it will be from my nostalgia for music. In my dreams I imagine that I am playing the piano. In my sleep I hear the music of Tchaikovsky and Chopin. . . . Sometimes I don't want to wake up."

Dyakov further notes: "Upon the directives of the high authorities, Topilin was exempt from general work in the forced labor camp. This was to save his fingers." As if "saving his fingers" would matter after some ten years of life in a labor camp.

In 1954 the Soviet State Music Publishing House began to work on a volume of some seven hundred pages devoted to *S. Prokofiev, Materials, Documents, and Reminiscences.* Published six years later, it includes Prokofiev's autobiography, his mother's short memoir written down by Lina and Boris Bashkirov at Ettal in 1923, letters and documents as well as a memoir by Myra Mendelson, and the reminiscences of his friends and fellow musicians.

Shostakovich, Khachaturian, and Kabalevsky headed the list of musicians who contributed to this volume. All three chose not to mention the 1948 event, as did the performers to whom Prokofiev had dedicated some of his works and who had advanced their careers by including them in their concert repertories. Neither David Oistrakh in his memoir entitled "About the Dear and Unforgettable One," nor

* "50 years after the Revolution that changed the World: Russia Today," *Look,* October 3, 1967.
† Moscow: Izdatelstvo Sovietskaya Rossiya, 1966.

Emil Gilels in his contribution entitled "The Great Compatriot," nor Mstislav Rostropovich in "My Encounters with Prokofiev" had said a word about it.

Svyatoslav Richter was the only exception. Though he could count on his fingers the few times he had been with Prokofiev, he had the courage to go on record by writing the following in his memoir "About Prokofiev": "The year 1948 had arrived. To me, personally, the attitude taken at that time against Prokofiev's works was incomprehensible."

But musicians are only one fraction of the "Soviet aristocracy," which includes painters, sculptors, actors, ballet dancers, and writers. While the government or the Communist Party might be censoring only one of the units, it is also serving a warning on the rest. And since the writers are, in Stalin's words, "the engineers of human souls," their voice is of paramount importance. But most of the capable and talented authors were "liquidated" during the purges. Among the few who survived, Ilya Ehrenburg, a staunch advocate of the Soviet regime, had managed to save his life by escaping to Spain "to report about the Spanish Civil War."

Yet even in 1955, two years after Prokofiev's death and at the time when, following Khrushchev's new policy, Ehrenburg was proudly writing *The Thaw*—the thaw after the freeze of Stalin's tyranny—he did not dare come forward like Emile Zola in his "J'accuse!" Instead, in an article entitled "He [Prokofiev] Knew How to Listen to the Times," which Ehrenburg had contributed to the reminiscences in the abovementioned volume, he wrote this carefully worded paragraph:

He [Prokofiev] scorned a Western world in which he was glorified. He wanted to work for his own people and the future. He had weathered many a trial. He was a great human being, and posterity will not be able to understand our difficult and glorious period of life without intently listening to the works of Sergei Prokofiev, and contemplating his extraordinary fate.

Perhaps in this veiled insinuation Ehrenburg meant to say what he thought of the Communist Party's ignominious behavior toward Prokofiev. Still, he lacked the courage to state the simple truth, in some such plain words as these: "If you, the masters of our lives and destinies, had died on the day when you gave us liberty and the opportunity to share the wealth of the works of our great artists, you would have been remembered with reverence and gratitude, but because since then you have been throttling the very spirit of these artists, you will be damned by the generations to come."

Instead, Nestyev gave the Russian people the following "official" record in his book on Prokofiev, published in 1957:

Critical opinions of the last stages of Prokofiev's creative ability were divided. Some, among those abroad, like Olin Downes in the United States and Gerald Abraham in England, attempted to prove that the direction taken by the composer toward lyricism and simplicity, and the rejection of his former excesses in sound signified the decline, poverty of imagination, and distorted individuality of his creative ability. According to them, Prokofiev was forced by the decree of the Central Committee of the Communist Party to write such music. The absurdity and mendacity of such statements are obvious.

Our own critics maintained that during the past five years Prokofiev had reached the *"heights of achievement"* in realistic and mass-level style.

Aware of the danger to himself as a critic and musicologist because of the ever changing policies of the Communist Party, Nestyev was careful in voicing his own opinion:

The path taken by Prokofiev during 1948–1953 signified, of course, neither a decline in his artistic ability, nor a victorious ascension to some unsurpassed heights. It was, most probably, the beginning of a new stage in his creative development which had a special value. His striving for pacification, keen observation, predominance of lyricism and gentle humor, and clear expression in his last compositions was not in the least surprising. These characteristics were often noticeable in his former works, but now they appeared with far more force.

In further summarizing the composer's last years, Nestyev would have sounded rhapsodic if his "official" record were not so cynical. Prokofiev's last years were uneventful, he says. He rarely left his country home or his apartment in Moscow. He no longer experienced either great triumphs or sharp encounters with the opponents of his works. His illness had curtailed his activities: he did not visit the Composers' Union, did not attend the concerts, did not conduct, almost never played the piano, and did not answer telephone calls. He had even completely abandoned chess.

But as if to show that Prokofiev lacked for nothing, Nestyev says that at his country home Prokofiev had a radio and a phonograph with records:

Prokofiev listened intently to broadcasts of the novelties in Soviet music, created after February of 1948; with great interest followed Shostakovich's "The Song of Forests," Miaskovsky's Twenty-seventh Symphony, Arutunian's Cantata "About the Fatherland," and Kabalevsky's Violin Concerto, and was sincerely jubilant about their success.

And putting the final touch to his analysis of Prokofiev's last years, Nestyev reports that after several other attacks of his illness, "which almost sent him to the grave" and at times partially paralyzed his speech, Prokofiev had been granted a pension by the government on April 22, 1952 (one year before his death). Nestyev concludes with:

This act on the part of the government proves once more the care with which the Soviet government showed its concern about one of the most talented Russian composers.

How touching.

One does not need to be an astute psychologist to understand Prokofiev's state of mind upon his return home from the session with the Central Committee of the Communist Party. He was not living in a country in which he could say to a State Department, "If you will mind your business, I will mind mine." And as for the critics' incoherent gibberish about his works, it would have been beneath his dignity to stoop so low as to be willing to take Khrenikov's compositions as a model for his own work. The latest decree of the Communist Party and the servile attitude of his critics posed to him the same old question which he himself had already asked in a published article upon his return to Russia in 1936, at the time of the first attack by Zhdanov: "Am I expected to write symphonies and operas in the genre of 'Marusya has taken poison. . . .' "

He had written the letter necessary to gain peace, and then returned to work on the opera he had already started when he was so rudely interrupted by the summons from the Communist Party.

This time he had chosen A. Polevoy's novel *The Story of a Real Man*. With Myra Mendelson he had written a libretto into which were incorporated the major subjects of the story, using some of the original text of the novel. The opera, in four acts, eleven scenes, was to be performed at the Kirov Theatre in Leningrad. Prokofiev now hoped that since it was on a contemporary Russian subject, it would serve as his positive answer to the criticism he had recently received.

He said that he wished to introduce into the opera easily understood episodes: "I intend to write trios, duets, and contrapuntally developed choruses, for which I am using extremely interesting documents of northern Russian folk songs. Clear and simple melodies and as much as possible simple harmonization—these are the other elements for which I strive in this opera."

He worked on the score during the spring and most of the summer of 1948, and finished the orchestration on August 11. On December 3 it was auditioned in his presence at the Kirov Theater. It was a fiasco. Prokofiev had underestimated the influence of the recent criticism of his work. It still rang in the ears of the performers, who had prepared the opera in a hurry and without enthusiasm. "I listened and could not recognize my own music. They were not playing *my* music," he said. On doctors' orders, Prokofiev was not allowed to attend the discussions that took place after the audition, but Myra Mendelson and Samosud reported to him the cruel and unjust remarks and decision that had been made.

The negative verdict, the rejection of the opera, was a new blow to Prokofiev's morale, not only because of all the work and time he had spent on it, but because it did not succeed in fulfilling his hope of reversing his critics' attitude.

On December 28, 1948, Khrenikov made the principal speech at a plenary session of the Union called to discuss musical development since the Communist Party issued its February 11 decree. Prokofiev, Khrenikov said, was out of tune with the vast majority of Soviet composers who have "entered onto a new path." He said that there were still formalist vestiges in the works of several composers, but that this clinging to formalism was clearly illustrated in Prokofiev's *The Tale of a Real Man*. After hearing some excerpts from the opera, Khrenikov said the composer had still failed to eliminate his "bourgeois formalism," and denounced the opera for its "anti-melodious content, and lack of understanding of Soviet heroism and Soviet humanity."

The opera will not be performed, concluded Khrenikov, and nine years later, echoing his "master's voice," Nestyev noted in his biography of Prokofiev that it remained in the composer's personal briefcase. Both Khrenikov and Nestyev were mistaken in their prognosis. Although the score underwent several cuts, reducing the eleven scenes to three acts instead of the original four, it has been constantly performed at the Bolshoi since its first performance on October 8, 1960.

Taking advantage, however, of the presence in Leningrad of Prokofiev and of representatives of the Committee of the Arts, the Kirov Theatre arranged an audition for the second part of *War and Peace*. The opera was performed without stage sets, costumes, or make-up, and some of the scenes were omitted, but as Samosud recalled later there was no point in arguing—the main thing was to succeed in obtaining an acceptance for a production.

Again Prokofiev had to remain in his room at the hotel and wait for Myra Mendelson and Samosud to bring him the news. This time the jury decided to produce one of the two parts of the opera, and when Prokofiev heard this, he immediately sketched a possible plan for a one-evening performance. He spoke of cutting the overture, and at least five or six scenes of the total eleven. "His desire to see the production of the opera was so intense," Samosud observed, "that he was ready to do anything: cut, rewrite, and omit as much as was required, so long as he was assured a production." Promising to do a second version of the opera, although it was not going to carry out his original conception, he returned home with a heavy heart, for in addition to everything else, Myra Mendelson could not prevent him from hearing about the death of his friends Asafiev and Eisenstein.

When Boris Volsky, who had worked as a mixer during Prokofiev's collaboration with Eisenstein on *Ivan the Terrible*, visited him at Nicolina Gora to ask him to write music for another film, Prokofiev shook his head: "Since the death of Sergei Eisenstein, I consider my motion-picture activities terminated." Besides, he told Volsky, he had already made so many plans for future work that he doubted whether he would be able to complete them because of doctors' restrictions.

Ever since his *Romeo and Juliet* had been performed by the Kirov Ballet in Leningrad, he had been contemplating writing a ballet with his old friend Lavrovsky on the "Don Juan" theme. It is interesting that when Ulanova had suggested to him a ballet based on "Snow Maiden," Prokofiev had refused, saying that he would not think of competing with the one already written by Rimsky-Korsakov. Yet now he found no objection to the fact that the "Don Juan" idea had been used by Cherubini, Cimarosa, and Mozart, among others, and that Gluck had composed a *Don Giovanni* ballet. For the libretto Lavrovsky and Prokofiev considered at various times the versions of Byron, Perruci, Shadwell, Mérimée, and, of course, Pushkin's *The Stone Guest*.

Their plans had gone so far that they had already cast Ulanova as Doña Anna, when one day Lavrovsky, who was spending the summer of 1949 near Prokofiev's country home, called on his friend with another idea for a ballet. He spoke of Peter Bazhov's small volume *Malachite Box*, a collection of "tales" from the Ural Mountain region. To his surprise, Prokofiev told him that he also had been thinking about it ever since Myra Mendelson had brought the book from the library and read aloud several "tales." "A long time ago, while I was abroad, I had often thought of the Urals, and daydreamed of the wild beauty of that region," Prokofiev said.

The two friends spent the rest of the day on the terrace of Prokofiev's home, planning a future production of the ballet. "You know," Prokofiev said, "I have a feeling that very soon I am going to be tortured by the major themes of this ballet." And indeed, a few days later Prokofiev, impatient to share the results of his inspiration with his friend, went down the road to meet Lavrovsky. Much excited and conducting with his cane as if there were an orchestra before him, he sang a melody that was to be given to one of the characters of the ballet. "In the overture," he explained, "this theme will be introduced by trumpets." And he was so pleased with it that during the evening he kept going to the piano to play it over and over again.

They were both fascinated by the exotic folklore character of Bazhov's narrative and the wealth of the well-drawn characters in his "tales." While Myra Mendelson and Lavrovsky were composing a libretto from several of the "tales," Prokofiev made an extensive study of the folklore of the Ural region.

He became so engrossed in his work that by the end of March 1949, less than six months later, he had completed the score. *The Stone Flower* and *A Worker in the Mountains* were the two Ural tales used by Prokofiev and his librettists as the basis for the ballet, which was a combination of the realistic and the fantastic. Since his return from his unnerving experience in Leningrad, Prokofiev's working hours were even more restricted by doctors, but his collaboration with Lavrovsky progressed at remarkable speed. Occasionally they would reach an impasse, however, as when Lavrovsky asked Prokofiev to compose music for a scene around a gypsy dance. Prokofiev agreed that such a scene was necessary, "but please," he said to Lavrovsky, "tell me as clearly as you can your plans for this scene, because I must admit I never thought of writing gypsy music. I know nothing about gypsies; I have never heard them."

Prokofiev did not mean literally that he did not know "gypsy music" or had never heard it. Like every other Russian, he had heard it all his life—for it is a favorite of amateur singers and night-club entertainers—but it belongs to a second form of Russian popular music that Prokofiev did not care to use in his compositions or to be influenced by.

At first Lavrovsky told Prokofiev in detail about the action in the scene, even showing him some steps of the dance and tried to sing appropriate melodies. But this method brought no desirable results, for the themes that Prokofiev offered were much too dry and unconvincing as gypsy music. Lavrovsky even collected whatever gypsy music he could find to steer Prokofiev in the right direction. When Prokofiev finally went to the piano to improvise his own variation, he suddenly stopped: "Please forgive me. Let me close the windows. I simply cannot allow such sounds to come out of Prokofiev's home."

Somehow, this type of music was so alien to him that he had great difficulty in composing the dance, and whenever Lavrovsky inquired about his progress, Prokofiev replied, "When my friends hear what I am composing and ask me about it, I tell them that Lavrovsky's taste has been ruined and he forces me to write such stuff." The ballet gained the jury's approval when, with Ulanova in the title role, it was auditioned at the Bolshoi in June 1949.

But not so Prokofiev's musical treatment of the subject. Again he was not present at the discussion that followed the audition, but Lavrovsky was. The jury severely criticized Prokofiev's work, maintaining that the music did not reflect the high artistic value of the picturesque style of Bazhov's "tales," and that it was much too somber and heavy, unsuitable for dancing.

"A great many thoughtless, hasty, and tactless opinions were voiced," Lavrovsky recalled later. But at that time, when Prokofiev's health was visibly worsening, Lavrovsky could not report to Prokofiev the jury's true reaction. To spare Prokofiev's feelings and health, Lavrovsky said, he concealed from him a "great deal," just as did Myra Mendelson, who was well informed about everything concerning the ballet and who, with her natural sensitivity, always tried to shield Prokofiev from everything unpleasant.

But the jury let Prokofiev know that they found his music to be written in an authentic Russian style, and in their praise they went so far as to compare it with Rimsky-Korsakov's *Sadko*. Whereupon Prokofiev, gratified at last by a success, plunged with renewed enthusiasm into the orchestration of the score's six hundred or so pages. He delivered the completed work in record time to the Bolshoi, but there the manuscript remained on the shelf, since the jury obviously never meant a word of their praise. Even for the Bolshoi Theatre it was too soon after "the 1948 event" to produce a Prokofiev work.

It was Prokofiev's last ballet, and his last work for theatrical production. It had become evident that his case was hopeless: no one was going to have his name on their billboards, no matter how hard he tried to fulfill the Communist Party's prescriptions for composing. The tragedy was that he was not only a prisoner of the state, he was a prisoner of his talent as well. He could not lay aside his pen and spend the rest of his days living the life of a country squire. He had to compose as long as he breathed, regardless of what happened to his work.

Well aware of Prokofiev's chagrin over the Bolshoi's "delays" in the production of his ballet, Lavrovsky often spoke to him of *Othello*, which he planned for a future Shakespearean ballet production. "I am afraid of such a production. I am afraid of Iago," Prokofiev said as he had once before. "He is so terrifying and repulsive, and would cost so much of my strength that I am afraid of him." Then, as an afterthought he added, "Of course, this work might be interesting, but . . . what is the sense of writing ballets, if they are left on the shelf? Why don't you go ahead with the production of *The Stone Flower?* Then I promise to start immediately working on *Othello*." Such was Prokofiev's desire to see *The Stone Flower* produced, that he was willing to pay the high price of contemplating the character of Iago.

"Alas," Lavrovsky said, "this promise was not to be fulfilled." The première of *The Stone Flower*, was not until February 12, 1954, a year after the composer's death. But in 1952 Prokofiev was destined to hear again about a possible production of the ballet.

35

There were long periods in which Prokofiev was strictly forbidden to work. He was given treatments, massages, and medications, but the constant recurrence of splitting headaches and dizziness sapped his strength. Nevertheless, he continued to work on what he called a "starving diet" of one hour per day.

At one of the concerts he was allowed to attend, Prokofiev heard the twenty-five-year-old Mstislav Rostropovich play his Cello Concerto, which, when performed by Berezovsky in November, 1938, had been a complete failure. In the green room Prokofiev told Rostropovich that after carefully listening to the concerto, he had decided to rewrite it; but although Rostropovich reminded him of this several times, he did nothing about it, and instead sent him a cello sonata, which he had composed in his "spare time" while working on his last ballet. He asked Rostropovich to come to Nicolina Gora to play it for him, and after this initial meeting Prokofiev finally decided to rewrite the Cello Concerto.

He told Rostropovich to bring him some cello compositions, "regardless of their quality" but containing interesting passages and using extensively a modern cello technique. But after he had examined some cello works by Popper and Davidov that Rostropovich had brought, he jokingly remarked to the young cellist, "What sort of music have you brought me?" and invited Rostropovich to spend the summer at his home, so that in close association with the cellist he could work on the concerto.

During the two summers he spent at Nicolina Gora, Rostropovich could closely observe the composer at work. He was surprised by the

patience with which Prokofiev, following his suggestions, would sometimes rework large sections of a composition. While he used his short
working hours for writing down melodies or making sketches for various compositions he had planned, he nevertheless was as meticulous as
ever about every detail in the composition. He considered Rostropovich's suggestions just as seriously as he had Eisenstein's when, during
their collaboration on films, he could not "palm off" something from
his old compositions, or Lavrovsky's "nagging" because he could not
satisfy him with his version of a gypsy rhapsody, or when consulting
Samosud on a new version of *War and Peace.*

Rostropovich was amused by Prokofiev's vivid conception of the
sounds of various instruments separately and in groups. Prokofiev told
him that the low notes played pianissimo on a tuba reminded him of
fat and greasy beetles that he would carefully take into his hand and
place from one note to another. He also said that in his orchestration
of his Cello Concerto the string quintet that follows the cello solo part
sounded to him like "poor relatives."

But Rostropovich also witnessed the constant deterioration of Prokofiev's health, even though Prokofiev never complained and tried to
follow the well-ordered routine of his daily life. He never asked his
doctors about the state of his health or whether his life was in danger.
He was only interested in the relationship of his illness to his work,
and as soon as the threat of putting him to bed and forbidding him to
work had passed, his spirits rose, he became gay, he joked and promised to be an obedient patient (in a special notebook he recorded
every time he took a prescribed medicine).

But he could not help "cheating" his doctors. He would often leave
the dinner table and go to his study to write down a melody or a few
words indicating the way an orchestration had come to his mind, or he
would make similar notes on the margins of a newspaper, which he
was allowed to read. He told Rostropovich that after a long struggle
with the doctors, he had managed to get permission to listen occasionally to broadcasts or to records that were sent to him.

And when he was allowed to work only twenty to thirty minutes
twice a day, when he had barely recovered from one of the attacks of
illness, when, pale and shaky from bloodletting he would beg his doctor to let him write down a melody because it was tormenting him, he
began to compose Winter Bonfire, a symphonic suite for children
based on verse written by Samuel Marshak, who was a popular author
of books for children. He wrote it in a vein similar to his two other
compositions for children: *Children's Music,* a collection of twelve
short piano pieces, and *Peter and the Wolf.*

In the eight parts of the suite he created short symphonic pictures on Marshak's subject—the children's excursion on a Sunday: their departure on a train, the snow-covered landscape they see from the window, "waltz on the ice," followed by the "winter bonfire and the children's meeting around it," a quiet winter evening, and finally a march and their return home on the train.

As soon as he had completed the score, which he was doing in addition to his work on the Cello Concerto, he started an oratorio, "On Guard for Peace," for symphony orchestra and children's chorus. Again he used Marshak's verses for the ten-part composition: (1) "The earth had just recovered from the thunder of war," (2) "Who today is ten years old?" (3) "Stalingrad—the city of glory," (4) "Let it be a reward to the heroes," (5) "We do not need war," (6) "The pigeon of peace," (7) "A lullaby," (8) "A peaceful celebration," (9) "A conversation in the atmosphere," and closing with the last part, (10) "The whole world is ready for the war against war."

Both suites were given on December 19, 1950, at the Hall of Columns at the Home of the Unions. Samosud's performance with the Symphony Orchestra of the U.S.S.R. and children's chorus won applause from the audience. This time Prokofiev, spending a sleepless night at home, did not need to worry when he asked Myra Mendelson, "Will they understand what I have tried to say?"

"I was not searching for the theme of this composition. I did not choose it from among other subjects; it was born from life, from its boiling state, from everything that surrounds us, from everything that disturbs me as well as everybody else," Prokofiev explained later. "In this work I wanted to express my thoughts about peace and war, my conviction that there will be no war, that the people all over the world will stand up for peace, will save civilization, our children, our future. . . ."

For both suites Prokofiev was awarded the Second Stalin Prize, given for the works of 1950. This might have been Stalin's part of the bargain for the letter Prokofiev had written in 1948 in reply to the decree of the Central Committee of the Communist Party and for his "good behavior." But what is more tragic and cruel in life than the words "too late?"

It was "too late" to tell Sergei Prokofiev that he could compose satisfactorily for "the need of his people." He would have welcomed with more pleasure being told the Central Committee's decree against him which had condemned most of his works had been revoked. To the last day of his life he continued to hope for it. The revocation of the decree and the admission that it had been made erroneously did not come until 1959, six years after his death, six years after Stalin's death, and after Khrushchev had launched an orgy of denunciations against Stalin's regime.

It was "too late" for Prokofiev to share with his last and closest friend the news about the prizes, for after a long illness Miaskovsky had died in August 1950, four months before the performance at the Hall of Columns.

Before it was "too late," fearing that at any time he might be again put to bed and forbidden to work, Prokofiev began to take an inventory of his works, to dictate to Myra Mendelson a complete list of them, and to prepare the manuscripts to be sent to the state archives. Most of his works had been published and performed "for better or worse," but there was *one* still in manuscript—he had even written a third version of it—*War and Peace*.

"I am willing to reconcile myself to the failure of any of my compositions," he said to Kabalevsky shortly before his death, "but if you only knew how much I wish for a production of *War and Peace*." It was "too late" when it was given by the Bolshoi in 1959 and then became a permanent addition to the theatre's repertory. It was "too late" when only several selected scenes from the opera were broadcast on February 4, 1953, a month before his death. "It is better to have even a part of it than nothing at all," Prokofiev remarked, but the doctors guarding him from excitement, would not let him listen to the broadcast.

In his novel *Clim Samgin* Maxim Gorky says, "Ah, but there are no 'simple people.' Some pretend to be simple, but actually they are like algebra problems with three or many unknowns." The chief questions concerning Prokofiev that had puzzled the Western world were: Why did he return to Russia? and since he obviously could not leave the country later, how did he feel about it after what had happened personally to him? At the time of his return to Russia he had clearly answered the first question, but as for the second, perhaps we should look for the answer in his article in *News* (a magazine in English), published in Moscow in 1951. It clearly shows that Prokofiev remained a great patriot and a man who was proud of his country's achievements.

At the end of 1951 an incident—publicized by an Associated Press dispatch—that took place in the United States created so much excitement in Moscow musical circles that Prokofiev felt called upon to write a letter to the editor; it developed into his "credo." Since this was the last exposé of his views concerning his own art and art in general, I feel compelled to quote it in full, though it is occasionally repetitious:

I have never been nor concertized in the American town of Salt Lake City in the State of Utah. Even in 1938 when, at the invitation of some of my American friends, I visited the United States, to my regret I did not have an opportunity to visit this city, whose inhabitants, we might presume, love music as much as anybody else in the world. Recently I heard of an example showing this love of music in the life of this town.

According to the Associated Press correspondent, the conductor of the Salt Lake City Symphony Orchestra, Maurice Abravanel, had reported to the police a telephone call he had received from a strange individual who threatened to molest and kill him if the orchestra played Prokofiev's Fifth Symphony, as announced on the program. The correspondent added that the Directors of the orchestra left the program unaltered.

Of course, this strange incident in the Salt Lake City musical life is not significant enough to warrant much discussion. But this sad story concerns me personally. Why should Prokofiev's Fifth Symphony cause such a violent reaction? As far as I know, this symphony is warmly received by American audiences, it was often successfully performed by the Boston Symphony Orchestra, the New York Philharmonic under the direction of Arthur Rodzinsky, as well as other orchestras. I have the recordings of these performances. And then . . . suddenly an incident in Salt Lake City. Why was the conductor who intended to perform the Fifth Symphony threatened? Is it possible that it was because this musical work glorifies the freedom of the human spirit?

In the Fifth Symphony I wished to glorify man as free and happy, his mighty strength, his noble spirit. I would not say that I searched for this theme, it was born in me and required expression. I wrote the music which developed and filled my soul. And is it this music or is it the idea that does not please certain men in the State of Utah. Most probably, they prefer music which besmirches man, and dulls his senses.

Recently, as I was putting my musical library in order, I came across some of my works published in various countries. I found the Seventh Piano Sonata with Olin Downes' commentaries, published in New York. (I also have the recordings of several American musicians who have performed this sonata.) I also discovered my symphonic fairy tale Peter and the Wolf with Harold Sheldon's commentaries (in 1938 I conducted myself this work in Boston). I found many other compositions including the Violin Sonata, the cantata Alexander Nevsky, recorded by Eugene Ormandy with the Philadelphia Orchestra. . . . All these, of course, were works of a different genre, thematical coloring, and technical ornamentation. But all of them are united by one idea—they speak of man and were created for him. I am convinced that this is the reason for their attraction for people of many countries, including those in the United States.

Not long ago I wrote an oratorio: On Guard for Peace. Again I did not search for this theme. It was born from life itself, its boiling state, from everything surrounding me and everybody else.

Usually I spent the summers in my country home, near Moscow. I know very well the road which leads from the center of Moscow to its suburbs, and out beyond the city limits, along the old and new forests, above the rivers and rye fields. Here is one of the fields: a new combine gleans the high rye. Ten kilometers further on, a group of red-cheeked children are playing on the greensward supervised by stern governesses. This is a kindergarten for children whose parents are working in the Moscow factories. We drive further on from my country home toward Moscow. Along the road special cranes are planting many old limetrees, and then—new buildings, new homes. Right near Moscow the austere outlines of the new, truly remarkable building of the Moscow University. This is an everyday picture of Soviet life.

I know that everything I observe on this short distance from my country house to Moscow is typical of the life of our country. I know eminent scientists, who have temporarily left their laboratories to go to Central Asia to build a canal in Turkmenia. I know young engineers who, after their graduation in Moscow, hurry to the shores of the Volga, Don, and Dnieper rivers to build electrical plants. I have many acquaintances and friends. They write books, cultivate gardens, build houses. And their lives are filled with the poetry of peaceful labor. From this, so to speak, the theme of my oratorio was born.

What is, then, the content of this modest composition? It speaks of the difficult days during the Second World War, of the great trial which fell upon the shoulders of our people. Then, the next part of it is dedicated to Stalingrad, victory over the enemy, and to the happy childhoods of our children. I wanted to express my thoughts about war and peace, my firm conviction that there will be no war, that people all over the world will stand guard for peace, save civilization, our children, our future. Perhaps I am going into too many details of the biography of my oratorio, but in this modest composition all the principles which I have mentioned above found their expression.

At present I am at work on a poem for a large symphony orchestra. It is dedicated to the joining of the two Russian rivers: the Volga and the Don. Where did this theme come from? It was suggested by life.

Our people have a great many songs about these rivers. To these now are added new ones singing of man's great feats in "conquering" nature.

In the United States and Western Europe there is a great deal of talk about the mission of the artist, about the freedom of his creative talent. Can an artist stand aside from life? Can he close himself in a "tower" [an ivory tower], can his subjective emotions limit his creations, or should he be there where he is needed, where his words, his music, his paintings or sculpture would help people to live better and more happily?

Let us consider the creative activities of Beethoven and Shakespeare,

Mozart and Tolstoy, Tchaikovsky and Dickens—those titans of the human spirit and thought. Does their greatness not consist precisely in the fact that these men of their own free will gave their mighty talent to the service of mankind? Are not their immortal creations marked by this trait?

When I was in the United States and in England, I often heard discussions about whom music should serve, what should the composer write about, what should direct his creative ability. I am convinced that a composer, a poet, sculptor, or painter is called upon to serve man and the people. They must beautify man's life and defend it. Before anything else they must be a "citizen of their art," glorify man's life and lead him to a happy future. Such, in my opinion, is the indisputable code of art.

I might be reproached for repeating well-known axioms, and for my discussion on being irrelevant to what had happened in Salt Lake City. But I believe that there is an inner relation between the two.

Before writing this article, I inquired about the subjects which inspire my colleagues. And I hear that in the near future Dmitri Shostakovich intends to write a composition dedicated to the great industrial achievements of the Soviet people. Tikhon Khrenikov already had begun writing about the triumph of peace all over the world. [This is the only time, to my knowledge, Prokofiev ever mentioned Khrenikov as a composer.] Yuri Shaporin, who has devoted the past few years to his opera *Decembrists,* is now working on a cantata on the texts of the Russian classical and contemporary poets. The young and talented composer Nikolai Peyko, a pupil of the late eminent composer Miaskovsky, is writing a symphonic poem for orchestra, soloists and chorus on the subject of Morning of our Fatherland. . . .

The Soviet composers work for the people, and their peaceful lives is the main theme of their music.

In the strange incident which took place in the American town of Salt Lake City, I see the proof of the rightness of our chosen path. Our music endeavors to imbue man with an assurance of his strength and his future. This is why our music is rejected by those who plan to destroy this future and jeopardize man's peace by new bloody wars. But they are helpless to silence our songs, our symphonies of peace and work—I am convinced of this for, after all, my Fifth Symphony *was* played in Salt Lake City.

Prokofiev was right when he said that the incident in Salt Lake City was not worthy of mention. The average Russian knew no more about Salt Lake City than an American knows about the Russian town of Tula. There is no doubt that it was "officially" brought to Prokofiev's attention and perhaps suggested his reply. The official interpretation of Prokofiev's reaction, however, is given by Nestyev in his book; he quoted only those sentences from the article that could support this interpretation. In order to show Prokofiev's "wrath" in his letter to the *News,* Nestyev substitutes a word here and there of his own. And he continues his comments with, "Gravely ill musician with a great passion branded the 'knights of the cold war' across the ocean."

Far from showing his wrath, Prokofiev's article is written in a dignified style, alien to that used in the official Soviet commentaries. Neither in this letter nor in On Guard for Peace, had he suggested burying the United States, as the peace-loving Khruschev had threatened. (In Prokofiev's composition the main idea—"we don't want war" —is sung by a ten-year-old boy.)

Finally, Nestyev concludes his official commentaries with this benevolent sentence: "Prokofiev's article, lashing at the enemies of culture, signifies his matured political activity"—a magnanimous acceptance officially granted "too late" to the composer who was not beginning a career, but was nearing the end of his life.

Meanwhile, Prokofiev continued to follow a work program that he had already made when he refused Volsky's offer to write for a film—a program obviously little influenced by the Communist Party's decree. He made two orchestral suites from *The Stone Flower* score, rewrote his Fifth Piano Sonata, and began his Seventh Symphony— compositions that could not endanger the Soviet state or affect the well-being of the Soviet people.

And then one day Lavrovsky brought good news, the Bolshoi was contemplating a performance of *The Stone Flower*, but Prokofiev would have to do some revisions in the score and compose additional material. Delighted, he set to work on everything that was required. Against his better judgment he agreed to alter the original orchestration in some parts of the score, although "it will merely be louder, and will vulgarize and besmirch the score," he said. Still, looking forward to his first ballet production since *Cinderella*, he worked with enthusiasm.

On the day of his sixtieth birthday the Composers' Union organized a small concert at which Richter gave the first performance of the Ninth Sonata—the one dedicated to him by the composer, the one which after its first reading at Prokofiev's home in 1946 Richter thought was "much too simple." Since that time, he had learned to love the work: the more he played it, the more attached to it he became—its simplicity, clarity and even its intimate character made him refer to it as "sonata domestica."

Prokofiev was too ill to attend the concert. "At present I don't feel well. I have been ordered to bed and forbidden to work," he wrote in a few lines to his friends. He listened to the concert over the telephone.

Two days later his birthday was further commemorated at a festive evening at the Composers' Union. Speeches were made by the representatives of the Committee of the Arts and the Bolshoi, and by several composers. This time his Moscow apartment was connected with the hall by two-way radio, and Prokofiev was allowed by his doctors to reply briefly to his well-wishers.

A few months later he felt stronger, and on February 18, 1952, the doctors permitted him to attend Rostropovich's first performance at the Grand Hall of the Moscow Conservatory of the recently completed Cello Concerto. Prokofiev had agreed to let Richter conduct the orchestra.

It was Richter's debut at the conducting desk. He had recently broken a finger on his right hand and was recovering from the excitement of performing Ravel's Concerto for the Left Hand, when he heard of the unexpected assignment. Kyril Kondrashin gave him a few lessons in conducting, but this did not free Richter of his foreboding. "It is easy to talk about it! To conduct Prokofiev's work—what a proposition!" Richter said.

Rostropovich asked Prokofiev not to attend the rehearsals—saying that it would paralyze the two young performers—and Prokofiev agreed to come only to the concert. Although the members of the Moscow Youth Orchestra were well disposed toward Richter's debut as a conductor, the rehearsals were not without a few "conflicts" between the conductor and his men. "Some of them," Richter said, "made surprised and ironical grimaces caused by the harshness of the orchestral sound, and Rostropovich's solo part, extremely difficult and 'modern,' put the cellists in the orchestra into a hilarious mood." To have at least some moral support, Rostropovich agreed that no matter what happened during the performance, he would smile at Richter whenever he came to a rest in his own part.

When Richter came on stage, he froze. He looked before him: there was no grand piano. Where was he to go? flashed through his mind. And he stumbled as he reached the conductor's platform. The audience gasped. Richter, realizing his ridiculous appearance, suddenly regained his sense of humor and calmed down. Rostropovich and Richter were greeted with an ovation, which disturbed Richter: applause in advance—a bad omen, he thought. He did not realize that the ovation was directed to the work of a composer who was then present, and of whose troubles the audience was well aware.

"What I most feared did not happen—the orchestra began *together*," Richter said later. "The rest seemed as if in a dream. From the great nervous strain, we were completely exhausted after we had finished playing, and so completely lost our heads that we did not call

Prokofiev on the stage. But he came up to the platform and shook our hands."

The concerto was not a success—the audience barely applauded, and the critics tore it to pieces—but Prokofiev was pleased. " 'Now I am happy. Now we have a conductor for my other compositions,' Prokofiev remarked in his businesslike way," Richter said later.

By March 20 Prokofiev had completed the piano score of the Seventh Symphony, but he was not well enough to transcribe it into an orchestral score. Following his indications, Anatoly Vedernikov not only had the orchestral score ready by the first week of July, but also had made a four-hand piano arrangement of it, which he and Richter played at the Composers' Union. Prokofiev was not able to be present at this initial performance of his latest work, and he anxiously waited at home for Kabalevsky's report on the musicians' reaction.

On the following day Kabalevsky found Prokofiev in bed, not well. He kept asking Kabalevsky about details of the performance, and beamed when he heard about its success. As if he suspected Kabalevsky of trying merely to comfort him, he made him repeat his account several times. "And the music is not much too simple?" he asked. Prokofiev was referring to his original plan to write a Symphony for Children, but which in the course of his work had developed into the Seventh.

Three months later, in October, Prokofiev managed to go to the Hall of Columns, where Samosud conducted the first public performance of the symphony. This was the last time Prokofiev attended a concert at which one of his works was performed. Neither the audience nor the critics who had acclaimed the symphony were searching for programmatic content in the work. They were ready to accept it purely as a symphony, lyrical in its character, youthful in its spirit. In 1959 it was posthumously awarded the Lenin Prize.

During these last winters Prokofiev lived in his Moscow apartment, where it was easier to be in constant contact with Lavrovsky—with whom he was working on additional material for the production of *The Stone Flower*—and because of the availability of medical help in case of emergency. "I am looking forward with great pleasure to meeting with the members of the Bolshoi and the Stanislavsky Theatres for our work together on the ballet *The Stone Flower* and the opera *War and Peace*," he wrote in one of his last notes.

The rehearsals of the ballet which began on March 1, 1953, gave extra impetus to Prokofiev's already high spirits. Disregarding everybody's warnings, he worked intensely with all his energy, putting the final touches to rewritten scenes and new material for the ballet. On

May 5, on his way to a rehearsal, Lavrovsky stopped by for a few minutes to see Prokofiev. Prokofiev was at work on the score. Lavrovsky left him, promising to call later and let him know how the rehearsal had gone.

In the afternoon Prokofiev interrupted his work to receive his daily visit from his doctor, Elena Tepper; later, to get some fresh air, he accompanied her to the clinic where she was working. He talked to her about *The Stone Flower* and also about his future plans. Smiling, he added, "But don't worry, I promise to be a good boy and will not upset the prescribed regime, although sometimes it is very difficult to tear oneself from work."

Two hours later Dr. Tepper was urgently summoned to Prokofiev's home. Her help came too late. He had died from suffocation.

Prokofiev's death passed almost unnoticed by the Russians, for the press was entirely preoccupied with the death of Josef Stalin, who died on the same day, at nine in the evening, three hours after Prokofiev.

On the following day Prokofiev's remains were placed at the Central Composers Home, where on March 7 a memorial service was held in a small hall. Kabalevsky, Shostakovich, Shaporin, Lavrovsky, Khachaturian, the motion picture director Vera Stroyeva, and several others offered eulogies. Because the musicians could not find among Prokofiev's works anything except cheerful themes not suited to the occasion, David Oistrakh played the first and third movements from the composer's Violin Sonata, and Samuel Feinberg played Bach.

Richter, who was returning from a concert in Tbilisi, learned of Prokofiev's death in Suhumi, where his plane was grounded because of an unusual snowstorm, thus preventing him from reaching Moscow in time for the funeral.

"Many young people were present in the hall," Nestyev notes in his book, but Khrenikov's name was not mentioned: the General Secretary of the Organizational Committee of the Soviet Composers' Union, General Andrei Zhdanov's lackey, apparently was not delegated this time to represent the Central Committee of the Communist Party.

The day of the funeral was cold, damp, and somber. The cortege slowly made its way though the Moscow streets, where the workers were preparing a pompous state funeral for Stalin. Prokofiev was buried in the cemetery of Novo-Devichy Monastery near the graves of his friends Asafiev and Miaskovsky.

On August 24, 1909, when at the age of nineteen he was unaware of what his life and career had in store for him, Prokofiev had written to

Miaskovsky in St. Petersburg, "Recently I thought of your last Song, in which somebody wanted to sleep, but preferred to become a stone."

For his music Miaskovsky had chosen Michelangelo's quatrain "Caro m'è'l sonno":

> Be silent, I beg you, do not dare awaken me;
> Oh, in this criminal and dishonored century
> One should neither feel, nor live—an enviable fate. . . .
> It is consoling to sleep, but more so to become mere stone.

Perhaps the future generations—those Ilya Ehrenburg advised "to contemplate Prokofiev's extraordinary fate"—will find it appropriate to use this quotation as an epitaph on Sergei Prokofiev's grave.

APPENDIX

The following is the text of an editorial that appeared in *Pravda*, January 29, 1936.

With the general cultural development of our country there grew also the necessity for good music. At no time and in no other place has the composer had a more appreciative audience. The people expect good songs, but also good instrumental works, and good operas.

Certain theaters are presenting to the new culturally mature Soviet public Shostakovich's opera *Lady Macbeth* as an innovation and an achievement. Musical criticism, always ready to serve, has praised the opera to the skies and given it resounding glory. The young composer, instead of hearing serious criticism, which could have helped him in his future work, hears only enthusiastic compliments.

From the first minute, the listener is shocked by deliberate dissonance, by a confused stream of sounds. Snatches of melody, the beginning of a musical phrase, are drowned, emerge again, and disappear in a grinding and squealing roar. To follow this "music" is most difficult; to remember it, impossible.

Thus it goes, practically throughout the entire opera. The singing on the stage is replaced by shrieks. If the composer chances to come on the path of a clear and simple melody, he throws himself back into a wilderness of musical chaos—in places becoming cacophony. The expression which the listener expects is supplanted by wild rhythm. Passion is here supposed to be expressed by noise. All this is not due to lack of talent, or to lack of ability to depict simple and strong emotions in music. Here is music turned deliberately inside out in order that nothing will be reminiscent of classical opera, or have anything in common with symphonic music or with simple and popular musical language accessible to all. This music is built on the basis of rejecting opera—the same basis on which "Leftist" art rejects in the theater simplicity, realism, clarity of image, and the un-affected spoken word—which carries into the theater and into music the most negative features of "Meyerholdism" infinitely multiplied. Here we have "Leftist" confusion instead of natural human music. The power of

319

good music to infect the masses has been sacrificed to a petty-bourgeois, "formalist" attempt to create originality through cheap clowning. It is a game of clever ingenuity that may end very badly.

The danger of this trend to Soviet music is clear. Leftist distortion in opera stems from the same source as the Leftist distortion in painting, poetry, teaching, and science. Petty-bourgeois "innovations" lead to a break with real art, real science, and real literature.

The composer of *Lady Macbeth* was forced to borrow from jazz its nervous, convulsive, and spasmodic music in order to lend "passion" to his characters. While our critics, including music critics, swear by the name of socialist realism, the stage serves us, in Shostakovich's creation, the coarsest kind of naturalism. He reveals the merchants and the people monotonously and bestially. The predatory merchant woman who scrambles into possession of wealth through murder is pictured as some kind of "victim" of bourgeois society. Leskov's story has been given a significance it does not possess.

And all this is coarse, primitive, and vulgar. The music quacks, grunts, and growls, and suffocates itself in order to express the love scenes as naturalistically as possible. And "love" is smeared all over the opera in the most vulgar manner. The merchant's double bed occupies the central position on the stage. On this bed all "problems" are solved. In the same coarse, naturalistic style is shown the death from poisoning and the flogging—both practically on stage.

The composer apparently never considered the problem of what the Soviet audience expects and looks for in music. As though deliberately, he scribbles down his music, confusing all the sounds in such a way that his music would reach only the effete "formalists" who had lost their wholesome taste. He ignored the demand of Soviet culture that all coarseness and savagery be abolished from every corner of Soviet life. Some critics call this glorification of merchants' lust a satire. But there is no question of satire here. The composer has tried, with all the musical and dramatic means at his command, to arouse the sympathy of the spectators for the coarse and vulgar inclinations and behavior of the merchant woman, Katerina Ismailova.

Lady Macbeth is having great success with bourgeois audiences abroad. Is it not because the opera is non-political and confusing that they praise it? Is it not explained by the fact that it tickles the perverted taste of the bourgeoisie with its fidgety, neurotic music?

Our theaters have expended a great deal of energy on giving Shostakovich's opera a thorough presentation. The actors have shown exceptional talent in dominating the noise, the screaming, and the roar of the orchestra. With their dramatic action they have tried to reinforce the weakness of melodic content. Unfortunately, this has served only to bring out the opera's vulgar features more vividly. The talented acting deserves gratitude, the wasted efforts—regrets.

APPENDIX

Chronology of Prokofiev's Works*

1896		First attempt to compose a piano piece—"Indian Gallop"
1897		March, Waltz and Rondo—the first compositions written down by the composer himself
1898	FEBRUARY	First "score": a march for four hands
1900	FEBRUARY–JUNE	*The Giant,* an opera written to his own plot (Sontsovka)
1900	DECEMBER–SPRING	Opera *Desert Island,* written to his own plot
1902	JANUARY JAN. 23/FEB. 5 SUMMER	First Little Songs from a series of pianoforte pieces (Sontsovka)
	JULY–NOVEMBER	Symphony in G major, the first attempt to write a symphonic work

* Compiled by Semyon Schlifstein (Moscow: State Publisher's "Music," 1959).

1903	JULY–OCTOBER	Opera *Feast During the Plague*, after Pushkin. Sonatas for Violin and for pianoforte—the first experiments (Sontsovka)
1906	MAY	March in F-minor (Fifty-fourth Little Song), which was later reworked and included in the piano cycle, Op. 12
1907	JUNE 30	Finished the opera *Undine*, after De La Motte Fouqué in V. Zhukovsky's translation (started in April 1904)
1907– 1908		Four piano pieces: Fairy-Tale, Badinage, March, The Phantom, reworked later to form Op. 3
1908		Four piano pieces: Reminiscence, Élan, Despair, Suggestion diabolique later reworked to form Op. 4
	SUMMER	Symphony in E-minor. The Andante from the symphony was later incorporated in the Fourth Sonata for Piano, Op. 29
1909	SUMMER	Four études for pianoforte, Op. 2. (Sontsovka; finished in St. Petersburg in September)
	AUGUST	Sonata for piano, Op. 1 Sinfonietta, Op. 5. (2nd version—April 1915; 3rd, Op. 48—1929)
1912	WINTER	First Piano Concerto, Op. 10 (the score was finished on Jan. 25/Feb. 7, 1912)
1912	APRIL	Toccata for piano, Op. 11
	AUGUST– SEPTEMBER	Second Sonata for piano, Op. 14 (completed on Aug. 28/Sept. 10 in Kislovodsk)
1912– 1913	DECEMBER– APRIL	Second Piano Concerto, Op. 16 (rewritten in Ettal in 1923)

	SEPTEMBER	Opera *Maddalena*, after M. Lieven's play (1st version—1911) Ten pieces for piano, Op. 12 (composed in 1906—1913)
1914	JUNE	"Sarcasms," five pieces for piano, Op. 17 (started in 1912)
	SEPTEMBER	*The Ugly Duckling*, after Hans Christian Andersen's fairy tale, for voice and piano, Op. 18
1914–1915	OCTOBER–JANUARY	Work on the ballet *Ala and Lolli*
1915	APRIL–AUGUST	Work on the ballet *The Buffoon* (*Who Outbuffooned Seven Buffoons*), after A. Afanasyev's Russian tales. Romances for voice and piano, Op. 23
	JULY–AUGUST	*Ala and Lolli* (Scythian Suite) for symphony orchestra, Op. 20. Began working on the piano cycle "Visions fugitives," Op. 22, Nos. 5, 6, 10, 16, 17
	NOVEMBER	Began working on the opera *The Gambler*, based on F. Dostoyevsky's story
1916	APRIL	Finished the piano score of *The Gambler*
	OCTOBER	Finished the score of *The Gambler* Continued work on "Visions fugitives"— Nos. 2, 3, 7, 12, 13, 20
	OCT. 31/NOV.13–NOV. 3/16	Five romances to words by A. Akhmatova for voice and piano, Op. 27
1917	FEBRUARY	Finished "Visions fugitives"
	SPRING	Third Sonata for piano, Op. 28 ("From Old Notebooks," 1907)
	SUMMER	First Violin Concerto (conceived in 1915)

	AUTUMN	Fourth Sonata for piano, Op. 29 (Kislovodsk; "From Old Notebooks," 1908)
	SEPT. 10	Finished the score of the Classical Symphony, Op. 25 (Yessentuki); the first themes were composed in 1916, the entire music and part of the score—in the summer of 1917
1917– 1918		Cantata (Call of the Ancients) "Seven, They Are Seven" to the poem by Konstantin Balmont, Op. 30 (Petrograd-Kislovodsk; started in September, 1917, second version—Paris, 1933)
1918	DECEMBER	"Old Granny's Tales" for piano, Op. 31. Four pieces for piano, Op. 32
1919	JAN.–OCT. 1	Opera *Love for Three Oranges*, after the tale by Carlo Gozzi
	DECEMBER	Started work on the opera *The Flaming Angel*, after the poem by Valery Bryusov
1920	SUMMER	Rewriting and orchestration of the ballet *The Buffoon* (Mantes)
1921	SUMMER	Third Piano Concerto, Op. 26 (Bretagne; some of the musical themes were composed in 1913, 1916, 1917)
1922	MARCH	Finished the work on sketches for *The Flaming Angel* (finished in 1923)
	APRIL	Symphonic suite The Buffoon
1923	JUNE	Fifth Sonata for piano, Op. 38 (finished in Paris in December; second version, Op. 135 1952—1953)
1924	JULY	Quintet for oboe, clarinet, violin, viola and double-bass, Op. 39 (written for a one-act ballet, *The Trapeze*)
	AUGUST–SEPTEMBER	Work on the Second Symphony, Op. 40 (the orchestral score was finished in Bellevue, France, on May 19, 1925)

1925	AUGUST–SEPTEMBER	Work on the ballet *Le Pas d'acier* (the score—1926)
1926	SUMMER	Orchestration of *The Flaming Angel*. Overture for chamber orchestra of 17 musicians, Op. 42
1927	SEPTEMBER	Completed *The Flaming Angel*
	OCT. 11	Rewriting of *The Gambler* (finished in March, 1928)
1928	JULY–OCTOBER	Third Symphony, Op. 44
	NOVEMBER	Rough sketches of the ballet *The Prodigal Son*
1929	FEBRUARY	Finished the piano and the orchestral scores of *The Prodigal Son*
1930	SUMMER	Finished the Fourth Symphony, Op. 47 (Started in March, 1929; new version, Op. 112—1947)
	DECEMBER	Finished the String Quartet, Op. 50
1931	JUNE	Ballet *On the Dnieper* (or *Sur le Borysthène;* the greater part was composed in the autumn of 1930) Fourth Concerto for Piano (left hand), Op. 53
1932	WINTER– SPRING	Fifth Piano Concerto, Op. 55
	AUTUMN	Sonata for Two Violins, Op. 56
1933	SUMMER	*Lieutenant Kijé,* incidental music for the film (Paris; suite—July 1934, Burgry) The Symphonic Song, Op. 57 (Paris)
1934	JANUARY	*Egyptian Nights,* music for the play staged by the Moscow Kamerny Theatre (Paris; suite—the summer of 1934)
1935	MAY 16	Scenario of the ballet *Romeo and Juliet,* after the play by Shakespeare (Leningrad) Second Violin Concerto, Op. 63 (begun in Paris, finished in Baku in August)

	SUMMER	*Romeo and Juliet* (the piano score finished on Sept. 8) "Music for Children," twelve easy pieces for piano, Op. 65 (Polenovo)
1936	APRIL	Finished the orchestration of the ballet *Romeo and Juliet* *Romeo and Juliet*, First and Second suites *Peter and the Wolf*, symphonic fairy-tale
	SUMMER	Music for the film *Queen of Spades* and for the plays *Boris Godunov* in the Meyerhold Theatre and *Yevgeni Onegin* in the Kamerny Theatre. Three romances to words by Pushkin, Op. 73 (Polenovo) Russian Overture for symphony orchestra Op. 72
1937	APR. 15	Cantata for the Twentieth Anniversary of October (begun in 1936) *Romeo and Juliet*, ten pieces for piano, Op. 75 Songs of Our Days, suite for soloists, mixed chorus, and symphony orchestra, Op. 76
1938	MAY	Started work on music for Sergei Eisenstein's film *Alexander Nevsky*
	DECEMBER	First Sonata for Violin and Piano, Op. 80 (finished in 1946)
1939	MARCH–JUNE	Cantata *Alexander Nevsky* Op. 78 Opera *Semyon Kotko*, after V. Katayev's story "I, Son of the Working People" (piano score finished on June 28)
1939	SEPT. 10	Finished the orchestration of *Semyon Kotko*
	AUTUMN	Dythyramb for mixed chorus and orchestra, Op. 85
	OCT. 17	Finished the autobiography "Childhood" (begun on July 1, 1937)

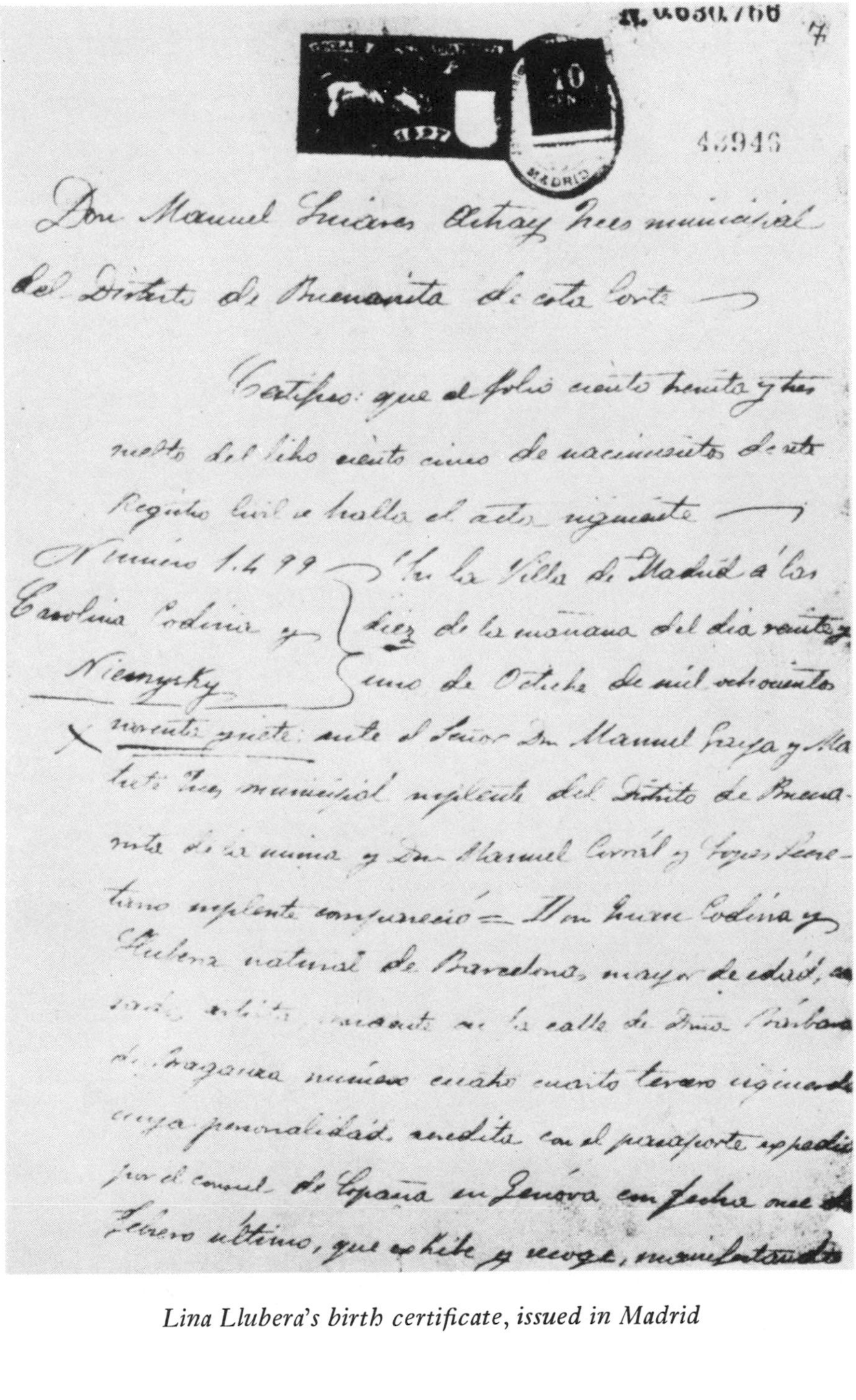
Don Manuel Suárez Ochoa Juez municipal del Distrito de Buenavista de esta Corte —

Certifico: que al folio ciento treinta y tres vuelto del libro ciento cinco de nacimientos de este Registro Civil se halla el acta siguiente —

Número 1.499 — Carolina Codina y Niemysky — En la Villa de Madrid á las diez de la mañana del dia veinte y uno de Octubre de mil ochocientos noventa y siete: ante el Señor Don Manuel Fraga y Martí Juez municipal suplente del Distrito de Buenavista de la misma y Don Manuel Corral y Rojas Secretario suplente compareció = Don Juan Codina y Llubera natural de Barcelona, mayor de edad, casado, artista, residente en la calle de Doña Bárbara de Braganza número cuatro cuarto tercero izquierda cuya personalidad acredita con el pasaporte expedido por el consul de España en Genova con fecha once de Febrero último, que exhibe y recoge, manifestando

Lina Llubera's birth certificate, issued in Madrid

el nacimiento de una niña con objeto de que
se inscriba en el Registro Civil y al efecto como pa-
dre de la misma declaró = Que dicha niña na-
ció en la casa del declarante á las seis de la mañana de ayer = Que es hija legítima del que
declara y de su mujer Doña Olga Niemysky
y Wehrle natural de Woronesh (Rusia) mayor de edad, residente con su marido. = Que es
nieta por línea paterna de Don Juan Codina
y de Doña Isabel Hubena naturales de Barcelona y por la materna de Don Ladislao Niemysky y de Doña Carolina Wehrle, naturales el prime-
ro de Vilna (Rusia) y la segunda de Colmar
(Francia) = Y que á la referida niña se le po-
ne el nombre de Carolina. = Presenciaron
esta inscripción los testigos Don Manuel Piedra
y Ruiz natural de la provincia de Zamora
domiciliado San Vicente ocho y diez y Don Raimundo Carral y Bartito natural de Monforte
provincia de Lugo, domiciliado Ventura Rodriguez
ocho, mayores de edad, casados empleados =

Leída este acta se sella y firman con el Señor
Juez, certifico = Hay un sello = Manuel Gaya =
Juan Codina = Raimundo Caral = Manuel Tieda
= Manuel Corral _____
Concuerda con su original a que me remito. Y para
que conste expido la presente en Madrid a veinte y
ocho de Diciembre de mil ochocientos noventa y siete.

Ministry of Interior document, issued in Munich, attesting to Lina Llubera's Spanish citizenship as indicated in her passport

B.

Nr. *5* .

[handwritten] am *[handwritten]* ten
Oktober [handwritten] tausend neunhundert *[handwritten]*

Vor dem unterzeichneten Standesbeamten erschienen heute zum Zwecke der
Eheschließung:

1. der *[handwritten: Sergei Sergejewitsch Prokofieff]*

der Persönlichkeit nach _____
_____ *[handwritten]* kannt,

_____ Religion, geboren am *[handwritten]* _____
April [handwritten] des Jahres tausen: *[handwritten]* hundert
[handwritten] zu *Sonzowka Ekaterinoslaw*
Rußland _____

wohnhaft in *[handwritten]* _____
Sohn de _____

wohnhaft in _____

2. die *[handwritten: Fräulein Codina Carolina]* _____

der Persönlichkeit nach _____
_____ *[handwritten]* kann*

_____ Religion, geboren am *[handwritten]* ten
Oktober [handwritten] des Jahres tausend *[handwritten]* hundert
[handwritten] zu *Madrid*
Spanien _____

wohnhaft in *[handwritten]* _____

*Application for marriage license by Sergei Prokofiev and Caroline
Codina (Lina Llubera)*

Miterschienen waren:

1. _____,

der Persönlichkeit nach _____ .... kannt.

2. _____,

der Persönlichkeit nach _____ .... kannt.

D...... Miterschienene zu 1 erklärt: Hiemit erteile ich als _____

.... meine Einwilligung zu der

beabsichtigten Eheschließung.

D...... Miterschienene zu 2 erklärt:

....

_____

Zum Schluß erklären die Verlobten: Wir versichern hiemit, daß — andere als die
in dieser Verhandlung erwähnten — Ehehindernisse unserer Eheschließung nicht entgegenstehen.

Insbesondere versichere~~n~~ *wir beide* ...., an Eidesstatt [1]),
daß *wir beide ledigen Standes u. gegenseitig nicht*
verwandt u. verschwägert sind.

II. Das Aufgebot wird sonach erlassen in *der Gemeinde* *Ettal*

....

~~und mit Schreiben an die betreffende Gemeindebehörde postfrei übersendet, beziehungs-~~
~~weise erhält d..... Verlobte Abschrift des Aufgebots behufs Einrückung in das zu~~

.... ~~erscheinende (verbreitete) Zeitungsblatt~~

....

~~oder es wird eine Bescheinigung der Ortsbehörde zu~~
~~gemäß § 47 Abs. 2 des Reichsgesetzes vom 6. Februar 1875 über die Beurkundung des~~
~~Personenstandes und die Eheschließung beigebracht.~~

Vorgelesen, genehmigt und unterschrieben

Serge Prokofieff

Caroline Codina

Der Standesbeamte:

[signature]

---

[1]) Hier wäre veranlaßten Falles anzugeben, ob Kinder der Verlobten vorhanden sind, zu denen sich der Verlobte als Vater bekannt hat — bekennen wird.
[2]) An Eidesstatt sind die Versicherungen von den Standesbeamten nur über bestimmte Tatsachen und nur dann abzunehmen,
wenn es nach den gesetzlichen Bestimmungen (vergl. § 45 Abs. 4 des Personenstandsgesetzes) zulässig und nach den obwaltenden Umständen
erforderlich erscheint.

Protokoll

aufgenommen zu Ettal am 14. September 1923

Betreff:
Absicht zur Eheschließung zweier ...

Gegenwärtig:
Die Unterzeichneten.

Es erscheinen heute
vor dem unterzeichneten Standesbeamten

der russische Staatsangehörige
Sergewitsch *Prokofieff*, ledig,
geb. am 24. April 1891, griechisch-
katholischer Konfession, Komponist,
z. Z. wohnhaft in Ettal, dem unterzeichneten Standesbeamten persönlich
bekannt

und

die spanische Staatsangehörige
Caroline *Codina*, ledig,
geb. 20. Okt. 1897, evang. luth.
Konfession, Künstlerin, z. Z. wohnhaft
in Ettal, dem unterzeichneten Standesbeamten persönlich bekannt

und geben an daß sie
miteinander die Ehe eingehen
wollen. Sie stellen deshalb an das
Evg. Ministerium die Bitte das
Aufgebot und ... das Ehefähig-
keitszeugnis.

Serge Prokofieff
Caroline Codina

Zur Beglaubigung

...

Declaration of intention to marry

Standesamt __Ettal__

Beilage A.
(Min.-Entschl. v. 30. Dez. 1899.)

Heiratsregister Nr. .... 19 ....

Aufgebotsverzeichnis Nr. .... 19 ....

.... Beilagen.

I. Verhandelt

__Ettal__ am 14 ten __September__ 19 23

Vor dem unterzeichneten Standesbeamten erscheinen heute und beantragen das Aufgebot für ihre Eheschließung:

Bräutigam: 1. Der¹) *Komponist Prokofieff Sergueiff*

(Rufname und sämtliche Vornamen, Rufname unterstrichen, sowie Beruf oder Gewerbe)

der Persönlichkeit nach .... *be*kannt,

geboren am 24 ten __April__ 18 91 zu *Sontzowka Ecatarinoslaw*

Regierungsbezirk, Kreis, Oberamt, Bezirksamt *Rußland*

griech. kath. Religion, Sohn des zu *Petersburg*

Vater des Bräutigams: ¹) lebenden verstorbenen *Michel Sergei Prokofieff*

und dessen zu *Ettal* ²) lebender

Mutter des Bräutigams: verstorbener Ehefrau *Maria Prokofieff*

geborenen *Jitkoff*

wohnhaft ³) seit *1. April 1922* in *Ettal*

.... straße Hs.-Nr. .... , vorher innerhalb der

letzten sechs Monate wohnhaft in ——

staatsangehörig in *Rußland*

⁴) noch ledig, ~~verheiratet gewesen mit~~ ....

~~geschieden seit~~ ....

Prokofiev's marriage license

Braut: 2. die *) ~~Krüsplerin~~ *Codina Carolina*

(Familien- und sämtliche Bornamen (Rufname unterstrichen), sowie Beruf oder Gewerbe)

der Persönlichkeit nach _____ be kannt,

geboren am *20* ten *Oktober 1897* zu *Madrid* _____

~~Regierungsbezirk, Kreis, Oberamt, Bezirksamt~~ *Spanien*

~~evang. kil.~~ ~~Christ~~ Religion, Tochter des *) zu *New York*

Vater der Braut: *) lebenden ~~verstorbenen~~ *Michel Juan Martin Codina*

und dessen zu *New York* *) lebender

Mutter der Braut: ~~verstorbener~~ Ehefrau *Olga Codina*

geborenen *Niemyski*

wohnhaft *) seit *9. VIII 1922* in *Cassel*

Straße Hs.-Nr. _____ , vorher innerhalb der

letzten sechs Monate wohnhaft in _____

staatsangehörig in *Spanien*

*) noch ledig, ~~verheiratet gewesen mit~~

~~geschieden seit~~

Die Verlobten, gegen deren Verhandlungsfähigkeit Bedenken sich nicht ergaben, wurden auf die Bestimmungen über die Erfordernisse zur Eheschließung *) hingewiesen und, soweit erforderlich, mit ihrem Inhalt bekannt gemacht. Sie überreichen in beglaubigter Form folgende Urkunden *):

1) ihre Geburtsurkunden:

a) *nicht vorhanden, Geburtsbescheinigung bestätigt durch ein derselben als ersetzend*

b) *der Braut.*

2) die zustimmende Erklärung derjenigen, deren Einwilligung nach dem Gesetze erforderlich ist, nämlich:

a) ——————

b) ——————

3) an weiteren Nachweisungen:

a) *2 Reisepässe.*

b)

c)

d)

*) Anzugeben sind Stand oder Gewerbe der Verlobten und ihrer Eltern und sämtliche Bornamen, soweit sie bekannt sind Nichtzutreffendes ist zu streichen.

3. der _Schriftsteller_ Boris Baschkiroff

der Persönlichkeit nach _____

_____ be kannt,

34 Jahre alt, wohnhaft in _Lottek_ _____

_____

4. der _Mutter_ Maria Prokofieff _____

_____

der Persönlichkeit nach _____

_____ be kannt,

52 Jahre alt, wohnhaft in _Lottek_ _____

_____

Der Standesbeamte richtete an die Verlobten einzeln und nach einander die Frage:

ob sie die Ehe mit einander eingehen wollen.

Die Verlobten bejahten diese Frage und der Standesbeamte sprach hierauf aus,

daß sie kraft des Bürgerlichen Gesetzbuchs nunmehr rechtmäßig verbundene Eheleute seien.

Vorgelesen, genehmigt und _unterschrieben_

Serge Prokofieff

Caroline Prokofieff geb. Co

Boris Baschkiroff

Maria Prokofieff

Der Standesbeamte.

Schichtel Martin

Nr. 43946.

München, den 5. Oktober 1923.

B.Staatsministerium der Justiz.

B.Staatsministerium des Innern.

An

das Standesamt

Ettal.

Betreff:

Eheschliessung von Ausländern im Inlande.

Mit der Vorlage des Bezirksamts Garmisch vom 1.Oktober 1923 Nr.4236.

Gebühr 1 000 000 000 M.

Der vermutlich keinem Staate angehörende Sergewitsch Prokofieff und die spanische Staatsangehörige Caroline Codina in Ettal werden für die Eheschliessung miteinander von der Beibringung der im Art.91 a Abs.1 und II des Ausführungsgesetzes zum

./.

9

Nr. 43946.

Eheschliessung . . . Prokofieff . . . .

Die auf der Entschliessung vermerkte Gebühr von 1000000000 M.

wolle erhoben und unter Angabe obenstehender Geschäftsnummer an das

Staatsministerium der Justiz in München (Postscheckkonto: München 9648)

eingesendet werden.

Die Entschliessung ist den Beteiligten nicht vor Bezahlung

der Gebühren auszuhändigen.

Geheimes Expeditionsamt

des Staatsministeriums der Justiz.

Receipt for Prokofiev's marriage certificate fee

1940	FEBRUARY	Sixth Sonata for Piano, Op. 82 (begun in Kislovodsk in the summer of 1939, finished in Moscow on February 11, 1940)
	SUMMER–AUTUMN	Opera *Betrothal in a Nunnery*, after Sheridan's play *The Duenna*
1941	APRIL	Set to work on the ballet *Cinderella*, based on Perrault's fairy tale libretto by N. Volkov
	APR. 12	Original plan of the libretto for *War and Peace*, after Leo Tolstoy's novel
	JULY	Work on a detailed libretto for *War and Peace*
	BEGINNING OF AUGUST	Songs, a march (Kratkovo)
	AUG. 15	Began working on the music for *War and Peace*
	OCT. 12	Finished The Year 1941 suite for symphony orchestra, Op. 90
	NOV. 12	Finished the first six scenes from *War and Peace*
	NOV. 17	Began working on the seventh scene from *War and Peace*—"On the Eve of the Battle of Borodino"
1941	NOVEMBER	Second Quartet for string instruments, on Kabardinian themes, Op. 92
1942	JAN. 12	Finished the scene "On the Eve of the Battle of Borodino"
	APR. 13	Finished the piano score of the opera *War and Peace*
	APRIL–MAY 2	Seventh Sonata for piano, Op. 83 (begun in the summer of 1939)
	MAY 3	Started the orchestration of *War and Peace*

	MIDDLE OF JUNE—	*Ivan the Terrible,* music for S. Eisenstein's film
	END OF NOVEMBER	Revision of *War and Peace,* "Ballad of the Boy Who Remained Unknown" to words by P. Antokolsky (orchestrated in 1943)
1943	MARCH	Finished the orchestration of *War and Peace*
	JUNE	Sonata for flute and piano, Op. 94 (transcription for violin and piano—1944) Finished the piano score of *Cinderella*
1944	SPRING–SUMMER	Finished the orchestration of *Cinderella*
	JULY–AUGUST	Fifth Symphony, Op. 100 Eighth Sonata for piano, Op. 84 (begun in the summer of 1939) (Ivanovo State Farm)
	OCT. 16	Arrangement of Russian folk songs, two volumes, Op. 104.
1945	JUNE 23–OCT. 9	Sketches for the Sixth Symphony, Op. 111
	SEPT. 29	Finished the score of the "Ode on the End of the War" (Ivanovo State Farm)
	NOV. 21, 24	Music for Part II of the film *Ivan the Terrible*
1946	SPRING	Composition of a new scene for *War and Peace*—"Ball in the Home of an Aristocrat"
1946–1947	WINTER	Composition of a new scene for *War and Peace*—"Council of War in Fili"
1947	FEB. 18	Finished the orchestration of the Sixth Symphony (Nicolina Gora; begun on Dec. 10, 1946)
	AUTUMN	Ninth Sonata for piano, Op. 103 (Nicolina Gora); started in the summer of 1945 in the Ivanovo State Farm

	OCT. 11	Sonata for violin solo, Op. 115
	OCT. 23	Began working on *Story of a Real Man*, after the novel by B. Polevoi
1948	MAY 11	Finished the piano score of *Story of a Real Man*
	AUG. 11	Finished the orchestration of *Story of a Real Man*
	SEPT. 18	Began working on the ballet *Tale of the Stone Flower*, after the tale of P. Bazhov
1949	MARCH 24	Finished *Tale of the Stone Flower* Sonata for violoncello and piano, Op. 119
1949–1950	OCTOBER–JANUARY	*Winter Bonfire*, a symphonic suite to words by S. Marshak
	SPRING–AUTUMN	"On Guard of Peace," oratorio to words by S. Marshak
1951	APR. 21	Symphony-Concerto for violoncello and orchestra, Op. 125 (final version—1952)
1952	MARCH 20	Finished the piano score of the Seventh Symphony, Op. 131 (Moscow)
	JULY 5	Finished the orchestration of the Seventh Symphony (Nicolina Gora)
	OCT. 11	Completed the final version of the opera *War and Peace*—introduced changes and made some additions to scenes 1, 10, 11 and 12
1953	MARCH 5	Final version of the Adagio, "The Joy of Katerina's Meeting with Danila," from the ballet *Tale of the Stone Flower*

Bibliography

Barmin, Alexander, *One Who Survived* (New York: Putnam's, 1945).

Boston Symphony, Prokofiev's letter to Tikhon Khrenikov, General Secretary of the Soviet Composers' Union, translated by Nicolas Slonimsky, November 5, 1948.

Dyakov, Boris, *Povest o Perezhitom* (Story of My Experiences) (Moscow: Publishers of Soviet Russia, 1966).

Dukelsky, Vladimir [Vernon Duke, pseud.], *Listen Here* (New York: Obolensky, 1963).

Ehrenburg, Ilya, *Memoirs: 1921–1941* (Cleveland and New York: World, 1963).

"50 Years After the Revolution that Changed the World: Russia Today," *Look*, October 3, 1967.

Evgenia Ginsburg, *Journey into the Whirlwind* (New York: Harcourt, Brace & World, 1967) (published originally as *Krutoy Marshrout* by Arnoldo Mondadori Editore, Milano, 1967).

Hanson, Lawrence and Elisabeth, *Prokofiev: A Biography in Three Movements* (New York: Random House, 1964).

Haskell, Arnold L., *Diaghilev* (New York: Simon & Schuster, 1935).

Lifar, Serge, *Serge Diaghilev, His Life, His Work, His Legend* (New York: Putnam's, 1940).

Nabakov, Nikolai, *Old Friends and New Music* (Boston: Atlantic Monthly Press, 1951).

Nestyev, Israel V., *Sergei Prokofiev, His Musical Life* (New York: Alfred A. Knopf, 1946); *Prokofiev* (Moscow: State Music Publishers, 1957; English translation, Stanford, Calif.: Stanford University Press, 1960).

331

Sergei Prokofiev 1953–1963 Statyi i Materialy (Articles and Materials) (Moscow: All-Union Publishers Soviet Composer, 1962).

Sergei Prokofiev (a book of photographs with Russian and English text) (Moscow: State Publishers "Music," 1965).

Schlifstein, Semyon, ed., *S. S. Prokofiev: Materialy, Documenti, Vospominaniya* (Moscow: State Music Publishing House, 1961; second edition).

Sabaneyev, Leonid, *Modern Russian Composers* (New York: International Publishers, 1927); *S. I. Taneyev* (Paris: Tair, 1930); *Moi Vospominaniya o Scriabine* (My Recollections of Scriabin) (Moscow: State Publishers, 1925).

Seroff, Victor I., *Rachmaninoff* (New York: Simon & Schuster, 1950); *Dmitri Shostakovich* (New York: Alfred A. Knopf, 1943).

Stevens, Edmund, *This Is Russia, Uncensored* (New York: Didier, 1950).

Yelagin, Yuri, *Dark Genius* (A biography of Vsevolod Meyerhold) (New York: Chekhov Publishing House, 1955); *Taming of the Arts* (New York: Dutton, 1951).

Wallach, Erica, *Light at Midnight* (New York: Doubleday, 1967).

INDEX

Abraham, Gerald, 284–285, 301
Abravanel, Maurice, 311
Afanasiev, Alexander, 87
Alchevsky, Ivan, 88
Alexander II, Czar, 183
Alexandrev, A. H., 260
Alliluyeva, Nadezhda, 249
Alliluyeva, Svetlana, 190, 190n.
Alpers, Ludmilla, 51
Alpers, Vera, 50–54, 56–60, 65, 236
Alpers, Vladimir, 51
Altschuler, Modest, 105–106, 110
Andersen, Hans Christian, 3, 84, 218
Andreyev, Nikolai, 78–79
Andreyeva, Anna Zherebzova, 78–79, 84
Anisfeld, Boris, 104
Ansermet, Ernest, 127
Antokolsky, Paul, 256
Arensky, Anton, 30, 39, 72
Arutunian, Alexander, 301
Asafiev, Boris (pen name Igor Glebov), 76, 85, 118, 136, 138, 165, 304, 317
Aslanov, A. P., 65
Auer, Leopold, 138
Auric, Georges, 127, 132

Babel, Isaak, 192

Bach, Johann Sebastian, 67, 143
Balakirev, Mili, 33–34, 57
Balmont, Konstantin, 95, 118–119, 246
Barère, Georges, 259
Barmin, Alexander, 249 n.
Barto, Agini (Agnes), 204–205
Bashkirov, Boris, see Verin
Bashkirov, Vladimir, 122
Bazhov, P., 304, 306
Beethoven, Ludwig van, 10, 27, 35, 48, 63, 75, 104, 115, 130, 161, 174, 191, 229, 253–254, 278, 287 312
Berezovsky, Leonid, 221–222, 307
Beria, Lavrenti, 194, 232, 248, 250, 286, 295, 299
Berlioz, Hector, 175
Bernhard, Alexander, 40
Birman, Serafima, 231–233
Bizet, Georges, 230
Blech, Leo, 136
Blok, Alexander, 277
Bobrova, Tatyana, 205
Bolm, Adolf, 104
Borodin, Alexander, 21, 33, 49, 121, 135, 226
Brahms, Johannes, 34, 72–73, 163, 190, 214